Critical Survey of Long Fiction

Novelists of the Jewish Culture

Editor

Carl Rollyson
Baruch College, City University of New York

Salem Press
Ipswich, Massachusetts • Hackensack, New Jersey

Cover photo:
Philip Roth (Hulton Achive/Getty Images)

978-1-4298-3694-4

CONTENTS

CONTRIBUTORS

Randy L. Abbott
University of Evansville

Dan Barnett
Original Contributor

Allan Chavkin
Texas State University-San Marcos

Frank Day
Original Contributor

Grace Farrell
Butler University

Howard Faulkner
Original Contributor

L. H. Goldman
Original Contributor

Jay L. Halio
Original Contributor

Pierre L. Horn
Wright State University

Julie Husband
SUNY-Buffalo

Sheila Golburgh Johnson
Santa Barbara, California

Lothar Kahn
Original Contributor

Steven G. Kellman
Original Contributor

Howard A. Kerner
Polk Community College

Rebecca Kuzins
Pasadena, California

James C. MacDonald
Original Contributor

Dennis Q. McInerny
Original Contributor

Charles E. May
California State University, Long Beach

Laurence W. Mazzeno
Alvernia College

Vasa D. Mihailovich
University of North Carolina at Chapel Hill

Bruce Olsen
Clarksville, Tennessee

Allene Phy-Olsen
Austin Peay State University

Deborah D. Rogers
Original Contributor

June H. Schlessinger
Original Contributor

Charles L. P. Silet
Iowa State University

J. David Stevens
Seton Hall University

Richard Tuerk
Texas A&M University-Commerce

Novelists of the Jewish Culture

The Critical Survey series provides students and general readers with in-depth profiles of major authors in one of the major literary genres or forms—in this case, long fiction. While the profiled authors may have written in other genres as well, sometimes to great acclaim, the focus of this volume is on their most important works as they relate to fiction.

As in the other volumes of the Critical Survey series organized upon ethnic and cultural identity, this volume offers readers a broad overview of authors, living and dead, who have achieved both national and international renown. While the focus of this collection falls mostly upon authors writing in the English language, it recognizes that Jewish fiction comprises writers from a wide variety of nationalities, including Israeli, Polish, Russian, Canadian, and American, writing in languages such as Croatian, Hebrew, Hungarian, Yiddish, and Italian.

In its focus upon authors writing in the last 125 years, this volume attends to representations of Jewish experience and the formation of varied contemporary Jewish identities. As seen in the work of writers like Ukrainian-born Sholom Aleichem to American novelist Philip Roth, Jewish culture and identity have undergone radical changes and yet still contend with the same basic concerns. Assimilation, individual and cultural identity, and rebellion against tradition are some of the more foundational themes of Jewish fiction in the twentieth century, themes that have been reinvented and redeveloped as the world has changed since the end of World War II.

World War II and the Holocaust have had a tremendous impact on Jewish literature, particularly in Europe. Holocaust survivors such as the Italian novelist Primo Levi and the Romanian author Aharon Appelfeld offer unique perspectives on what it meant to be a part of the Jewish identity in the mid-twentieth century by virtue of the ordeals they suffered. Both writers addressed their experiences directly through autobiography and obliquely through long fiction, and although the realities of their internment are not always explicit, the death camps are seldom far from the hearts and minds of their characters.

The list of Jewish writers who have risen to prominence since 1945 is also a list of the most influential writers in the canon of contemporary world literature, including, among many others, Bernard Malamud, Cynthia Ozick, Isaac Bashevis Singer, Philip Roth, Saul Bellow, and Chaim Potok. Through their popular and award-winning work, these writers have added their own perspectives on national identity and what it means to be Jewish, and have ensured that the voice of the Jewish individual and culture continues to be a major part of the growing and changing body of world literature.

What becomes clear, upon surveying the broad scope of literary texts and personal experience, is that Jewish authors continue to wrestle with the same issues as their predecessors, translating personal experience into storytelling that has found a permanent place within the literary tradition.

SHMUEL YOSEF AGNON

Shmuel Yosef Czaczkes

Born: Buczacz, Galicia, Austro-Hungarian Empire (now Buchach, Ukraine); July 17, 1888
Died: Rehovoth, Israel; February 17, 1970
Also known as: Shmuel Yosef Czaczkes

PRINCIPAL LONG FICTION

Hakhnasat kala, 1931 (*The Bridal Canopy*, 1937)
Bi-levav yamim: Sipur agadah, 1935 (*In the Heart of the Seas: A Story of a Journey to the Land of Israel*, 1947)
Sipur pashut, 1935 (*A Simple Story*, 1985)
Oreach nata lalun, 1939 (*A Guest for the Night*, 1968)
Temol shilsom, 1945 (*Only Yesterday*, 2000)
Shirah, 1971 (*Shira*, 1989)
Bachanuto shel Mar Lublin, 1974

OTHER LITERARY FORMS

Many of the works written by Shmuel Yosef Agnon (AHG-nahn) are available in two comprehensive collections, both titled *Kol sippurav shel Shmuel Yosef Agnon*. The first volume of the first collection appeared in 1931 in Berlin. The collection included two novels, *The Bridal Canopy*, parts 1 and 2, and *A Simple Story*, and three collections of short stories, *Me-az ume-'ata* (1931; from then and from now), *Sipure ahavim* (1931; stories of lovers), and *Beshuva vanachat* (1935; with repentance and joy). This edition was expanded to eleven volumes: Volumes 7 and 8, including the novel *A Guest for the Night* and a collection of stories, *Elu ve'elu* (1941; of this and that), were printed in Jerusalem. Volumes 9 through 11, published both in Jerusalem and Tel Aviv, included the novel *Only Yesterday* and two more volumes of short stories, *Samukh venir'e* (1951; near and apparent) and *Ad hena* (1952; *To This Day*, 2008). The second comprehensive collection of Agnon's work was published in Tel Aviv in eight volumes, seven of them in 1953 and another in 1962.

In addition to his fiction, Agnon published a number of nonfiction works. They include *Yamim nora'im* (1938; *Days of Awe*, 1948), an anthology of High Holiday traditions; *Sefer, sofer, vesipur* (1938; book, writer, and story), excerpts on booklore from various sources; *Atem re'item* (1959; *Present at Sinai: The Giving of the Law*, 1994), a compilation of rabbinic responsa; and *Sifrehem shel tsadikim* (1961; tales of the Zaddikim), stories of the Baal Shem Tov and his disciples. Posthumous publications of Agnon's works include the two novels *Shira* and *Bachanuto shel Mar Lublin* (in Mr. Lublin's store); three collections of stories, one concerning Agnon's hometown in

Shmuel Yosef Agnon
(The Nobel Foundation)

Galicia, titled *'Ir u-melo'ah* (1973; a city and the fullness thereof), and two others, *Lifnim min hachomah* (1975; inside the wall) and *Pitche dvarim* (1977; introductions); a book of Agnon's letters and speeches, *Meatsmi el atsmi* (1976; from myself to myself); and a work tracing Agnon's family tree, *Korot batenu* (1979; pillars of our house). Some of his works have been translated into French, Spanish, and German.

Achievements

Affectionately known in Israel by the acronym "Shai," Shmuel Yosef Agnon was during his lifetime, as one critic notes, "uncontestably the dean" of Hebrew letters. He is widely read and almost a household word in Israel but is not as well known to English-speaking audiences. His works, although deceptively simple, are so complex that they do not lend themselves well to translation. He was a prolific writer, the author of more than one hundred tales, yet for many years relatively few of his major works were available in English translation.

Agnon is unique in many respects: He was a religious Jew who wrote fiction rather than biblical commentaries, an intellectual writer who appeals to the simple as well as to the highly sophisticated. Most of his writings appeared in local periodicals, either in Europe or in Israel, prior to their incorporation in the volumes of collected works. In his extraordinary Hebrew prose style, which assimilates biblical phrases and talmudic parables, Agnon insists on a return to Jewish sources. He is an allusive writer who writes with the erudition of his rabbinic background, using the language of the Jewish scholar. His Hebrew is classical rather than modern. Agnon's works have a timeless, dreamlike, magical quality that takes them beyond the reality he presents. The issues with which Agnon deals are not explicit; they are veiled in layers of symbolism, making his works so elusive that scholars are reluctant to attempt translations. The surface of his fiction, however, is realistic, offering a detailed picture of Eastern European Jewry of the nineteenth and twentieth centuries.

Agnon was the recipient of numerous honors and prizes. In 1966, with poet Nelly Sachs, he received the Nobel Prize in Literature—the first time this award was granted to a Hebrew-language writer.

BIOGRAPHY

The oldest of five children, Shmuel Yosef Agnon was born Shmuel Yosef Czaczkes in the small village of Buczacz in Eastern Galicia (a small East European province that has belonged alternately to Poland and to Austria). His father, Shalom Mordecai, an ordained rabbi, earned his livelihood as a fur merchant. Religiously, the family was traditionally observant; economically, it was strongly bourgeois; culturally, it was erudite in Jewish literature. Agnon received a traditional and liberal education, studying the Talmud, Midrash, Jewish medieval philosophers, and Hasidic and rabbinic lore as well as the early Galician enlightened writers, modern Hebrew and Yiddish literature, and German literature. His broad education developed in him two loves, which became his modus vivendi: his love for literature and for Zion.

In his Nobel Prize speech, Agnon claimed that he wrote his first poem at the age of five as a tribute to his father, who was away on a business trip, because he missed him. His early interest in writing was no doubt generated by a desire to emulate both his father, who wrote poetry and scholarly articles, and his cousin, Hayim Czaczkes, a writer whose works were often published in the Galician press. He was fortunate that his family was well-off and did not need his help in its support, and he was encouraged to pursue his own interests. At fifteen, he published his first poem in the Kraków Hebrew weekly. By the time he was eighteen, he was considered a promising young writer.

Agnon, a strong Zionist, left for Palestine in 1907, and although he returned to Buczacz twice, in 1913 and in 1930, he could stay only for short periods. His journey to Eretz Yisrael, the Land of Israel, was a difficult one, requiring a train trip to Trieste and then a sea voyage to Jaffa. Agnon's short novel *In the Heart of the Seas* records this hazardous trip. Upon entering Palestine, he settled in Jaffa, the scene of a number of his stories, including his first published tale in 1908, titled "Agunot" ("Deserted Wives"). Following a trend adopted by earlier Hebrew writers, such as Mendele Mokher Sefarim (pseudonym for Shalom Jacob Abramovich) and Sholom Aleichem (pseudonym for Sholom Rabinowitz), young Shmuel Yoseph Czaczkes signed this tale with the name of "Agnon," adopting it officially as his family name in 1924.

It is significant that he chose this particular name, for it would seem to indicate his own relationship to the world. In Jewish law, the *agunah*, or deserted woman, is not free to remarry, because she has not been divorced. She is anchored in a relationship that can last forever. This image of being in limbo was pursued a decade after Agnon's story by S. Ansky in his classical drama *The Dybbuk* (1916; English translation, 1917) and some thirty-five years later by Saul Bellow in his depiction of the *Dangling Man* (1944). In all three cases, the characters are not free. They are constricted by invisible threads that they do not control and cannot sever. This condition is not a form of alienation, an estrangement from a person or society; rather, it suggests an eternal rootedness that cannot be easily extirpated. At the age of twenty, Agnon felt like the *agunot* of his tales: uprooted, yet eternally bound to his native village of Buczacz and the world of his youth. In 1911, he moved to Jerusalem and settled permanently in that city, even though he left it for one extended period and other brief periods. He was proclaimed an honorary citizen of Jerusalem in 1962.

Agnon went to Berlin in 1913. The time he spent in Germany proved to be very significant to him. (He made a brief trip to his hometown to visit his ailing father, who died November 20, 1913. His mother had died earlier, in 1908.) There he met Zalman Schocken, a merchant and Zionist and patron of the Jewish arts who became Agnon's admirer, his patron, and his sole publisher. Agnon was one of those fortunate artists who never had to struggle for a livelihood and was thus free to concentrate on his writing.

Germany was then a hub of cultural activity, and Agnon moved in a dynamic circle of philosophers, writers, Zionist leaders, and industrialists. In 1920, he married Esther Marx, a member of one of Germany's most respected Jewish families. The couple moved to Homburg, where their two children were born, a daughter, Emunai, in 1921, and a son, Hemdat, in 1922. Agnon's years in Germany were productive ones, but in 1924 his home there was destroyed by a fire that consumed much of his unpublished material. He never entirely recovered from the trauma of this loss. In his Nobel speech, he claimed to have lost, at that time, not only everything he had written after he left Israel but also a rare library of four thousand Hebrew books. After the fire, he returned to Jerusalem alone, sending his wife and children to her parents' home. In 1925, his family joined him, and they made their home in Talpiot, a suburb of Jerusalem. Agnon was busy at this time working on his epic novel *The Bridal Canopy*.

In 1929, Agnon lost his home again, this time to marauding Arabs, who attacked numerous Jewish settlements in that year. The family escaped unhurt, but his house and library were in shambles. In a letter to his friend Schocken, he described the scene and wrote that he was able to save his manuscripts, but most of his archives and the history of Eretz Yisrael were destroyed. His new library of three thousand books, many of which he had inherited from his father-in-law, also suffered: Books had been "overturned and scattered and torn" in the attack.

The loss of his home a second time was a crushing blow to Agnon. The family spent four months at his wife's sister's home in Bat Galim, near Haifa. In January, 1930, Agnon traveled to Germany to see Schocken, who had decided to publish Agnon's collected works. During this time, Agnon also made a trip to Buczacz. He stayed only a week, but this trip provided the material for his novel *A Guest for the Night.*

The Berlin edition of his collected works was enthusiastically received, and from that time on, Agnon's life was a series of artistic and critical triumphs. Since his death in Israel on February 17, 1970, his daughter has edited a number of his works, many of which have been published by Schocken Books.

ANALYSIS

Two dominant forces ruled Shmuel Yosef Agnon's life: the Torah as the essence of a meaningful life and Eretz Yisrael, the Land of Israel, as the ancestral homeland for the Jew. On a personal basis, Agnon integrated these passions into his existence at an early age. He was brought up in a religious home. For a brief time, he abandoned his piety, but he shortly realized that his life was empty without it. He returned to his Orthodox ways and lived as a Jew committed to the Torah, albeit in secular surroundings. He made Eretz Yisrael his home when most religious Jews still looked upon the Holy Land as a suitable burial place but not a place to live. They felt that settlement in Israel could take place only with the advent of the Messiah.

On an artistic level, Agnon's early works, those that are best known and have been widely translated, present a nostalgic evocation of the milieu of the Eastern European shtetl—specifically, his native village of Buczacz. The works that are set in the nineteenth century depict a hermetically sealed community governed by piety and love and watched over by the omnipresent and benevolent Almighty. Agnon, however, was a man of his times, fully aware of contemporary events and their effects on the Jewish community. Eretz Yisrael is a motif in all of his works, which reflect the ongoing dissolution of the shtetl as it became increasingly vulnerable to the intrusions of the age. Although Agnon made brief visits to Buczacz as an adult, all of his works are drawn from his childhood memories of his hometown. The images are at times ebullient and joyful, as in *The Bridal Canopy*; at times fanciful, as in *In the Heart of the Seas*; and at other times somber and depressing, as in *A Guest for the Night.*

THE BRIDAL CANOPY

The Bridal Canopy is the first novel of a trilogy in which Agnon deals with the experience of Eastern European Jewry. Written in 1931 (although based on a short story completed in 1920), a time of upheaval between two major wars, the novel focuses on the Jewish community in Galicia of the 1820's. In a mood of fantasy and nostalgia, Agnon presents a work that is both realistic and unrealistic: realistic in its depiction of the Jewish milieu, the piety of the Jew, and his devotion to the Torah; unrealistic in its childlike attitude toward life, where the concerns of men are limited to the amassing of a bridal dowry and to the telling of tales of past saints and wonder-workers.

The theme of this major work, as suggested in the title, is the brotherhood of the Jewish people, which is achieved through the upholding of God's commandments, especially those of charity and hospitality. The original title, *Hakhnasat kala*, a Hebrew idiom meaning bridal dowry, was loosely translated as *The Bridal Canopy* for the English translation of the novel by I. M. Lask, but this is misleading. The focus of the work is on the collection of the dowry; the wedding itself, which takes place under the "bridal canopy," is of relatively minor significance. Agnon deals with the marriage process, which involves not only the protagonist, Reb Yudel, but also the entire Jewish community. All participate in the preservation of the social institution of marriage and in the fulfillment of God's commandment of procreation. The bridal dowry, an ancient concept—well known in the time of Abraham, who sent his servant, Eliezer, loaded with gifts, to seek a wife for his son, Isaac—is an integral element of the traditional Jewish marriage.

With this initial novel, Agnon falls into the category of Jewish writers who depict Jewish social institutions humorously. Many of them, such as Yosef Perl and Mendele Mokher Sefarim, writing during the period of the Haskalah—the Enlightenment—parodied and satirized traditional Jewish customs. Agnon's novel more closely resembles the work of Israel Zangwill, who in the late nineteenth century wrote the marvelously funny work *The King of Schnorrers* (1894), depicting, with a combination of humor and love, the Jewish mendicant, who is considered a vital aspect of the community. It is through him that the community is able to fulfill God's commandment of charity. The protagonist, the schnorrer, never allows the community to forget that he is the instrument of their salvation. Similarly, in Agnon's work, Reb Yudel, by raising a bridal dowry for his daughter, allows the community to participate both in hospitality to a stranger and in charity to the poor. Through the peregrinations of Reb Yudel, one sees a cohesive Jewish community, its members flawed but united, a community wherein each is his brother's keeper.

The plot is simple, if somewhat improbable. Provoked by his wife's complaints, the protagonist leaves the relative comforts of his home and the house of study in his native village of Brod and travels to various neighboring communities to raise enough money for the bridal dowry of his eldest daughter. He is accompanied by his faithful friend, the wagon-driver Nota, and Nota's trusty and intelligent horses, Mashkeni and Narutza. (These names whimsically play on a passage in the Hebrew Bible's Song of Songs, where the beloved says to her betrothed, "Draw me after thee"—*mashkeni*—"and we will run together"—*narutza*.) After spending months on the road, he yearns for a return to the simple life and decides to make up for lost time by settling in at an inn, studying the Torah, and using the collected dowry money to pay for his stay. While at the inn, he is mistaken for a wealthy man who coincidentally happens to bear his same name and lives in the same town as he does. This mistaken identity is the vehicle for the ensuing events: an alliance in the form of an engagement with a wealthy family, the return to his home, the inadvertent intercession of the aristocratic Yudel Nathanson, who unwittingly becomes the patron of Yudel the Hasid, the discovery of the treasure in a cave, the wedding itself, Yudel's blessed and prosperous life, and his eventual settling in the Land of Israel.

Agnon's language in *The Bridal Canopy* is a combination of the Yiddish vernacular and biblical and postbiblical Hebrew. It was the medium of popular Hebrew texts of the seventeenth, eighteenth, and nineteenth centuries and also the language of the pious Jew of the period depicted. Eclectic in style, the novel is essentially a series of tales or anecdotes held together by the tale of Reb Yudel. Most of the tales in *The Bridal Canopy* were published as individual stories; some are well integrated into the novel, whereas others seem superimposed. These tales are, at times, didactic, at other times fanciful. Some are folktales; others are Agnon's own creations. The narrative of Reb Yudel's odyssey and the tales within the narrative illuminate the character of the protagonist and the inhabitants of the community of Brod, his hometown, and those whom he meets in the neighboring villages. The tale within the tale is also symbolic of the Jew within the Jewish community: Each has his or her own personality, and together they make up a larger entity.

The novel itself is a depiction not so much of Reb Yudel as it is of the entire environment he traverses. It establishes Agnon's posture in his fictive world as well, an attitude of respect for religious tradition in spite of instances of hypocrisy and ignorance. The work is divided into two parts. Book 1 deals with the departure of Reb Yudel, the raising of the bridal dowry, and the quest for a successful match for his daughter; book 2 deals with his return home and the wedding.

The opening chapter describes Reb Yudel's high spiritual aspirations and his lowly material circumstances. He lives in an unfurnished cellar. His only possession is a rooster, known as Reb Zerach, that functions at the beginning of the work simply as an alarm clock, awakening Reb Yudel at dawn for the morning worship. At the end of the work, it becomes clear that the rooster's function is a more subtle one.

Reb Yudel's character, as the work progresses and he becomes a wanderer, combines three Jewish stock figures: the *batlon* (the idler), the *meshulach* (the messenger or schnorrer), and the *maggid* (the itinerant preacher and storyteller). Reb Yudel, a *batlon*, known affectionately, if somewhat ironically, as "the Chasid," the student, is one of that society's pious men who is incapable of earning a living and spends all day in the house of study. Agnon indicates his attitude toward the protagonist (and the work itself) by referring to him by the descriptive diminutive "Reb Yudel" or "little Jew." It is the name given to a child or to one of lowly stature, *dos kleine Mensch*, and lacks the reverence that would be found in the scholar's appellation. At no time is the character referred to as "Rav Yehuda ha Chasid"—Rabbi Judah, the pious. Agnon wants his audience to recognize the humble nature and childlike quality of his protagonist as well as the inherent comedy of the work. This is reflected not only in Yudel's naïveté but also in his attitude toward life and the world at large, an attitude indicated in the subtitle of the book, *The Wonders of Reb Yudel, the Chasid from Brod . . .* , which supports the mood of fantasy and nostalgia in which this novel was written. Reb Yudel is not a saint and does not perform miracles, but he depends on and believes in miracles. Like a child, Reb Yudel interprets experiences and expressions in their most literal contexts. Like the unscholarly, nonsaintly individual, he misquotes the sages, misapplies biblical and talmudic sayings, and misassesses situations.

Agnon's depiction of Reb Yudel is not harshly critical. Reb Yudel represents a world that no longer exists, a world that was reassuring in its simplicity, in its belief in the goodness of God and humankind, a world where one could spend one's life recounting the marvels of the sages while enjoying the hospitality of one's host and brethren. Some critics find a troubling ambiguity in the novel, an uncertain combination of acceptance and rejection of the world so painstakingly delineated. Readers are likely to feel this ambiguity only if they mistake Agnon's comedy for criticism. In fact, Agnon wrote as a devoted traditionalist; he makes this obvious in his depiction of Heshel, the *maskil*, the man of the Enlightenment whom Reb Yudel meets during his odyssey. Heshel, ready to discard tradition without replacing it with anything substantial ("Grammar is the foundation of the world," he claims), receives the harshest treatment of any character in the work. He begins as a wealthy man, and Yudel goes to him for a contribution to his bridal fund, but he ends in a state of abject penury, ill clothed, pockets empty, starving. He comes as a beggar to the wedding of Yudel's daughter. The point Agnon makes is obvious: Life is impoverished when it is devoid of tradition. In contrast to Heshel, Reb Yudel, the believer, is amply rewarded for his faith with material fortune, a prosperous life with its spiritual culmination in the Land of Israel, where he settles in his old age.

It has been suggested that *The Bridal Canopy* is modeled on Miguel de Cervantes' *Don Quixote de la Mancha* (1605, 1615) and that Agnon treats his protagonist ambivalently, as both saint and fool. Actually, Agnon's style, like Sholom Aleichem's, more closely resembles that of the American humorist Mark Twain in its use of the vernacular, folk humor, tall tale, literal interpretation of metaphor, and comic treatment of cloistered religion. The protagonist, Reb Yudel, is not a romantic; he does not fight windmills, nor does he reach for the impossible dream, as does Don Quixote. He is a firm believer in the beneficence and magnanimity of God and has utmost faith that all of his needs will be met, and, ultimately, they are. This is not a romantic concept but a religious one.

The Bridal Canopy is an eclectic work. In his Nobel speech, Agnon voiced his indebtedness to the Jewish sources: to the Bible and to its major commentator, Rashi; to the Talmud and *Shulhan ʿarukh*; to Jewish sages and authorities on Jewish law; to medieval poets and thinkers, especially Moses Maimonides; and to contemporary Hasidim and pious men with whom he had spent time.

In the Heart of the Seas

In the Heart of the Seas, the second of the trilogy begun with *The Bridal Canopy*, is a shorter novel that has much in common with its predecessor. The time period of the second novel is the same as that of the earlier work, about 1820; the milieu, the city of Buczacz (instead of the village of Brod) in Galicia. While *The Bridal Canopy* ends with Reb Yudel's ascent to the Holy Land, *In the Heart of the Seas* begins with the last-minute preparations for the departure of a group of pious Hasidim who have decided to emigrate to Eretz Yisrael. The work deals with the journey itself, the perils, trials, and anguish involved in this trip, and the determination of the pilgrims in spite of all hardships.

It is a tale that commingles reality and fantasy. In 1934, the year the novel was published, Agnon was witness to the Fifth Aliya (ascent to the Land of Israel), which brought some 250,000 Jews to the country. Most of them were refugees from Nazi Germany who managed to leave before all exits were closed. They were not necessarily religious people; they were those who had the means and the foresight to leave. In *In the Heart of the Seas*, Agnon reflects on what it would be like to emigrate to the Holy Land out of love and religious commitment rather than the political necessity of the times. It is a fantastic concept. The single individual may move whenever he or she desires, but communities of people are not so mobile and will reestablish themselves, or move from the security of their environment, only when forced to do so. This was the case with the Jewish community of Eastern Europe. *In the Heart of the Seas* is a wistful tale with a realistic veneer.

The work assumes even greater significance if considered in the context of the secular writings of the Hebraists and the cultural climate of the time. Zionism was viewed mainly as a secular and political movement within the Jewish world and was frowned upon by religious Jews who, like the rabbi of Buczacz in *In the Heart of the Seas*, believed that it was sacrilege to go to Israel prior to the coming of the Messiah. Agnon takes the traditional image of Zion, which the ancient poets and pietists glorified in psalms and poetry, and transforms it into a realistic destination of the pious Hasidim of this Eastern Galician village.

Although the action takes place in the early part of the nineteenth century, the author includes himself as one of the travelers. He is the last to join the group. He is mentioned by name, Rabbi Shmuel Yosef, the son of Rabbi Shalom Mordechai ha-Levi, who is married to a woman named Esther and who has a penchant for storytelling. The tale is related by an omniscient narrator who is replaced at times by the author's own persona. He purports to be chronicling the adventures of a man named Chananiah exactly as he heard them.

On a literal level, Chananiah is the character who frames the story. The story starts with him and ends with him. Chananiah—meaning "God has graced"—is a saintly mysterious stranger, an evanescent figure. He joins the group of Hasidic pilgrims to the Holy Land. Before they start out on their journey, he tells them his own story, a tale of robbers, immoral men, and their hideouts in a country that knows no Sabbath; the chief of the villains wears phylacteries (leather boxes containing biblical passages that are traditionally worn by Orthodox Jews during prayer), even though he is not Jewish. Chananiah is a jack-of-all-trades; he emerges in time of need to help the travelers with their preparations, making boxes for their belongings while keeping his own in a kerchief. He disappears for the voyage itself but is seen riding the waves on this same kerchief, and he reaches the destination much before his fellow travelers. He also appears on the last page of the work, where the narrator states that the book is a tribute to the memory of Chananiah. This would seem to suggest a realism that is contradicted by the subtitle of the story, *Sipur agadah* (*An Allegorical Tale*). In its allegorical context, the work suggests that all of life is a pilgrimage fraught with dangers and hardships, cloaked in mystery. The good, those "graced by God," will ride the rough seas under his aegis, protected by his garment. The work, then, becomes a tribute not to the evanescent Chananiah of this particular tale but to all of those Chananiahs who embark on the journey into time or who journey from night to day, from ignorance to illumination, donning the protective mantle of God's covering, the Torah.

Chananiah is also the author himself, who narrates allegorical tales for the reader to interpret. The kerchief is the imagination of the author, which can take him over the seas, or back in time, or anywhere he desires to go.

The style of this work is, like that of *The Bridal Canopy*, eclectic. Agnon draws from biblical sources, the book of Jonah, Psalms, Song of Songs, the Midrash, among others, and also from travel literature describing voyages to the Holy Land, especially a work published in 1790 titled *Ahavat Zion*, an autobiographical account of Rabbi Simcha of Zalozitz's voyage to Eretz Yisrael. Less fanciful than *The Bridal Canopy* despite its allegorical quality, *In the Heart of the Seas* acts as a bridge to the realism and sobriety of the last novel of the trilogy, *A Guest for the Night*, Agnon's greatest work.

A GUEST FOR THE NIGHT

In *A Guest for the Night*, Agnon changes his mode of storytelling from the comic and fanciful to the tragic. Originally published in daily installments in *Ha'aretz*, a Tel Aviv newspaper, from October 18, 1938, to April 7, 1939, the novel reflects the unrelenting gloom that pervaded both Europe and Palestine during this period.

Agnon, distraught upon losing his home for the second time, made a sentimental journey to his native village of Buczacz in 1930, attempting to recapture some of the serenity and security of his childhood. He was unsuccessful; within five days, Agnon realized that he could not reenter the protective womb of his childhood. The key to his security was not to return to or re-create a chimerical past but to build a strong foundation in the present, to ensure a firm and stable future. The novel is an extended re-creation of this visit. It deals with the return of the narrator to his native town of Shibush (the Hebrew word for "error") after his home in Jerusalem has been destroyed by Arab marauders. It is a bleak work, evincing none of the gaiety and merriment of Agnon's previous novels. Realistically drawn, it reveals Agnon at the height of his powers.

In a complex interweaving of historical and psychological themes, Agnon develops the idea that an adult's recollection of childhood is best left to the imagination. Reality belongs to the present, and the real present can never be as beautiful as the imagined past. The theme of the ēgun, the "dangling man," is used to convey the character of the protagonist. He is a man in limbo, ejected from his home, estranged from his family. Just as the *agunah*, the deserted woman, is still tied down to her evanescent husband, and just as the dangling man dangles from the end of an imperceptible cord, so the protagonist of *A Guest for the Night* is securely linked to the home and land from which he flees, to the family from which he separates and the traditions that bind him for all time.

Early in the novel, the narrator is given the key to the *bet midrash* (house of study) by the townspeople of his native village. On a literal level, the key opens the door to the house of study. The narrator, however, misplaces the key immediately and must have a new one made. The old key turns up once again at the end of the story, when the narrator has returned to Jerusalem; his wife finds it in a corner of his suitcase. The villagers have no need for the key. Most of the old-timers have left town, and those who remain await an opportune moment to leave. The new key suggests that the house of study needs new life to restore its grandeur. The narrator's presence is temporary, and his effect on the town is limited. Symbolically, the old key represents the old tradition, which has served the townspeople in the past but seems to be in disharmony with the present time and inadequate to meet contemporary needs. One character's story of a wartime comrade who was shot while still wearing his phylacteries illustrates this point. That the old key reappears at the end of the story, when the protagonist has returned to his home in Jerusalem, suggests Agnon's concept of tradition: It recedes into the background when it is unceremoniously dropped; it will, however, resurface eventually to take its necessary place within one's life. On a psychological level, the key opens the door for the narrator to a secure world where he can close himself off from harm, and although he allows everyone to enter, he knows that whoever comes is a countryman and friend. The four walls of the house of study represent a return to the secure embrace of his childhood.

Eretz Yisrael is another primary theme in this work. Agnon settled in Israel during the time of the Second Aliya, the second wave of Zionist emigration to Israel, which spanned the decade from 1904 to 1914. Those who participated in this *aliya* (literally, "ascent") were mainly from Eastern Europe. Many of them became workers and settled in the port city of Jaffa, where Agnon himself settled before moving to Jerusalem. Others settled in existing *moshavim* (agricultural settlements) or established kibbutzim. Agnon depicts this period of Zionism in *A Guest for the Night* in his portrayal of the members of the Jewish pioneer group preparing themselves for life in Israel by working as a group on a farm in Poland and also in vignettes of the various members of the Bach family, including the patriarch, Reb Shlomo Bach, who settles in Israel in his old age. The narrator has left Israel after the attack on his home, but he considers his leaving a form of therapy and not a permanent emigration. He expresses his love for Eretz Yisrael by the tales he tells and by his positive attitude toward the Holy Land in conversations with various members of the community. In fact, at one point he says that one of the reasons he does not like to visit with the local rabbi is that he is disturbed by the rabbi's antagonism toward Israel.

In *The Bridal Canopy*, Reb Yudel's journey to Israel is the culmination of his life, and he settles there in his old age. In *In the Heart of the Seas*, an entire Hasidic group, a quorum of ten, moves to the Holy Land. In *A Guest for the Night*, young and old strive to achieve the same goal. Not all are fortunate in their endeavors. Some cannot make it for familial, economic, or political reasons. Zvi, the young man who prepares himself for life in the Land of Israel by working on a farm in Poland, cannot afford the cost of proper papers and attempts to enter the country illegally; he is turned back by the British. Some who do make it are disillusioned and do not stay, as is the case with Yerucham Freeman. In fact, Yerucham Freeman's harsh criticism of the protagonist's relationship to Israel and his influence on others illuminates another theme of this work: illusions and realities.

For most of the Jews of Eastern Galicia (and, for that matter, worldwide), the Land of Israel at this period was indeed a dream, the subject of poetry, literature, prayers, and communal deliberations. It gave direction to one's life, but it remained generally an unattainable quest, an illusion, as it were. The narrator of this work, having settled in the Land of Israel while still a youth, transforms this illusion into a reality for his community. He becomes an exemplar for others and, in time, personifies Israel itself. Yerucham Freeman also falls in love with the Land of Israel, but he does not realize that he is exchanging one illusion for another. For this reason, he cannot find fulfillment when he does emigrate to the Holy Land. Entering the new country, he finds that the narrator has left for a sojourn abroad. This information shatters Yerucham's dream, which was thoroughly interwoven with its personification, and (expelled from the Land of Israel for communist activities) he returns to his native village to gain a foothold in reality.

The narrator makes a similar movement, but for opposite reasons. Reality for him is the home he has established for himself in the Land of Israel, encompassing both its beauty and its harshness. The narrator would like to erase its harshness by returning to a state of illusion—a return to his childhood and his juvenile vision of the Holy Land. His prolonged stay in Shibush demonstrates that one cannot go "home" again, one cannot recapture the past. The narrator arrives in Shibush on the eve of Yom Kippur, the most solemn day in the Jewish calendar, a day of judgment for all. By bringing the narrator in at the onset of this holy day, Agnon suggests that the protagonist needs to take stock of himself and repent for his sins, the most obvious of which is his decision to leave his family and home in the Land of Israel. Just as Shibush is no longer the place that he knew, so must Israel take a more realistic place in his life. Reality may at times be beautiful, but it is also brutal.

All the themes of the novel coalesce within a historical perspective spanning two time periods. The work was written during a six-month span from October, 1938, to April, 1939, a period that witnessed the upheaval of the Jewish communities in Europe prior to the outbreak of World War II and the ultimate destruction of the shtetl way of life. Indeed, *A Guest for the Night* has been referred to as "an elaborate elegy on the lost shtetl culture."

The story itself takes place in 1930, a time between wars, a time when the entire European world had not had a chance to recover from the devastating effects of the maelstrom of World War I before it was thrown into another cycle of death and destruction. The Jewish community was caught in this vertigo. Agnon's work captures all the bleakness of this "no exit" situation: Europe, the shtetl, could no longer be the home of the Jew, and Eretz Yisrael, the Land of Israel, was not considered a viable alternative. As a British mandate, Palestine was inhospitable and unsympathetic to Jewish immigration, while the Yishuv, the Jewish settlement in Israel, was not developed sufficiently to be a replacement for the Jewish community of the shtetl. Agnon re-creates this dilemma in the narrative of *A Guest for the Night*. Allegorically, the title (taken from Jeremiah 14:8) suggests the historical situation of the Jew, who comes as a guest to a foreign country, intending to stay for a short while, and remains for as long as he can maintain his status as a guest; then, when the realities of life force him to do so, he leaves.

Agnon is above all a storyteller, and although the mood of *A Guest for the Night* differs from that of *The Bridal Canopy*, the style is characteristically Agnon's. In both works, the inn or the house of study represents the centrifugal force of the novel: The protagonist employs his vantage point as a hotel guest to narrate his own tales and the tales of the people with whom he comes in contact or allows them to tell their own tales. The protagonists of both novels are passive characters and sedentary people; they are not adventure seekers. Agnon's heroes are humble, gentle, and compassionate people who are imbued with a love and fear of God and a love for their fellow human beings. Their tales comprise the chronicles of the Jewish people.

Agnon's later works continue to reflect on the situation of the Jew in modern society. Although the Holocaust is not a major theme of his works, it is an underlying current in many of his novels. In *A Guest for the Night*, the gloom and sterility of the village seem to foreshadow the destruction of the culture about to take place. Agnon's next novel, *Only Yesterday*, set in Palestine in the early part of the twentieth century, symbolically suggests, with its protagonist's being eaten by a mad dog, the fate of the Jewish people.

Perhaps what has endeared Agnon so much to his people is the love that he expresses for them throughout his writings and his understanding and compassion for their situation, one of uprootedness, which he echoed in the name he adopted for himself. In a fluctuating, chaotic world, his steadfast traditionalism, coupled with his artistic complexity, is appreciated by a general audience as well.

L. H. Goldman

OTHER MAJOR WORKS

SHORT FICTION: "Agunot," 1909 (English translation, 1970); "Vehaya he-'akov lemishor," 1912; *Me-az ume-'ata*, 1931; *Sipure ahavim*, 1931; "Ha-mitpahat," 1932 ("The Kerchief," 1935); *Sefer hama'asim*, 1932 (reprints 1941, 1951); "Pat Shelema," 1933 ("A Whole Loaf," 1957); *Beshuva vanachat*, 1935; *Elu ve'elu*, 1941; *Shevu'at emunim*, 1943 (*Betrothed*, 1966); *Ido ve'Enam*, 1950 (*Edo and Enam*, 1966); *Samukh venir'e*, 1951; *Ad hena*, 1952 (*To This Day*, 2008); *Al kapot hamanul*, 1953; *Ha-Esh veha'etsim*, 1962; *Two Tales*, 1966 (includes *Betrothed* and *Edo and Enam*); *Selected Stories of S. Y. Agnon*, 1970; *Twenty-one Stories*, 1970; *'Ir u-melo'ah*, 1973; *Lifnim min hachomah*, 1975; *Pitche dvarim*, 1977; *A Dwelling Place of My People: Sixteen Stories of the Chassidim*, 1983; *A Book That Was Lost, and Other Stories*, 1995.

POETRY: *Agnon's Alef Bet: Poems*, 1998.

NONFICTION: *Sefer, sofer, vesipur*, 1938; *Yamim nora'im*, 1938 (*Days of Awe*, 1948); *Atem re'item*, 1959 (*Present at Sinai: The Giving of the Law*, 1994); *Sifrehem shel tsadikim*, 1961; *Meatsmi el atsmi*, 1976; *Korot batenu*, 1979.

MISCELLANEOUS: *Kol sippurav shel Shmuel Yosef Agnon*, 1931-1952 (11 volumes); *Kol sippurav shel Shmuel Yosef Agnon*, 1953-1962 (8 volumes).

BIBLIOGRAPHY

Aberbach, David. *At the Handles of the Lock: Themes in the Fiction of S. J. Agnon*. New York: Oxford University Press, 1984. Sets out the major patterns in Agnon's writing on a work-by-work basis and features discussion of his novels as well as his short fiction. Includes detailed notes and a list of references.

Band, Arnold J. *Nostalgia and Nightmare: A Study in the Fiction of S. Y. Agnon*. Berkeley: University of California Press, 1968. Covers Agnon's literary development text by text and is very useful for the historical background to, and context of, Agnon's work. Discusses Agnon's life and his career as a writer and includes both primary and secondary bibliographies, informative appendixes, and a general index.

_______. *Studies in Modern Jewish Literature*. Philadelphia: Jewish Publication Society, 2003. Anthology of Band's essays written from the 1960's to the early twenty-first century includes a section titled "Modern Hebrew Literature" that includes four essays devoted to discussion of Agnon's work.

Ben-Dov, Nitza. *Agnon's Art of Indirection: Uncovering Latent Content in the Fiction of S. Y. Agnon*. New York: E. J. Brill, 1993. Discusses a number of themes in Agnon's work; of particular interest is a chapter titled "The Web of Biblical Allusion." Includes bibliography and index.

Fisch, Harold. *S. Y. Agnon*. New York: Frederick Ungar, 1975. Part of a series on literary greats, this work includes a useful chronology and a brief biography of Agnon's life. An in-depth discussion of individual writings follows the biographical section. Supplemented by notes, primary and secondary bibliographies, and an index.

Fleck, Jeffrey. *Character and Context: Studies in the Fiction of Abramovitsh, Brenner, and Agnon*. Chico, Calif.: Scholars Press, 1984. Places Agnon's work alongside that of his contemporaries, especially in the first chapter, "Modern Hebrew Literature in Context." Focuses on one of Agnon's novels in another chapter, "Man and Dog in *Only Yesterday*."

Green, Sharon M. *Not a Simple Story: Love and Politics in a Modern Hebrew Novel.* Lanham, Md.: Lexington Books, 2001. Examines Agnon's novel *A Simple Story* and argues that Agnon was a Jewish nationalist and secular modernist whose critical depictions of modern Jewish life were not meant to demean Jews; rather, the author's intention was to demonstrate how the Jewish community could thrive by recapturing its sense of self-respect, heroism, and romantic love.

Hochman, Baruch. *The Fiction of S. Y. Agnon*. Ithaca, N.Y.: Cornell University Press, 1970. Presents a detailed interpretation of Agnon's major works, placing them in the context of the time and place in which they were written. A primary bibliographical note aids readers in locating translations of the original works, and notes on all the chapters are supplied at the end of the book, as is an index.

Negev, Eilat. *Close Encounters with Twenty Israeli Writers*. London: Vallentine Mitchell, 2003. Negev, a literary correspondent for the Israeli journal *Yedioth Achronot*, presents twenty profiles of prominent contemporary Israeli writers, including Agnon, based on her interviews with the writers and other research.

Shaked, Gershon. *Shmuel Yosef Agnon: A Revolutionary Traditionalist*. New York: New York University Press, 1989. Details Agnon's progression as a writer, including biographical events that influenced his development and analysis of his novels. Includes index, notes, and select bibliography.

SHOLOM ALEICHEM

Born: Pereyaslav, Russia (now Pereyaslav-Khmelnitsky, Ukraine); March 2, 1859
Died: New York, New York; May 13, 1916
Also known as: Sholom Naumovich Rabinowitz

PRINCIPAL LONG FICTION

Natasha, 1884
Sender Blank und zayn Gezindl, 1888
Yosele Solovey, 1890 (*The Nightingale*, 1985)
Stempenyu, 1899 (English translation, 1913)
Blondzne Shtern, 1912 (*Wandering Star*, 1952)
Marienbad, 1917 (English translation, 1982)
In Shturm, 1918 (*In the Storm*, 1984)
Blutiger Shpas, 1923 (*The Bloody Hoax*, 1991)

OTHER LITERARY FORMS

Sholom Aleichem (ah-LAY-kehm) is best known for his short narratives, impressionistic sketches, and literary slices of life. The stories surrounding two of his characters—Tevye, the milkman, and Menahem-Mendl, the unsuccessful jack-of-all-trades—are frequently brought together in collections that form episodic but coherent wholes. The adventures of a third character, Mottel, the cantor's son, are sometimes published as young adult fiction, though divisions of Aleichem's audience according to age distinctions are artificial. Aleichem's stories have been published throughout Europe, in Israel, and in the United States. At least eight separate compilations are now available in English.

Some of Aleichem's writings, descriptions, or reactions to events and people are difficult to classify and are sometimes labeled simply "miscellany." Even his autobiography—*Fun'm yarid*, 1916 (*The Great Fair: Scenes from My Childhood*, 1955)—contains as much fantasy as fact. Although he had planned the book for many years, it was left incomplete at his death and covers only his youth.

ACHIEVEMENTS

Sholom Aleichem is regarded as one of the founders of Yiddish literature and is perhaps the most beloved writer in that language. While his longer fiction adds little to the development of the novel, even these works demonstrate the strengths for which he is loved throughout the Jewish world. Although, like most educated East European Jews of his time, he began by writing in Hebrew, the language of sacred learning and of scholarship, he soon discovered that Yiddish was the proper vehicle for relating the exploits of people like those he had known in his youth. The wisdom, the humor, and even the foolishness of these folk could be fully captured only as they actually spoke. In his hands, this despised "jargon" became a vivid, lively, literary instrument. Fluent in the Russian language, and a correspondent with Leo Tolstoy and Anton Chekhov, Aleichem brought to Yiddish fiction the compassion for the insulted and injured that was such a dominant note in classic Russian fiction.

By the end of the twentieth century, Yiddish was spoken only in small pockets of the United States, East Europe, and Israel, and was spoken chiefly by older people. The Yiddish newspapers had almost disappeared, and the theater was preserved only as a relic. Though much of the humor was lost in translation, Aleichem's writing survived and reached large Gentile as well as Jewish audiences in English, Russian, Hebrew. and other languages. Aleichem's fictional characters were introduced to even wider audiences with the popularity of his Broadway musical *Fiddler on the Roof* (pr. 1964), adapted from his Tevye tales, and an operatic adaptation of the novel *The Nightingale* (music by Noam Elkies and libretto by Jeremy Dauber), which was performed at Harvard University in 1999.

Aleichem's central value, though, is his preservation in fiction of a milieu that has vanished, of a people dispersed through pogroms, immigration, revolution, assimilation, and the Holocaust. His books are populated by rabbis, cantors, religious teachers, and kheder students, and yet his books have social and political dimensions. The society of the shtetl (a small Jewish townlet) is already changing in these writings. Revolutionaries who identify themselves as Russians more than as Jews and seek to rid their lives of czars, bishops, and rabbinical tyrants alike begin to appear in his novels. Other characters dream of wealth in America, while Zionists preach a return to the land of their spiritual ancestors.

Along with a large continuing readership, Aleichem has received many posthumous honors, including, in his name, statues in Russia's Kiev and Moscow and a street in New York City. His likeness is also on postage stamps in East Europe and Israel. His home in Kiev is now a place of literary pilgrimage.

BIOGRAPHY

Sholom Aleichem was born Sholom Naumovich Rabinowitz in 1859 in Pereyaslav, Russia (now in Ukraine), to a family of means, although family fortunes fluctuated during his childhood as they did throughout his entire life. His family moved to Voronkov, a small town nearby, which would be the model for his fictional town of Kasrilevke. Even though he received a traditional Jewish religious education, his father was aware of his talents and made sure they were supplemented by training at a Russian secondary school.

Sholom was thirteen years old when his beloved mother died. According to Jewish custom, it was not long before he had a stepmother; in this case, she could have stepped from the tales of the Brothers Grimm. However, she inspired his first published Yiddish work, a dictionary of humorous curses commonly uttered by stepmothers.

Because of the precarious financial situation of his family, young Sholom accepted a position as a government rabbi, an elected but despised functionary who mediated between the czarist government and the Jewish community. Later he was able to find more congenial employment as tutor to Olga Loyeff, daughter of a wealthy Jewish family. Falling in love and fearing her father's disapproval, Aleichem and Loyeff eloped. Their marriage lasted until his death.

Around 1883, Sholom wrote a humorous sketch that appeared in a Yiddish paper under the pseudonym Sholom Aleichem, a Hebrew greeting meaning "Peace unto you." He used the pseudonym initially as an apology for not writing in Hebrew, but he would come to use this pen name exclusively, just as he would continue to write in Yiddish. As business concerns and stock-market speculation took him to cities such as Kiev, Odessa, Paris, and Vienna, his writing continued, with brief narratives, character sketches, extended anecdotes, and even poems. Also a skilled reader, he was soon in demand as a performer, reading his own stories.

As times became ever more difficult in the Pale of Settlement (the area of the czarist empire in which Jews were permitted to live), immigration to the United States became an attractive possibility. In 1905, a devastating pogrom in which many Jews perished convinced Aleichem to relocate his family to the United States, where he was widely read and the Yiddish theater promised a decent livelihood.

It was in his later years that Aleichem aspired to be a playwright. His ear for the rhythms of speech of many different personalities, along with his imaginative portrayal of different character types, would seem to have fitted his work for the stage. However, he had limited success in the American Yiddish theater.

Even as his sales mounted on two continents, Aleichem, who was not an especially skilled businessman, received limited royalties and often was compelled to earn his living with lectures and readings. Never fully at home in the United States, he died in New York City in 1916. Enormous crowds attended his funeral, acknowledging him as a folk hero. His plays met with some acclaim after his death.

Analysis

Sholom Aleichem excelled in character development. The personalities of his protagonists unfold through their thoughts, desires, dreams, worries, and hopes; their interactions with others; and, most of all, through their speech. Their language—a lively, colloquial Yiddish—is rhythmic and rustically poetic. They curse one another, express affection, identify with animals, misquote Scripture, and misuse Talmudic lore, though, even in their innocent, or calculated, mangling of Scripture and tradition, they often reveal a higher folk wisdom.

Because Aleichem was basically a writer of short impressionistic sketches, it is difficult to diagram a clear plot in his narratives. He was largely indifferent to the literary architecture required of longer works. His novels, often picaresque, are therefore disjointed and episodic. He may introduce a character, leave him or her for several chapters, take up another character, and only later return to the first. The natural environment is rarely or only briefly described, yet the little towns and bustling cities through which his characters move come alive as they struggle to survive in whatever setting God has placed them.

The most famous Aleichem characters struggle with poverty, dream of what it would be like to be rich, and ultimately accept their plight. They are not, however, above arguing with the Deity. There is frequently a nearly magical, even mystical element in some of Aleichem's writing, which may reflect the influence of his grandfather, a Hasidic Jew and Kabbalistic mystic.

Preferring the epistolary narrative form or the monologue, Aleichem allows his protagonists to speak for themselves. Sometimes they address their unseen listener respectfully, but the author appears rarely to interfere with them. This encourages the reader to laugh with rather than at the characters so compassionately presented. In his novels, Aleichem appears to be telling rather than writing a story.

It has been customary to refer to Aleichem as the Jewish Mark Twain. There is a story, almost certainly apocryphal, of his meeting with the American humorist: When introduced, Twain is modestly rumored to have said "I understand that I am the American Sholom Aleichem." Certainly, in their use of first-person narrative, often in dialect, to individualize their fictional creations and bring out the humor of situations, the two are similar. They are alike in their kindly satire, as they comment on the foibles of society. However, Aleichem, as several critics have suggested, might more appropriately be compared to Charles Dickens, who displays, as does Aleichem, a stoic quality of writing and a "laughter through tears" humor.

In the Storm

An early short novel presented as if it were a two-act play, *In the Storm* is a story of three different families who live together at one address in Russia in 1905. In the background are revolution, pogroms, and riots. The characters try to cope through assimilation, religion, and rebellion against tradition. Jews of three different social classes further represent different economic orders. One family is headed by a prosperous businessman who bullies his way through the Jewish community; another father is a struggling druggist, trying to assimilate. The third head of household is a shoemaker, very conscious of his poverty. Although there is little sustained action, the novel is a fine mirror of its time and place.

Stempenyu

Stempenyu, the novel's title character, is a fiddler, with the soul of an artist. He has made an unfortunate marriage to Friedl, a shrew. He meets the gentle Rachel, and the two fall in love. She, too, is unhappily married, to a rich young man who ignores her in his enthusiasm for Talmudic study. Stempenyu and Rachel meet only a few times, once significantly against a monastery wall, and their love is never consummated. Rachel's virtue is, in fact, rewarded, when her husband is exhorted by his mother that his family is as important as his religion. While the chief interest of the novel is its examination of Jewish life in the Pale of Settlement, with its arranged marriages, the narrative also enables Aleichem to express his rejection of sentimental romances and the adulterous tradition of "love in the Western world." In Jewish life, readers are reminded, love comes in marriage, not before or apart from it.

WANDERING STAR

Aleichem's final attempt at sustained fiction allowed him to express his opinion of actors, the Yiddish stage, and theatrical promoters. This novel is strung together by a thin love story about two youths who escape their oppressive homes to become wandering performers. The main interest of *Wandering Star*, however, resides in descriptions of the magic of theater, reflections on the differences between sacred and secular music, and a lively review of the history of Yiddish theater. Aleichem focuses on the theater's origins in Romania to its degeneration in New York City at the hands of impresarios more interested in money than in Jewish folk art.

THE BLOODY HOAX

The Bloody Hoax is a novel based on a real event, known as the Beiliss affair, in which a Ukrainian Jew was accused of a ritual murder in 1911. In Aleichem's recasting of events, two friends, one Jewish and the other Gentile, decide to exchange places in order to expand their experience of life. The Gentile boy initially encounters problems through his inability to speak Yiddish, but his trouble really begins with the surfacing of "the blood libel," an unfounded but pervasive accusation made against Jews in times of persecution. He is accused of using Gentile blood to make Passover bread. Despite its serious subject, the novel is marketed as a comedy, and it is especially notable in its treatment of Russian Jewish intellectuals and the Zionist movement at the beginning of the twentieth century.

Allene Phy-Olsen

OTHER MAJOR WORKS

SHORT FICTION: *Tevye der Milkhiger*, 1894-1914 (*Tevye's Daughters*, 1949; also known as *Tevye the Dairyman*); *Menakhem-Mendl*, 1895 (*The Adventures of Menachem-Mendl*, 1969); *Der farkishnefter Shnayder*, 1900 (*The Bewitched Tailor*, 1960); *Mottel, Peyse dem Khazns*, 1907-1916 (*The Adventures of Mottel, the Cantor's Son*, 1953); *Jewish Children*, 1920; *The Old Country*, 1946; *Inside Kasrilevke*, 1948; *Selected Stories of Sholom Aleichem*, 1956; *Stories and Satires*, 1959; *Old Country Tales*, 1966; *Some Laughter, Some Tears*, 1968; *Holiday Tales of Sholem Aleichem*, 1979; *The Best of Sholom Aleichem*, 1979 (Irving Howe and Ruth R. Wisse, editors); *Tevye the Dairyman and the Railroad Stories*, 1987; *The Further Adventures of Menachem-Mendl*, 2001.

PLAYS: *A Doktor*, pr. 1887 (*She Must Marry a Doctor*, 1916); *Yakenhoz*, pr. 1894; *Mazel Tov*, pr. 1904; *Tsuzeyt un Tsushpreyt*, pr. 1905; *Die Goldgreber*, pr. 1907; *Samuel*

Pasternak, pr. 1907; *Stempenyu*, pr. 1907; *Agenten*, pb. 1908; *Az Got Vil, Shist a Bezem*, pb. 1908; *Konig Pic*, pb. 1910; *Shver Tsu Zein a Yid*, pb. 1914; *Dos Groyse Gevins*, pb. 1915 (*The Jackpot*, 1989); *Menshen*, pb. 1919; *Der Get*, pr. 1924; *The World of Sholom Aleichem*, 1953; *Fiddler on the Roof*, pr. 1964.

NONFICTION: *Fun'm yarid*, 1916 (*The Great Fair: Scenes from My Childhood*, 1955); *Briefe von Scholem Aleichem und Menachem Mendl*, 1921.

BIBLIOGRAPHY

Butwin, Joseph, and Frances Butwin. *Sholom Aleichem*. Boston: Twayne, 1977. A general review of the life and work of Aleichem, with insightful descriptions of all major writings and critical reactions to them. Part of Twayne's World Authors series.

Halberstam-Rubin, Anna. *Sholom Aleichem: The Writer as Social Historian*. New York: Peter Lang, 1989. A scholarly consideration of Aleichem's reconstruction of his native East European Jewish community written as a background study for the Broadway production of *Fiddler on the Roof*.

Howe, Irving. *World of Our Fathers: The Journey of the East European Jews to America and the Life They Found and Made*. New York: Simon & Schuster, 1976. A thorough examination of East European Jewish immigrants in the United States, the role of Yiddish in their lives, and their love of the Yiddish theater and Yiddish writers. This is the world Aleichem entered in his later years.

Liptzin, Solomon. *A History of Yiddish Literature*. New ed. Middle Village, N.Y.: Jonathan David, 1985. A thorough survey of the entire sweep of Yiddish literature and Aleichem's dominant place within it. Especially helpful are the discussions of characteristic Yiddish humor and the problems of translation. Equally pertinent is the examination of the rise and ultimate decline of Yiddish as a language of literature, theater, and cultural exchange.

Samuel, Maurice. *The World of Sholom Aleichem*. New York: Random House, 1973. A readable reconstruction of the world about which Aleichem wrote, the towns and villages of the Jewish Pale of Settlement. Illustrations are taken from the writings of Aleichem, in a demonstration of the ways in which fiction can imaginatively recapture an actual time and place now vanished.

Silverman, Erica, and Mordicai Gerstein. *Sholom's Treasure: How Sholom Aleichem Became a Writer*. New York: Farrar, Straus and Giroux, 2005. An illustrated biography aimed at younger readers. Covers events of the author's early life, including his problems with a difficult stepmother and his fascination with Jewish folklore.

Waife-Goldberg, Marie. *My Father, Sholom Aleichem*. New York: Schocken Books, 1971. A loving, carefully prepared biography of the author by his youngest daughter. Waife-Goldberg discusses the reception of Aleichem's works, the fluctuations in his career, and his sometimes-precarious financial situation even after he became famous as a writer.

AHARON APPELFELD

Born: Czernowitz, Romania (now Chernovtsy, Ukraine); February 16, 1932

Principal long fiction

Ke-ishon ha-'ayin, 1972
Badenheim, 'ir nofesh, 1975 (*Badenheim 1939*, 1980)
Tor ha-pela'ot, 1978 (*The Age of Wonders*, 1981)
Kutonet veha-pasim, 1983 (*Tzili: The Story of a Life*, 1983)
Nesiga mislat, 1984 (*The Retreat*, 1984)
Be-'et uve-'onah ahat, 1985 (*The Healer*, 1990)
To the Land of the Cattails, 1986 (also known as *To the Land of the Reeds*)
Al kol hapesha'im, 1987 (*For Every Sin*, 1989)
Bartfus ben ha-almavet, 1988 (*The Immortal Bartfuss*, 1988)
Katerinah, 1989 (*Katerina*, 1992)
Mesilat barzel, 1991 (*The Iron Tracks*, 1998)
Timyon, 1993 (*The Conversion*, 1998)
Layish, 1994
Unto the Soul, 1994
'Ad she-ya'aleh 'amud ha-shahar, 1995
Mikhreh ha-kerah, 1997
Kol asher ahavti, 1999 (*All Whom I Have Loved*, 2006)
Masa' el ha-horef, 2000
Polin erets yerukah, 2005 (*Poland, a Green Country*, 2005)
Pirhe ha-afelah, 2006 (*Blooms of Darkness*, 2006)

Other literary forms

Aharon Appelfeld's writing career began with poetry published in the 1950's and progressed through short stories to novellas and longer fiction. He has been a prolific writer in Hebrew of countless poems, hundreds of stories, and more than twenty volumes of fiction and essays. Many of his short stories have been published in English-language periodicals, and one collection is available in English, *In the Wilderness* (1965). Like his longer fiction, Appelfeld's short stories revolve principally around the events preceding and following the Holocaust and deal in large part with Jews separated from the mainstream who manage to maintain themselves in a non-Jewish world. Prominently mentioned in significant discussions of his work are the stories "Berta," "The Journey," "The Betrayal," "The Pilgrimage to Kazansk," "Regina," "Kitty," and "1946."

Achievements

Although Aharon Appelfeld has been published since the 1950's and emerged in the 1960's as a leading Israeli writer, it was only in the 1980's that his genius was recognized outside Israel, with the publication of several of his novels in English. Prior to that time, however, he had been recognized with several major Israeli awards, including one for his poetry in 1960 and the Bialik Prize in 1978. He was also the recipient of the Israel Prize for Literature in 1983 and the National Jewish Book Award for fiction in 1989. His autobiography *The Story of a Life* (2004) was awarded the Prix Médicis in France, and in 2005 Appelfeld received the Nelly Sachs Prize, a literary award presented every two years by the German city of Dortmund.

Most critics writing in English have concentrated on Appelfeld's reputation as one of the great voices of the Holocaust (Alan Mintz asserts that "Greenberg and Appelfeld are the two great writers of the Holocaust in Hebrew literature") and on his writing techniques of simplicity and understatement and their relationship to the techniques of Franz Kafka. Appelfeld himself has commented on these evaluations of his work, disagreeing in part with both: "I am not writing what is called 'Holocaust literature.' . . . I'm just telling stories about Jews—to Jews—at a certain period in their history. . . . If my work has echoes of both *Kohelet* [Ecclesiastes] and Kafka, that's because I see them both in the tradition of Jewish minimalist literature." Appelfeld's writing achievements are perhaps characterized better by Irving Howe: "No one surpasses Aharon Appelfeld in portraying the crisis of European civilization both before and after the Second World War. . . . He is one of the best novelists alive."

BIOGRAPHY

Aharon Appelfeld was born in Czernowitz, Bukovina, Romania, in 1932, into an assimilated Jewish family whose language of choice was German. When Appelfeld was eight, he and his family were removed from their environment. His mother was taken by the Nazis, and he was separated from the rest of his family and shipped to a concentration camp in Transnistria, from which he escaped. After three perilous years of wandering through the forests of Eastern Europe with temporary stays with various refugees along the way, he joined the Russian army in 1944, at age eleven, in the Ukraine as a field cook. At twelve, Appelfeld joined a gang of war orphans who made their way south, living off the land. He was the youngest member and was to remain in touch with others of the gang. Upon their arrival in Italy, the gang members were befriended by a priest and lived for a time at his church, singing in the choir. After this interlude, the gang went on to Naples, where they met a Youth Aliya group and were persuaded to go to Israel. Appelfeld has related that the gang's last night in Naples was spent at a brothel, where he sat up all night in a chair.

After his arrival in Israel in 1947, Appelfeld began writing poetry in his newly acquired language, Hebrew. The Jerusalem editor to whom he sent his poetry corrected it and rejected it for three years, after which time the editor instructed the poet not to send him any more poetry until he learned to write Hebrew. Ten years later, in 1960, Appelfeld has noted, he received an award for his poetry, the award named after the same editor, who had recently died.

In 1962, Appelfeld's first short-story collection was published by an eccentric publisher who had not read the material but liked the author's looks. The book, although not distributed to bookstores initially, enjoyed critical acclaim and started Appelfeld's literary career as a short-story writer and novelist. A graduate of Hebrew University in Jerusalem, Appelfeld teaches Hebrew literature at Ben Gurion University of the Negev in Beersheba, Israel, and makes his home in a suburb of Jerusalem.

ANALYSIS

Careful analysis of Aharon Appelfeld's writing suggests that his works consist of detailing different elements of one story, his own story. The seemingly autobiographical aspects of these novels, however, reveal Appelfeld's unusual ability to retell visions and motifs in ever-changing and fascinating literary hues and designs. Appelfeld himself has said,

> It's usually pointed out that I draw on my own experience for my stories and novels. I acknowledge that. Yet I have no interest in writing autobiography. . . . Memory can't create a story; the author must. So I objectify my own experience by recreating it in the stories of others.

As noted above, critics have also referred to Appelfeld as one of the great producers of Holocaust literature. Although accurate, that judgment is ironic, for Appelfeld never specifically names or addresses events of the Holocaust in his writing. Nevertheless, in his sparsely written recounting of the pre-Holocaust period, the author evokes the horrors to come by stirring the memories and imagination of those who read with a historical perspective. In like manner, in his stories about those who survived the years of hiding or after being "sucked into" railroad cars, both recurring motifs in Appelfeld's works, he forces the reader's imagination to develop the pictures he never paints but that are responsible for the broken, imperfect souls of the post-Holocaust experience. Appelfeld himself has spoken of this technique: "You can never understand the meaning of the Holocaust. You can just come to the edges of it. If you wrote about it directly, you'd end up trivializing it."

The novels discussed below, in fact, can be placed into two simple categories: those that describe pre-Holocaust European Jewish society and begin and end with no hope for the future (*Badenheim 1939* and *The Retreat*) and those that seem to indicate that the return to roots, the finding of the true secrets of Jewishness, permits the survival of youth into the post-Holocaust period (*The Age of Wonders, Tzili, To the Land of the Cattails*). All these novels share a common base of retold experience, literary techniques, motifs, themes, and symbols, woven into magic by a masterful storyteller. The retold experience is Appelfeld's own life and its connection with the Holocaust. Although, as stated earlier, the Holocaust is never named and its too-familiar scenes of horror are never drawn, the dreamlike superimposition of allegory and realism immerses the reader in visions of impending horror. The reader's historical memory and imagination fill in what Appelfeld's novels do not provide, especially since the understated, simple, spare, and matter-of-fact text demands these additions.

Appelfeld's images and themes are recurrent. The most devastating images recall, with chilling understatement and deceptively simple, direct language, the naïve willingness of European Jews to accept resignedly the events, indignities, and humiliations that preceded the Holocaust, and their destructive self-abnegation and anti-Jewish behavior. Appelfeld accents these characteristics by emphasizing stereotypical differences between pre-Holocaust Jews and non-Jews. Jews were timid figures whose long faces were pale from lack of outdoor activity and whose bodies were undeveloped by physical exercise. On the one hand were the intellectual Jews who had assimilated into Western European culture, abandoning their traditions and the Yiddish language; on the other hand were the *Ostjuden* (Jews from the east, Poland in particular), who lacked refinement and who were known for their single-minded pursuit of mercantile occupations and their observance of traditional ways. The two groups disliked each other intensely. Travel, trains, disdaining intellectuals, culpable *Ostjuden*, forests, abandoned children, lost mothers, ugly fathers, unpleasant Jewish characteristics, and the coarse, peasantlike behavior of non-Jews—these are the recurring motifs that Appelfeld weaves into an allegorical but realistic fictional world that intensifies the reader's vision of the Holocaust. These recurrent themes testify to the ugliness of prewar Jewish society, its emphasis on assimilation and self-hate, its rejection of the essence of Judaism, its inability to "raise a hand" against its oppressors. Opposed to this are the themes of inner peace, salvation, and even survival achieved through the finding and acceptance of the secrets of basic Judaism.

Recurrent symbols and motifs include forests and nature—havens in Appelfeld's own life, symbolizing peace and safety. Trains and other forms of transportation, by contrast, lead to uncertain destinations usually invoking premonitions of the impending Holocaust. Love of books and humanizing education, as opposed to rigidly enforced study in the Austrian *gymnasium*, indicate characters' acceptance of Judaism and humanism, whereas descriptions of people eating usually indicate coarse, peasantlike cruelty to man and beast and are associated with non-Jews. Although the novels discussed here are based on retold experience and recurrent themes, symbols, and motifs, each also presents a different view of the same problems, thus affording a multifaceted, in-depth analysis of factors preceding the Holocaust. Although readers can share Appelfeld's stories, they are also left to complete them and draw their own conclusions.

BADENHEIM 1939

Badenheim 1939, the first of Appelfeld's novels to be translated into English, recounts with chillingly understated simplicity the naïve response by a broad spectrum of Jews to unmistakable warning signals just prior to the Holocaust. By not using historical terminology for the victims, the victimizers, or the impending events, Appelfeld increases the horror of his story: The reader is wrenched by historical knowledge of the impending disaster posed against the unawareness of the victims and their almost giddy efforts to ignore what is clear.

The book opens in 1939 as the Austrian resort town of Badenheim slips from sluggish winter into tentative spring, bringing with it a mélange of sybaritic visitors who wait for the entertainment to begin. Dr. Pappenheim, the "impresario," is responsible for providing summer-long entertainment for the guests, many of whom are regulars at Badenheim. To introduce his major theme of willful Holocaust unawareness, Appelfeld introduces the character of Trude, wife of the pharmacist. Like an unwelcome Elijah, Trude is consumed by what the others view as a manic-depressive illness that allows her no peace, as she is obsessed by her vision of a "transparent . . . poisoned and diseased world" in which her absent daughter is "captive and abused" by her non-Jewish husband. She also describes the resort-goers as "patients in a sanitorium."

Additional disharmonies surface when Dr. Pappenheim is disappointed by the musicians' greed and he himself displays melancholic longing for his *Ostjuden* Polish roots. Even more ominous is the increasingly authoritative role taken by the Sanitation Department, which "took measurements, put up fences and planted flags" as "porters unloaded rolls of barbed wire, cement pillars, and all kinds of appliances." Characteristically, the naïve vacationers interpret these preparations as signs of a particularly successful summer festival; otherwise, "why would the Sanitation Department be going to all this trouble?" The palpably clear answer is accentuated by the appearance of the twin performers, "tall, thin and monkish," whose forte is the death poetry of Rainer Maria Rilke and who "rehearsed all the time with morbid melody throbbing in their voices."

The themes of assimilation and levels of Jewishness surface when a "modest announcement" appears on the notice board, saying that all citizens who are Jews must register with the Sanitation Department by the end of the month. Heated discussions among the guests about who must comply, based upon class distinctions that elevate the importance of Austrian Jews and denigrate the *Ostjuden*, increase strife.

All the while, the Sanitation Department has continued its work. It now holds detailed records of each person's heritage and begins to display inviting posters of Poland. Concurrently, the department prohibits access to or exit from the town, stops all incoming and outgoing mail, and closes the resort pool. As fear and despair begin to envelop the people, "an alien orange shadow gnawed stealthily at the geranium leaves," and the Jews are put into quarantine.

What has been considered up to this time as disease or infection, an unnamed fear in some hearts such as Trude's, becomes real. Delusions disappear and weaker people ignore basic social rules as they loot the pharmacy and consume all the food. The musicians steal the hotel dishes, and even the dogs become uncontrollable. At the same time, another force begins to operate in the face of chaos. With the common experience of deprivation and fear of the unknown future, the edges of dissension among the people start to smooth and closer common bonds draw the captives together.

Badenheim 1939 ends with the recurring Appelfeld image of trains and journeys signaling a hopeless future. Still uncomprehending, the victims refuse to recognize the facts, clinging to the illusion that deportation to Poland is only a "transition." Old and young Austrian Jews, *Ostjuden*, and those who are part Jewish are "all sucked in as easily as grains of wheat poured into a funnel [into] four filthy freight cars." The last irony is voiced by Dr. Pappenheim, who observes, "If the coaches are so dirty it must mean that we have not far to go."

THE AGE OF WONDERS

Badenheim 1939 re-creates Appelfeld's memory of the European pre-Holocaust world, but the narrator's voice is objective; the characters in this novel cannot be linked directly with Appelfeld or with those around him. *The Age of Wonders*, Appelfeld's second book in English translation, on the other hand appears to be closer to fictionalized biography; in it Appelfeld's own feelings are more visible. *The Age of Wonders* also affords the reader a view of both the pre-Holocaust and the post-Holocaust periods, and as a result it is a more complete and stronger novel than its predecessor.

In the first part of *The Age of Wonders*, the "ugly orange fog" felt in *Badenheim 1939* is an omnipresent, identifiable antagonist. The viscous, threatening suffocator of the pleasure-seeking vacationers in Badenheim is a major character in *The Age of Wonders* as it envelops and destroys Austrian-Jewish lives in pre-Holocaust Vienna. Repeated evocations of Jewish decadence prior to the war enforce the realization that the horror could perhaps have been averted had the Jews reversed the course of assimilation and self-hatred.

The three-year prewar history of a doomed intellectual family in Vienna is reviewed and dispassionately related by the only child, whose name, Bruno, is not revealed until the second part of the book. The action begins with the mother and Bruno traveling by train from their last carefree summer vacation in a forested, "little known retreat." The first clear indication of the impending Holocaust comes when all the passengers who are non-Christian by birth are commanded to leave the train and register during an unscheduled stop at an old sawmill.

Appelfeld's recurring theme of Jewish alienation from Jews is introduced when Bruno's relatives come to celebrate his eleventh birthday. Cousin Charlotte, who has been fired from her position as an actor with the National Company, represents the reality of Jews being ostracized from the Austrian culture and also Jewish self-delusion (she acts foreign roles). Uncle Carl Landman, an attorney, expresses his outrage at Jewish "vulgarity"; some Jews refuse the customs of the prevailing culture. Bruno's Uncle Salo represents the Jewish merchant who flirts with Gentile women and is despised by the intellectuals, such as Landman and Bruno's father. The party ends with bitter debate about what Jewish life should be and displays of hate among the guests; the gathering represents a microcosm of Jewish life before the Holocaust and seems to indicate that Appelfeld sees these divisions as a precursor to the Holocaust.

Bruno's father, a nationally known and acclaimed author/intellectual, despises observant Jews and the *Ostjuden* entrepreneurs, whom he charges with "dark avarice" and whom he believes "should be wiped off the face of the earth, because they ruin everything they touch." Speaking of his own heritage, he says, "My Jewishness means nothing to me." Ironically, the father's anti-Semitism, which is a theme in his own works, is used against him by another, similarly minded Jew. Michael Taucher destroys the author's reputation and career via repeated attacks in the press. Supported by non-Jewish editors who allow Taucher all the space he can fill, the critic finally writes, about Bruno's father, "the Jewish parasite must be weeded out," and then, having served his purpose, he himself disappears.

Another important thread that unwinds as months go by is the high attrition rate among traditionally observant Jews, as the older generation dies off and the younger traditionalists feel the scorn of their contemporaries. When Bruno's Aunt Gusta dies and is buried according to traditional Jewish rites, Bruno describes the scene as "ugly and shameful."

Kurt Stark, a sculptor and longtime friend of Bruno's father, illustrates the almost militant Jewish opposition to the contemporary traditionalists who wanted to preserve religious observance and practices. In a theme shown in several of Appelfeld's works, notably *To the Land of the Cattails*, Stark, the son of a Jewish mother and an Aryan father, seeks refuge from his "tortured [and] cruel perplexities" by conversion to Judaism. In spite of all the difficult hurdles, Stark reaches his goal, but he and his life are horribly altered. After his circumcision, he barely exists in the Paul Gottesman Almshouse for Jews, a dreadful place devoid of spiritual or physical beauty and inhabited by old, dying men. Stark has become a stereotypical Appelfeld Jew—retiring, weak, pale, and unhealthy—whereas before his conversion he had been the stereotypical Aryan—strong, robust, and physically aggressive.

With the family's growing sense of isolation and their increasingly frequent contacts with homeless, dispossessed Jews, Bruno's father seeks escape by appealing to non-Jewish friends. He is representative of the male characters in Appelfeld's works, most of whom are neither strong nor admirable. Bruno's mother, on the other hand, like Tzili in *Tzili* and Toni and Arna in *To the Land of the Cattails*, gathers strength and courage to do what she can to maintain order, even after her husband abandons the family and escapes to Vienna and a non-Jewish woman. In one of the most violent scenes in Appelfeld's fiction available in English, all of the town's Jews are herded into and locked in the synagogue, where the frenzied prisoners decide that the rabbi, who represents Judaism, is the source of their misery and beat him almost to death.

Book 1 of *The Age of Wonders* shares the hopelessness of *Badenheim 1939* but appears to place the blame for the coming disaster on the Jewish people themselves, their assimilation, and their self-chosen alienation from Judaism. In Bruno and his family can be seen the autobiographical elements of Appelfeld's own separation from mother and father prior to the Holocaust, and the images of Bruno's summer vacations in the forest as restorative and saving are unmistakably autobiographical.

The darkness of book 1 is mitigated by book 2, which introduces hope through survival. Book 2 takes up the same motif with which book 1 begins and ends: Bruno is again on a train, but now he is alone, returning thirty years later to the town of his birth, Knospen, Austria. Bruno comes back with memories of the war years mentioned only in reference to towns—Auschwitz and Thereisenstadt—with the burden of a wife and a failing marriage in Jerusalem, and with an inherited and continuing dislike of Jews as part of his emotional foundation. Although his reason for returning is unclear to both Bruno and the reader, what Bruno experiences is depressingly morbid. Bruno finds only the memories of his town of birth and revisited aspects of the countryside pleasant. In contrast, memories of people and places such as school, perhaps some of them once pleasant, become unwholesome and diseased in revisitation.

The Henrietta Bar, which Bruno frequents and leaves "dull with drink," reveals unpleasant postwar realities. As bizarre as the four swarthy Singapore midgets who entertain bar patrons, not with their talent but with their freakish appearance and wild dancing, are the strange, half-breed waitress and her friends, half-Jewish misfits who have no real identity or past other than their existence. Among these Bruno discovers a half cousin, a bastard daughter of his Uncle Salo. Finally, he confronts old Brum, a prototype of prewar denial and cowardice who echoes Bruno's father. Demanding that Bruno leave because he is stirring up "evil spirits . . . Jews again . . . the old nightmare," Brum arouses unexpected violence in Bruno by stating, "My hatred for Jews knows no bounds." Bruno hits the Jewish anti-Semite in the face and displays no emotion except vengeance as the old man, a both real and symbolic specter of the past, lies bleeding on the ground.

Never going back to see what happens to Brum, Bruno quietly leaves town early the next morning. The phrase "It's all over" echoes in his mind as epiphany relieves Bruno of a heavy emotional burden. Ironically, even though the Jews Bruno meets on his return initially repel him, he becomes increasingly tolerant of their weaknesses. In a total reversal, Bruno becomes violent against the disease of prewar Jews—the same one he himself had displayed—Jewish anti-Semitism.

Unlike *Badenheim 1939*, *The Age of Wonders* reflects hope and rebirth after death. Bruno, by surviving and returning to his roots, finds truth and reaffirms the faith of his long-dead Aunt Gusta. He becomes a vibrant, unafraid, and robust Jew. The antithesis of prewar stereotypical Jews who hated themselves, their heritage, and would not raise their hands against attack, Bruno undergoes conversion and remains strong and vital.

Tzili

Appelfeld's third novel to appear in English translation, *Tzili*, continues in the pattern of *The Age of Wonders* with a strong autobiographical element, pre- and post-Holocaust segments, and the tempering of pessimism by the survival of youth. Appelfeld's use of allegory in *Tzili* sets it apart from his other novels. The minimalist approach places an even greater responsibility on the reader to interpret meaning while multiple levels of interpretation are added to each word and scene. This approach makes *Tzili* possibly the most rewarding reading of the novels discussed here.

As a young child, Tzili is ignored by her invalid father and shopkeeper mother and is left during summer days to sit alone behind the shop in the dirt and ashes. Feebleminded and unable to learn when she is finally sent to school at age seven, Tzili is scolded by her parents, who are extremely anxious that their children attain high academic goals, and she is ridiculed by her Gentile classmates, who are particularly gleeful at the spectacle of a Jewish child who cannot learn. The parents engage an old Jewish tutor to instruct their youngest child in Jewish customs and laws, but Tzili can manage only to repeat the Judaic formulas drilled into her by rote. Her tutor appreciates the irony, wondering "why it had fallen to the lot of this dull child to keep the spark [of Judaism] alive." Indeed, only the tutor's visits keep the child from total wretchedness. Unintentionally, as a last resort, her parents have unwittingly provided Tzili with the source of her future salvation as well as her present strength—a strong faith.

When troops appear just outside town, the family deserts Tzili; after charging her to "take care of the property," the rest of them flee to what they mistakenly believe will be safety. Tzili survives an undescribed night of massacre, but her family is never mentioned again. Indeed, Tzili repeatedly escapes death as if she were divinely protected. In a long, circular journey that never takes her far from her birthplace, Tzili moves from childhood to young adulthood. Her survival is both a celebration of indomitable human courage and an allegorical reference to the undying spirit of Judaism, as she survives as if by miracles a series of deadly episodes during the Holocaust years.

When the war ends, Tzili is fifteen, pregnant, and abandoned by her lover-companion, Mark. She falls into the company of liberated but disturbingly petty, quarreling Jews. They ignore Tzili's pain and their own as they travel, but, surprisingly, when Tzili's fragile condition prevents her from keeping up with the group, a fat, former cabaret dancer demands that the group stop for the girl, and they do. A stretcher is constructed, upon which Tzili is carried aloft for the rest of the long journey amid "a rousing sound, like pent-up water bursting from a dam." The stretcher bearers are joined by the entire group, who roar, "We are the torch bearers." Tzili, symbol of the Jewish spark noted by her former tutor, unites the group, gives them strong purpose, and helps them survive. Tzili's destiny ultimately leads her aboard a ship bound for Palestine, perhaps with others of the group. While the fate of her assimilated parents and intellectually superior siblings is unknown, the "chosen" child is saved for entrance to the Chosen Land, Palestine.

THE RETREAT

In *The Retreat*, except for the restorative nature of the forest and other recurring motifs, Appelfeld seems to eliminate the strong autobiographical elements seen in *The Age of Wonders*, *Tzili*, and *To the Land of the Cattails* as well as their theme of youth and survival. Instead, this book is an echo of *Badenheim 1939*, concentrating, in a very different environment, on the ugliness of the pre-Holocaust Jewish milieu and the assimilation and breakdown of Jews and their community because of self-hatred. There is no hint of a future, no youth present who, like Tzili, can be viewed as a living symbol of the enduring spirit of Judaism. The chilling shadow of the Holocaust comes closer as the narrative continues, and the only hope offered is that the Jews in the Retreat, an isolated mountaintop house that has been established as an "Institute for Advanced Study," will help one another and will not abandon anyone; in a time of extremes, they discover that they need one another for support and comfort.

Lotte Schloss, the novel's protagonist, is the listener among the other castoffs at the Retreat; she is a prototype of the metamorphosis and becomes an important part of the group's final support system. The "great Balaban," founder of the institute, envisions his Retreat as a place where Jews can learn to divest themselves of their ugly Jewish characteristics and become more like the Gentiles around them. Thwarted in this goal, Balaban dies unmourned, but ironically he has prepared the members of the group to shift for themselves, help one another, and therefore survive.

At the end of *The Retreat* a faint glimmer of hope for survival through unity appears, but Appelfeld destroys any possibility of salvation: "At night, of course, people were afraid. But they helped one another. If a man fell or was beaten, he was not abandoned." Unity is all the group has.

TO THE LAND OF THE CATTAILS

Appelfeld returns to autobiographical material in his fifth novel published in English, *To the Land of the Cattails*. Its blend of allegory and realism explores what Appelfeld has called a "a love story between a mother and a son," and it ends, as did Appelfeld's own childhood, with the mother lost and leaving her son to find his own way to Jewishness. Although this narrative ends before the Holocaust is at its height, it shares with *The Age of Wonders* and *Tzili* a sense of fulfillment in the characters' acceptance of their Jewishness, and it marks a further development of Appelfeld's almost mystical ability to evoke the Holocaust while never naming it or describing it concretely.

To the Land of the Cattails, interspersing flashbacks and current happenings, recounts a two-year journey during which the two major characters undergo dramatic metamorphoses. In the autumn of 1938, thirty-four-year-old Toni Strauss (née Rosenfeld) and her fifteen-year-old son, Rudi, begin a long journey by horse and carriage from the bustling city of Vienna back to the mother's birthplace of Dratscincz, Bukovina, on the river Prut. Rudi resembles his father, a Gentile "through and through," in appearance and interests. Toni is fearful lest her son also become callous and brutal and abandon her, as his father had fourteen years earlier. She therefore resolves to return to her parents, whom she has not seen since she eloped at seventeen with August Strauss, a Gentile. In addition to fulfilling her own yearning to return from exile, Toni also has a "strong wish for [Rudi] to be Jewish."

Although Rudi considers himself a Jew, Toni tells him at the beginning of their journey, "Certainly you are a Jew, but you need a few more things, not many, not difficult . . . you are a Jew in every fibre of your being. And here, in these regions, you will learn the secret easily." Thus the story of Rudi's metamorphosis begins. In the course of their long journey, however, Rudi returns to his Gentile roots rather than becoming more Jewish. Toni watches the transformation with dread. Her own total commitment to Judaism accomplished, she decides to go on alone to her parents' home. Rudi soon follows after her, but his mother is gone, having been "easily sucked in" with other compliant Jews to waiting railway cars and an unknown future.

Rudi wanders off, blaming his mother for leaving him and angry that she did not wait for him, but he suddenly understands what he has guessed, that his mother is in danger. That understanding begins the final stage of Rudi's metamorphosis, achieved through his friendship with Arna, a thin, thirteen-year-old Jewish girl who also has been separated from her family. Arna believes in God and teaches Rudi the ways of observant Jews; she has brought him a "kind of hidden promise." Rudi falls critically ill, and as Arna takes care of him, he wishes for death. During his illness, he hears Arna intone "Hear, O Israel."

Rudi learns the Jewish secrets well, so well that his physical presence changes to match his spiritual change. His gait, which was once swaggering and self-assured, is different after his illness. In fact, Rudi is so different that "he himself did not know how much he had changed." As the narrative ends and the transformation is complete, Rudi and Arna stand at a railroad station watching a train approach: "It was an old locomotive, drawing two old cars . . . the local apparently. It went from station to station, scrupulously gathering up the remainder." Hope remains that Rudi and Arna, young, vigorous, and secure in their Jewishness, will somehow survive the ensuing Holocaust years and share what they have learned with a future generation.

June H. Schlessinger

OTHER MAJOR WORKS

SHORT FICTION: *'Ashan*, 1962; *Ba-gai ha-poreh*, 1963; *In the Wilderness: Stories*, 1965; *Kefor 'al ha-arets*, 1965; *Be-komat ha-karka'*, 1968; *Adne ha-nahar*, 1971; *Ke-me a edim*, 1975; *Shanim ve-sha ot*, 1975.

NONFICTION: *Masot be-guf rishon*, 1979; *What Is Jewish in Jewish Literature? A Symposium with Israeli Writers Aharon Appelfeld and Yoav Elstein*, 1993; *Beyond Despair: Three Lectures and a Conversation with Philip Roth*, 1994; *Sipur hayim*, 1999 (*The Story of a Life*, 2004); *'Od ha-yom gadol: Yerushalayim, ha-zikaron vẹha-or*, 2001 (*A Table for One: Under the Light of Jerusalem*, 2005); *Encounter with Aharon Appelfeld*, 2003 (Michael Brown and Sara R. Horowitz, editors).

BIBLIOGRAPHY

Appelfeld, Aharon. *Beyond Despair: Three Lectures and a Conversation with Philip Roth*. Translated by Jeffrey M. Green. New York: Fromm International, 1994. Series of lectures contains useful biographical information on Appelfeld. In an interview that first appeared in *The New York Review of Books* in 1988, Roth and Appelfeld explore the biographical and literary sources of Appelfeld's works.

Bauer, Yehuda, et al., eds. *Remembering for the Future*. 3 vols. Elmsford, N.Y.: Pergamon Press, 1989. Includes many informative essays on Appelfeld, especially "Aharon Appelfeld and the Uses of Language and Silence," in which Lawrence I. Langer explores irony in Appelfeld's work, and "To Express the Inexpressible: The Holocaust Literature of Aharon Appelfeld," in which Nurit Govrin treats Appelfeld's fiction in the context of his essays.

Budick, Emily Miller. *Aharon Appelfeld's Fiction: Acknowledging the Holocaust*. Bloomington: Indiana University Press, 2005. Presents philosphical analyses of Appelfeld's major novels, including *Badenheim 1939*, *Tzili*, and *The Iron Tracks*, addressing how these fictional works support understanding of true historical events.

Fridman, Lea Wernick. "The Silence of Historical Traumatic Experience: Aharon Appelfeld's Badenheim 1939." In *Words and Witness: Narrative and Aesthetic Strategies in the Representation of the Holocaust*. Albany: State University of New York Press, 2000. Analyzes Appelfeld's novel *Badenheim 1939* along with other Holocaust literature to demonstrate how Appelfeld and other writers invent techniques to represent this "unrepresentable" tragedy.

Ramras-Rauch, Gila. *Aharon Appelfeld: The Holocaust and Beyond*. Bloomington: Indiana University Press, 1994. Provides biographical information on Appelfeld as well as critical discussion of his works.

Schwartz, Yigal. *Aharon Appelfeld: From Individual Lament to Tribal Eternity*. Translated by Jeffrey M. Green. Hanover, N.H.: University Press of New England/Brandeis University Press, 2001. Discusses three major themes in Appelfeld's work: the recovery of childhood and memory, the creation of place, and the religious stance of the Holocaust writer. Maintains that Appelfeld's underlying concerns transcend his experiences as a Holocaust survivor to include larger issues of Jewish identity.

Wisse, Ruth R. "Aharon Appelfeld, Survivor." *Commentary* 76, no. 2 (August, 1983): 73-76. Contains an early appraisal of Appelfeld's fiction.

SHOLEM ASCH

Born: Kutno, Poland, Russian Empire (now in Poland); November 1, 1880
Died: London, England; July 10, 1957
Also known as: Szulim Asz; Shalom Ash

PRINCIPAL LONG FICTION

Dos Shtetl, 1905 (*The Little Town*, 1907)
Amerike, 1911 (*America*, 1918)
Motke Ganev, 1916 (*Mottke the Thief*, 1917)
Onkl Mozes, 1918 (*Uncle Moses*, 1920)
Kiddush Hashem, 1920 (English translation, 1926)
Toyt Urteyl, 1926 (*Judge Not*, 1938)
Khayim Lederers Tsurikkumen, 1927 (*Chaim Lederer's Return*, 1938)
Farn Mabul, 1927-1932 (*Three Cities*, 1933)
Der Tilim Yid, 1934 (*Salvation*, 1934)
Three Novels, 1938 (includes *Uncle Moses*, *Judge Not*, and *Chaim Lederer's Return*)
The Nazarene, 1939
The Apostle, 1943
Ist River, 1946 (*East River*, 1946)
Mary, 1949
Moses, 1951
Der Novi, 1955 (*The Prophet*, 1955)

OTHER LITERARY FORMS

Although Sholem Asch (ahsh) is remembered chiefly as a novelist, much of his early work consists of dramas. When *Der Got fun Nekome* (pr. 1907; *The God of Vengeance*, 1918) was performed on Yiddish stages in Russia and Poland, Max Reinhardt, who understood Yiddish, decided to produce it at the Deutsche Theater. This was the first time that a Yiddish work had appeared in the international literature. This play, in which a brothel owner purchases a Torah to place in his daughter's room, hoping it will protect her from the impurities in the apartment below, was widely condemned as sacrilegious. Many other dramas followed, including adaptations of such novels as *Mottke the Thief*, which enjoyed considerable success on Yiddish stages.

Asch also published *From Many Countries: The Collected Stories of Sholem Asch* (1958) and other collections of short fiction, as well as an autobiographical essay, *What I Believe* (1941), in which he reacted to criticism levied against him by the Jewish community.

Sholem Asch
(Library of Congress)

ACHIEVEMENTS

Until 1950, Sholem Asch was indisputably the best-known, most translated, most successful Yiddish writer. More than anyone before him, he managed to inject the Yiddish word into world culture, making the world aware of a major literature that had been unjustly ignored. This broader world sometimes seemed more kindly disposed to him than the segment of his Jewish readers who objected to his delineation of the seamier aspects of Jewish life in some works and to his sympathetic treatment of Christianity in others. The bulk of his Jewish readers remained faithful and recognized in him a lover of the poor and weak, a God-seeker, a gentle soul keenly aware that humans did not live by bread alone.

In spite of his high regard for Christianity, Asch remained faithful to Jewish life and tradition, acutely aware of the anti-Semitism all around him. While his characters accept this intolerance as a fact of life, Asch himself could not always assume the same stance. He returned a medal awarded to him by the Polish government when he realized that the policies of that government permitted a heightened anti-Jewish feeling.

A student of the revered I. L. Peretz, whose influence he acknowledged as late as 1951, Asch went beyond the teachings of this master and dealt with topics that Yiddish literature had theretofore avoided. His work marks an abandonment of the rational ways that the Jewish enlightenment had made obligatory for Jewish writers. Like Isaac Bashevis Singer, who replaced him as *the* Yiddish writer on the world stage, Asch was attracted to folkloristic and irrational elements. Because of the diversity of his oeuvre, critics have found it difficult to classify Asch. There is the Romantic who idealized the life of simple

Jews and insisted on the primacy of tradition and faith in faith; there is the naturalist who brilliantly depicted the milieus of thieves, jugglers, and prostitutes; there is the didactic moralist who strove to teach the meaning of the good life. There is even a hint of the publicist who fought Hitlerite anti-Semitism by underscoring the basic nobility of Jewish existence and demonstrating the common bonds uniting Judaism and Christianity. This very multiplicity suggests Asch's enduring appeal.

BIOGRAPHY

The tenth child of a pious and prosperous Hasid, Sholem Asch underwent an early formal education in Hebrew language and literature, especially the Bible. His progress indicated sufficient promise for his father to entertain hopes for him in a rabbinic career. As a teenager, Asch came upon his first secular book and became "enlightened." He found employment as a scribe, writing letters for the illiterate, which likely gave him unique insights into the human psyche. At the same time, he was teaching himself German, Russian, and Polish and reading whatever books by major writers became available to him.

At the age of sixteen, Asch visited Peretz, whose stories he had admired, and requested that the master comment on his own efforts, which he was then writing in Hebrew. Peretz liked what he read but urged the youngster to change to Yiddish. Asch's first story, "Moshele," appeared in *Der Jud* in late 1900. A collection of Hebrew stories published in 1902 was followed in 1903 by another in Yiddish. (His writing then, as later, was colored by the dark and dingy places in which he had lived and the hunger he had suffered and which he was never to forget.) Asch married Mathilda Shapiro, the daughter of a teacher and minor poet. In 1904, he serialized his "poem in prose" *The Little Town* in *Der Freint*; in 1905, it was published as a book that quickly established him at the forefront of Yiddish writers.

Asch visited Palestine in 1907 and the United States in 1909. He was awed by biblical sites in Palestine and the evidence of Jewish and Christian events. In America, the landscapes impressed him, but he was repelled by the sweatshops, the tenements, and the quality of the life he observed.

In the ten years preceding World War I, Asch completed ten plays. He lived mostly in France but was forced to leave upon the outbreak of the conflict. In addition to *Mottke the Thief*, his wartime writing, emanating mostly from New York City, included *Uncle Moses*, a novel of immigrants in their initial years in New York.

After the war, Asch revisited Eastern Europe as the representative of a Jewish relief agency. He was horrified by the slaughter of Jews at the hands of Cossacks and White Russians. What he saw reminded him of a seventeenth century Ukrainian slaughterer of Jews whose soldier-peasants terrorized the countryside. The result was the first of his historical novels, *Kiddush Hashem* (sanctification of the name).

In the words of Sol Liptzin, Asch in the postwar years continued "glorifying Jewish deeds of brotherly love and quiet heroism." Before Adolf Hitler rose to power, Asch believed that contrasting such quiet deeds of Jews with the crude Hitlerite reliance on force would be his way of fighting the Nazi menace. *Salvation*, written in 1932, was the most spiritual novel he wrote, and he was embittered by its poor reception.

Asch's spiritual orientation, accompanied by the desire to strengthen the Jewish position, led to novels on Jesus (*The Nazarene*), Paul (*The Apostle*), and Mary (*Mary*). These works alienated his Jewish readers, who feared a case of apostasy at a time when Hitler was decimating European Jewry. *The Nazarene* was published in English before a Yiddish publisher would touch it. The controversy continued for nearly a decade. The resilience of European Jews and the establishment of a Jewish state tore Asch out of his isolation and prompted him to turn to *Moses*, which he had begun long before and had laid aside in favor of his Christian novels.

In 1954, having lived in the United States and France, Asch settled permanently in Israel, where he wrote *The Prophet* (1955). As the chronicler of a world that had disappeared, Asch became again an object of admiration—a condition that his insatiable ego demanded. In 1957, he suffered a mild stroke. While in London for an operation, he died before surgery could be performed.

ANALYSIS

Nearly all of Sholem Asch's works are related, in a broad sense, to some religious concern. His many themes are clearly intertwined: the simple, traditional life of the Jew; saintliness in the quest for God and service to humans; the ugliness of poverty but the distinct possibility of meaningful beauty even in poverty; the emptiness of a purely material existence; the Jewish roots of Christianity and the need to close the gap between the two faiths. In fact, faith in both its meanings—trust in God and different institutionalized ways of reaching Him—is a thread running through all of Asch's works, but especially his later works.

THE LITTLE TOWN

Even in his first major work, *The Little Town*, Asch had romanticized the inwardness of Jewish life in the shtetl, a different approach from the ridicule usually heaped upon the backward enclaves in literature. Asch perceived nobility and charm in the poverty-ridden, filth-infested shtetl.

Similarly, Asch dealt with spiritual and sacrificial heroism before dealing with it directly in *Kiddush Hashem*. Living far out in the Padolian steppe, a Jewish innkeeper, Mendel, dreams of the day when other Jews will join him in the town and enable him to build a synagogue and lead a Jewish existence. Mendel eventually overcomes the threats of the local priest, and a small but flourishing Jewish community comes into being. Mendel and the congregation are dangerously sandwiched between the machinations of the Catholic priest and the Greek Orthodox priest. The former is intent on humbling the latter. What better means of debasing his rival than to force him to go to the Jew Mendel to obtain the key to his own church? In his frustration, the Orthodox priest threatens Mendel: Sooner or later "the little brothers" will come to liberate the peasants from the Polish lords and the filthy Jews.

The little brothers eventually come, under the leadership of Bogdan Chmelnitzky, and lay waste not only to Mendel's but also to every Jewish community far and wide. Mendel's attachment to his synagogue is such that he refuses to leave, but the rabbi reminds him that the synagogue is only stone, while a human life is a human life. Mendel's Jews flee, joining the stream of refugees; they put up a heroic fight with virtually no weapons. They are finally conquered through the betrayal of the Polish lords, who are only too willing to sacrifice their Jewish allies in the mistaken belief that they can thereby save themselves.

Through Mendel and his family, which includes a learned son and his beautiful wife, Asch depicts the simplicity and piety of Jewish life and the Jews' willingness to live and die for "the sanctification of the name." Jews are offered a chance to save their lives by bowing before the Cross, but they will bow only before their one and only God. All resist the easy way out, sacrificially preferring to suffer cruelty, death, and martyrdom. Although the body may be destroyed, the will and spirit are indestructible. Asch only implies that the Jews' imperishable faith in God has ensured their survival in the past and will ensure it in the future.

Charles Madison has stated that "Asch's compassionate brooding gives the tragic tale the poignant quality of imaginative truth." This critic has also distinguished between two forms of martyrdom—Mendel's, which is not a pure martyrdom in that it is wholly passive, and his daughter-in-law's, which is active: She persuades the Cossack captor who loves her that he should shoot her, on the pretense that no bullet can hurt her.

KIDDUSH HASHEM

Kiddush Hashem is perhaps Asch's only novel in which religious motifs and Jewish historical destiny, especially the Jews' suffering for their survival as a group, fuse successfully. The structure of the novel, on the other hand, is awkward, which prevents it from becoming the masterpiece it might have been.

MOTTKE THE THIEF

If *The Little Town* and *Kiddush Hashem* are, to use Liptzin's words, in a Sabbath mood, *Mottke the Thief* is decidedly workaday. Asch abandons the idealized Jews of earlier works to offer such sad human specimens as Blind Layb and Red Slatke, Mottke's parents. Layb is a vicious, irresponsible father whose only guidance to his child is the lash, which he uses freely and cruelly. Not only is Jewish life imperfect in *Mottke the Thief*, in spite of some obedience to forms and tradition, but it also exists on the lowest levels of humanity. Asch shows an exceptional virtuosity in this novel. The first half combines picaresque with gargantuan, larger-than-life features; the second half is Zolaesque in its depressing naturalism. The abused Mottke, first open enough to seek affection even from a curious dog, is transformed into a callous pimp and murderer, a development that calls for considerable skill, which Asch demonstrates in good measure.

Asch's earlier work might have given rise to the impression that there was something do-goodish in the writer, that his feet were not firmly planted on the ground. With the creation of Mottke, this impression was swept aside. From the moment Mottke joins a group of vaudevillians, uses and abuses them, seduces or is seduced by Mary, the rope dancer, and competes with the treacherous Kanarik, he becomes a character apart from any that Asch had previously created. The erstwhile thief's descent into total depravity continues. With Mary's help, he kills Kanarik, assumes Kanarik's identity, and acquires his own small staff of prostitutes. Yet the Mottke who had once enjoyed something of a Jewish upbringing, however atypical, is not wholly dead. He is fatally attracted to a decent girl, and his love generates decent impulses that have long been submerged. The desire for chastity, piety, and living in the love of and reverence for God, however, has been resurrected too late. Perhaps Mottke's conversion, which comes to naught, is not the most persuasive part of the book; in any case, Mottke is betrayed by the sweet girl he loves. Yet even in the novel's variety of depressing settings, Asch still emerges as a man with a profound faith in faith.

SALVATION

Salvation, a story of the saintly Jekhiel and his quest for God and ways of serving humanity, is more in the mainstream of Asch's fiction than is *Mottke the Thief*. It is probably the most purely "spiritual" of Asch's novels—a term he himself used to describe it—and he attributed its relative failure with the reading public to the refusal of the modern world to address spiritual questions.

Jekhiel's father was a Hasid who left his wife and younger son to join his rabbi in study. Jekhiel was a deep disappointment to him, for, unlike Jekhiel's older brother, Jekhiel has failed to grasp the subtleties of the Talmud. Jekhiel, oppressed by a sense of failure, helps his mother eke out a bare living in the marketplace. She dies, and the youngster serves as tutor to an innkeeper's children, to whom he teaches the elements of the Hebrew language. Jekhiel is heartened one day by a wise stranger, who tells him that knowing the Psalms, with their simple yet warm teachings, is every bit as important in the sight of God as the subtle shadings of talmudic disputation. Soon Jekhiel is known as the Psalm-Jew (which was, indeed, the original Yiddish title of the novel).

In this first half of *Salvation*, Asch poses several questions, to which his answers are clear. He is not enamored of the father, who puts study—however strong an ethic in Jewish tradition—ahead of his familial obligations; Asch does not place learning the Talmud above simpler aspects of the Jewish obligation to ponder the ways of God. A cold, rational approach to religion attracts him less than a warmer, human, perhaps less rational mode.

Jekhiel, without wishing it, develops a following of his own, becoming the rabbi of the Psalms, simple and humble. He is also known for miracles, for which, however, he claims no credit. On one occasion, Jekhiel, under great pressure, commits God to giving a child to a hitherto barren woman. A girl is born. When Jekhiel's wife dies shortly thereafter, the pious rabbi sees it as a sign from Heaven. He leaves home and, in the manner of ascetic saints of all faiths, roams the countryside in rags. He is finally recognized and forced to return.

The years pass, and the girl whose birth he had promised has grown to maturity and fallen in love with a strapping young Polish soldier. They plan to marry. In preparation for her conversion to Catholicism, she enters a convent. There is consternation in the girl's family. Torn by conflicting pressures, the girl jumps to her death. Jekhiel, who had fought the conversion, is troubled for the second time: Has he overstepped proper bounds again? Was not human life and the search for God more precious than the particular way of reaching Him: the Jewish or the Christian?

Asch's implied tolerance of intermarriage again brought him into conflict with his Jewish readers. *Salvation* paved the way for a work that would nearly lead to a rupture with these readers: the story of Jesus of Nazareth, whose emphases within Judaism were not that different from those of Jekhiel the Psalm-Jew.

THE NAZARENE

The problem of Christian anti-Semitism is omnipresent in the oeuvre of Sholem Asch. Considering the author's vision of Jesus, an extension of his characterization of Jekhiel, it is not surprising that Asch often felt bitter about the crimes against Jews committed in the name of the saintly Nazarene. Throughout *The Nazarene*, Asch has his Rabbi Jeshua repeat that he has not come to destroy the Law but to fulfill it. Jeshua observes all but one or two of the ritual commandments, but it is his failure to observe those that his wealthy detractors use against him. Asch's Jesus is learned in the Torah; the character appears to be depicted in the tradition of the great teacher Hillel; he has infinite wisdom and compassion. If, in spite of its strengths, *The Nazarene* fails to satisfy completely, that failure must be attributed to the nature of the subject.

Jeshua as a man, as a self-revealed Messiah, and as a Son of Man (interpreted to mean the Son of God) is a difficult fusion to achieve. Asch is as successful as any novelist who has ever attempted it or, for that matter, biographers and interpreters. There are times, however, when Jeshua, ever mysterious—now very human, now very enigmatic, even furtive—suggests ever so slightly the religious charlatan. Yet this was far from Asch's intent and has not been the impression of all readers.

Jeshua's teachings are within the frame of Jewish tradition, but as he himself says, the fulfillment of that tradition requires new interpretations and emphases. The occasional impressions of hucksterism are held only by the more cynical modern reader, reacting to Jesus' refusal to answer questions directly, to speak in parables only, to select carefully his moments of healing and revealing, to satisfy the doubts of the most searching and spiritually avid of his disciples and admirers. Rabbi Jeshua has a talent for the grand gesture and for the attention-getting phrase or figure of speech, but this image is not one created by Asch; it is, rather, inherent in the subject matter, which he derives entirely from New Testament sources. There are few famous sayings of Jesus that are not quoted, and the endless quotations, although necessary, at times slow the pace of the narrative.

Asch underscores the innovations of the teachings of Jesus: compassion for the poor, the sick, the neglected; the emphasis on the spirit, not the forms, of observance; the primacy of faith; a piety that adds to fervor of the divine humility and an all-encompassing pity; and an involvement in the affairs of humans. Jesus attacks privilege, be it hereditary or earned. The task of involving oneself in the suffering of others must be never-ending; it must lead to the more fortunate assisting those who are suffering. Rabbi Jeshua's leniency toward the sinner, reassurance of the untutored and ignorant, and forbearance vis-à-vis those who have disappointed him all contribute to making him an innovative teacher and preacher. In the end, Jeshua dies, like so many of Asch's noble characters, for the sanctification of the name.

Asch was attracted to the story of Jesus on an early trip to Palestine, but he did not turn to writing it until decades later, when the need for closer Jewish-Christian ties seemed to him highly desirable. The device he finally employed for telling it was ingenious: A half-demented anti-Semitic Polish scholar, imagining that he was Pontius Pilate's right-hand man, relates the first third of the novel. Judas Ischariot, Jesus' most learned disciple, whom Asch rehabilitates in the novel, tells the next third in the form of a diary. The final third, recounted by a Jewish disciple of Nicodemus, a rabbi sympathetic to Jeshua, reports on the political and religious evasions within the Sanhedrin and Pilate's desire to rid himself of the troublemaking revolutionary.

Again, Asch displays his mastery of painting different milieus. The messianic craving among lowly and wealthy Jews, the Roman cynicism toward this strangest of peoples, the Jews, the doings in the Temple, the political rivalries between priests and scholars, the evocation of historical figures, the atmosphere of Jesus' preaching and reception in Gali lee—all come alive in Asch's prose. If Rabbi Jeshua is only partly convincing, it is because his dual status as man and Messiah may well elude even the most skillful of writers.

EAST RIVER

Set on New York's East Side, another radically different milieu, *East River* is hardly one of Asch's better novels. The writing, even the syntax, appears a bit sloppy, and the work bears the marks of haste. The novel does, however, pull together many of Asch's most typical themes and interests: the poor sorely tried, and not by poverty alone; one son given to learning, the other to practical pursuits; traditional Jewish religious learning transformed into secular equivalents; anti-Semitism and the need for Jewish-Christian dialogue; the spirit of a religion versus its mere forms. Intermarriage, which unleashed a minor religious war between contending religious leaders in *Salvation*, is treated here with sympathy and understanding.

To be sure, Moshe Wolf, symbol of the old life, cannot reconcile himself to his wealthy son's intermarriage, but neither can he accept—in spite of, or because of, his own poverty—this son's exploitation of Jewish and Christian workers. Wolf, a near saint, accepts with love and understanding the burdens imposed on him by God: his beloved older son's crippling polio, this son's failure to use his dazzling intelligence to study Scripture, applying it instead to secular ideas, which often frighten the traditional Jew in him. Wolf's wife, Deborah, thoroughly Americanized, has more understanding for the tycoon son than for the "cripple." For her, the former has succeeded; the latter, with his superfluous learning, is useless.

The Catholic girl who originally loved the cripple but then married the tycoon is treated sympathetically and is ultimately accepted by Wolf as a God-loving, God-seeking human being. Mary breaks with her pathologically anti-Semitic failure of a father and leads her husband back to the ways of decency and righteousness. Mary's relationships with her father and husband are not credible and detract seriously from any power the novel might have. Yet for whatever it is worth, Mary convinces her husband not to live only for himself or even his immediate family, but to enlist himself in the war against poverty, injustice, and cruelty. The old lesson is repeated here in less subtle form: Humans do not live by bread, or money, alone.

Asch's daring in tackling milieus that cannot have been close to him is admirable: a grocery store, Tammany Hall, sweatshops, synagogue politics, Jewish-Irish relations, the garment industry. It is interesting to speculate what this book would have been like at the height of Asch's literary power. A courageous failure, it testifies to the profoundly ecumenical spirit of his fiction.

Lothar Kahn

OTHER MAJOR WORKS

SHORT FICTION: *From Many Countries: The Collected Stories of Sholem Asch*, 1958.

PLAYS: *Tsurikgekumen*, pr. 1904; *Der Got fun Nekome*, pr. 1907 (*The God of Vengeance*, 1918).

NONFICTION: *What I Believe*, 1941; *One Destiny: An Epistle to the Christians*, 1945.

BIBLIOGRAPHY

Brodwin, Stanley. "History and Martyrological Tragedy: The Jewish Experience in Sholem Asch and Andre Schwarz." *Twentieth Century Literature* 40 (1994): 72-91. An excellent comparative analysis of Asch's novel *Kiddush Hashem* and Andre Schwarz-Bart's *Le Dernier des justes*. The novels focus on the biblical injunction of *Kiddish hashem*, in which both the Jewish individual and the Jewish community are called upon to sanctify the name of God by suffering martyrdom.

Fischthal, Hannah Berliner. "Christianity as a Consistent Area of Investigation of Sholem Asch's Works Prior to *The Nazarene*." *Yiddish* 9 (1994): 58-76. Focuses on how Asch treated Christianity in the works he wrote prior to *The Nazarene*, his controversial 1939 novel based on the life of Jesus Christ.

Lieberman, Herman. *The Christianity of Sholem Asch*. New York: Philosophical Library, 1953. Lieberman, a columnist for the Yiddish-language newspaper *Forward*, provides a scathing denunciation of *The Nazarene*, claiming that Asch's novel about the life of Jesus "may lure away ignorant Jewish children into worshipping foreign gods."

Norich, Anita. *Discovering Exile: Yiddish and Jewish American Culture During the Holocaust*. Stanford, Calif.: Stanford University Press, 2007. Studies the writings of Asch and other Jewish authors who published works in both Yiddish and English during the Holocaust to demonstrate how the Yiddish- and English-speaking worlds of the 1930's and 1940's drew upon each other for inspiration.

Siegel, Ben. *The Controversial Sholem Asch: An Introduction to His Fiction*. Bowling Green, Ohio: Bowling Green State University Press, 1976. Often cited as the best introduction to Asch's life and work, this book is especially good for its examination of the controversy that followed the publication of *The Nazarene*. Includes a chronology, bibliography, and detailed index.

Slochower, Harry. "Franz Werfel and Sholem Asch: The Yearning for Status." In *No Voice Is Wholly Lost: Writers and Thinkers in War and Peace*. New York: Creative Age Press, 1945. This essay is another good comparative analysis to be read in conjunction with that of Stanley Brodwin.

Stahl, Nanette, ed. *Sholem Asch Reconsidered*. New Haven, Conn.: Beinecke Rare Book and Manuscript Library, Yale University, 2004. Reprints lectures delivered at a conference held at Yale in 2000, in which Yiddish literary critics reevaluated Asch's work. Includes a discussion of his christological novels, plays, and American fiction, as well as his novels dealing with the radical change and dislocation experienced by European Jews at the beginning of the twentieth century. Also includes an overview of Asch's life by his great-grandson, David Mazower.

Steinberg, Theodore. L. "Sholem Asch's *Three Cities*." In *Twentieth-Century Epic Novels*. Newark: University of Delaware Press, 2005. Steinberg analyzes *Three Cities* and four novels by other authors to demonstrate how the novels' themes and contents, especially their heroic elements, qualify them as modern epics.

SAUL BELLOW

Born: Lachine, Quebec, Canada; June 10, 1915
Died: Brookline, Massachusetts; April 5, 2005

PRINCIPAL LONG FICTION

Dangling Man, 1944
The Victim, 1947
The Adventures of Augie March, 1953
Seize the Day, 1956
Henderson the Rain King, 1959
Herzog, 1964
Mr. Sammler's Planet, 1970
Humboldt's Gift, 1975
The Dean's December, 1982
More Die of Heartbreak, 1987
A Theft, 1989
The Bellarosa Connection, 1989
The Actual, 1997 (novella)
Ravelstein, 2000
Novels, 1944-1953, 2003 (includes *Dangling Man*, *The Victim*, and *The Adventures of Augie March*)
Novels, 1956-1964, 2007 (includes *Seize the Day*, *Henderson the Rain King*, and *Herzog*)

OTHER LITERARY FORMS

In addition to his many novels, Saul Bellow published short stories, plays, and a variety of nonfiction. His stories have appeared in *The New Yorker*, *Commentary*, *Partisan Review*, *Hudson Review*, *Esquire*, and other periodicals, and his collections of short stories include *Mosby's Memoirs, and Other Stories* (1968) and *Him with His Foot in His Mouth, and Other Stories* (1984). His full-length play *The Last Analysis* was produced for a short run on Broadway in 1964, and three one-act plays, *Orange Soufflé*, *A Wen*, and *Out from Under*, were staged in 1966 in the United States and Europe. Another one-act play, *The Wrecker*, was published, though not staged, in 1954. Throughout his career, Bellow wrote numerous articles on a variety of topics. In 1976, he published an account of his trip to Israel, *To Jerusalem and Back: A Personal Account.*

ACHIEVEMENTS

Often described as one of America's most important novelists, Saul Bellow earned enormous critical praise and a wide readership as well. He was awarded the Nobel Prize in

Saul Bellow
(The Nobel Foundation)

Literature in 1976. His popularity is, perhaps, surprising, because his novels do not contain the usual ingredients one expects to find in best-selling fiction—suspense, heroic figures, and graphic sex and violence. In fact, his novels are difficult ones that wrestle with perplexing questions, sometimes drawing from esoteric sources such as the anthroposophy of Rudolf Steiner and the psychology of Wilhelm Reich. One of America's most erudite novelists, Bellow often alluded to the work of philosophers, psychologists, poets, anthropologists, and other writers in his fiction. He once stated that modern novelists should not be afraid to introduce complex ideas into their work. He found nothing admirable about the anti-intellectualism of many modern writers and believed that most of them failed to confront the important moral and philosophical problems of the modern age. Opposed to the glib pessimism and the "complaint" of the dominant tradition of modern literature, Bellow struggled for affirmation at a time when many writers viewed such a possibility as merely an object of ridicule.

In contrast to many other American writers, who produced their best work when they were young and then wrote mediocre or poor fiction as they grew older, Bellow is known for the consistent high quality of his work. Moreover, his fiction reveals an immense versatility. In his work, one finds highly structured Flaubertian form as well as picaresque narrative, naturalistic realism as well as romance.

Bellow earned a reputation as a master of narrative voice and perspective, a great comic writer (perhaps the best in America since Mark Twain), and a fine craftsman whose remarkable control of the language allowed him to move easily from the highly formal to the colloquial. Most important, his novels illuminate the dark areas of the psyche and possess immense emotional power. Bellow once complained that many contemporary authors and critics are obsessed with symbolism and hidden meanings. A literary work becomes an abstraction for them, and they contrive to evade the emotional power inherent in literature. Bellow's novels do not suffer from abstraction; they deal concretely with passion, death, love, and other fundamental concerns, evoking the whole range of human emotions for his readers.

BIOGRAPHY

Saul Bellow was born Solomon Bellows (he later dropped the "s" from his last name) in Lachine, Quebec, Canada, on June 10, 1915, the youngest of four children. Two years before, his parents, Abraham and Liza (Gordon) Bellows, had emigrated to Canada from St. Petersburg, Russia. The family lived in a very poor section of Montreal, where Bellow learned Yiddish, Hebrew, French, and English. In 1923, Bellow was diagnosed with tuberculosis and spent half a year in Montreal's Royal Victoria Hospital. When he was nine years old, the family moved to Chicago, where they lived in the tenements of Humboldt Park.

In 1933, after graduating from Tuley High School, Bellow entered the University of Chicago. Two years later he transferred to Northwestern University, where he received a bachelor's degree with honors in sociology and anthropology. In 1937, he entered the University of Wisconsin at Madison to study anthropology but left school in December to marry Anita Goshkin and to become a writer. He was employed briefly with the Works Progress Administration Writers' Project and then led a bohemian life, supporting himself with teaching and odd jobs. During World War II, he served in the merchant marine and published his first novel, *Dangling Man*.

After publishing his second novel, *The Victim*, Bellow was awarded a Guggenheim Fellowship in 1948, which enabled him to travel to Europe and work on *The Adventures of Augie March*, parts of which he published in various periodicals before publishing the novel in 1953. This third novel won the National Book Award for fiction in 1953 and established Bellow as one of America's most promising novelists.

After his return from Europe in 1950, Bellow spent a large part of the next decade in New York City and Duchess County, New York, teaching and writing before moving back to Chicago to publish *Herzog*. While *Seize the Day* and *Henderson the Rain King* did not receive the critical attention they deserved, *Herzog* was an enormous critical and financial success, even becoming a best seller for forty-two weeks and selling 142,000 copies, making Bellow wealthy for the first time in his life. *Herzog*, which prompted several thousand readers to send letters to the author pouring out their souls, is not only Bellow's masterpiece but also the most autobiographical of his novels. The impetus for the novel was the breakup of his second marriage, to Sondra Tschacbasov, because of her affair with his best friend, the writer Jack Ludwig. Although the novel reveals all of the important episodes of Bellow's life up to the time of the writing of *Herzog*, its primary focus is on the triangle of Herzog (Bellow), an academic suffering from writer's block, his beautiful and strong-willed wife Madeleine (Sondra), and the flamboyant charlatan Valentine Gersbach (Ludwig). The shameless Gersbach pretends to be Herzog's best friend and even provides marital counseling for the despondent husband while cuckolding him.

The next two novels, *Mr. Sammler's Planet* and *Humboldt's Gift*, helped increase Bellow's reputation but also created some controversy. *Mr. Sammler's Planet* was critical of the excesses of the late 1960's, and some complained that Bellow had become a reactionary. Although Bellow opposed the Vietnam War, he found it difficult to identify with the "counterculture." *Humboldt's Gift* disturbed some critics, who complained that Bellow's interest in the ideas of Austrian social philosopher Rudolf Steiner indicated that he was becoming an escapist; it was a mistaken assumption. An ardent supporter of Israel, Bellow traveled to that country in 1975 and published an account of his journey, *To Jerusalem and Back*. In 1976 he was awarded the Nobel Prize in Literature. Winning the Nobel Prize did not result in a loss of Bellow's creativity, and he published important books in the 1980's and 1990's, especially *The Dean's December*, *More Die of Heartbreak*, and *The Actual*, which challenge conventional thinking on political, aesthetic, and philosophical matters. His final novel, *Ravelstein*, published in 2000, prompted controversy, as it revealed that Bellow's close friend Allan Bloom (Abe Ravelstein in the novel) was gay and probably died as a consequence of acquired immunodeficiency syndrome (AIDS).

Bellow was married five times; he had three sons by his first three wives and, at the age of eighty-four, a daughter by his fifth wife. After living in Chicago for many years, he moved to Massachusetts in 1994, where he became a professor of literature at Boston University. Bellow died in Brookline, Massachusetts, in 2005 at the age of eighty-nine.

ANALYSIS

Saul Bellow's mature fiction can be considered a conscious challenge to modernism, the dominant literary tradition of the age. Bellow viewed modernism as a "victim literature" because it depicts alienated individuals who are conquered by their environments. According to Bellow, this "wasteland" tradition originated in the middle of the nineteenth century with the birth of French realism and culminated in the work of Samuel Beckett and other nihilistic contemporary writers. This victim literature reveals a horror of life and considers humanist values useless in a bleak, irrational world. Modernism assumes that the notion of the individual self that underlies the great tradition of the novel is an outmoded concept and that modern civilization is doomed.

First novels

Bellow's first two novels owe a large debt to the wasteland modernism that he would explicitly reject in the late 1940's. *Dangling Man* is an existentialist diary that owes much to Fyodor Dostoevski's *Notes from the Underground* (1864). The demoralized protagonist, Joseph, is left "dangling" as he waits to be drafted during World War II. A moral casualty of war, he has no sense of purpose and feels weary of a life that seems boring, trivial, and cruel. Excessively self-conscious and critical of those around him, he spends most of his time alone, writing in his journal. He can no longer continue his past work, writing biographical essays on philosophers of the Enlightenment. Although he is alienated, he does realize that he should not make a doctrine out of this feeling. The conclusion of the novel reveals Joseph's ultimate failure to transcend his "victimization"; he is drafted and greets his imminent regimentation enthusiastically.

Bellow's next novel, *The Victim*, also depicts a passive protagonist who is unable to overcome his victimization. As Bellow admitted, the novel is partially modeled on Dostoevski's *The Eternal Husband* (1870) and uses the technique of the doppelgänger as Dostoevski does in *The Double* (1846). Bellow's novel presents the psychological struggle between Asa Leventhal, a Jew, and Kirby Allbee, his Gentile "double." A derelict without a job, Allbee suggests that Leventhal is responsible for his grim fate. Leventhal ponders the problem of his guilt and responsibility and tries to rid himself of his persecuting double. Despite his efforts to assert himself, he is still "dangling" at the end of the book—still a victim of forces that, he believes, are beyond his control.

The Adventures of Augie March

After his second novel, Bellow became disenchanted with the depressive temperament and the excessive emphasis on form of modernist literature. He had written his first two novels according to "repressive" Flaubertian formal standards; they were melancholy, rigidly structured, restrained in language, and detached and objective in tone. Rebelling against these constricting standards, Bellow threw off the yoke of modernism when he began to write his third novel. The theme, style, and tone of *The Adventures of Augie March* are very different from those of his earlier novels, for here one finds an open-ended picaresque narrative with flamboyant language and an exuberant hero who seeks to affirm life and the possibility of freedom. Whereas the environment has a profound influence on Joseph and Asa Leventhal, Augie refuses to allow it to determine his fate. During the course of many adventures, a multitude of Machiavellians seek to impose their versions of reality on the good-natured Augie, but he escapes from them, refusing to commit himself.

With his third novel, then, Bellow deliberately rejected the modernist outlook and aesthetic. The problem was to find an alternative to modernism without resorting to glib optimism. It seems that he found an alternative in two older literary traditions—in nineteenth century English Romantic humanism and in a comedy that he considered typically Jewish. Unlike the fiction of the modernists, which denigrates the concept of the individual, Bellow's fiction asserts the potential of the self and its powerful imagination, which can redeem ordinary existence and affirm the value of freedom, love, joy, and hope.

While comedy in Bellow's fiction is a complex matter, its primary function seems to be to undercut the dejection that threatens his heroes. The comic allows Bellow's protagonists to cope with the grim facts of existence; it enables them to avoid despair and gain a balanced view of their problematic situations. Comedy, the spirit of reason, allows them to laugh away their irrational anxieties. Often Bellow seems to encourage his worst anxieties in order to bring them out into the open so that he can dispose of them through comic ridicule.

Seize the Day

Whereas *The Adventures of Augie March* presents Bellow's alternative to a "literature of victimization," his subsequent novels can be regarded as probing, exploratory studies in spiritual survival in a hostile environment. *Seize the Day* is a much more somber novel than *The Adventures of Augie March*. Bellow felt that his liberation from Flaubertian formalism had gone too far, and that he must use more restraint in his fourth novel. He realized that Augie was too effusive and too naïve. The protagonist of *Seize the Day* is similar to the protagonists of the first two novels, but while Tommy Wilhelm is a "victim," Bellow's attitude toward him is different from his attitude toward Joseph and Asa Leventhal. In his fourth novel, Bellow sought to show the spiritual rebirth of such a "victim."

The short novel, divided into seven parts, presents the day of reckoning in the life of Wilhelm, a forty-four-year-old former salesman of children's furniture whose past consists of a series of blunders. Living in the Hotel Gloriana (which is also the residence of his wealthy father, Dr. Adler), Wilhelm feels that he is in a desperate situation. He is unemployed and unable to obtain money from his unsympathetic father. He gives his last seven hundred dollars to be invested for him by the mysterious psychologist Dr. Tamkin, a man who has become not only his surrogate father and financial adviser but also his instructor in spiritual and philosophical matters. Furthermore, Wilhelm's wife, Margaret, from whom he is separated, is harassing him for money. Depressed and confused by the memories of his failures in the past and absorbed by his problems in the present, Wilhelm needs love and compassion. Dr. Adler, Dr. Tamkin, and Margaret all fail him.

Seize the Day is a harsh indictment of a money-obsessed society, where a father is unable to love a son who is unsuccessful. Tamkin's speech on the two souls, no doubt the most important passage in the novel, helps clarify Bellow's social criticism. The psychologist argues that there is a war between a person's "pretender soul," the social self, and the "real soul." When the pretender soul parasitically dominates its host, as is common in modern society, the individual becomes murderous. If the individual is true to the real soul, however, and casts off the false pretender soul, he or she can learn to love and "seize the day."

Bellow shows that all of the characters in the novel are products of an exploitative, materialistic society—all are dominated by their pretender souls. Dr. Adler has fought his way up the economic ladder to success. Revered by the residents of the Hotel Gloriana, he is full of self-love. He desires to spend his remaining years in peace and refuses to acknowledge his paternal obligation to his desperate son. Wilhelm's appeals for money are actually pleas for some sign of paternal concern. He provokes his father, trying to disturb the polite barrier of aloofness that the old man has constructed to prevent any kind of real communication between father and son. While Wilhelm is a difficult son for a father to cherish, Dr. Adler is a coldhearted man who has no real affection for his son, or for anyone else except himself. When, at the end of the novel, Wilhelm begs his father for some kind of sympathy, the hard-boiled Adler brutally rejects him, revealing his hatred for his "soft" son.

Dr. Adler's failure as a father results in Wilhelm's turning to the strange psychologist Dr. Tamkin. Down on his luck, Tamkin is a confidence man hoping to make easy money. He is another one of Bellow's eccentric fast-talkers, full of fantastic stories and philosophical and psychological insights. Wilhelm is attracted to Tamkin not only because he is a father figure who promises to save him from his dire financial crisis but also because he is one man in a cynical society who speaks of spiritual matters. The direct result of Tamkin's advice is the loss of Wilhelm's money, but while the doctor is a phony whose flamboyant personality enables him to dupe the naïve ex-salesman, he does indirectly allow Wilhelm to obtain a kind of salvation.

Wilhelm is the only character in the novel who is able to forsake his pretender soul. He is a product of society as the other characters are, but he is different from them in his instinctive distaste for the inveterate cynicism at the heart of society. Accepting society's definition of success, he considers himself a failure. He suffers immensely and constantly ponders his life and his errors in the past, yet while he can at times degenerate into a buffoon indulging in self-pity and hostility, he is also attracted to the idealism that Tamkin occasionally expounds.

A significant moment occurs near the end of the novel when Wilhelm suddenly feels a sense of brotherhood with his fellow travelers in the New York subway. For once he has transcended his self-absorption, though he is immediately skeptical of this intuitive moment. At the very end of the novel, another heightened moment occurs in which he does make the breakthrough foreshadowed in the subway scene. Having lost all of his money, he pursues into a funeral home a man who resembles Tamkin. Suddenly he finds himself confronting a corpse, and he begins to weep uncontrollably. He weeps not merely out of self-pity, as some have suggested, but for humankind. Understanding that death and suffering are an inextricable part of the human condition, he feels humility and is able to overcome his excessive self-absorption. He is finally able to cast off his pretender soul. The work concludes with a powerful affirmation and suggests an alternative to the spiritual death of a materialistic, predatory society.

HENDERSON THE RAIN KING

Bellow's next novel, *Henderson the Rain King*, is the first fully realized work of his maturity. It is Bellow's first novel of which one can say that no other writer could have conceived it, much less written it. Although it has some characteristics of the picaresque, the fable, and the realistic novel, *Henderson the Rain King* assumes the most widely used form for longer works during the English Romantic era—the quest romance. The tone of the novel is somewhat different from that typically found in the quest romance, however; it is exuberant and comic, and the book is full of wit, parody, farce, and ironic juxtapositions.

The novel might be seen as Bellow's version of Joseph Conrad's *Heart of Darkness* (1902). Like Conrad's Marlow, Eugene Henderson recalls his journey into the heart of Africa and his bizarre adventures there, which culminate in his meeting with a Kurtz-like instructor who has a profound influence on him. Whereas Kurtz reveals to Marlow the human potential for degradation, Dahfu conveys to Henderson the human promise of nobility. With its allusions to William Wordsworth, Samuel Taylor Coleridge, Percy Bysshe Shelley, and William Blake, the novel affirms the possibility of the individual's regeneration by the power of the human imagination; it is a trenchant rejection of Conrad's pessimism.

The novel can be divided into three basic parts: Chapters 1-4 depict Henderson's alienation; chapters 5-9 present his journey to the African tribe of the Arnewi; and chapters 10-22 portray his journey to the African tribe of the Wariri and his spiritual regeneration. The first section presents Henderson's discursive recollections of his life before he set out for Africa, in which he attempts to reveal the reasons for the journey. While these chapters provide a plethora of information about him, he is never able to articulate the reasons for his "quest," as he calls it. Bellow is suggesting in this section that there are no clear-cut reasons for the African journey. Henderson leaves his wife and family for the African wilderness because of his dissatisfaction with his meaningless existence. A millionaire with tremendous energy but no scope for it, Henderson has spent most of his life suffering or making others suffer. Middle-aged, anxious about his mortality, and unable to satisfy the strident inner voice of "I want, I want," he leaves for Africa, hoping to burst "the spirit's sleep," as he phrases it, echoing Shelley's *The Revolt of Islam* (1818).

With his loyal guide Romilayu, he first visits the Arnewi tribe. These people are "children of light" who represent a healthy existence; they are gentle, peaceful, and innocent. Queen Willatale, who rules the tribe, informs Henderson that man wants to live—"grun-tu-molani." It is an important message for Henderson, but he soon demonstrates that he is unable to follow Willatale's wisdom. Desiring to help the tribe, whose water supply has been infested by frogs, he decides to kill the creatures. His bomb is too powerful and destroys the cistern as well as the frogs. Henderson has violated the code of the Arnewi, who abhor violence and have love for all living creatures.

After Henderson leaves the Arnewi, he visits the Wariri, "the children of darkness," who are violent and hostile, reminiscent of the predatory society of Bellow's earlier novels. He does meet one extraordinary individual, however, and establishes a friendship with him. King Dahfu is a noble man who completes Henderson's education begun with the Arnewi. He perceptively observes that Henderson's basic problem is his avoidance of death: He is an "avoider." Dahfu helps him by persuading him to go down into a lion's den to overcome his anxiety over mortality. Dahfu believes, too, that Henderson can absorb qualities of the lion and slough off his porcine characteristics. Dahfu is another one of Bellow's eccentric teachers who speaks both wisdom and nonsense. His greatest importance for Henderson is that he embodies the nobility of human beings, who can by the power of the imagination achieve spiritual regeneration. At the end of the novel, Henderson finally bursts the spirit's sleep and leaves Africa for America. He has a sense of purpose and can love others. He plans to become a physician and will return home to his wife.

HERZOG

Herzog is by most accounts Bellow's best and most difficult novel. It is a retrospective meditation by a middle-aged professor who seeks to understand the reasons for his disastrous past. A complex, discursive work, pervaded by sardonic humor, it defies traditional labeling but owes a debt to the novel of ideas, the psychological novel, the epistolary novel, and the romantic meditative lyric. *Herzog* is a meditative work in which the protagonist compulsively remembers and evaluates his past, striving to avoid complete mental breakdown. There are reminiscences within reminiscences, and the story of Moses Herzog's life is related in fragments. Bellow's method enables the reader to see how Herzog's imagination recollects and assembles the fragments of the past into a meaningful pattern.

Distraught over his recent divorce from his second wife, Madeleine, Herzog has become obsessed with writing letters to everyone connected with that event as well as to important thinkers, living and dead, who concern him. He associates his domestic crisis with the cultural crisis of Western civilization, and therefore he ponders the ethics of Friedrich Nietzsche as well as those of his psychiatrist, Dr. Edvig. Herzog's letter writing is both a symptom of his psychological disintegration and his attempt to meditate on and make sense of suffering and death.

At his home in the Berkshires, Herzog recalls and meditates on the events of his recent past; the five-day period of time that he recalls reveals the severity of his psychological deterioration. His mistress, Ramona, believes that a cure for his nervous state can be found in her Lawrentian sexual passion, but he considers her "ideology" to be mere hedonism; impulsively, he decides to flee from her to Martha's Vineyard, where he has friends. After arriving there, the unstable professor leaves almost immediately and returns to New York. The next evening he has dinner with Ramona and spends the night with her, waking in the middle of the night to write another letter. The following morning he visits a courtroom while waiting for a meeting with his lawyer to discuss a lawsuit against Madeleine. Hearing a brutal child-abuse and murder case causes the distraught professor to associate Madeleine and her lover with the brutal child murderers; he flies to Chicago to kill them. As he spies on them, he realizes his assumption is absurd and abandons his plan. The next morning he takes his young daughter Junie for an outing but has a car accident and is arrested by the police for carrying a gun. He confronts an angry Madeleine at the police station and manages to control his own temper. Later, he is released and returns to his run-down home in the Berkshires, and the novel ends where it began.

Interspersed within these recollections of the immediate past are memories of the more distant past. By piecing these together, one learns the sad story of Herzog's domestic life. Feeling a vague dissatisfaction, the successful professor divorced his first wife, Daisy, a sensible midwestern woman, and began affairs with a good-natured Japanese woman, Sono, and the beautiful, bad-tempered Madeleine. After marrying Madeleine, Herzog purchased a house in the Berkshires, where he intended to complete his important book on the Romantics. Soon they returned to Chicago, however, where both saw a psychiatrist, and Madeleine suddenly announced that she wanted a divorce. The shocked Herzog traveled to Europe to recuperate, only to return to Chicago to learn that Madeleine had been having an affair with his best friend and confidant the whole time their marriage had been deteriorating.

Herzog's grim past—his disastrous marriages and the other sad events of his life that he also recalls—becomes emblematic of the pernicious influence of cultural nihilism. Herzog is devoted to basic humanist values but wonders if he must, as the ubiquitous "reality instructors" insist, become another mass man devoted to a brutal "realism" in the Hobbesian jungle of modern society. His antipathy for the wastelanders' cynicism is strong, but he knows his past idealism has been too naïve. Repeatedly, the "reality instructors" strive to teach ("punish") Herzog with lessons of the "real"—and the "real" is always brutal and cruel. Sandor Himmelstein, Herzog's lawyer and friend, proudly announces that all people are "whores." It is an accurate description not only of Himmelstein but also of his fellow reality instructors. Their cynical view is pervasive in modern society, in which people play roles, sell themselves, and seduce and exploit others for their own selfish ends.

The turning point of the novel is Herzog's revelation in the courtroom episode. Intellectually, he has always known about evil and suffering, but emotionally he has remained innocent. His hearing of the case in which a mother has mistreated and murdered her son while her lover apathetically watched is too much for him to bear; here is a monstrous evil that cannot be subsumed by any intellectual scheme. In a devastating moment the professor is forced to realize that his idealism is foolish.

At the end of the novel, Herzog has achieved a new consciousness. He recognizes that he has been selfish and excessively absorbed in intellectual abstractions. A prisoner of his private intellectual life, he has cut himself off from ordinary humanity and everyday existence. He sees that his naïve idealism and the wastelanders' cruel "realism" are both escapist and therefore unacceptable attitudes; they allow the individual to evade reality by wearing masks of naïve idealism or self-serving cynicism. The exhausted Herzog decides to abandon his compulsive letter writing and to stop pondering his past. The threat of madness has passed, and he is on the road to recovery.

Mr. Sammler's Planet

Mr. Sammler's Planet is a meditative novel of sardonic humor and caustic wit. The "action" of the novel centers on the protagonist's recollection of a brief period of time in the recent past, though there are recollections of a more distant past, too. Once again the mental state of the protagonist is Bellow's main concern. Like Herzog, Artur Sammler has abandoned a scholarly project because he finds rational explanations dissatisfying; they are unable to justify suffering and death. The septuagenarian Sammler is yet another of Bellow's survivors, a lonely humanist in a society populated by brutal "realists."

This seventh novel, however, is not merely a repetition of Bellow's previous works. Sammler is detached and basically unemotional, yet he reveals a mystical bent largely absent in Bellow's other protagonists. He is drawn to the works of Meister Eckhart and other thirteenth century German mystics. While he does not literally believe in their ideas, he finds reading their works soothing. His religious inclination is a recent phenomenon. Sammler had been reared in a wealthy, secular Jewish family in Kraków, Poland. As an adult, he became a haughty, cosmopolitan intellectual, useless to everyone, as he readily admits. On a visit to Poland in 1939, when the Germans suddenly attacked, he, his wife, and others were captured and ordered to dig their own graves as the Nazis waited to murder them. Although his wife was killed in the mass execution, miraculously Sammler escaped by crawling out of his own grave. After the war ended, Sammler and his daughter Shula were rescued from a displaced persons camp by a kind nephew, Dr. Elya Gruner, who became their patron.

The experience of the Holocaust destroyed what little religious inclination Sammler possessed, but in his old age he has become concerned with his spiritual state. Unfortunately, it is difficult to pursue spiritual interests in a materialistic society hostile to them. The basic conflict in the novel is between Sammler's need to ponder the basic questions of existence—a need accentuated by the dying of the noble Gruner—and the distractions of modern-day society. In the primary action of the novel, Sammler's main intention is to visit the dying Gruner, who finds Sammler a source of great comfort. Several "accidents" distract Sammler from his goal, and on the day of his nephew's death, he arrives too late.

The "accidents" that encumber Sammler reveal clearly the "degraded clowning" of contemporary society. Sammler is threatened by a black pickpocket who corners the old man and then exposes himself. In the middle of a lecture he is shouted down by a radical student who says that Sammler is sexually defective. His daughter Shula steals a manuscript from an Indian scholar, and Sammler must waste precious time to recover it. Even Gruner's self-centered children, who have little compassion for their dying father, distract Sammler by their thoughtless actions.

Opposed to Gruner, who is part of the "old system" that esteems the family, the expression of emotion, and the traditional humanist values, is the contemporary generation, a kind of "circus" characterized by role-playing, hedonism, amorality, self-centeredness, and atrophy of feeling. Despite its flaws, Bellow sympathizes with the "old system." The novel concludes after Sammler, despite the objections of the hospital staff, goes into the postmortem room and says a prayer for Gruner's soul.

HUMBOLDT'S GIFT

As in Bellow's previous novels, the tension and the humor of *Humboldt's Gift* have their origins in the protagonist's attempt to free himself from the distractions of contemporary society and pursue the needs of his soul. The protagonist, Charlie Citrine, strives to define for himself the function of the artist in contemporary America. He tries to come to terms with the failure and premature death of his onetime mentor, Von Humboldt Fleisher, who had the potential to be America's greatest modern poet but achieved very little. Charlie wonders if the romantic poet can survive in a materialistic society; he wonders, too, if he can overcome his fear of the grave and exercise his imagination. A writer who has squandered his talent, Charlie has intimations of terror of the grave and intimations of immortality. He spends much time reading the anthroposophical works of Rudolf Steiner; although he is skeptical of some of Steiner's more esoteric teachings, he is sympathetic to the spiritual worldview of anthroposophy, even finding the notion of reincarnation persuasive.

The primary nemesis of Charlie's spiritual life is Ronald Cantabile, a small-time criminal. Renata, Charlie's voluptuous mistress, Denise, his ex-wife, and Pierre Thaxter, a confidence man, are also major distractions. When Charlie, on the advice of a friend, refuses to pay Cantabile the money he owes him from a poker game, the criminal harasses him. In fact, the proud, psychopathic Cantabile refuses to leave Charlie alone even after he agrees to pay him the money. He continually humiliates Charlie and even tries to involve him in a plot to murder the troublesome Denise.

Denise, Renata, and Thaxter also distract Charlie from pondering the fate of Humboldt and meditating on fundamental metaphysical questions. Hoping Charlie will return to her, Denise refuses to settle her support suit and continues to demand more money. When Charlie is forced to put up a two-hundred-thousand-dollar bond, he is financially ruined, and the loss of his money results in the loss of the voluptuous Renata, who decides to marry a wealthy undertaker. A third disillusioning experience involves Thaxter, who has apparently conned Charlie. Charlie had invested a small fortune in a new journal, *The Ark*, which was supposed to restore the authority of art and culture in the United States. Thaxter, the editor of *The Ark*, never puts out the first issue and has, it appears, stolen the money. His confidence game symbolizes America's lack of respect for art and culture, impractical subjects in a practical, technological society.

Charlie does, however, overcome these "distractions." Humboldt's posthumously delivered letter, accompanied by an original film sketch (his "gift") and a scenario that the two had written at Princeton years before, provides the genesis for Charlie's salvation. The original film idea and the scenario of their Princeton years enable Charlie to attain financial security, but, more important, Humboldt's letter provides the impetus for Charlie's decision at the end of the novel to repudiate his past empty life and pursue the life of the imagination. Humboldt's ideas, bolstered by the poetry of Blake, Wordsworth, and John Keats, enable Charlie to avoid the fate of the self-destructive artist. He decides to live in Europe and meditate on the fundamental questions—in short, to take up a different kind of life.

When, at the end of the novel, Charlie gives Humboldt and the poet's mother a proper burial, Bellow suggests that Charlie's imagination is ready to exert itself and wake him from his self-centered boredom and death-in-life. The final scene of the novel promises Charlie's spiritual regeneration.

THE DEAN'S DECEMBER

Bellow's 1982 novel *The Dean's December* is "a tale of two cities," Chicago and Bucharest, in which the protagonist, a dean at an unnamed college in Chicago, ponders private and public problems. Albert Corde experiences at first hand the rigid penitentiary society of the Communist East as well as the anarchic society of the non-Communist West, which seems on the verge of disintegration. The novel is a protest against the dehumanization of the individual. The East has enslaved its population, while the West has "written off" its doomed "Underclass." Like *Humboldt's Gift*, this novel can be seen as a kind of retrospective crisis meditation in which the protagonist attempts to come to terms with an immensely complex and threatening "multiverse," as Augie March calls it.

The complicated plot defies a succinct summary, but the basic situation can be outlined. The dean and his wife, Minna, arrive in Romania to visit her dying mother. Corde tries to help his despairing wife, who is unable to reconcile herself to the grim reality of her mother's death. He also ponders the controversy that he has provoked in Chicago. The dean has published two articles in *Harper's* in which he has commented on the political and social problems of the city. The articles outrage the powerful members of Chicago society, and the administration of his college disapproves of the controversy that the dean has provoked. Moreover, Corde creates another controversy when he pressures the police to solve the murder of a white graduate student, Rickie Lester. A sensational trial, a "media circus," is the result of the dean's search for justice.

While, more than any other novel by Bellow, *The Dean's December* is concerned with contemporary public issues, especially the vile conditions of the inner city, it is also concerned with the spiritual state of the individual. In fact, Bellow suggests that there is a connection between the spiritual malady of the individual and the spiritual anarchy of society. The novel is a protest against not only people's lack of political freedom but also the spiritual enslavement that is the result of their inability to see clearly and to experience reality. Corde implies that this inability to experience reality is largely a product of "seeing" the world with a kind of reductive journalism completely lacking in imagination. Disgusted with contemporary journalism that provides only substitutes for reality, Corde intends to incorporate "poetry" into writing. The novel suggests that in Corde's kind of poetic vision there is hope for the spiritual rebirth of the individual and society.

MORE DIE OF HEARTBREAK

Three years after the publication of his collection *Him with His Foot in His Mouth, and Other Stories*, Bellow published *More Die of Heartbreak*. This comic novel does not have a highly structured plot; rather, it might be best described as an elaborate monologue from the overstimulated mind of the bachelor narrator, Kenneth Trachtenberg. Kenneth, an expert in Russian history and culture, is preoccupied with his uncle, Benn Crader, a renowned botanist. The only important "action" in the novel revolves around the attempt of Dr. Layamon, his daughter Matilda, and her fiancé Benn Crader to "extort" money from Benn's relative, Harold Vilitzer, a political racketeer in bad health. Years before, Vilitzer had cheated the Crader family in a real estate deal. The greedy Dr. Layamon sees his daughter's marriage to Benn as a marvelous opportunity to acquire a fortune if Benn will agree to pressure Vilitzer for the money the corrupt politician stole from the Crader family. Although he wants to please his beautiful fiancé and her father, Benn is not enthusiastic about the plan. As the narrator suggests, Benn is a man who should be in search of "higher meanings." At the end of the novel, Benn flees from the Layamons to the North Pole to carry out his research. The implication is that now he will be able to pursue his neglected aesthetic and metaphysical goals.

A THEFT

After being rejected by two periodicals because it was "too long," the short novel *A Theft* was published in 1989 as a paperback original. Like so many of Bellow's works, the plot of this 109-page novel is subordinate to Bellow's interest in character. Just as *Seize the Day* might be considered an intimate psychological exploration of Wilhelm, *A Theft* is a detailed exploration of the soul of the heroine, Clara Velde. Clara was brought up on old-time religion but has led a disorganized life, including disappointing love affairs, suicide attempts, and four marriages. Her fourth marriage is not successful, and she is actually in love with an "old flame," Ithiel Regler, a Henry Kissinger-like high-powered adviser to statesmen. For Clara, transcendent love between her and Ithiel is symbolized by an emerald ring that he gave her years ago. When this ring is stolen, Clara finds herself in a troubling search for it and experiences a kind of spiritual quest as well. She feels a special sense of kinship with her self-possessed au pair, Gina. In its epiphany-like quality, the conclusion of the novel is reminiscent of *Seize the Day.*

THE BELLAROSA CONNECTION

Another paperback original, the short novel *The Bellarosa Connection* is narrated by the wealthy founder of the Mnemosyne Institute in Philadelphia. The institute instructs businesspeople and others in the use of memory. The narrator, a retired widower, focuses his immense powers of recollection on two relatives who haunt him—Harry and Sorella Fonstein. Harry narrowly escaped the Nazi death camps, thanks to the Broadway producer Billy Rose, who made use of his gangster connections in Italy to help Fonstein and others escape to freedom. Billy Rose's generosity is particularly noteworthy, the narrator implies, because the Broadway producer has a sleazy reputation.

In the United States, Harry marries the intelligent, capable Sorella and becomes successful but is frustrated by Rose's repulsing Harry's repeated attempts to meet him and express his gratitude. The central scene of the novel is the dramatic encounter between Sorella and Rose, in which the determined woman attempts to coerce the stubborn producer into meeting her husband by threatening to reveal sordid details of Rose's private life. Despite Sorella's "blackmail," Rose refuses to meet Harry. Bellow in this short novel is pondering how the assimilation of Jews into American life can corrupt not only their values but also their souls. Sorella reflects: "The Jews could survive everything that Europe threw at them. I mean the lucky remnant. But now comes the next test—America." Apparently the United States proves "too much" for at least some of them.

THE ACTUAL

The novella *The Actual* is narrated by Harry Trellman, an introspective man in his sixties who grew up in a lower-middle-class Jewish neighborhood in Chicago. His father was a simple carpenter; his mother's family was wealthy. Harry was put in an orphanage despite the fact that both his parents were alive because his hypochondriacal mother did not have the time to care for him; she spent much time abroad and in the United States at various sanitariums looking for a cure for her disease of the joints. The bills for sojourns abroad and at home were paid by the mother's family; her brothers were successful sausage manufacturers who could pay for the cures she took at Bad Nauheim or Hot Springs, Arkansas. After the Korean War, the government sent Harry to study Chinese at a "special school." He spent a number of years in the Far East, the final two in Burma, where he made business connections, and then returned to Chicago, where he had "unfinished emotional business."

Although the precise source of Harry's income is not clear, apparently he is well-off. Semiretired and without financial concerns, Harry is nevertheless far from being content. For more than four decades he has loved Amy Wustrin, whom he first knew in high school. When Harry returned to Chicago after his Far East sojourn, he and Amy met again. Despite for Harry a momentous sexual encounter in which he kissed Amy "under the breast and inside the thigh," the relationship did not progress. After divorcing her first husband, Amy married Jay Wustrin, Harry's best friend in high school. Neither Jay nor Amy paid much heed to the marriage vows, and the result was a bitter divorce that culminated in Jay's playing tapes in divorce court of Amy's adulterous lovemaking in which one could hear her orgasmic cries. None of this disheartening history dampened Harry's ardent love for Amy.

Harry and Amy are brought together by the ninety-two-year-old billionaire Sigmund Adletsky, for whom Amy is working as an interior decorator and Harry as adviser in his "brain trust." Harry accompanies Amy in her emotionally arduous task of exhuming Jay's body from his cemetery plot next to the grave of Amy's mother so that Amy can bury her father there. (A practical joker with nihilistic proclivities, Jay had purchased the plot from Amy's father.) In the grave scene that concludes the novel, the withdrawn intellectual Harry takes decisive action by confessing his love for Amy and asking her to marry him. This scene is reminiscent of the conclusion to *Humboldt's Gift*, when the protagonist in the cemetery achieves an epiphany and the work ends with the implication that the protagonist, keenly aware of mortality and the death-in-life of his past existence, will be spiritually reborn.

Ravelstein

Bellow's final novel, *Ravelstein*, is heavily autobiographical and explores the relationship between the narrator Chick (Bellow) and his good friend Abe Ravelstein, a fictional portrait of Allan Bloom, whose book *The Closing of the American Mind* (1987) was a surprise best seller and made the University of Chicago professor wealthy and famous. This novel prompted some controversy when it was published because it revealed that Bloom was gay and probably died of complications from AIDS. Some people felt that Bellow acted unethically by "outing" Bloom and invading his privacy. Bellow seems to have anticipated this objection to the writing of *Ravelstein*, for early in the novel the dying Ravelstein encourages his friend Chick to write a book about him after he dies and be as ruthless as Chick wants in exposing his flaws and weaknesses. It is likely that the iconoclastic Bloom encouraged Bellow to write a candid book about him that would eschew all romanticizing and sentimentality.

The form of the novel owes debts to the genres of biography, memoir, and roman à clef. In addition to the narrator and Ravelstein, other characters in the novel also have real-life counterparts, including Bellow's fifth wife, Janis Freedman, as Rosamund; his Romanian-born fourth spouse, Alexandra Tulcea, as Vela; the conservative thinker Leo Strauss as Davaar; the sociologist Edward Shils as Rakhmiel Kogon; former assistant secretary of state Paul Wolfowitz as Philip Gorman; and political scientist Werner Dannhauser as Ravelstein's close friend Morris Herbst.

Unlike *The Victim* or many of Bellow's other stories, plot is unimportant in this novel;

portrayal of character and the exploration of ideas are the primary interests. Bellow is concerned, too, with exploring the interior life of the narrator, who is preoccupied with the problem of nihilism in its various forms and disguises. The narrator wrestles with the problem of how a good person should react to evil in the modern world. Chick seems to regard Ravelstein as his mentor—this dying intellectual comes to embody Jewish humanism that places the highest importance on the worth of human life and the value of the individual; in contrast is the murderous nihilism of the World War II period that resulted in the horrors of the Holocaust. The meandering meditative mind of the narrator repeatedly returns to the anti-Semitism of the twentieth century, which represents the evil that is the opposite of the goodness that Ravelstein embodies.

Ravelstein is a death-haunted book that describes not only the final illness of the narrator's dear friend but also the illness that comes very close to killing the narrator. Like Bellow, who nearly died from an illness similar to the narrator's, the narrator survives to write this portrait of his friend. The book concludes with the narrator's recollection of his and Ravelsteins's discovery of a huge flock of tropical parrots surviving in the midwestern winter. This epiphany suggests that the narrator has finally reconciled himself to the profound loss of his friend and that he can affirm existence in all its inexplicable strangeness and mysterious beauty.

Allan Chavkin

OTHER MAJOR WORKS

SHORT FICTION: *Mosby's Memoirs, and Other Stories*, 1968; *Him with His Foot in His Mouth, and Other Stories*, 1984; *Something to Remember Me By: Three Tales*, 1991; *Collected Stories*, 2001.

PLAYS: *The Wrecker*, pb. 1954; *The Last Analysis*, pr. 1964; *Under the Weather*, pr. 1966 (also known as *The Bellow Plays*; includes *Out from Under*, *A Wen*, and *Orange Soufflé*).

NONFICTION: *To Jerusalem and Back: A Personal Account*, 1976; *Conversations with Saul Bellow*, 1994 (Gloria L. Cronin and Ben Siegel, editors); *It All Adds Up: From the Dim Past to the Uncertain Future*, 1994.

EDITED TEXT: *Great Jewish Short Stories*, 1963.

BIBLIOGRAPHY

Atlas, James. *Bellow: A Biography*. New York: Random House, 2000. Full and accessible biography was written with the cooperation of its subject. Includes bibliography and index.

Bach, Gerhard, ed. *The Critical Response to Saul Bellow*. Westport, Conn.: Greenwood Press, 1995. Substantial collection presents two to five reviews and essays on each of Bellow's novels. Includes an informative editor's introduction, a chronology, and an interview with Bellow.

Bigler, Walter. *Figures of Madness in Saul Bellow's Longer Fiction*. New York: Peter Lang, 1998. Examines the psychological makeup of Bellow's characters. Includes bibliographical references.

Bloom, Harold, ed. *Saul Bellow*. New York: Chelsea House, 1986. Omnibus of reviews and essays on Bellow's work gives a good sense of the early critical responses. Includes commentary by writers such as Robert Penn Warren, Malcolm Bradbury, Tony Tanner, Richard Chase, and Cynthia Ozick.

Cronin, Gloria L. *A Room of His Own: In Search of the Feminine in the Novels of Saul Bellow*. Syracuse, N.Y.: Syracuse University Press, 2001. Approaches Bellow's novels from the perspective of French feminist theory, providing many provocative insights on gender in the works and analyzing Bellow's characters with attention to the nuances of language. Unlike some critics, Cronin avoids a reductionist reading of Bellow's work that sees the novels as the product of a biased male point of view.

Freedman, William. "Hanging for Pleasure and Profit: Truth as Necessary Illusion in Bellow's Fiction." *Papers on Language and Literature* 35 (Winter, 1999): 3-27. Argues that Bellow's realism is a search for truth, not the discovery of it. Discusses how Bellow deals with the question of whether the individual is isolated or a member of a human community. Contends that for Bellow the value of literature is the ceaseless search for truth in a world that promises truth but seldom provides it.

Halldorson, Stephanie S. *The Hero in Contemporary American Fiction: The Works of Saul Bellow and Don DeLillo*. New York: Palgrave Macmillan, 2007. Juxtaposition of the works of two major American writers who are rarely linked results in an insightful examination of the meaning of the hero and the antihero in modern culture.

Kiernan, Robert. *Saul Bellow*. New York: Continuum, 1989. Provides a useful chronology of Bellow's life and production. Traces the writer's development from *Dangling Man* to *More Die of Heartbreak*. Among the best books on Bellow for the general reader.

Leroux, Jean-Francois. "Exhausting Ennui: Bellow, Dostoevsky, and the Literature of Boredom." *College Literature* 35, no. 1 (Winter, 2008): 1-15. Explores the theme of ennui, a major element in Bellow's work, and the influence of the novels of Fyodor Dostoevski on Bellow's outlook.

Miller, Ruth. *Saul Bellow: A Biography of the Imagination*. New York: St. Martin's Press, 1991. Traces Bellow's travels, linking the author's life to his work. Contains useful appendices, a bibliography, a listing of interviews, and a table of contents from *The Noble Savage*, a journal edited by Bellow.

DANILO KIŠ

Born: Subotica, Yugoslavia (now in Serbia); February 22, 1935
Died: Paris, France; October 15, 1989

PRINCIPAL LONG FICTION

Mansarda, 1962 (English translation, 2008)
Psalam 44, 1962
Bašta, pepeo, 1965 (*Garden, Ashes*, 1975)
Peščanik, 1972 (*Hourglass*, 1990)
Grobnica za Borisa Davidoviča, 1976 (*A Tomb for Boris Davidovich*, 1978)

OTHER LITERARY FORMS

In addition to novels, Danilo Kiš (keesh) published two books of short stories that are sometimes mistakenly labeled as novels: *Rani jadi* (1970; *Early Sorrows: For Children and Sensitive Readers*, 1998) and *Enciklopedija mrtvih* (1983; *The Encyclopedia of the Dead*, 1989). His short stories lose some of their significance in that Kiš often wrote his novels as collections of related stories, thus blurring the line between the two genres. His attempts at television drama, *Noć i magla* (1968; night and fog), *Papagaj* (1969; parrot), and *Drveni sanduk Tomasa Wulfa* (1974; wooden trunk of Thomas Wolfe), have been less successful than his other works. Kiš also was an essayist and polemicist, advocating new approaches to literature and expounding his own views on literary art. His *Po-etika* (1972; poetics), *Po-etika, knjiga druga* (1974; poetics, book two), and especially *Čas anatomije* (1978; a lesson in anatomy) are examples of a spirited and passionate defense of his own works against detractors. In addition, the essays trace for younger writers the path to a more modern approach to writing. Kiš also skillfully translated the works of some major writers from the original French, Hungarian, and Russian.

ACHIEVEMENTS

Danilo Kiš belongs to the generation of Serbian writers who burst upon the literary scene in the mid-1960's with a fresh outlook on literature and with surprisingly mature works. As one of the most articulate and cosmopolitan among them, he was able to bring down the barriers of traditionalism and provincialism prevalent in Serbian prose up to that time. To be sure, that process had begun before Kiš's generation, but it reached its full potential with that generation, finally bringing Serbian prose into the mainstream of contemporary world literature. His second important contribution can be seen in his highly accomplished style. His seemingly simple yet rather sophisticated realism, broad erudition, and uncanny dexterity with words made him the undisputed leader among the Serbian writers in the second half of the twentieth century. With these qualities, Kiš has appealed to readers beyond his homeland, resulting in translations of his works into many languages. Among other awards, he received the French Legion of Honor medal as a Knight of the Arts and Literature.

BIOGRAPHY

Danilo Kiš was born in Subotica, a northern city of Yugoslavia (now in Serbia) near the Hungarian border, on February 22, 1935, of a Jewish father and a Montenegrin mother. His family was subjected to terror during World War II, which his father and other relatives did not survive. He spent his childhood in Novi Sad until the infamous massacre of Serbs and Jews in 1942, after which he fled to his father's home village in Hungary. After the war, working on farms and voraciously reading adventure, mystery, and crime books, he nurtured his imagination and the love for books that eventually brought him to Belgrade University, from which he graduated in 1958 with a degree in comparative literature. As a young lecturer, Kiš spent two years in Bordeaux, France, an experience that led to a long-standing love affair with that country. He lived and worked in Paris for most of his adult life, until his death from lung cancer in 1989.

ANALYSIS

In most of his works, Danilo Kiš is preoccupied with the suffering of people during wartime, especially those the hardest hit—Jews and other minorities. He does not dwell on suffering per se but rather on what war forces the victims to do under such unusual circumstances. The mistreatment of the innocent and their outward dehumanization offer them a chance to observe their past and to arrive at some rudimentary understanding of the meaning of existence. This process pertains even to those who suffered in peacetime at the hands of oppressors, since their suffering, too, was often the result of war. By transforming the tragic fate of specific individuals into general experience, Kiš imbued his works with universality and pathos. His sophisticated approach to both form and subject matter raises the artistic value of his works.

MANSARDA

Kiš's first work, the short novel *Mansarda* (the attic), did not foreshadow his primary concerns discussed above. The work of a novice, *Mansarda* reveals the ebullience of a writer flexing his muscles. One impressionistic chapter follows another in no discernible order. The characters find it difficult to separate reality from hallucinations. There is hardly any plot, and the themes crystallize only after a tortuous course of events. What the novel does show, however, is the age-old problem of young people in search of identity amid growing pains, and the seductive and often tragic combination of love and suicide. The central feature of this fledgling yet remarkably mature work is the metaphor of an attic, where the protagonist lives, to which he constantly returns yet from which he is pulled down to earth, where he must face the reality of everyday existence. *Mansarda* did not solve this perennial dilemma, but it promised more mature accomplishments by the young author.

PSALAM 44

In *Psalam 44* (Psalm 44) appears for the first time the theme that would recur in most of Kiš's subsequent works. Written in a more controlled style than *Mansarda, Psalam 44* depicts, in an almost entirely realistic fashion, a few hours in a Nazi concentration camp during the last days of World War II. Again, Kiš does not so much describe what happens to the main characters—a captive Jewish doctor forced to ply his trade in the camp and a young Jewish girl who has just given birth to their child—as he does reveal their thinking and feelings. Tortured by their tense inner world and the bizarre real world crumbling around them, they are nurtured by the concern and help they receive from other inmates and, most important, by their own love, which conquers all obstacles. The author does not succumb to this potentially trite subject matter, nor does he moralize. Resisting these temptations, Kiš creates a deeply felt artistic document of humankind's inhumanity toward humans.

GARDEN, ASHES

In his third novel, *Garden, Ashes*, Kiš's main theme gains full force. Through the reminiscences of his dolorous childhood, he builds a monument to the memory of his remarkable father—to his memory because, a victim of a pogrom, he left the child's world before there could be a closer, more prosaic relationship. The father was an eccentric and an incorrigible dreamer, a frustrated genius, a poet, a philosopher, a grotesque Don Quixote, a drunkard, a proud squanderer of his many gifts, a giant among Lilliputians, and a misplaced wanderer from some exotic land. He was the focal point of the child's imagination and preoccupations for a long time.

The father's most important function, as far as the boy is concerned, was to impress on the child's feverish imagination a firm belief that life is not what it seems to be—a sequence of cruel, frightful, seemingly meaningless events—or that at least it does not have to be so. The fact that the father was always an alien among the people around him only enhances the boy's awe and love for him. The tragic circumstances of his disappearance and the passage of time have added an aura of pathos and unreality to the already unreal experiences of a growing boy—learning to accept and cope with his father and his memory. The reader is left with the feeling that the bonds between the precocious child and his wayward father are indestructible and that the father's shadow will accompany the child's every step into adulthood.

These events are related by Kiš in a poetic tone and with an accomplished style. He incorporates many modern techniques, skillfully blending reality and dream and following the rampant imagination of a gifted, painfully sensitive child. The result is more than another confessional, cathartic farewell to childhood by a young man who has outgrown it: It is, rather, an artistic creation with a life of its own. The exceptional beauty and richness of the language come through even in translation.

HOURGLASS

Kiš returns to this, by now more or less constant, theme in his next novel, *Hourglass*. There are, however, significant differences, seen primarily in the noticeable maturation in the author's style and in his approach to the theme. While in *Garden, Ashes* and in the short-story collection *Early Sorrows* the reminiscences of Eduard Sam are those of a son, in *Hourglass* the father, or E. S. as he is called, appears in his own right, telling his own story. The telling of the story also marks an advance for Kiš: While in earlier works the narrative mode was personal, sentimental, and often poetic, this novel features a dazzling variety of narrative devices.

The novel is composed of several sections—"Pictures from a Journey," "Notes of a Lunatic," "Investigation," and "The Investigation of Witnesses"—that represent various approaches to reality and that recur in the novel when particular approaches are being used. The novel ends with a letter written by the protagonist that can be seen as his last will. Each chapter has a specific function that corresponds to the author's varying points of view. In the first of these chapters, impressions of various objects that meet the observer's eye are given in minute detail, underlining one possible method of observation—the purely realistic one. In "Notes of a Lunatic," reality is seen through the mind and emotions of a victim of persecution and suffering. Here the author penetrates the realistic surface created by the previous method.

In the chapters on investigation, Kiš employs a purely dramatic technique of direct questions and answers used in a criminal investigation, thus underscoring the unspeakable tension under which every moment of the protagonist's life is spent. Yet these different approaches are intrinsically related through the author's constant return to the same object in a different guise, as if to say that there is only one reality but there are different perceptions of it. While it is true that this technique makes the novel somewhat complex and at times difficult to follow, it is also true that Kiš is willing to experiment and that the experimentation has added a new dimension to his craft.

In the last analysis, however, the significance of *Hourglass* lies not so much in its artistic virtuosity as in the treatment of the theme that has preoccupied Kiš ever since he began to write: the tragedy of men involved in conflict with one another, whether because of race, religion, politics, or greed. Kiš sees the atrocities and the ensuing suffering in World War II as inevitable as long as humans continue to ignore the need for understanding, compassion, and respect for each other, no matter what the circumstances. The universality of these concerns, combined with its artistic virtues and complexity, make *Hourglass* not only one of the most important achievements in modern Serbian writing but also one of the outstanding works on a central theme of postwar European literature.

A TOMB FOR BORIS DAVIDOVICH

That Kiš is not interested exclusively in the atrocities committed during World War II in his homeland is confirmed by his next novel, *A Tomb for Boris Davidovich*. The focus here shifts to the few years before the outbreak of the war in the Soviet Union—a period during which that country experienced one of the worst cases of humankind's inhumanity to humans, the infamous purges of the so-called dissidents. That the main victims are again Jews is both coincidental and purposeful; while many of the purge victims were Jewish, many others were not. In Kiš's vision, Boris Davidovich is again a universal symbol, as was Eduard Sam in the previous works.

The novel is composed of seven seemingly loosely related stories that, on a closer look, reveal an organic unity. The author follows the crisscrossing paths and intertwined destinies of several people, most of whom again fall victim to persecution through no fault of their own. Yet it is peacetime, and the persecutors are not Nazis. Kiš thus returns to one of the basic lessons of *Hourglass*: Humans will commit the same crime, regardless of motives, if they lose respect for the dignity of their fellow humans. People do not have to be officially at war to exterminate one another; they can do it whenever they take it upon themselves to be the final judges of others or, what is yet more deadly, gods on Earth.

Five of the stories in *A Tomb for Boris Davidovich* deal with the victimization of the Jewish revolutionaries in the Soviet Union. The sixth goes back six centuries, to medieval France, where another Jew, not coincidentally bearing the initials of Boris Davidovich, succumbs to persecution. The only way to combat this perennial evil is through courage and constant resistance, which is exactly what the protagonist of the last story, a Soviet writer, lacks in his refusal to face reality.

Kiš employs here a mixture of facts and fiction, a method new to the literatures of Yugoslavia. His reliance on historical facts provoked widely publicized accusations of plagiarism, which he was able to refute easily by pointing out that, though relying on facts, he gave them artistic garb, weaving them into the intricate web of his imagination.

The combination of significant subject matter and artistic prowess in almost all of his works established Kiš's reputation as one of the best among the contemporary Eastern European writers. What makes him even more important was his ability to transcend narrow regional boundaries and to appeal to readers of all persuasions. Kiš was indeed the most accomplished and modernistic of all contemporary Yugoslav writers.

Vasa D. Mihailovich

OTHER MAJOR WORKS

SHORT FICTION: *Rani jadi*, 1970 (*Early Sorrows: For Children and Sensitive Readers*, 1998); *Enciklopedija mrtvih*, 1983 (*The Encyclopedia of the Dead*, 1989).

TELEPLAYS: *Noč i magla*, 1968; *Papagaj*, 1969; *Drveni sanduk Tomasa Wulfa*, 1974.

NONFICTION: *Po-etika*, 1972; *Po-etika, knjiga druga*, 1974; *Čas anatomije*, 1978; *Homo Poeticus*, 1983; *Gorki, talog iskustva*, 1990; *Homo Poeticus: Essays and Interviews*, 1995; *Skladište*, 1995.

Bibliography

Birnbaum, Marianna D. "History and Human Relationships in the Fiction of Danilo Kiš." In *History, Another Text: Essays on the Fiction of Kazimierz Brandys, Danilo Kiš, György Konrád, and Christa Wolf*, edited by Marianna D. Birnbaum and R. Trager-Verchovsky. Ann Arbor: University of Michigan Press, 1988. A general analysis of the topics of human relations and history in Kiš's novels. Also examines Kiš's short-story collection *The Encyclopedia of the Dead.*

Brodsky, Joseph. Introduction to *A Tomb for Boris Davidovich*, by Danilo Kiš. New York: Penguin Books, 1980. Brodsky, a poet and winner of the Nobel Prize in Literature, provides valuable information about Kiš in his introduction to *A Tomb for Boris Davidovich.*

Czarny, Norbert. "Imaginary-Real Lives: On Danilo Kiš." *Cross Currents: A Yearbook of Central European Culture* 3 (1984): 279-294. Czarny discusses Kiš's work in terms of artistic objectivism and irony.

Kiš, Danilo. *Homo Poeticus: Essays and Interviews*. Translated by Michael Henry Heim, Ralph Manheim, and Francis Jones. Edited by Susan Sontag. New York: Farrar, Straus and Giroux, 1995. A collection of Kiš's interviews and nonfiction writings that provides an excellent insight into his thinking and his aesthetics. Among the topics he discusses are nationalism, Judaism, the dangers of censorship, the dilemmas of Central European identity, and the work of writers Vladimir Nabokov and Jorge Luis Borges.

Review of Contemporary Fiction 14, no. 1 (1994). This issue contains a number of articles on Kiš, along with a few of his poems, excerpts from his fiction, and essays. In "Danilo Kiš: An Introduction," Brooke Horvath analyzes Kiš's work, placing him in the context of Central European literature and literary history. Some of the other articles provide analyses of *Hourglass* and some of his short stories and discuss the function of memory and history in his fiction.

Stavans, Ilan. *The Inveterate Dreamer: Essays and Conversations on Jewish Culture*. Lincoln: University of Nebraska Press, 2001. Although Jewish writers are scattered throughout the globe and write in many different languages, Stavans seeks to find some commonalities that would provide the definition of a "modern Jewish literary tradition." Part of his exploration includes an analysis of the work of Kiš.

Vuletić, Ivana. *The Prose Fiction of Danilo Kiš, Serbian Jewish Writer: Childhood and the Holocaust*. Lewiston, N.Y.: Edwin Mellen Press, 2003. Vuletić discusses Kiš's conception of the novel and closely examines his "family triptych"—the novels *Garden, Ashes* and *Hourglass* and the short-story collection *Early Sorrows*. She places the trilogy within the context of Serbian and European late modernism and describes how the three books are unified by their thematic and narrative aspects.

ARTHUR KOESTLER

Born: Budapest, Hungary; September 5, 1905
Died: London, England; March 3, 1983
Also known as: Artúr Kösztler

Principal long fiction

The Gladiators, 1939
Darkness at Noon, 1940
Arrival and Departure, 1943
Thieves in the Night: Chronicle of an Experiment, 1946
The Age of Longing, 1951
The Call Girls: A Tragi-Comedy with Prologue and Epilogue, 1972

Other literary forms

Among his nonfiction works, Arthur Koestler (KEHST-luhr) published four autobiographical volumes—*Spanish Testament* (1937), later abridged as *Dialogue with Death* (1942); *Scum of the Earth* (1941); *Arrow in the Blue: The First Volume of an Autobiography, 1905-1931* (1952); and *The Invisible Writing: The Second Volume of an Autobiography, 1932-1940* (1954)—as well as an autobiographical essay on his disillusionment with Communism found in *The God That Failed* (1950), edited by Richard Crossman and with additional essays by Richard Wright, Ignazio Silone, Stephen Spender, Louis Fischer, and André Gide. Koestler's nonfiction works exceed twenty-five volumes, divided roughly between social-historical commentary and the history of science. He also wrote one play, *Twilight Bar: An Escapade in Four Acts* (pb. 1945). Koestler's first five novels, along with most of his other books, have been reissued in the Danube edition, published in England by Hutchinson and in the United States by Macmillan.

Achievements

Arthur Koestler will be remembered as an apostate to the Left who dramatized in *Darkness at Noon* and in his autobiographical works the integrity of many Communist intellectuals in the 1930's and the anguish they suffered under Soviet leader Joseph Stalin. As a novelist, he is generally a skilled storyteller, putting conventional techniques to the service of philosophical themes. Although none of his novels were best sellers in the usual sense, *Darkness at Noon*—translated into thirty-three languages—has been reprinted many times, and its appeal shows no sign of slackening. It continues to be read widely in college and university courses and is probably one of the most influential political novels of the twentieth century, despite the fact that comparatively little academic literary criticism has been devoted to it. Indeed, Koestler's novels—even *Darkness at Noon*—are perhaps kept alive more by political scientists and historians than by professional students of literature.

Arthur Koestler
(National Archives)

Aside from being an accomplished novelist of ideas, Koestler was one of the finest journalists of his age, often producing works as controversial as his political fiction. Typical of his best essays is the piece in *The Lotus and the Robot* (1960) on "Yoga Unexpurgated" (noted as being "far too horrible for me to read" by William Empson in his review); like many other of his best essays, "Yoga Unexpurgated" will maintain its readability. *The Sleepwalkers: A History of Man's Changing Vision of the Universe* (1959), a survey of early scientific thought with emphasis on Renaissance astronomy, is part of a trilogy (with *The Act of Creation*, 1964, and *The Ghost in the Machine*, 1967) on the understanding of the human mind, and it ranks as Koestler's most suggestive effort at research and speculation. Even more controversial than his psychological studies, although a wholly different kind of work, is *The Thirteenth Tribe* (1976), which revived the thesis that the Jews of Eastern Europe are descended from the ancient Khazar Empire. Scholarly reviews of Koestler's research tended to be severe. *The Case of the Midwife Toad* (1971) reveals sympathies for neo-Lamarckian philosophy, and *The Roots of Coincidence* (1972) surveys the claims of parapsychology, ending with a plea "to get out of the straitjacket which nineteenth-century materialism imposed on any philosophical outlook."

Although he flirted with crank notions, to the detriment of his credibility, Koestler was neither a crank nor a dilettante. His renegade vision has enlivened contemporary arts and letters for several decades, and it is likely that this force will continue to be felt for several more.

Biography

Arthur Koestler was born Artúr Kösztler on September 5, 1905, in Budapest, Hungary, the only child of middle-class Jewish parents. He was precocious in math and science and closer to his mother than to his father, an eccentric, self-taught businessman. When Koestler was in his teens, the family moved to Vienna, Austria, and he attended the university there as a science student. After four years, he left school without a degree and went to Palestine, where he joined a Zionist movement for a while before obtaining a correspondent's job with the Ullstein newspapers of Germany. He advanced rapidly in journalism, becoming, in 1930, the foreign editor of *B.Z. am Mittag* and the science editor of *Vossische Zeitung* in Berlin, partly as a result of his success as a reporter on the *Graf Zeppelin* flight to the North Pole in 1931.

In December, 1931, Koestler became a member of the German Communist Party, and less than one year later he gave up his position with Ullstein and spent several weeks traveling in the Soviet Union. He then spent three years in Paris working for the Comintern, leaving for Spain at the outbreak of the Spanish Civil War in 1936. His marriage to Dorothy Asher in 1935 lasted only two years before they were separated, eventually to be divorced in 1950. While in Spain for the Comintern in 1937, Koestler was captured by the Nationalists and sentenced to execution. Thanks to the British press, he was freed after three months, and he published an account of his experiences, *Spanish Testament* (1937). By the next year, he was in France again, where he resigned from the Communist Party in disillusionment with Stalinism and the show trials. During that time, he wrote *Darkness at Noon*. After escaping from Nazi internment in France, he fled to Britain and spent 1941 to 1942 in the British Pioneer Corps.

After *Darkness at Noon* was published, Koestler was in Paris at the center of the uproar it caused among members of the French Left. (Simone de Beauvoir's roman à clef, *The Mandarins*, in 1954, makes vivid this period in French intellectual life.) In the late 1940's, Koestler became a leader among anti-Communist voices in the West, twice visiting the United States to lecture, as well as enjoying an appointment between 1950 and 1951 as a Chubb Fellow at Yale University. After his divorce in 1950, he married Mamaine Paget. In 1952, he took up residence in America for two years, during which time he published his autobiographical volumes *Arrow in the Blue* and *The Invisible Writing*. He was divorced in 1953.

One phase in Koestler's career ended in 1955, when he indicated in *Trial of the Dino-*

saur, and Other Essays that he was finished writing about politics. At that time, his interest turned to mysticism and science, and he tried in his writings on extrasensory perception (ESP) to narrow the gap between natural and extrasensory phenomena. He married Cynthia Jefferies in 1965. After World War II, Koestler had become a naturalized citizen of England, and his adopted country honored him by making him a Commander of the Order of the British Empire (C.B.E.) in 1972 and a companion of literature (C.Lit.) in 1974. Koestler and his wife died in London, England, on March 3, 1983, both victims of apparent suicide.

ANALYSIS

All of Arthur Koestler's works, both fiction and nonfiction, reveal a struggle to escape from the oppressiveness of nineteenth century positivism and its later offshoots. *The Yogi and the Commissar, and Other Essays* (1945) sums up the moral paradox of political action. The Yogi, at one extreme, represents a life lived by values that are grounded in idealism. The Yogi scorns utilitarian goals and yields to quietism; his refusal to intervene leads to passive toleration of social evil. The Commissar, committed to dialectical materialism, ignores the shallow ethical concerns of the historically benighted middle class and seeks to function as an instrument of historical progress. History replaces God, and human suffering is seen as an inevitable step toward the ultimate historical synthesis rather than as an element of God's mysterious purpose. For the Commissar, the end justifies the means, and it is this ethical position that is debated most effectively in *The Gladiators*, *Darkness at Noon*, and *Arrival and Departure*.

In his postscript to the Danube edition of *The Gladiators*, Koestler points out that these novels form a trilogy "whose leitmotif is the central question of revolutionary ethics and of political ethics in general: the question whether, or to what extent, the end justifies the means." The question "obsessed" him, he says, during the seven years in which he belonged to the Communist Party and for several years afterward. It was his answer to this question that caused him to break with the party, as he explains eloquently in his essay in *The God That Failed*. The city built by the rebellious slaves in *The Gladiators* fails because Spartacus does not carry out the stern measures necessary to ensure the city's successful continuation. In *Darkness at Noon*, the old revolutionary Rubashov is depicted as trying to avoid the error Spartacus made, but ending up lost in a maze of moral and ethical complications that destroy him.

Behaviorist psychology is congenial to the materialism of Communist revolutionary ethics, and Koestler attacks its claims heatedly. Indeed, Koestler's interest in mysticism, the occult, and parapsychology was an attempt to find an escape route from the deadly rationalism that makes humans a mere clockwork orange. As far back as 1931, Koestler was investigating psychometry with as much curiosity as he brought to his journalistic accounts of the exploding universe. His answer to the behaviorists is laid out in *The Ghost in the Machine*, and it is clearly a theological answer. Koestler implies here that evolution is purposive, hence the theological nature of his understanding of life. A problem remains, however; Koestler argues that the limbic system of the brain is at odds with its neocortex, resulting in irrational decisions much of the time. Humans are thus as likely to speed to their own destruction as they are to their fulfillment. Koestler's unorthodox answer to humans' Manichaean internal struggle is deliberate mutation by chemical agents. The same topic is fictionalized quite successfully in *The Call Girls*.

The Gladiators

Koestler's first novel, *The Gladiators*, was written in German and translated into English by Edith Simon (Koestler's later novels were published in his own English). The source of the novel is the sketchy account—fewer than four thousand words all together—of the Slave War of 73-71 B.C.E. found in Livy, Plutarch, Appian, and Florus. Koestler divides his narrative into four books. The first, titled "Rise," imagines the revolt led by the Thracian gladiator Spartacus and a fat, cruel Gaul named Crixus. They march through Campania looting and adding more defectors to their band. In book 2, "The Law of Detours," after the destruction of the towns Nola, Suessula, and Calatia, the rebels are twenty thousand strong, or more, and approaching the peak of their power. The unruly faction, however, has spoiled the movement's idealism by its ransacking of these towns, and Spartacus is faced with a decision: Should he let this group go blindly into a foolhardy battle with the forces of the Roman general Varinius, or should he counsel them and enforce a policy of prudence? In his deliberations he is aided by a wise Essene, a type of the imminent Christ, who tells him that of all God's curses on man, "the worst curse of all is that he must tread the evil road for the sake of the good and right, that he must make detours and walk crookedly so that he may reach the straight goal." He further tells Spartacus that for what the leader wants to do now, he needs other counselors.

Despite the Essene's warning, Spartacus follows the "law of detours." Later that night, he confers with Crixus, and although no details of their talk are given, it is clear that Crixus is going to lead the lawless to their unwitting deaths in a confrontation with Varinius. This sacrifice of the unruly faction, however justified, is a cynical detour from honor. Later, however, when the Thracian Spartacus, already pressed by food shortages in the Sun State after a double cross by the neighboring city, is faced with a rebellion against his policies by the Celts, he proves to be insufficiently ruthless: He still retains the idealism with which he began the revolution. Koestler sums it up in his 1965 postscript: "Yet he shrinks from taking the last step—the purge by crucifixion of the dissident Celts and the establishment of a ruthless tyranny; and through this refusal he dooms his revolution to defeat." Book 3, "The Sun State," recounts the conflicts that lead up to Spartacus's defeat, and the gladiators' humiliation and crucifixion are narrated in book 4, "Decline." Although Koestler's characters are wooden, *The Gladiators* is a satisfying historical novel; the milieu is well sketched, and Spartacus's dilemmas are rendered convincingly.

DARKNESS AT NOON

Darkness at Noon, Koestler's masterpiece, is the story of an old Bolshevik, Rubashov, who is called before his Communist inquisitors on charges of heresy against the party. He is interrogated first by Ivanov, who is himself executed, and then by Gletkin, and at the end he is killed by the inevitable bullet in the back of the neck. The novel is divided into three sections, one for each hearing Rubashov is given, and a short epilogue titled "The Grammatical Fiction." In addition to the confrontations between Rubashov and his questioners, there are flashbacks from Rubashov's past and extracts from his diary; the latter provide occasions for Koestler's meditations on history. The narrative is tight and fast moving, and its lucid exposition has surely made it one of the most satisfyingly pedagogic novels of all time. Many readers shared the experience of Leslie Fiedler, who referred to *Darkness at Noon* in his review of *The Ghost in the Machine*, admitting that "Koestler helped to deliver me from the platitudes of the Thirties, from those organized self-deceptions which, being my first, were especially dear and difficult to escape."

Speaking of the "historical circumstances" of *Darkness at Noon*, Koestler explains that Rubashov is "a synthesis of the lives of a number of men who were victims of the so-called Moscow Trials." Rubashov's thinking is closest to that of Nikolai Bukharin, a real purge victim, and Rubashov's tormentor, Gletkin, had a counterpart of sorts in the actual trial prosecutor Andrei Vishinsky. (Robert Conquest's *The Great Terror*, 1968, provides useful details of the real trials.)

Two main theses are argued in *Darkness at Noon*: that the end does not justify the means, and that the individual ego, the *I*, is not a mere "grammatical fiction" whose outline is blurred by the sweep of the historical dialectic. The events that cause Rubashov great pain and guilt involve two party workers whose devotion is sacrificed to the law of detours. Little Loewy is the local leader of the dockworkers' section of the party in Belgium, a likable man whom Rubashov takes to immediately. Little Loewy is a good Communist, but he is ill used by the party and eventually destroyed in an act of expediency. When the party calls for the workers to resist the spreading Nazi menace, Little Loewy's dockworkers refuse to handle cargoes going out from and coming into Germany.

The crisis comes when five cargo ships from Russia arrive in the port. The workers start to unload these boats until they discover the contents: badly needed materials for the German war effort. The workers strike, the party orders them back to the docks, and most of the workers defect. Two years later, Mussolini ventures into Africa, and again a boycott is called, but this time Rubashov is sent in advance to explain to the dockworkers that more Russian cargo is on its way and the party wants it unloaded. Little Loewy rejects the duplicity, and six days later he hangs himself.

In another tragedy of betrayal, Rubashov abandons his secretary, Arlova, a woman who loves him and with whom he has had an affair. When Arlova's brother in Russia marries a foreigner, they all come under suspicion, Arlova included. Soon after, she is called back to oblivion in Russia, and all of this happens without a word from Rubashov. As these perfidies run through his mind, Rubashov's toothache rages intensely. Ivanov senses Rubashov's human sympathies and lectures him on the revolutionary ethic:

> But you must allow that we are as convinced that you and they would mean the end of the Revolution as you are of the reverse. That is the essential point. The methods follow by logical deduction. We can't afford to lose ourselves in political subtleties.

Thus, Rubashov's allegiance to the law of detours leads him into a moral labyrinth. He fails to heed that small voice that gives dignity to the self in its resistance to the degrading impersonality of all-devouring history and the behaviorist conception of human beings.

Arrival and Departure

In *Arrival and Departure*, Koestler's third novel, Peter Slavek, age twenty-two, stows away on a freighter coming from Eastern Europe and washes up in Neutralia (Portugal) in 1940. He is a former Communist who has been tortured by fascists in his home country, and he is faced in Neutralia with four possibilities: reunion with the party, with whom he is disillusioned; joining the fascists, who present themselves as the shapers of the true brave new world; flight to America; or, finally, enlistment with the British, whose culture is maimed but still represents a "brake" on the madness overtaking Europe.

Homeless and confused, Peter meets two women. Dr. Sonia Bolgar, a native of his country and friend of his family, gives him a room and looks after him while she is waiting for the visa that will take her to America. Her lover, Odette, is a young French war widow with whom Peter has a brief affair until Odette leaves for America. Her departure precipitates a psychosomatic paralysis of one of Peter's legs, symbolic of the paralysis of will brought on by his conflicting urges to follow her and to commit himself again to political action. Sonia, who is an analyst and reduces all behavior to the terms of her profession, leads Peter through a deconstruction of his motives that exposes their origins in childhood guilt feelings. His self-insight cures his paralysis, just as his visa for America is granted. He prepares to leave, but at the last moment he dashes off the ship and joins the British, who parachute him back into his own country in their service.

Much of *Arrival and Departure* is artistically inert, but it does have a solid point to make. Although Fyodor Dostoevski's name is never mentioned in *Arrival and Departure*, the novel is Koestler's response to Dostoevski's *The Possessed* (1871-1872), which depicts revolutionaries as warped personalities, dramatizing their neuroses and grudges in political action. For Koestler, human motives are more complex:

> "You can explain the messages of the Prophets as epileptical foam and the Sistine Madonna as the projection of an incestuous dream. The method is correct and the picture in itself complete. But beware of the arrogant error of believing that it is the only one."

Arrival and Departure is, then, a subtle commentary on the motivation of revolutionaries, rejecting any claims to exclusivity by psychoanalysis and psychobiography.

THIEVES IN THE NIGHT

A far more absorbing novel than *Arrival and Departure* is *Thieves in the Night*, an account of the establishment of the commune of Ezra's Tower in Palestine. Many of the events are seen from the perspective of one of the commune's settlers, a young man named Joseph who was born and educated in England. His father was Jewish, his mother English, and this mixed heritage justifies Koestler's use of him as a voice to meditate on the Jewish character and the desirability of assimilation. As a novelistic study of a single character, *Thieves in the Night* is incomplete, but as a depiction of the personal tensions within a commune and as an essay on the international politics wracking Palestine in the period from 1937 to 1939, it is excellent.

The British policy formulated in the 1939 White Paper is exposed in all its cruelty. This policy—perhaps influenced by romantic conceptions of the Arab world—shut down the flow of immigrants into Palestine, leaving the Jews exposed and helpless in Europe. At the novel's end, Joseph has joined the terrorist movement and is engaged in smuggling Polish Jews off the Romanian cattle boats that are forbidden to unload their homeless cargo. In its musings on terrorism, *Thieves in the Night* seems to back off from the repudiation of the doctrine that the end justifies the means. Koestler always faced these issues honestly, and *Thieves in the Night* is as engrossing—and as cogent—in the twenty-first century as it was in 1946.

THE AGE OF LONGING

Published in 1951 and set in Paris in the mid-1950's, *The Age of Longing* describes a time of spiritual disillusionment and longing for an age of faith. The narrative opens on Bastille Day and focuses on three characters: Hydie, a young American apostate from Catholicism, who kneels on her prie-dieu (prayer desk) and laments, "LET ME BELIEVE IN SOMETHING"; Fedya Nikitin, a security officer with a rigid commissar mentality; and Julien Delattre, poet and former party member.

The relationship between Hydie and Fedya occupies much of the novel, with Hydie's ache for religious solace played off against Fedya's unquestioning faith in Communism. Hydie is American, naïve, and innocent; she is seeking experience on which to base faith. Fedya is the son of proletarian revolutionaries from Baku, Azerbaijan, a son of the revolution with the instincts of a true commissar. He seems to have been programmed with party clichés. When the two become lovers, Fedya humiliates Hydie by treating her as a mere collocation of conditioned responses. She then turns against Fedya and, finally understanding his true assignment as a spy, tries to shoot him but botches the job. Regardless of whether their relationship has allegorical significance, the unfeeling commissar is one of Koestler's most effective characterizations. At one point, Fedya asks a young school friend why she likes him, and the answer is, "Because you are clean and simple and hard like an effigy of 'Our Proletarian Youth' from a propaganda poster."

The third main character, Julien Delattre, is in many ways Koestler's self-portrait.

Delattre has given up his allegiance to the "God that failed," and he tells Hydie that "My generation turned to Marx as one swallows acid drops to fight off nausea." He finds his mission in warning others about the ideological traps that he has successfully escaped, and one of the best scenes in the novel comes when he takes Hydie to an evening meeting of the Rally for Peace and Progress. The centerpiece of the session is Koestler's satiric depiction of Jean-Paul Sartre, who appears as the pompous theoretician Professor Pontieux. Author of a fashionable work of postwar despair, "Negation and Position," Professor Pontieux "can prove everything he believes, and he believes everything he can prove."

The Age of Longing ends with an image appropriate to its theme. A funeral party is proceeding past the graves of Jean de La Fontaine, Victor Hugo, and others when air-raid sirens start screaming. "The siren wailed, but nobody was sure: it could have meant the Last Judgment, or just another air-raid exercise."

THE CALL GIRLS

More than twenty years passed between the publication of *The Age of Longing* and that of *The Call Girls*, Koestler's last novel. During those two decades, Koestler's interests had shifted from ideology to science and human behavior. The "call girls" of the title are prominent intellectuals—mostly scientists but including a poet and a priest—nomads of the international conference circuit. Koestler puts them all together in a Swiss mountain setting and sets them to talking about ideas. They have been summoned by one of their members, Nikolai Solovief, a physicist, to consider "approaches to survival" and to send a message to the president of the United States. Unfortunately, the meeting degenerates into a series of uncompromising exchanges between behaviorists and nonbehaviorists. Only Nikolai and Tony, the priest, are able to accommodate themselves to the claims of both reason and faith, and rancor replaces the objective search for truth. *The Call Girls* is an entertaining exposition of the various options available to those seeking enlightenment today.

Readers of *The Ghost in the Machine* and Koestler's work on ESP will recognize in the arguments of Nikolai and Tony those of Koestler himself. Koestler always staged his intellectual dramas in the dress of irreconcilable opposites—the Yogi and the Commissar, ends versus means—and here the protagonist is clearly spirit and the antagonist matter. His call girls demonstrate that there is still life in this old conflict.

Frank Day

OTHER MAJOR WORKS

PLAY: *Twilight Bar: An Escapade in Four Acts*, pb. 1945.

NONFICTION: *Spanish Testament*, 1937; *Scum of the Earth*, 1941; *Dialogue with Death*, 1942; *The Yogi and the Commissar, and Other Essays*, 1945; *Insight and Outlook: An Inquiry into the Common Foundations of Science, Art, and Social Ethics*, 1949; *Promise and Fulfillment: Palestine, 1917-1949*, 1949; *Arrow in the Blue: The First Volume of an Autobiography, 1905-1931*, 1952; *The Invisible Writing: The Second Volume of an Autobiography, 1932-1940*, 1954; *Trial of the Dinosaur, and Other Essays*, 1955; *Reflections on Hanging*, 1956; *The Sleepwalkers: A History of Man's Changing Vision of the Universe*, 1959; *The Lotus and the Robot*, 1960; *Hanged by the Neck: An Exposure of Capital Punishment in England*, 1961 (with C. H. Rolph); *The Act of Creation*, 1964; *The Ghost in the Machine*, 1967; *The Case of the Midwife Toad*, 1971; *The Roots of Coincidence*, 1972; *The Challenge of Chance: Experiments and Speculations*, 1973 (with Sir Alister Hardy and Robert Harvie); *The Heel of Achilles: Essays, 1968-1973*, 1974; *Life After Death*, 1976 (with Arthur Toynbee et al.); *The Thirteenth Tribe*, 1976; *Janus: A Summing Up*, 1978; *Bricks to Babel: Selected Writings with Comments*, 1981; *Stranger on the Square*, 1984 (with Cynthia Koestler).

EDITED TEXTS: *Suicide of a Nation? An Enquiry into the State of Britain Today*, 1963; *Drinkers of Infinity: Essays, 1955-1967*, 1968 (with J. R. Smythies); *Beyond Reductionism: New Perspectives in the Life Sciences*, 1969 (with Smythies).

Bibliography

Cesarani, David. *Arthur Koestler: The Homeless Mind.* New York: Free Press, 1999. A thorough reassessment of Koestler's ideas and writings that also explores, among other subjects, his Jewish background, relationships with women, and political activities. Includes a bibliography and an index.

Goodman, Celia, ed. *Living with Koestler: Mamaine Koestler's Letters, 1945-1951*. New York: St. Martin's Press, 1985. A vivid personal view of Koestler, documented by Koestler's second wife, Mamaine Paget.

Hamilton, Iain. *Koestler: A Biography*. Reprint. New York: Macmillan, 1985. This lengthy biography, favorable to Koestler, is arranged year by year in the fashion of a chronicle and breaks off around 1970. Many events have been retold partly on the basis of interviews, Koestler's papers, and firsthand accounts.

Harris, Harold, ed. *Astride the Two Cultures: Arthur Koestler at Seventy.* London: Hutchinson University Library, 1975. This collection of essays by authors sympathetic to Koestler provides nearly equal coverage of the writer's involvement in literary and in scientific activities. The essays include discussions of the Koestler the novelist and his book *Darkness at Noon.*

Judt, Tony. "Arthur Koestler, the Exemplary Intellectual." In *Reappraisals: Reflections on the Forgotten Twentieth Century.* New York: Penguin Press, 2008. Judt includes a discussion of Koestler in this book, which seeks to inform twenty-first century readers about the social thought and socially motivated activism of the twentieth century.

Koestler, Cynthia. *Stranger on the Square.* New York: Random House, 1984. A joint memoir by Cynthia and Arthur Koestler, left unfinished at their deaths.

Marton, Kati. *The Great Escape: Nine Jews Who Fled Hitler and Changed the World.* New York: Simon & Schuster, 2006. Koestler was among the Hungarian Jews who left

Hungary between World War I and II to escape Fascism. Marton recounts Koestler's journey to the United States and his accomplishments as an author.

Pearson, Sidney A., Jr. *Arthur Koestler.* Boston: Twayne, 1978. Although a bit sketchy on matters of biography, this work deals with basic issues in Koestler's writings and has some trenchant and interesting discussion of political themes. Also helpful are the chronology and a selected annotated bibliography.

Perez, Jane, and Wendell Aycock, eds. *The Spanish Civil War in Literature.* Lubbock: Texas Tech University Press, 1990. References Koestler throughout. Peter I. Barta's essay "The Writing of History: Authors Meet on the Soviet-Spanish Border" specifically discusses *Darkness at Noon*, providing an excellent grounding in the political history from which Koestler's fiction evolved.

Sperber, Murray A., ed. *Arthur Koestler: A Collection of Critical Essays.* Englewood Cliffs, N.J.: Prentice-Hall, 1977. Both positive and negative reactions appear in this fine sampling of critical work about Koestler's literary and scientific writings. Among those commentators represented by excerpts here are George Orwell, Saul Bellow, Edmund Wilson, Stephen Spender, and A. J. Ayer.

Sterne, Richard Clark. *Dark Mirror: The Sense of Injustice in Modern European and American Literature.* New York: Fordham University Press, 1994. A substantial discussion of *Darkness at Noon* is included in this book, which analyzes literature that treats the conflict between "natural" ethical law and more "realistic" concepts of justice.

PRIMO LEVI

Born: Turin, Italy; July 31, 1919
Died: Turin, Italy; April 11, 1987
Also known as: Damiano Malabaila

PRINCIPAL LONG FICTION

La chiave a stella, 1978 (*The Monkey's Wrench*, 1986)
Se non ora, quando?, 1982 (*If Not Now, When?*, 1985)

OTHER LITERARY FORMS

Associated with Holocaust literature, Primo Levi (LAY-vee) was a novelist, short-story writer, essayist, and poet, although he is known primarily for his memoirs. These include *Se questo è un uomo* (1947; *If This Is a Man*, 1959; revised as *Survival in Auschwitz: The Nazi Assault on Humanity*, 1961) and *La tregua* (1963; *The Reawakening*, 1965). Levi himself, in a preface, characterizes his collection of stories *Moments of Reprieve* (1986) as a record of experiences left out of *If This Is a Man* and *The Reawakening*. (Most of these autobiographical short stories were previously published in 1981 in *Lilit e altri racconti*.) *Il sistema periodico* (1975; *The Periodic Table*, 1984), a collection of autobiographical pieces unified by its organization according to the chemical elements, mixes traditional genres. Levi's poems about his experiences during the Holocaust are collected in *Shema: Collected Poems* (1976). Additional poems are collected in *L'osteria di Brema* (1975). His early pseudonymous short-story collections *Storie naturali* (1966) and *Vizio di forma* (1971) combine autobiography, science fiction, and fantasy to describe his experiences after the war. Levi's essays are collected in *La ricerca della radici* (1981; *The Search for Roots: A Personal Anthology*, 2001).

ACHIEVEMENTS

An Italian Jew who survived the Nazi death camp Auschwitz, Primo Levi is widely acclaimed as a fictional, historical, and autobiographical chronicler of the Holocaust and its aftermath. Highly praised by such important writers as Umberto Eco, Italo Calvino, Studs Terkel, Claude Lévi-Strauss, Irving Howe, Alfred Kazin, Philip Roth, and Saul Bellow, Levi's work is distinguished by the author's attempt to understand his wartime experiences and by a compassionate, sensitive, and astonishingly optimistic view of humanity. Levi's epigraph for *The Periodic Table* is a Yiddish saying: "Troubles overcome are good to tell." Levi's works are ample proof of the proverb, his life a testament of the resilience of the human spirit. In recognition of his many achievements, Levi won Italy's prestigious Premio Bagutta, Viareggio, Strega, and Campiello literary prizes.

Biography

Primo Levi was born on July 31, 1919, in Turin, Italy, to a cultured middle-class couple, Ester and Cesare Levi. Levi attended the University of Turin and in 1941 received his Ph.D. in chemistry. A Jew in occupied Italy during World War II, he joined the Italian Resistance and was soon arrested for anti-Fascist activities. Upon discovering that Levi was a Jew, the German SS deported him to their death facility in Auschwitz. There, where number 174517 was tattooed on his left arm, he remained until the concentration camp was liberated in 1945. For his survival, he credited luck, which manifested itself in terms of his health, which was good most of the time he was in Auschwitz and poor at precisely the right moment (when the Germans fled the concentration camp, taking with them all "healthy" prisoners). In addition, he worked as a chemist part of the time he was in Auschwitz, and his friend, an Italian bricklayer, smuggled extra food to him.

After the war, Levi found employment as technical director of a paint factory. In 1947, Levi married Lucia Morpurgo, a teacher, who helped him adjust to his new life. Still deeply depressed, he turned to writing in an attempt to understand his concentration camp experience. The Holocaust turned the chemist into the writer. Levi later described his time in Auschwitz as "the fundamental experience of my life." He went on to say, "I knew that if I survived, I would have to tell the story." In 1947, he chronicled his imprisonment at Auschwitz in *If This Is a Man*, and later, in *The Reawakening*, he described his bizarre, circuitous journey home from Poland. Many of his other works, including *Shema*, *Moments of Reprieve*, and *If Not Now, When?* were also inspired by the Holocaust. In 1977, Levi devoted himself to writing full time. He died in his hometown of Turin on April 11, 1987, survived by a son, Renzo, a physicist, and a daughter, Lisa, a biologist.

Analysis

Most of Primo Levi's work (with the exception of *The Monkey's Wrench*) can be placed within the genre of Holocaust literature. As a survivor of Auschwitz, Levi blended personal reminiscence and reflection to depict his major preoccupation, the unfathomable horror that was the Holocaust. Almost totally devoid of self-pity, Levi reserved his concern for others. He never indulged in luridness or melodrama. Rather, his tone is clear, straightforward, and moderate—his passion, muted. Although his writing deals with the deepest of human emotions and feelings, it remains restrained in a manner that makes for a quiet intensity, which is only emphasized by his subtle (if somewhat startling) humor. Through his unflinching and careful use of detail, he presents a picture of human degradation. Despite the bleakness inherent in Levi's usual subjects, however, his portrayal leads not to bitterness but, astoundingly, to a compelling affirmation of life, to a sense of faith in humanity, to a compassionate understanding of both victims and victimizers, and, finally, to a powerful and moving vision of the dignity of humankind.

The Monkey's Wrench

Although Levi's first piece of long fiction, *The Monkey's Wrench*, represents a divergence from his usual concerns (and therefore is lighter and even more amusing in tone), it still reflects Levi's life experiences, and Levi himself is one of the main characters. This work has been widely classified as a novel. In actuality, however, *The Monkey's Wrench* defies classification, being a combination of autobiography and long and short fiction. Indeed, in an interview with Philip Roth, Levi implied that he did not consider *The Monkey's Wrench* to be a novel. The work is, perhaps, best regarded as a collection of short stories linked by a narrative situation: The unnamed narrator/writer, who represents Levi, for the most part listens to and records stories related by Faussone, the protagonist and Levi's self-styled alter ego. This frame automatically emphasizes the complex relationship between storyteller and listener, between writer and reader.

In the street-smart, cocky, energetic Faussone, Levi created one of his most fully realized characters. An itinerant steelworker, Faussone (like Levi and the narrator) comes from Turin. In seemingly artless monologues, Faussone articulates his devotion to work, a passion he shares with the narrator, who finds, "If we except those miraculous and isolated moments fate can bestow on a man, loving your work (unfortunately, the privilege of a few) represents the best, most concrete approximation of happiness on earth." In fact, the central metaphor of the novel has to do with the relationship between life and work, whether the comparison is to rigging, to chemistry, or to writing.

Like Levi, the narrator is a chemist (a paint specialist) and author from Turin. Just as Levi became a full-time writer in 1977, the narrator (who, in describing his writing generally alternates between the languages of rigging and of chemistry) relates his last adventure as a chemist and marks his impending transition:

> With nostalgia, but without misgivings, I would choose another road . . . the road of the teller of stories. My own stories . . . then other people's stories . . . his [Faussone's], for example. . . . it was possible that, having spent more than thirty years sewing together long molecules . . . I might have learned something about sewing together words and ideas.

If Not Now, When?

If in his previous works Levi depended primarily on his own individual experience, *If Not Now, When?* is based on the true story of Jewish partisans who banded together to fight the Nazis. Levi described this deliberate new direction in his writing in his interview with Roth: "I had made a sort of bet with myself: after so much plain or disguised autobiography, are you, or are you not, a full-fledged writer, capable of constructing a novel, shaping characters, describing landscapes you have never seen? Try it!" In *If Not Now, When?* for the first time Levi imagines rather than recalls events surrounding the Holocaust. He reconstructs a people (Yiddish-speaking Eastern European Jews whom

Levi had not known before his concentration camp experience), a period (World War II), a setting (the countryside of Eastern Europe), and even a language (Yiddish) to celebrate the active resistance of the Jews, arguing against the commonly held notion that all Jews passively submitted to their fate at the hands of their Nazi murderers. Levi outlined his intentions thus:

> I wished to assault a commonplace still prevailing in Italy: a Jew is a mild person, a scholar (religious or profane), unwarlike, humiliated, who tolerated centuries of persecution without ever fighting back. It seemed to me a duty to pay homage to those Jews who, in desperate conditions, had found the courage and the skills to resist. . . . I cherished the ambition to be the first (perhaps only) Italian writer to describe the Yiddish world.

The story begins in 1943 as two Russian Jews—Mendel, one of the main characters, a resourceful and philosophical watchmaker whose wife has been slaughtered by the Nazis, and Leonid, an uncommunicative young concentration camp escapee—try to elude the Nazis. Living hand-to-mouth as they travel over marshes, forests, and countryside, they join with various ragged groups of refugees, stragglers, and partisans attempting both to survive and to fight the Germans. Eventually, the two meet a group of Jewish partisans, the Gedalists, named for their leader, Gedaleh. This courageous band—comprising a wide variety of Polish and Russian men and women, from former Soviet soldiers to fugitives of Nazi roundups and concentration camps—aims to survive, to harm the Germans, and eventually, to reach Palestine. Traveling over much of the same territory Levi himself crossed on his protracted journey home from Auschwitz (chronicled in his memoir, *The Reawakening*), the partisans get as far as Italy before the novel ends, as does the war in Europe, in August, 1945.

The novel oscillates in atmosphere from romantic to epic. The tone is not indignant, but rather reflective, understated, and at times quietly humorous. What distinguishes this work from most Holocaust literature is that Levi rarely details the German atrocities that form the backdrop of this story. Explicitly, "this story is not being told in order to describe massacres." Nevertheless, images of the grotesqueness of the Holocaust are a silent presence, almost more notable in their absence. As one character explains to another, "It's the first rule. . . . If we kept on telling one another what we've seen, we'd go crazy and instead we all have to be sane, children included."

Action-packed, tense, and suspenseful, the plot of this stirring war story is (like the plot of *The Reawakening*) picaresque. Levi is a master of the episodic, a painter of poignant vignettes. As they travel westward from Russia to Italy, their springboard to Palestine, the Gedalists risk considerable danger to sabotage the Germans, engaging in a series of rear-guard acts of harassment and guerrilla warfare—from ambushing trains to liberating concentration camps—that are variously amusing, frightening, exciting, and moving.

If Not Now, When? is also a novel of character, however. In fact, Levi later confessed, "For the first and only time in my life as a writer, I had the impression (almost a hallucination) that my characters were alive, around me, behind my back, suggesting spontaneously their feats and their dialogues." Irrepressible and courageous, individual members of the Gedalists are sharply and insightfully drawn. The characters are made all the more vivid and striking through a series of elegant and wonderful metaphors.

Mendel's character is the most fully developed, and, as the third-person narrator, continually presents his innermost thoughts. This is in direct contrast to the presentation of the elusive Gedaleh, whose interior consciousness, and consequently his character, remains remote. Introduced as "the legendary leader" of the partisan group, Gedaleh, with his violin as talisman, is appropriately mysterious and heroic.

As for the group itself, the narrator presents the inner thoughts of the band as a whole, expressive of a developing Jewish collective consciousness. It is here that Levi strikes a chord of universality: The possibility for community, camaraderie, mutual responsibility, and unity emerges as the final lesson to be learned from the Holocaust and from all of Levi's works. Perhaps this lesson is best expressed in the words of Rabbi Hillel: "If I am not for myself, who will be for me? If I am for myself alone, what am I? If not now, when?"

Deborah D. Rogers

OTHER MAJOR WORKS

SHORT FICTION: *Storie naturali*, 1966; *Vizio di forma*, 1971; *Lilit e altri racconti*, 1981; *Moments of Reprieve*, 1986; *The Sixth Day, and Other Tales*, 1990; *L'ultimo Natale di guerra*, 2000; *A Tranquil Star: Unpublished Stories of Primo Levi*, 2007.

POETRY: *L'osteria di Brema*, 1975; *Shema: Collected Poems*, 1976; *Ad ora incerta*, 1984 (*Collected Poems*, 1988).

NONFICTION: *Se questo è un uomo*, 1947 (memoir; *If This Is a Man*, 1959; revised as *Survival in Auschwitz: The Nazi Assault on Humanity*, 1961); *La tregua*, 1963 (memoir; *The Reawakening*, 1965); *Il sistema periodico*, 1975 (memoir; *The Periodic Table*, 1984); *La ricerca della radici*, 1981 (*The Search for Roots: A Personal Anthology*, 2001); *L'altrui mestiere*, 1985 (*Other People's Trades*, 1989); *I sommersi e i salvati*, 1986 (*The Drowned and the Saved*, 1988); *Conversazioni e interviste: 1963-1987*, 1997 (*The Voice of Memory: Interviews, 1961-1987*, 2001).

MISCELLANEOUS: *Racconti e saggi*, 1986 (stories and essays; *The Mirror Maker*, 1989).

BIBLIOGRAPHY

Angier, Carole. *The Double Bond: Primo Levi, a Biography*. New York: Farrar, Straus and Giroux, 2002. Definitive biography, meticulously researched over a ten-year period, recounts Levi's life, including the years after World War II when he wrote his novels and other works, and describes his complex temperament.

Anissimov, Myriam. *Primo Levi: Tragedy of an Optimist*. Translated by Steve Cox.

Woodstock, N.Y.: Overlook Press, 1999. Biography tells Levi's story primarily through his writing. Includes a glossary of terms associated with concentration camps as well as notes, bibliography, and index.

Benchouiha, Lucie. *Primo Levi: Rewriting the Holocaust.* Leicester, England: Troubador, 2006. Analyzes Levi's writings to demonstrate how his work was influenced by his time in Auschwitz. Argues that all of Levi's works in some way reflect his experiences of the Holocaust.

Cicioni, Mirna. *Primo Levi: Bridges of Knowledge.* Oxford, England: Berg, 1995. Good general introduction to Levi's work. Outlines the events of Levi's life well, despite the unavailability of many biographical details, owing to the Levi family's reluctance to release information about the writer. Bibliography lists primary and secondary materials written in English as well as foreign-language publications.

Gordon, Robert S. C. *Primo Levi's Ordinary Virtues: From Testimony to Ethics.* New York: Oxford University Press, 2001. Analyzes the ethical dimensions in all of Levi's work, charting his transition from concentration camp survivor to philosopher and ethicist. Includes bibliography and index.

_______, ed. *The Cambridge Companion to Primo Levi.* New York: Cambridge University Press, 2007. Collection of essays discusses the full range of Levi's works. Topics addressed include Levi's identity as a Jew and as a resident of Turin, Italy, his Holocaust writings, his science fiction, and his place in Italian literature.

Homer, Frederic D. *Primo Levi and the Politics of Survival.* Columbia: University of Missouri Press, 2001. Examines Levi's philosophy, his social and political views, and his place in Holocaust history, demonstrating how Levi became a significant political philosopher. Includes bibliography and index.

Patruno, Nicholas. *Understanding Primo Levi.* Columbia: University of South Carolina Press, 1995. Provides a good introduction to Levi's writing. Chapter 4 is devoted to *The Monkey's Wrench*, and chapter 5 analyzes *If Not Now, When?* Includes biographical information, critical analysis, bibliography, and index.

Tarrow, Susan R., ed. *Reason and Light: Essays on Primo Levi.* Ithaca, N.Y.: Cornell University Press, 1990. Collection of essays contains several pieces on Levi's fiction and on his relationship to the Holocaust and its literature. Includes bibliographical references.

Thomson, Ian. *Primo Levi: A Life.* New York: Holt, 2003. Close examination of Levi's life, with a focus on his writing, is achieved largely through interviews with his contemporaries. Valuable for its historical sensitivity.

BERNARD MALAMUD

Born: Brooklyn, New York; April 26, 1914
Died: New York, New York; March 18, 1986

PRINCIPAL LONG FICTION

The Natural, 1952
The Assistant, 1957
A New Life, 1961
The Fixer, 1966
The Tenants, 1971
Dubin's Lives, 1979
God's Grace, 1982
The People, 1989

OTHER LITERARY FORMS

While acknowledging the significant achievements of Bernard Malamud (MAL-uh-muhd) as a novelist, many critics believe that the most distinctive and enduring contributions the author made to American fiction are to be found in his short stories, particularly those collected in *The Magic Barrel* (1958) and *Idiots First* (1963). Malamud published three more volumes of short fiction in his lifetime: *Pictures of Fidelman: An Exhibition* (1969), a collection of six linked stories featuring the same protagonist; *Rembrandt's Hat* (1973); and *The Stories of Bernard Malamud* (1983), twenty-five stories largely drawn from previously published volumes. The posthumously published volume *The People, and Uncollected Stories* (1989) gathers a number of previously uncollected stories, most of them early pieces from the 1940's but also including two from the 1980's.

ACHIEVEMENTS

With novelists such as Saul Bellow and Philip Roth, Bernard Malamud is among the most distinguished of a number of Jewish writers who did much to set the tone of postwar American fiction. Malamud's singular achievement is to have captured the experience of Jews in the United States at a point of transition between cultures. His characters—not only the Jews but also their Gentile counterparts—are not yet quite a part of American culture, nor have they fully abandoned the old culture of which they are no longer members. Out of this sense of dislocation and the struggle to create a new life, Malamud created most of his early stories and novels. Although not all the novels have Jewish protagonists—the first two in fact do not—the dilemma is constant; the Gentile characters are as displaced and alienated as the Jewish ones. He received numerous awards for his fiction, including two National Book Awards and a Pulitzer Prize.

Biography

Bernard Malamud was born in Brooklyn to Russian immigrant parents. His father, like Morris Bober in *The Assistant*, was a small grocer, and the family moved around Brooklyn as business dictated. When Malamud was nine years old, he had pneumonia and began a period of intensive reading. Later, encouraged by his teachers, he also began writing short stories.

From 1932 to 1936, Malamud was a student at the City College of New York. He later began work on a master of arts degree at Columbia University, and, while teaching night school at Erasmus Hall, his own alma mater, he started writing in earnest. He married Ann de Chiara in 1945, and four years later he and his family moved to Corvallis, Oregon, where for twelve years Malamud taught English at Oregon State. A son was born before they left for Corvallis, a daughter after they arrived. While there, he published his first three books; after leaving, he wrote his satire of academic life in an English department, *A New Life*. Returning to the East in 1961, Malamud taught for many years at Bennington College in Vermont. He died in New York on March 18, 1986.

Analysis

In *The Natural*, Iris Lemon tells the protagonist that all people have two lives, "the life we learn with and the life we live with after that. Suffering is what brings us toward happiness." Although her statement requires qualification, it is a suggestive summary of the major theme of Bernard Malamud's work: the journey toward a new life, a journey marked by suffering, which may or may not be redemptive. In fact, however, Malamud's characters usually have three lives: one from which they have not learned and that they are attempting to leave behind, a life the reader sees in flashbacks and confessions as well as in brief opening scenes; a middle life, the learning life, which is the substance of the books; and the new life promised to successful characters at the end. Malamud's novels, then, are in the tradition of the bildungsroman, but they have older protagonists than do most American novels of education. What Malamud depicts in each of his novels is a renewed attempt to find new life and to convert suffering to meaning, a second journey toward knowledge.

Of the old life, Malamud usually shows his readers little. *The Natural* opens with a brief pregame sketch that quickly shows Roy Hobbs's past. In *The Assistant*, the reader sees the robbery for which Frankie Alpine will try to atone, and in *The Fixer*, there is a short portrait of Yakov Bok's past in his village. Malamud's characters are trying to forget the past, so even when it enters their minds, they try to shove it away. Moreover, Malamud's novels usually begin with a journey away from a past life. Whether European Jews coming to America or moving from their shtetl to Kiev, or whether American Jews traveling from New York to Oregon or baseball players leaving the country for the big city, Malamud's protagonists are always travelers, uneasy with their past, uncertain of their future. In fact, they often try to conceal their past: Alpine and Hobbs work conscientiously to obliterate the stories of their earlier lives. Yakov Bok drops his prayer things, a reminder of his old life and its ways, into a river. One of Malamud's most frequent devices is to have characters change their names in an attempt to escape their past identity. Bok, trying to pass as a Gentile, becomes Yakov Ivanovitch Dologushev, his initials ironically spelling "yid."

What all of Malamud's characters must learn, however, is that they have to accept responsibility for their past actions. Paradoxically, while the evil that his characters have done remains with them and so must be acknowledged, the good can be erased. At the end of *The Natural*, Roy Hobbs, a failure in his quest for a new life, discovers that for his part in throwing the league playoffs, all of his baseball records will be expunged from the record books.

The journey is always a quest, as the mythological base of *The Natural*, Malamud's first and prototypal novel, makes clear. The public part of the quest takes place in the world of men, and its lesson is that of law, of the inner check, of renunciation. Hobbs is a natural hitter, but he lacks good judgment, both on the field and off. Frankie Alpine in *The Assistant* continually steals from Morris Bober. Saving Bober's daughter Helen from being raped, he is unable to control his own sexual appetite and rapes her himself. "Why do Jews suffer so much?" he asks Morris Bober, and after replying that to live is to suffer, Morris adds, "I think if a Jew don't suffer for the Law, he will suffer for nothing." Although Alpine is not yet a Jew, he does suffer for nothing.

Acceptance of the law, curbing one's appetite, is the first lesson. As Levin thinks in *A New Life*, "Renunciation was what he was now engaged in. It was a beginning that created a beginning." Law alone is not enough, however, and Malamud's questers must pass a second test as well for their journeys to be successful: the test of love, of dream, of acceptance of life in its fullness and ambiguity. Helen Bober could marry Nat Pearl, studying to be a lawyer but lacking dreams, or she could choose Louis Karp, pure appetite, lacking law. She chooses neither, and at the novel's conclusion a chance remains for Frankie Alpine, who is learning what W. H. Auden calls a "law like love." In *A New Life*, Levin first picks up Henry James's *The American* (1877), a book that makes a case for renunciation, but Pauline Gilley, another man's wife whom Levin first renounces but later accepts, moves the discussion to William Dean Howells, who, like Malamud, prefers the economy of pain.

Another qualification to Iris Lemon's statement is necessary: Suffering is what *may* bring one toward happiness. The quest is not successful for all of Malamud's characters. Many of them, already displaced from their European homelands, refuse to undertake another journey. Others learn the wrong lesson from their old life. "*Rachmones*, we say in Hebrew," says Yakov Bok. "Mercy, one oughtn't to forget it." Many, particularly women (there are no Jewish mothers in Malamud), do forget it and harden their hearts. Still others, having undertaken the journey, are, like Roy Hobbs, too selfish ever to move beyond themselves.

Not only do Malamud's novels tell and retell the same story, but they do so with similar casts and with the same images. The protagonist is typically without a close family, sometimes orphaned. He is often a *schlemiel* or a *schlemazl*, always wanting to escape his past, but unlucky and clumsy in the attempt. He is likely to be self-deceived. Early in *The Assistant*, while still stealing, Alpine tells himself that he is "an honest guy." Later he says, "Even when I am bad I am good," inaccurately viewing himself as a man of stern morality.

Especially in the early novels and short stories, there is a father figure, and the learning relationship is dramatized in terms of an apprenticeship. These figures become less important in the later novels. By *A New Life*, a transitional book, both would-be father figures, the inane Fairchild and the more scholarly but weak Fabrikant, are failures. After *A New Life*, the questers are orphaned even in this middle life.

Malamud also makes frequent use of doubles, figures both actual and dreamed. Roy and Bump Baily, the player he replaces, are identified with each other: They share the same girl and the same fault. Frankie Alpine enacts in his dreams the crimes Ward Minogue, his darker opposite, actually commits. In *The Tenants*, Harry Lesser and Willie Spearmint (born Bill Spear—blacks also change names in Malamud) act out the common racial stereotypes, reverse them, and then destroy each other's work and life. An image from William Shakespeare's *King Lear* (1605-1606), each as the other's shadow, dominates the book.

Women in Malamud's work are of two types: the dark ladies (Memo Paris, who betrays Roy Hobbs, and Harriet Bird, who shoots him; Avis Fliss, who spies on Levin; and Zenaida, who gives false testimony against Bok) and the potentially redemptive ladies of the lake (Iris Lemon, Helen Bober, Pauline Gilley, Fanny Bick in *Dubin's Lives*). The function of the good women is in part to hear the hero's confession, enabling him to acknowledge his past, but the women confess too, and, as in Nathaniel Hawthorne, an earlier fabulist, the protagonists have the obligation to accept the women's ambiguous moral nature, a test they often fail. Roy, for example, who wants Iris's sympathy, is disquieted when she tells him that at thirty-three she is a grandmother.

Malamud is also consistent in his metaphors. The journey is often from a prison to freedom. Stores are identified as prisons; Alpine feels both imprisoned and entombed in Bober's grocery. Bok exchanges a shtetl for a prison but learns the meaning of freedom while he is confined. Levin says that if you make the wrong basis for your life, "you spend your whole life in jail," though he later realizes that the prison is himself.

Another metaphor involves moving from a mirror to a window—and beyond. Characters must not reject the mirror, refuse to see themselves as they truly are, as Irene Bell, née Belinsky, does when she refuses to look into a dropped mirror in *The Tenants*. Unfortunately, after they know themselves, the characters sometimes become so fascinated with their own image that they cannot move on. *The Natural* opens with Roy Hobbs on a train, striking a match to look out the window but seeing only his own reflection; throughout the novel, he never achieves any higher values than those centered on himself.

Progress, the attempt to make contact with another, is often symbolized by gazing through a window—transparent, but still dividing, the attempt finally a failure. A common example of this failure is voyeurism; Levin eyes Pauline Gilley's house and watches her through binoculars at a basketball game, while Gerald, her husband, watches several characters through the viewfinder of his camera. Lesser in *The Tenants* is watched through a keyhole. Frankie Alpine climbs an air shaft to watch through a window as Helen Bober showers, and William Dubin in *Dubin's Lives* sneaks to Fanny Bick's house to spy on her and her boyfriend through a window.

Consistent images are linked in Malamud's novels. They must have about them a touch of red or black, a reminder of their human imperfection. They are associated, often by their names, with flowers (Iris, though with Lemon), with birds (Harriet Bird, Avis Fliss), and with trees. The bad women have sore breasts (Memo, Avis) and are like trapped birds and twisted trees.

If there is a conversion—an acceptance of the old life and a promise of a new—it takes place in an isolated, natural spot, such as the park in the urban world of *The Assistant*, where Alpine tells Helen that the best part of Leo Tolstoy's *Anna Karenina* (1875-1877; English translation, 1886) is Levin's conversion in the woods; the lake in *The Natural* (Memo, the bad woman, is, however, associated with polluted waters); the woods in *A New Life*, where Malamud's Levin is converted; and the artificial jungle of *The Tenants*, where the meeting of Lesser and Spearmint ends in death. In *Dubin's Lives*, Dubin is running through the countryside when he first meets Fanny, and it is there that they finally make love.

Despite this consistency of theme, character, and image, Malamud's fiction changed during his career. The early works, with their blend of romance and realism, represent Malamud's best writing. About midway through his career, however, he seemed to have tired of his form; his novels became more discursive, his protagonists more articulate. On one hand, he moved toward experimentalism, but on the other hand, toward the novel of ideas. Quoting Herman Melville that to have a mighty novel, one needs a mighty theme, suggesting that "the purpose of a writer is to keep civilization from destroying itself," Malamud in his later novels reached obtrusively for significance. The protagonists of these later works are frequently blocked artists: the writers in *The Tenants*, the biographer in *Dubin's Lives*.

The Natural

Malamud's first novel, *The Natural*, is a fanciful combination of American baseball lore with the myth of the wasteland. Here, the wasteland is a New York baseball team, the Knights, whose coach, Pop Fisher, is the fisher king of the legend. The quester and protagonist of the novel is Roy Hobbs, his name meaning rustic king. Roy undergoes a double-edged test to see if he can bring life to the baseball team, but the center of the novel is what Roy himself does—or does not—learn from the tests, the chance of a new life for the quester. Though *The Natural* is in many ways the least Jewish of Malamud's novels, it is the prototype for the rest of his fiction; the story it tells and the patterns it uses are those that persist through Malamud's work.

The pregame section of the novel, the brief history of the past life in which Hobbs does not learn and that he will attempt to leave behind, opens with the image of Hobbs staring at his own reflection in the train window. This inability to look beyond himself, his egocentric view of the world, is Hobbs's undoing. Both parts of Roy's testing are also prefigured in this section, which is a microcosm of the novel as a whole. In the public test, Roy, a pitcher, is challenged by an established batting king, whom Roy strikes out as Malamud draws the mythic parallels. The cost of that success is that Roy slays his first father figure, his mentor who catches the pitches without adequate chest protection, is injured, and dies.

If Roy is partially successful in his physical challenge, he is not at all so in the world of moral choice. In the pregame section, he is questioned by the first of the women in the novel, Harriet Bird. The episode is based on the real-life shooting of a ballplayer. Harriet invites Roy up to her hotel room. She tests him with a series of questions about the value of his ambitions, but when Roy's self-centered answers reveal the limits of his aspirations—he plays only for his own glory—his unalloyed confidence is rewarded with a bullet. The section ends with a fantastic tableau: Harriet Bird doing a grisly nude dance around the fallen body of Roy Hobbs.

The nine inninglike sections of the novel that follow repeat more spaciously the double test the quester has to undertake to revitalize the team and prove himself worthy of a new life. When Roy arrives, everything is dismal: The Knights are losing, the players are dispirited, Pop Fisher is ailing. Even the drinking fountain produces only rusty water. Once Roy begins to play, however, the team's luck changes. Armed with his mythic bat, Wonder Boy, Roy hits five home runs and energizes the team. Rain falls, and the process of restoring life-giving water to the land begins. Roy, however, gets his chance to play only when another player, Bump Baily, is injured. Again, Roy's success depends on the suffering of another, suffering on which Roy is too willing to capitalize. Roy and Bump are doubles, Bump a darker projection of many of Roy's faults. As the fans and team-members point out, they share a common limitation: They play for themselves rather than for the team. The high point of Roy's career is Roy Hobbs Day, an event that occurs in the middle of this symmetrical novel. He is given a white Mercedes, a symbolic lancer on which he proudly rides around the stadium.

Roy's acceptance speech has only one theme, his own greatness, and from this triumph, Roy's downward path, indicated by his batting slump, begins. Although there are short times of solid hitting, as when Roy agrees to play for another, the on-field slump is accompanied by Roy's involvement with the illegal off-the-field dealings of the team's owner, who is setting up the throwing of the league playoffs, a fictive event modeled on the notorious "Black Sox" scandal of the 1919 World Series. Roy is in a world beyond his experience. Baffled by the owner's oily, cliché-ridden speeches, Roy participates in the fix. Although at the end of the playoff game Roy tries to play well to reverse the evil he has already done, it is too late; he can no longer free himself and strikes out. The story that begins with Roy striking out an aging star comes full circle with a new young pitcher striking out Roy.

In the private half of the test, Roy once again fails. As he has earlier made the wrong choice with Harriet Bird, he once again makes the wrong moral choices in this section of the novel. He becomes involved with the dark lady, Memo Paris, and they drive off together to a beach, even though the sign cautions danger, warning them of polluted water. There can be no symbolic cleansing here. Memo tries to explain the values she has learned from the suffering in her past, but what she has learned is solely to look out for herself. Roy wants to say something comparable about his own life, but he can think of nothing except more boasting about his future. When he returns to the ballfield after this episode, his grim future is apparent and his lack of control is magnified. The mystic meal is transformed into a large banquet where Roy eats so much he becomes too sick to play.

Memo's counterpart, the redemptive lady of the lake, is Iris Lemon. Like Memo and Harriet, she is associated with birds, flowers, and water, and as with Memo, the key scene involves a journey to the lake; Iris's role, however, is as potential savior of Roy. They drive together to a lake sheltered from the outside world, and it is there that Iris, too, questions Roy about his values, but she tries to lead him beyond boasting. She begins a confession of her own life. Although she is a grandmother at thirty-three, she has learned from her suffering, has transformed it into meaning. Roy is thirty-four, but something about Iris's confession repels him. They make love, and Iris becomes pregnant—she is the only fruitful woman in the novel—but Roy finally rejects her. In the last game of the playoffs, he sees her in the stands, but he is intent on trying to hit a dwarf who habitually heckles him from the bleachers. The ball instead hits Iris, who has stood to cheer for Roy. In the final scene between them, Iris tells Roy that she is pregnant, that he has created a new life for another at least, and she asks Roy to hit one for their child. It is too late, and Roy strikes out. He thinks of all the wrong choices he has made and wants to undo them, but he cannot.

In addition to the myth of the wasteland and the quest for new life, a central image of the novel occurs in a dream Roy frequently has. It involves Roy and his dog in a forest, a secluded place where he can follow his innermost thoughts without shame. Driving once with Memo, Roy thinks he sees a boy and a dog emerging from a woods, a boy whom Memo seems to hit. Whether she has or not, Memo speeds on—leaving behind her destruction of Roy's innocence and his illusions. In the forest he thinks he will lose his directions in order to find himself, lose his life in order to save it, but for Roy, whose middle life is marked with nothing but wrong choices, there is no salvation, no learning. The boy and his dog have vanished along with Roy's innocence, and he has rejected Iris, who could have saved him.

THE ASSISTANT

In Malamud's second novel, *The Assistant*, the surface of the myth is quite different. The pastoral world of baseball gives way to an urban business setting. The rustic king gives way to the petty thief, and the myth of heroic action on which the fate of many depends is replaced by the legend of a saint. Spaciousness is superseded by narrowness, movement by confinement. *The Natural* is often humorous and always marked by energy; even evil is active. In *The Assistant*, gloom and lethargy hand over every scene, and the despair is oppressive. The mythic parallels in *The Natural* are elaborate and schematic; in *The Assistant*, implicit and suggestive.

These differences sketched, however, *The Assistant* remains another telling of Malamud's basic myth. For most critics, it is his most successful; the fusion of romance and realism, of surface accuracy with poetic evocation, is seamless and compelling. Like Roy Hobbs, Frankie Alpine, the protagonist of *The Assistant*, is without parents. Both find older men from whom to learn, and both are partially responsible for their deaths. When the lessons they encounter involve renunciation, a check on their passions, they refuse to heed the wisdom. Both learn the wrong lessons from their suffering, at least for a time, and both cheat for financial gain. The two novels are stories of their protagonists' education, and they both open with a glimpse of the old life: Frankie Alpine and a friend rob Morris Bober, the Jewish shopkeeper to whom Alpine apprentices himself. That old life indicated, Malamud settles into the central concern of his books: the middle life, the learning life, where suffering may promise the characters a new and better future.

Frankie returns to the scene of his robbery and begins to help Morris Bober in the grocery store. The relationship between the two is one of father and son, typically cast as master-assistant, an educational apprenticeship. There are three pairs of natural fathers and sons in the novel, and they contrast with Frankie and Morris in their inadequacy. The most promising of these is that of Nat Pearl, one of Frankie's rivals for Helen Bober's affection, with his father. Nat becomes a lawyer, but although he rises financially, he is shallow compared to Alpine, and his treatment of Helen is unkind. Less successful is the relationship of the loutish Louis Karp with his father, who is trying to arrange a marriage between Louis and Helen. The worst is that between Detective Minogue, who investigates the burglary, and his son Ward, who, with Frankie, has perpetrated it.

What Frankie must learn from his surrogate father is stated in a crucial scene in which Frankie asks Morris why Jews suffer so much. Morris first answers that suffering is a part of human existence: "If you live, you suffer." He goes on, however, to indicate that suffering can be meaningful if one suffers not only *from* but also *for*: "I think if a Jew don't suffer for the Law, he will suffer for nothing." Frankie's question is ironically self-directed, for it is Alpine himself, the non-Jew, who is suffering more than he has to: He is suffering not only the existential guilt that comes with living but also the contingent guilt that comes from his own stealing. Like Roy Hobbs, Alpine cannot check his appetite, and he continues to steal from Morris even while trying to atone for the earlier robbery. Though he steals only small amounts, though he promises himself he will repay Bober, and though he assures himself that he is really a good man, Alpine continues to violate the law, and he suffers unnecessarily for this violation. At the end of the novel, Alpine becomes a Jew and replaces Bober in the store. This action is not, as some critics have suggested, the pessimistic acceptance of a Jew's suffering or a masochistic embracing of Morris's despair; it is rather an acknowledgment of guilt for the suffering Alpine has imposed on others and on himself and the resolve to be like a Jew in suffering *for* something, in making suffering meaningful.

Alpine must learn more than just law, however, for human needs are more complex than that. When Helen Bober meets Nat Pearl on the subway, he is carrying a thick law book; her own book seems to her protection, and when he asks what it is, she replies, Miguel de Cervantes' *Don Quixote de la Mancha* (1605, 1615). Like Quixote, she is a dreamer, unsatisfied with her life as it is, and it is this quality that she will share with Frankie and that draws them together. The dialectic that informs Malamud's work is represented here: the law book, from a discipline that recognizes human limitations and demands attention to the responsibilities of this world, and *Don Quixote*, the book that allows one to look beyond these limits and provides a model for noble action. Helen rejects Nat Pearl because the law is insufficient by itself. Her action is not, of course, a rejection of the law, for she rejects Alpine too, when he lives in a world of dreams, unbound by law, for his dreams lead him into actions the law forbids. The generative force is a synthesis of the two.

Helen is, then, the other person from whom Frankie will learn. That he has the capacity for knowledge and for gentle action—as well as for the lawlessness that has marked his life—is shown by his constant identification with St. Francis. He is from San Francisco, and his name resembles that of the saint. He looks at pictures of and dreams about St. Francis, striving for his quality of goodness. With Helen, too, though, Frankie must learn to moderate his passions; with her, too, he violates the law. A voyeur, like so many Malamud characters, he climbs an air shaft to watch her showering. The mirror having been replaced by a glass, the glass remains itself a partition, separating the dreamer from the object of his desires. More serious is his rape of Helen in the park. It is the low point of the novel: Morris fires Frankie; his business is failing, and Morris tries to commit suicide. Frankie looks at himself in the mirror, finds himself trapped inside a prisonlike circle, and hates himself for always having done the wrong thing. He returns to the store and resolves to bring it back to life for the hospitalized Morris. Although Helen and her mother do not like Frankie's return, they have little choice but to accept him, and although Frankie occasionally backslides, he makes firmer progress at controlling his passions.

Helen never fully accepts Frankie in the course of the novel, but she does reject her other suitors, and in a series of dreams, the reader discovers a tentative acceptance of Frankie: In his dreams, Frankie, like St. Francis, performs a miracle, turning a wooden rose he has carved and given to Helen into a real flower. In life, she has thrown the present away, but in the dream she accepts it. Helen, too, dreams of Frankie, out in the snow, making "a wife out of snowy moonlight."

Unlike *The Natural*, with its unambiguously pessimistic ending, *The Assistant* ends on a note of hope. Morris has died and Frankie has taken his place, and there is a suggestion that Frankie may be entrapped by the small grocery and the poverty of the Bobers' life, but there is also, in his conversion to Judaism and in his gradual winning of Helen's trust, a more powerful suggestion that he has learned the lessons of love and law, of dream and check, and that this middle life, for all its suffering, may indeed bring him toward happiness and offer him the promise of new life.

THE FIXER

The Fixer is Malamud's most ambitious novel, both because the reality he creates to embody his myth—the historical trial of a Russian Jew accused of murdering a Christian boy—is the most distant from his own experience and because the purposes of the tale, its philosophical underpinnings, are the most explicit and have the most scope.

As usual the novel opens with a journey. The main character, Yakov Bok, sees his travels, the leaving of his shtetl for a new life in Kiev, as an escape from his past. Bok attempts to strip away his Jewishness: He shaves his beard and cuts his earlocks. On the ferry across the river to his new hell, he drops his prayer things into the water. Like many of Malamud's characters, Bok is first adopted by an older man as an employee/foster son. This father figure, whom Yakov finds lying drunk in the snow, is without wisdom; indeed, he is a member of a militantly anti-Semitic organization. His daughter is the first woman with whom Bok becomes involved, but she also turns against Bok, accusing him of raping her. Because, however, she has written him letters avowing her love, even those who want to cannot believe her.

There are other dark women. On leaving the village, Bok is given a ride by a Jew-cursing Christian; he dreams of Lilith. The most powerful of these women is a member of a gang; she has killed her own son and accuses Bok of the deed and of a sexual assault on the boy. In this version of Malamud's story, not only does the father figure fail but there is also no redemptive counterpart of these betraying women to offer Bok hope or love.

Most of the novel takes place after the discovery of the murdered child's body and the imprisonment of Bok. The prison is a consistent metaphor in Malamud for the confined lives of his characters; Bok has left a figurative prison for a literal one. Malamud allows Bok escape through the agency of his mind, especially in his dreams. Like those of most of Malamud's characters, however, Yakov's dreams are full of bitterness and terror. If they provide him with a vision and a remembrance of life beyond the prison, they also remind him of the limits of his existence.

A second relief for Bok is that one of the Russian prosecutors, Bibikov, knows of Bok's innocence, and they share a philosophical discussion, its base in Baruch Spinoza, throughout the novel. Bok emphasizes that Spinoza, although he is a philosopher who asserts humanity's freedom, recognizes that people are limited; his name for that restrictive force is Necessity. The accumulated suffering in *The Fixer* is a powerful documentation of Necessity, and forces outside human control play a more significant role in this novel than in any other of Malamud's works.

If Necessity is so powerful, asks Bibikov, where does freedom enter? Bok replies that freedom lies within the mind: One rises to God when one can think oneself into nature. Bok also learns from one sympathetic guard, who quotes to him from the Bible that those who endure to the end will be saved. Yakov learns to endure, and he does so through the freedom his mind creates. He learns also that thoughtful endurance is not enough, for neither Bibikov nor that guard, Kogin, is allowed even to survive: Bibikov takes his own life, and Kogin is murdered.

Bibikov has explained to Bok that there is in Spinoza something Bok has missed, another kind of freedom, more limited but nonetheless real: "a certain freedom of political choice, similar to the freedom of electing to think." It is this freedom that Bok finally affirms. He has undergone the extreme suffering that Necessity entails. For most of the novel there is hope that in his mind he is at least free and can create new worlds, and there is hope that he will endure. The novel ends with a more political hope. Bok, at least in his dreams, elects to shoot the czar. He has created political freedom by electing to think of himself as free. Again he cites Spinoza that if "the state acts in ways that are abhorrent to human nature, it's the lesser evil to destroy it."

Much of *The Fixer* is a moving dramatization of these ideas, and much of it as well conforms to the basic pattern of Malamud's myth, which he has developed so often and so well. *The Fixer* is marred, however, and its faults suggest those that damage many of Malamud's later works. The philosophy seems too often grafted onto a rather static tale, the story itself an excuse for the ideas rather than the ideas a product of the story. The historical events have been distorted to fit the ideas. There is no reason Malamud should be bound by fidelity to historical truth, but all of his revisions seem to be in the direction of simplicity—not the simplicity that allows the novelist focus, but a simplicity that reduces moral complexity to schematism. All the intellectual weight of *The Fixer* is given to one set of people who hold one set of values; it is not simply that the novel presents good versus evil, but that it presents eloquent and intelligent good versus inarticulate and stupid evil.

In the novels that followed *The Fixer*, Malamud's problems with form and with integrating form and meaning became more noticeable. *The Tenants* suffers from inadequately worked-out ideas. *Dubin's Lives* is marred by structural redundancy and by a facile ending, although it features an articulate and convincing hero, a failed artist's search to find himself. Dubin's own life is finally one of promise, and that is the story Malamud knew to tell.

God's Grace

God's Grace is the story of Calvin Cohn, the only surviving human after humankind has destroyed itself in a nuclear war. The novel opens with Cohn aboard a ship, where he discovers another survivor, a chimpanzee. Most of the book is set on an island where they discover other chimps, a reclusive gorilla, and some baboons. Unlike *Dubin's Lives*,

God's Grace returns to the playfully fantastic style of Malamud's early stories, but like all of his work, it is another accounting of the middle life. For Cohn, the old life is completely dead; this is his new chance to re-create a life for himself—and for all the world. In part resembling Robinson Crusoe and his story of survival, *God's Grace* is more centrally a fable about Cohn's attempt to maintain his faith in a God who has allowed this destruction and his faith that humankind can develop order among the creatures that remain. He plays a record of his father singing, "They that sow in tears shall reap in joy," and that becomes Cohn's rationalistic credo.

When the chimpanzees begin talking, Cohn has a chance to verbalize his thoughts, but though this development would seem promising, Cohn's thoughts are insistently didactic. He is intent on teaching the animals to act morally, but his attempt fails: The tone darkens and the animals begin destroying each other and finally Cohn himself. His faith in the efficacy of reason to tame nature's cruelty is naïve, and just as he underestimates the darker passions, he omits love entirely from his list of virtues. In an ending reminiscent of the close of "The Magic Barrel," another story about the relationship of law and love, the gorilla George, who has remained outside the group, attracted only when Cohn is playing records of his cantor father's chanting, begins a Kaddish for the dead Cohn and his vanished dreams. Malamud asks perhaps too much of this work: The realism of survivorship does not always blend with the fantasy of animal speech; the playful beginning gives way too abruptly to the brutal ending, yet much that is sustained recalls Malamud's work at its best.

THE PEOPLE

At the time of his death, Malamud was working on a novel titled *The People*, having completed the first draft of sixteen of a projected twenty-one chapters. This unfinished work, published posthumously, is the story of a Jewish refugee who, like Levin in *A New Life*, is an anomalous figure set down in the American West. In *The People*, however, the time frame is the late nineteenth century, not the 1950's, and Malamud's protagonist is captured by a group of Native Americans whose chief and advocate he eventually becomes. Like *God's Grace*, *The People* is a fable, a darkly comic tale marked by the bleakness faintly laced with hope that characterizes Malamud's last works.

Howard Faulkner

OTHER MAJOR WORKS

SHORT FICTION: *The Magic Barrel*, 1958; *Idiots First*, 1963; *Pictures of Fidelman: An Exhibition*, 1969; *Rembrandt's Hat*, 1973; *The Stories of Bernard Malamud*, 1983; *The People, and Uncollected Stories*, 1989; *The Complete Stories*, 1997 (Robert Giroux, editor).

NONFICTION: *Talking Horse: Bernard Malamud on Life and Work*, 1996 (Alan Cheuse and Nicholas Delbanco, editors).

Bibliography

Abramson, Edward A. *Bernard Malamud Revisited.* New York: Twayne, 1993. Good general introduction to Malamud provides biographical information and individual chapters devoted to analyses of his first six novels. Includes selected bibliography and index.

Avery, Evelyn, ed. *The Magic Worlds of Bernard Malamud.* Albany: State University of New York Press, 2001. Wide-ranging collection of essays on Malamud and his writings includes personal memoirs by his friends and by members of his family as well as analyses of some of his novels.

Bloom, Harold, ed. *Bernard Malamud.* New York: Chelsea House, 2000. Collection of essays assesses the entire spectrum of Malamud's works, including analysis of *The Natural* and of Malamud's heroes. Includes a chronology of his life and a bibliography.

Cappell, Ezra. "Reflecting the World: Bernard Malamud's Post-Holocaust Judaism." In *American Talmud: The Cultural Work of Jewish American Fiction.* Albany: State University of New York Press, 2007. Chapter on Malamud is part of an examination of the fiction of American Jewish writers that focuses on how this fiction is linked to religious texts and traditions. Cappell argues that these writers can be viewed as creating a new form of Jewish rabbinic scripture.

Codde, Philippe. *The Jewish American Novel.* West Lafayette, Ind.: Purdue University Press, 2007. Malamud's novels are among those considered in this study of American Jewish novels that enjoyed unprecedented success in the post-World War II period. Discusses the possible reasons for this success.

Davis, Philip. *Bernard Malamud: A Writer's Life.* New York: Oxford University Press, 2007. First full-length biography of the author chronicles the events of his life, describes his writing methods, and connects the events of his life to his work. Also provides literary analysis of Malamud's novels and other fiction.

Field, Leslie A., and Joyce W. Field, eds. *Bernard Malamud and the Critics.* New York: New York University Press, 1970. Collection of critical essays addresses various topics, such as the Jewish tradition in Malamud's work and his use of myth, ritual, and folklore. Some contributors discuss specific novels and stories. A valuable resource for scholars interested in early Malamud criticism. Includes select bibliography and index.

Ochshorn, Kathleen. *The Heart's Essential Landscape: Bernard Malamud's Hero.* New York: Peter Lang, 1990. Presents discussion of each of Malamud's novels and his short-story collections. Ochshorn continues a trend in Malamud criticism that views his heroes as tending toward the *mensch* (good person) and away from the *schlemiel* (fool). Includes a bibliography.

Richman, Sidney. *Bernard Malamud.* Boston: Twayne, 1966. First book-length study of Malamud is a must for students who are starting to study the author's works. Systematically appraises each of Malamud's works through *A New Life* and devotes a chapter to Malamud's Jewishness. Includes some of Richman's personal correspondence with the writer and a select bibliography.

Smith, Janna Malamud. *My Father Is a Book: A Memoir of Bernard Malamud.* Boston: Houghton Mifflin, 2006. Malamud's daughter provides an intimate and candid account of her father's life and literary legacy, drawing on her own memories as well as on her father's letters and journals.

AMOS OZ

Born: Jerusalem, British Mandate of Palestine (now in Israel); May 4, 1939
Also known as: Amos Klausner

Principal long fiction

Makom aher, 1966 (*Elsewhere, Perhaps*, 1973)
Mikha'el sheli, 1968 (*My Michael*, 1972)
Laga 'at ba-mayim, laga 'at ba-ruah, 1973 (*Touch the Water, Touch the Wind*, 1974)
Menuhah nekhonah, 1982 (*A Perfect Peace*, 1985)
Kufsah shehorah, 1987 (*Black Box*, 1988)
La-da'at ishah, 1989 (*To Know a Woman*, 1991)
Matsav ha-shelishi, 1991 (*Fima*, 1993)
Al tagidi lailah, 1994 (*Don't Call It Night*, 1995)
Panter ba-martef, 1994 (*Panther in the Basement*, 1997)
Oto ha-yam, 1999 (*The Same Sea*, 2001)
Pit'om be-'omek ha-ya'ar, 2005
Haruze ha-hayim veha-mavet, 2007 (*Rhyming Life and Death*, 2009)

Other literary forms

Amos Oz is a widely regarded and well-known Israeli intellectual and writer. He has published essays on politics, literature, and other topics. His journalistic essays have appeared in the Israeli labor newspaper *Davar* and, beginning in the 1990's, the newspaper *Yedioth Ahronoth*. His nonfiction has been published in *The New York Times* and *The New York Review of Books*, and his political essays are collected in *Po va-sham be-Erets-Yisra'el bi-setav* (1982; *In the Land of Israel*, 1983) and *Israel, Palestine, and Peace: Essays* (1994). He also has published collections of literary essays, *Mathilim sipur* (1996; *The Story Begins: Essays on Literature*, 2000); short stories, *Artsot hatan* (1965; *Where the Jackals Howl, and Other Stories*, 1981); and novellas, *Har ha'etsah ha-ra'ah* (1976; *The Hill of Evil Counsel: Three Stories*, 1978). His remarkable memoir *Sipur 'al ahavah ve-hoshekh* (2002; *A Tale of Love and Darkness*, 2004) tells about coming-of-age in a period of violence.

Achievements

Amos Oz has written books in Hebrew and hundreds of articles and essays that have been translated into more than thirty-five languages. He was a visiting fellow at St. Cross College, Oxford, and an author-in-residence at Hebrew University of Jerusalem, Colorado Springs College, and Boston, Princeton, Tel Aviv, and Indiana universities. He was named Officer of Arts and Letters in France and honored with the French Prix Femina for best foreign novel published in France. In 1942, he won the German Frankfurt Peace

Prize, and the city of Frankfurt also awarded him the Goethe Prize in 2005 (an award earlier received by Sigmund Freud and Thomas Mann, among others).

In 2007, Oz won the Prince of Asturias Award of Letters, one of a series of annual prizes given in Spain by the Foundation Principe de Asturias since 1981 to individuals or entities who make notable achievements in the sciences, humanities, or public affairs. He earned his country's most prestigious literary prize—the Israel Prize for Literature—in 1998, the fiftieth year of Israel's independence. He received an honorary degree from the University of Antwerp, Belgium, in 2008, and in the same year received the Dan David Prize for Creative Rendering of the Past. Oz has been active in the Israeli peace movement, which works for a two-state solution to the Israeli-Palestinian conflict.

Biography

Amos Oz, born Amos Klausner in 1939, spent his early years in Jerusalem. Until the age of fifteen, he lived at No. 16 Amos Street, a place that plays a prominent part in his memoir *A Tale of Love and Darkness*. Yehuda Klausner and Fania Mussman, his father and mother, were Zionist immigrants from Eastern Europe. Much of his father's family was right-wing Zionist. Yehuda, who had studied history and literature in Lithuania, worked as a librarian and writer in Jerusalem. His maternal family emigrated from Poland to Haifa in 1934.

Although Oz's immediate family was not religious, he attended the community religious school, Tachmoni, instead of the alternative socialistic school because it was antithetical to his family's political views. He then attended the Hebrew high school in Rehavia. Oz's mother, who suffered from depression, committed suicide in 1952.

Oz was fourteen years old when he changed his last name from Klausner to Oz ("Oz" means strength and power in Hebrew). He left his father's home and joined Kibbutz Hulda, where he intended to work as a field laborer and live by the Zionist ideals of labor, equality, and simple living. However, he found himself increasingly drawn to study and writing and took leave from the kibbutz to complete a degree in literature and philosophy at Hebrew University. As time went on, royalties from his writing allowed him to perform less field work. In 1960, Oz married Nily Zuckerman, whose father was the librarian of the kibbutz. Oz completed his service in the Israeli Defense Forces in 1961, but he later fought in the Six Day War of 1967 and the Yom Kippur War of 1973.

Oz remained on the kibbutz until 1986, when he and his wife moved to the drier climate of southern Israel because of his son's asthma. In addition to being a prolific writer, Oz has been a professor of Hebrew literature at Ben-Gurion University of the Negev. Both his life and his writing are deeply rooted in his native land.

Analysis

Amos Oz's fiction is often concerned with domestic relationships, portrayed in a realistic manner. However, within this realistic facade, his characters struggle with internal conflicts between body and spirit, their own desires and social constraints, irrational impulses opposed to stability, and their faith in Israel tinged with skepticism. While they dream of perfection and long for the Messiah, they must navigate the dangerous reality of life in Israel. Most of Oz's novels are serious psychological studies, thoughtful and self-assured, and occasionally lightened by a mordant humor. Many of his characters believe they are living in a dream world, especially when people they believe they know suddenly behave in uncharacteristic ways.

In style, Oz is innovative. His novels take varying shapes, from *Black Box*, an epistolary novel, to the free-flowing lyricism of *The Same Sea*, which is told in poetic paragraphs that intersperse the past and the present, the near and the far. Among the story's extraordinary range of voices, the reader sometimes hears the ghostly voice of the deceased. Some of his novels have a claustrophobic feeling, which mirrors the claustrophobia of the intense familial relationships they portray.

MY MICHAEL

My Michael, published in 1968, became Oz's breakthrough work. *My Michael* is the story of its first-person narrator, Hannah Greenbaum, a thirty-year-old native of Jerusalem who is married to Dr. Michael Gonen, a geologist and, in Hannah's own words, a "good-natured man." Unlike traditional plots, this novel is structured by Hannah's slow decline into mental illness during her courtship and marriage.

Michael and Hannah meet when they are both students: he a third-year geology student and she a first-year student at Hebrew University. In the mornings she teaches at a kindergarten. One of the first clues to Hannah's instability is her relationship to her deceased father, whose presence in Hannah's mind is felt from the beginning of the novel, when she interrupts her story of how she and Michael met with the incongruous declaration that she has never loved anyone as much as her father. She also fondly recalls a bout of diphtheria she suffered when a child, from which she recovered reluctantly. Memories and fantasies of childhood are interspersed throughout her narrative.

Michael is an only child, and his family hopes he will be a scholar. After a brief courtship with Hannah, he proposes marriage. Hannah accepts, but she also realizes that Michael bores her. Their son, Yair, is born near the end of their first year of marriage. Hannah gives up her studies in literature at Hebrew University and Michael passes his exams, but money is still scarce. Hannah has a nervous breakdown, and when she is ill, Michael is called up for military duty in the 1956 war, giving Hannah new fantasies of military excursions mixed with news from the front. Eventually, her mental condition improves, and Michael returns from military duty. Their days settle down to routine: Michael finishes his thesis and Hannah is once again pregnant, yet she remains lost in fantasy and Michael remains unable to enter her interior world. *My Michael* is distinguished by the remarkable integration of Hannah's inner and outer worlds and its pattern of significant motifs woven delicately throughout the narrative.

Black Box

Black Box is written as a series of letters among Alex Gideon, his former wife Ilana, her new husband Michael, and Alex and Ilana's son Boaz. Interspersed with these letters are communications from Alex's lawyer Zakheim and from Ilana's sister Rahel, whose calm common sense is in direct contrast to Ilana's passionate temperament, which is still in thrall to her first husband. The novel is further enriched by Michael's constant quoting of scripture; reviews of Alex's new book, *The Desperate Violence: A Study in Comparative Fanaticism*; court records; and reports from a private investigator.

The sixteen-year-old Boaz is the apparent instigator of the plot. Ilana first writes to Alex, who is now a university professor in Chicago, to help her find Boaz, who has a penchant for physical violence and is often in trouble. A boy who deeply resents both his parents and Ilana's second husband (Michael), Boaz is gradually won over by Michael's ability to get his son out of trouble by using his vast network of relatives. Slowly, the reader recognizes that each character is a fanatic: Alex is a hardened officer with the Israel Defense Forces who is obsessed with terrorism, Ilana is a slave to masochistic sex, Michael is driven by his absolute religious devotion, and Boaz is ruled by his thirst for independence.

A "black box" is a term used to describe an airplane's recorders of flight data and cockpit communications. In the case of an airplane crash, for example, recorders are useful for the data they might reveal about the cause of that crash. The black box and its functions are apt metaphors for the novel, which centers on the correspondence between Alex and Ilana as they rehash their troubled marriage and divorce of seven years earlier, as well as their courtship. As the correspondence continues over the course of a year, Alex and Ilana gradually get over their bitterness toward each other. The wealthy Alex establishes Boaz in his own childhood home in Israel. Slowly, Boaz "finds" himself there, establishes a commune, and pursues farming and astronomy while rehabilitating his house. He remains an idealist and perhaps the truest embodiment of the Zionist tradition.

In the second half of the novel, the reader discovers that Alex is dying of cancer. He returns to his old home in Israel, where Boaz cares for him; Ilana and her young daughter also nurse him. Michael, at first outraged that Ilana has rejoined Alex, relents and gives both Ilana and Alex his blessing when Alex informs him that he has but a few months to live. Only in the proximity of death are these four strong characters able to find true reconciliation.

To Know a Woman

To Know a Woman is the story of Yoel Ravid, told in the omniscient third person but confined to the viewpoint of this tired, recently widowed and retired, forty-seven-year-old man. Employed for twenty-three years with the Israeli secret service, he was on an assignment in Helsinki, Finland, when his wife had a fatal accident. Perhaps because of his wife's death and the responsibility of taking care of his sixteen-year-old daughter, or perhaps because, as he says, his concentration is failing, he retires from his job and rents a house near Tel Aviv to live with his mother, mother-in-law, and daughter.

Yoel starts to fill the void first by tinkering around the house compulsively, performing small repairs. He expands his reach to the garden, while his mind is taken up with the past and attempts to understand his deceased wife and slightly impaired daughter. Recurrent images fill his mind, particularly of a paraplegic he saw on a street in Helsinki. He has an affair with an American neighbor who lives with her brother, his daughter finds a boyfriend, and he resists the efforts of the secret service to woo him into one last mission, one that would have been fatal. Occasionally, he gives in to paranoia; he has joyous moments when the sheer beauty of the landscape overwhelms him. His daughter moves out to live with her boyfriend, and although he has deep qualms about it, he heeds the advice of his friends and lets her set out on a life of her own.

Most important in this obsessive, claustrophobic novel, Yoel gives in to his real estate agent's suggestion to volunteer at the local hospital, and there he finds his true calling. Surrounded by bloodstains, filth, and odors of urine, excrement, and sweat, he finds these elements bring him a certain joy; he knows he is alive, removed from the empty life he had lived since his wife's death. He also discovers new powers in himself: He has the power to allay pain, soothe the distraught, and pacify the terrified. He is able to summon a mixture of compassion and firmness that the hospital patients need, and he is often called by doctors to calm a patient impervious to injections. The reader leaves this former spy using his trained ability of concentration to stare into the blackness of disease, trauma, and death, hoping for an occasional flicker of light.

Sheila Golburgh Johnson

Other Major Works

SHORT FICTION: *Artsot hatan*, 1965 (revised 1976; *Where the Jackals Howl, and Other Stories*, 1981); *Ahavah me'uheret*, 1971 (*Unto Death*, 1975); *Har ha'etsah ha-ra'ah*, 1976 (*The Hill of Evil Counsel: Three Stories*, 1978).

NONFICTION: *Be-or ha-tekhelet ha-'azah: Ma'amarim u-reshimot*, 1979 (*Under This Blazing Light: Essays*, 1995); *Po va-sham be-Erets-Yisra'el bi-setav*, 1982 (*In the Land of Israel*, 1983); *Mi-mordot ha-Levanon: Ma'amarim u-reshimot*, 1987 (*The Slopes of Lebanon*, 1989); *Shetikat ha-shamayim*, 1993 (*The Silence of Heaven: Agnon's Fear of God*, 2000); *Israel, Palestine, and Peace: Essays*, 1994; *Mathilim sipur*, 1996 (*The Story Begins: Essays on Literature*, 2000); *Kol ha-tikvot: Mahashavot 'al zehut Yisre'elit*, 1998; *Sipur 'al ahavah ve-hoshekh*, 2002 (*A Tale of Love and Darkness*, 2004); *How to Cure a Fanatic*, 2006.

CHILDREN'S LITERATURE: *Sumkhi*, 1978 (*Soumchi*, 1980).

Bibliography

Coetzee, J. M. "Whither Dost Thou Hasten." *The New York Review*, March 5, 1998. A review of Oz's novel *Panther in the Basement* that explores a repeated theme in his work:

A young boy is at a crossroads in his life, which coincides with a crossroads in the life of his nation.

Cohen, Joseph. *Essays and Interviews with Yehuda Amichai, A. B. Yehoshua, T. Carmi, Aharon Appelfeld, and Amos Oz.* Albany: State University of New York Press, 1990. Each chapter provides a critical look at the English translations of these Israeli writers. Each critique is rounded out by interviews with the five authors. Discusses the relationship of politics to literature, the responsibility of the writer, and the relationship between literature and life.

Mayot, Yair. *Somber Lust: The Art of Amos Oz.* Translated by Margaret Weinberger. Albany: State University of New York Press, 2002. Excellent critical study of Oz's fictional work. Part of the Modern Jewish Literature and Culture series.

CYNTHIA OZICK

Born: New York, New York; April 17, 1928

PRINCIPAL LONG FICTION

Trust, 1966
The Cannibal Galaxy, 1983
The Messiah of Stockholm, 1987
The Puttermesser Papers, 1997
Heir to the Glimmering World, 2004 (also known as *The Bear Boy*)

OTHER LITERARY FORMS

Cynthia Ozick's forte is short fiction, especially the novella; two of her novels, *The Cannibal Galaxy* and *The Puttermesser Papers*, were in fact developed from shorter pieces. Many of her stories have been collected in volumes such as *The Pagan Rabbi, and Other Stories* (1971) and *The Shawl* (1989). Although her literary reputation depends primarily on her fiction, Ozick has also published dozens of essays, largely dealing with the same major theme found in her fiction—that of Jewish identity. Both her essays and her short stories have appeared in such periodicals as *The New Yorker, Harper's, Partisan Review*, and *Salmagundi*. Her essays have been collected in a number of volumes, including *Art and Ardor* (1983), *What Henry James Knew, and Other Essays on Writers* (1993), *Portrait of the Artist as a Bad Character, and Other Essays on Writing* (1996), and *Quarrel and Quandary: Essays* (2000). Her poetry, which is also accomplished, has appeared in such publications as *Commentary, The Literary Review*, and *Epoch*. Her one play, *Blue Light* (based on Ozick's highly acclaimed short story "The Shawl"), had a staged reading in 1993 and a full production in 1994.

ACHIEVEMENTS

Cynthia Ozick has consciously reflected a major literary debate that has been ongoing since the mid-twentieth century. Although she began as a self-confessed worshiper at the shrine of art for art's sake and the formalistic standards represented by American novelist Henry James, in middle life she rebelled against that view. Increasingly, she asserted that an author should be actively engaged in judgment and interpretation and that a story should "mean" and not merely "be." In particular, she hopes to create a midrash, or fictive commentary, on Jewish life in the Diaspora. She sees the overvaluation of art as a form of "idolatry," a violation of the Second Commandment, and therefore a contradiction to "Jewish sensibility."

Ozick's fiction is thickly textured, allusive, and highly imaginative. Short accounts of her work do not do justice to her verbal energy and powerful range of reference. Regarded as one of the world's finest short-story writers, she has accumulated many honors, including the National Book Award, the American Academy of Arts and Letters Award, the PEN/Faulkner Award, and the O. Henry Award. In 2006, Ozick was on the short list for the Man Booker International Prize. Ozick has the unique honor of being the first writer to be awarded the Rea Award for the Short Story. Her work has been translated into most major languages.

BIOGRAPHY

Born of Russian Jewish immigrants, Cynthia Ozick was brought up in the Pelham Bay section of the Bronx in New York City, where her parents operated a pharmacy and managed to scrape by during the Great Depression. At P.S. (Public School) 71, she was a "luckless goosegirl, friendless and forlorn," and she was indifferent to her studies at Hebrew school.

After graduating from Hunter College High School, she attended New York University. She was determined to be a writer. At Ohio State University she wrote her master's thesis on Henry James, indicating her early dedication to that writer. "At twenty-two," she later wrote, "I lived like the elderly, bald-headed Henry James," a devotee of the sacredness of art. The product of this intense dedication was the 1966 novel *Trust*. Ozick was disillusioned with the shortcomings of her artistic accomplishment, "which did not speak to the Gentiles, for whom it had been begun, nor to the Jews, for whom it had been finished."

The essay "Toward a New Yiddish" (1970) marks an important turning point for Ozick, artistically, morally, and intellectually. Literature, she decided, is important not for formal reasons but because it lays out the specifics of life being lived. She attempted thereafter to write fiction that would interpret the "meaning" of Jewish life and the Jewish sensibility. This effort may be seen clearly in her novels and short fiction. In 1952, Ozick married Bernard Hallote. They made their home in Yonkers, New York, and they have one daughter, Rachel, a biblical archaeologist.

ANALYSIS

After her disappointment in her first novel, *Trust*, which took her fourteen years to write, Ozick felt that she did not have the time, given her methods of composition, to write another work of such length and complexity. *Trust* is a Jamesian novel in important respects: its theme of "Europe versus America," its concentration on upper-class characters, its situations of personal discovery, its virtuoso technical devices. *Trust* contains only one Jew, Enoch, a young man who, significantly, discovers his Jewish identity as well as a meaning of history different from that held by the Gentiles in his work cataloging Holocaust victims.

Expansions of Enoch's quest form the basis for Ozick's later work. In her essays, she announced a new direction: Literature is for the sake of humanity, she declared; it is not an idol of the imagination. Literature is a recognition of the particular. She denied the tenets of the dominant New Criticism and its "intentional fallacy," which declared that writers should dissolve their explicit intentions into the forms they discover. This artistic turnabout affected her subject matter. As she saw it, two standards distinguish the Jewish sensibility from that of the Gentiles: The Jews abjure idolatry, which is found not only in the worship of art but also in other secular religions such as Freudianism and Marxism, and they maintain a tradition of interpretive commentary, as evidenced by the Talmud. She seized upon English, now spoken by more than half the world's Jews, as the medium to replace the dying Yiddish language. What she meant by a Jewish literature in English was soon illustrated in her shorter fiction. In "The Pagan Rabbi," for instance, the protagonist, an assimilated Jew, visits a Hasidic community in New York State and is humbled by the spiritual commitment he finds there. A strong narrator, one with a broad knowledge of Jewish tradition and allusive powers, became her principal character.

THE CANNIBAL GALAXY

The Cannibal Galaxy clearly serves Ozick's aesthetic and moral program. The protagonist, Joseph Brill, had been a "hidden child" in a French convent during the Holocaust. In his youth he seeks to become an astronomer, to look *ad astra*, toward the cold heavens, to escape what he has experienced. He soon compromises his ambition, however; he emigrates to the United States and seeks mediocrity as his refuge—as principal of a middling school in the middle of the country, far from coasts and foreign dangers.

Brill's idol becomes the "Dual Curriculum," a mixture of Jewish and non-Jewish culture that finds a small, fashionable following but that to Ozick represents assimilation killing the roots of culture: "When a Jew becomes a secular person he is no longer a Jew." Brill's escape into dullness continues for years, but it is finally interrupted by the introduction of Hesther Lilt, a brilliant and aggressive intellectual. She is a self described "imagistic linguistic logician" who enrolls her daughter, Beulah, in his school. Hesther fascinates Brill and reminds him of his many compromises. He is particularly obsessed with the relationship between mother and daughter.

Beulah is an ordinary child, without any of the spark shown by her mother. How disappointed the mother must be, Brill thinks. In a central conversation, he accuses Hesther of failing her daughter because she lacks a maternal instinct. In return, she tells him that she is "nothing but maternal" and that he has stopped too soon in maintaining his hope for Beulah. Her obsession with Beulah's development is in fact her idol, and it finally cannibalizes her as Brill's idol has cannibalized him.

Brill, freed from his obsession with Hesther, marries another woman, fathers a son, and sinks into a stupor of boredom and frustration. One day years later he sees Beulah being interviewed on television. In a startling switch of personality, she has become a fashionable avant-garde artist. She publicly demeans her mother and ridicules her education at his school as meaningless. Hesther has accomplished the creation of her idol at the cost of destroying her relationship with her daughter. Brill's son, Nephali, meanwhile, seems enormously talented, a prodigy, everything Brill's idol-worshiping heart could have wished. As he develops into manhood, however, he becomes a mediocrity, "a business major at the University of Miami," showing none of his early promise. The end of Brill's life is a coma of boredom, a result of his having failed to meet life in its immediacy.

THE MESSIAH OF STOCKHOLM

In *The Messiah of Stockholm*, Ozick further examines the themes of the earlier novel in an entirely different background. Lars Andemening, a Polish refugee who has taken a Swedish name and who supports himself as a once-a-week book reviewer, believes himself to be the son of Bruno Schulz, a Polish Jewish writer and victim of the Holocaust with a phantasmagorical and prophetic style. Lars has no proof whatsoever of his identity, only his dreams and conjectures from Schulz's work. He seizes upon rumors of a lost manuscript by Schulz, *The Messiah*, and devotes his life to finding it. His quest leads him to Heidi, the proprietor of a bookstore, and Dr. Eklund, her shadowy husband, who is "an authority on texts." They too are refugees with uncertain background, and it is unclear why they should bother with the penniless and apparently deluded Lars. The mystery deepens when Adela, a woman representing herself as Schulz's daughter, appears with a manuscript she claims to be that of *The Messiah* in Schulz's own hand.

Dr. Eklund pronounces the text authentic, and Lars is confronted with a reality that lays waste the fragile structure of his fantasies. The text itself is a dreamscape of Schulz's hometown of Drohobycz, now emptied of people and dominated only by idols who have no one left to worship them. Finally the idols themselves are destroyed by a small bird carrying from the synagogue a bit of hay that had been slept on by a saintly Jew. The text, therefore, declares the fallacy of the idolatry of which Lars has been guilty.

Dr. Eklund urges Lars to use his newspaper column to introduce this literary discovery. Lars, however, denied his illusions and his special status in respect to Schulz, accuses Eklund and Adela of attempting a literary hoax—the actual truth about the manuscript hangs rather ambiguously. Lars burns the manuscript, figuratively burning the idolatrous dream out of his life. No longer does he see his father's eye peering down on him in his sleep. Like Joseph Brill, he sinks into a mediocrity without vision. His newspaper column, now devoted to popular writers instead of middle European visionaries, becomes a huge success. On a direct level, the novel seems to illustrate the truth of the Second Commandment. Questions remain, however—notably, has Lars fared better or worse without his illusions?

THE PUTTERMESSER PAPERS

Ozick developed *The Puttermesser Papers* into a novel from two stories about Ruth Puttermesser (her surname means "butter knife") that had appeared in her collection *Levitation: Five Fictions* (1982). Though the supernatural and the improbable had been common elements in her preceding fiction, in this work Ozick ventures freely into the fantastic, using material from the Kabbala, Jewish mystical writings dating back to the Middle

Ages. The novel's formlessness, improbability, and swift changes of direction show an increasingly greater distance from the ideals of Henry James.

In a manner that suggests Franz Kafka, the novel takes readers through Ruth Puttermesser's entire adult life. Initially she is a repressed, bookish woman, a lawyer and a bureaucrat in New York City's Department of Receipts and Disbursements, still living in the Bronx apartment in which she was brought up. She yearns for a Jewish identity, which her assimilated parents did not give her. She fantasizes a relationship with an imaginary Uncle Zindel and immerses herself in Hebrew and arcane Jewish lore.

When Ruth is forty-six, her regulated life is smashed into pieces. She loses her job in an unfair political maneuver; her married lover, Morris Rappoport, walks out on her; and she loses her beloved apartment to the arsonists of a changing neighborhood. Even her gums are giving way to periodontal disease. Then a miracle happens. From the earth and water of her flowerpots, combined with the sacred name of God, Ruth inadvertently creates a golem, a being whose creation ritual is described in ancient Jewish writings. The golem insists on being called Xanthippe, after the shrewish wife of Socrates, and wants to be regarded as Ruth's daughter.

The story becomes wildly comic. Through the golem's power, Ruth becomes mayor of New York. The city is magically transformed into something close to paradise on earth: Gangs disappear, graffiti is erased, and civility rules the streets. Xanthippe's powers turn to rebellion, however—the created idol, wanting to be human, demands more and more from Ruth—and the city once more decays. Ruth is compelled to return the golem to its original elements.

A major episode again illustrates the idolatry of art. Ruth, a fervent admirer of English novelist George Eliot (the pen name of Mary Ann Evans), wishes to find a mate similar to George Lewes, Eliot's married lover, with whom Eliot had a fabled romance of powerful mutual interests. She lures Rupert Rabeeno, who reproduces the paintings of the masters on postcards (a thoroughly noncreative activity) into a fascination with Eliot and Lewes. Rupert, the unimaginative duplicator, focuses instead on Johnny Cross, the man who tried to imitate Lewes after his death. Once again, Ruth's idolatrous attempts to incorporate meaning into her life lead to personal disaster. Rupert leaves her on their honeymoon in Venice—as Cross left Eliot in the same city.

The novel ends with Ruth in heaven. She had looked forward to a time when she could live entirely in her imagination, with all eternity to seek out the pleasures that fascinated her. Heaven itself, however, is a disappointment. Though everything is available there, nothing sustains itself. Ruth should have relied on the texture of life being lived. Idolatry and the uninterpreted life caused her suffering despite her goodwill.

Heir to the Glimmering World

A departure from many of Ozick's previous novels, which often call on the supernatural or fantastic as plot elements, *Heir to the Glimmering World* focuses on theme and character, centering on the Mitwissers, a family whose world is lost when they emigrate to New York from Germany in 1933. Professor Rudolph Mitwisser, the paterfamilias, was brought to New York by a small Quaker college under the misunderstanding that he would teach on a Christian sect called the Charismites. Mitwisser's passion and field of inquiry, however, is the Karaites, a small Jewish sect whose members take a fundamentalist approach to the Hebrew Bible and do not accept interpretation.

Rudolph's wife, Elsa, was a scientist and academic in Germany who finds refuge from her reduced circumstances in aberrant, sometimes even self-destructive, behavior. Distraught, she largely confines herself to her room and, like her husband, ignores the responsibilities of caring for their five children. It is left to their sixteen-year-old daughter, Anneliese, to care for her three younger brothers and her toddler sister.

Rose Meadows, the primary narrator of the novel and an orphan, arrives into the disarray of the Mitwisser household as an assistant to the professor. She is not entirely alone in the world, as she retains a tenuous link with her cousin Bertram, who took her in after her father's death. He turned Rose out when he fell in love with an active Communist, who eventually abandoned him for the cause. Thus Rose, at the time she is growing into adulthood, settles uneasily into the Mitwisser household as a place to get her bearings.

James A'Bair, a young alcoholic who was once the model for his father's successful series of children's books based on the Bear Boy, admires Rudolph Mitwisser's work and enjoys the chaotic family life so different from his own upbringing. He ingratiates himself with everyone in the family except Elsa, and serves as a financial benefactor to them. He narrates several of the chapters of his own life in a tone of sophisticated boredom that echoes the emptiness within.

Eventually, James seduces the innocent Anneliese, impregnates her, then takes his own life. Anneliese returns to the family home, in which Bertram, after falling on hard times, has found a haven. Bertram marries Anneliese, whose infant daughter inherits James A'Bair's large estate, allowing the family to partake of comfortable circumstances. Elsa, now a grandmother, rises to the occasion and returns to her role in the family.

Rose, realizing her work in the family is over, leaves to seek her fortune in Manhattan with the excellent secretarial skills she has developed during her time with Rudolph. Her experiences with the Mitwissers have confirmed her view of life as chaotic and subject to coincidence, luck, hope, and disillusionment, yet as Rose sets off for her own life, the reader feels confident she will find her way. By the end of this coming-of-age novel, it is clear that Rose will blossom by escaping the stagnant world of the Mitwissers.

Bruce Olsen
Updated by Sheila Golburgh Johnson

OTHER MAJOR WORKS

SHORT FICTION: *The Pagan Rabbi, and Other Stories*, 1971; *Bloodshed and Three Novellas*, 1976; *Levitation: Five Fictions*, 1982; *The Shawl*, 1989; *Dictation: A Quartet*, 2008.

PLAY: *Blue Light*, pr. 1994 (adaptation of her short story "The Shawl").

POETRY: *Epodes: First Poems*, 1992.

NONFICTION: *Art and Ardor*, 1983; *Metaphor and Memory: Essays*, 1989; *What Henry James Knew, and Other Essays on Writers*, 1993; *Fame and Folly: Essays*, 1996; *Portrait of the Artist as a Bad Character, and Other Essays on Writing*, 1996; *Quarrel and Quandary: Essays*, 2000; *The Din in the Head*, 2006.

EDITED TEXT: *The Best American Essays, 1998*, 1998.

MISCELLANEOUS: *A Cynthia Ozick Reader*, 1996.

Bibliography

Bloom, Harold, ed. *Cynthia Ozick: Modern Critical Views*. New York: Chelsea House, 1986. Excellent collection of essays includes brief reviews of Ozick's books as well as lengthy analyses. Provides much of value for both beginning students and scholars involved in the examination of complications of idea and form in Ozick's work.

Cohen, Sarah Blacher. *Cynthia Ozick's Comic Art: From Levity to Liturgy*. Bloomington: Indiana University Press, 1994. Places Ozick in the context of the Jewish comic tradition but argues that levity in her fiction must serve a higher purpose than laughter for laughter's sake, usually the satiric purpose of attacking vices, follies, and stupidity.

Franco, Dean J. "Rereading Cynthia Ozick: Pluralism, Postmodernism, and the Multicultural Encounter." *Contemporary Literature* 49, no. 1 (2008): 56-84. Scholarly study addresses Ozick's approach to human values in her fiction.

Friedman, Lawrence S. *Understanding Cynthia Ozick*. Columbia: University of South Carolina Press, 1991. Provides an informative critical study of Ozick's work, including in-depth discussion of her novels. Includes bibliography and index.

Kauvar, Elaine M. *Cynthia Ozick's Fiction: Tradition and Invention*. Bloomington: Indiana University Press, 1993. Examines the sources and contexts of Ozick's fiction, focusing on tensions between Hebraism and Hellenism, Western culture and Judaism, and artistic imagination and moral responsibility. Examines Ozick's relationship to psychoanalysis, feminism, and postmodernism.

Lowin, Joseph. *Cynthia Ozick*. New York: Twayne, 1988. Presents an excellent overview of Ozick's canon. Particularly valuable for beginning students whose knowledge of Holocaust literature and Ozick is limited. Offers perceptive and lucid analyses of her major works.

Nisly, L. Lamar. "Throwing Everything Off Balance: Ozick's Fantastic and O'Connor's Grotesque Portrayals of Mystery." In *Impossible to Say: Representing Religious Mystery in Fiction by Malamud, Percy, Ozick, and O'Connor*. Westport, Conn.: Greenwood Press, 2002. Discusses the different approaches that Ozick and Flannery O'Connor take in their fiction in their evocation of the experience of religious mystery.

Pinsker, Sanford. *The Uncompromising Fiction of Cynthia Ozick*. Columbia: University of Missouri Press, 1987. Excellent resource for readers new to Ozick's fiction provides brief analyses of the major works. Emphasizes postmodern aspects of Ozick's writing, particularly self-referential elements and the use of fantasy.

Powers, Peter Kerry. "Disruptive Memories: Cynthia Ozick and the Invented Past." In *Recalling Religions: Resistance, Memory, and Cultural Revision in Ethnic Women's Literature*. Knoxville: University of Tennessee Press, 2001. Discusses the influence of Ozick's ethnic identity on her fiction.

Seaman, Donna. "Life Sentences." *Los Angeles Times Book Review*, April 27, 2008. Offers an analysis of Ozick's body of work in addition to a review of her collection of short fiction *Dictation: A Quartet*.

CHAIM POTOK

Born: Bronx, New York; February 17, 1929
Died: Merion, Pennsylvania; July 23, 2002
Also known as: Herman Harold Potok; Chaim Tzvi

PRINCIPAL LONG FICTION

The Chosen, 1967
The Promise, 1969
My Name Is Asher Lev, 1972
In the Beginning, 1975
The Book of Lights, 1981
Davita's Harp, 1985
The Gift of Asher Lev, 1990
I Am the Clay, 1992
Old Men at Midnight, 2001 (3 novellas)

OTHER LITERARY FORMS

The book *Wanderings: Chaim Potok's History of the Jews* (1978) is a personal reconstruction of four thousand years of Jewish history. Chaim Potok (POH-tawk) also wrote essays and book reviews for Jewish and secular periodicals and newspapers. In January, 1988, his stage adaptation of *The Chosen* opened as a short-lived Broadway musical, with music by Philip Springer and lyrics by Mitchell Bernard. Potok wrote two picture books for young children, *The Tree of Here* (1993) and *The Sky of Now* (1995), both illustrated by Tony Auth. Potok also published essays and stories in various magazines and a collection of short stories about troubled young people, *Zebra, and Other Stories* (1998). In addition, he wrote a few full-length works of nonfiction, including *The Gates of November: Chronicles of the Slepak Family* (1996), the epic story of the families of Solomon Slepak, a Bolshevik and one of the founders of the Soviet Union. Slepak managed to survive all of Joseph Stalin's purges without being imprisoned. The book also focuses on his son, Volodya Slepak, a refusenik and one of the Russian Jews who applied for and was for years refused permission by the Soviet government to immigrate to Israel.

ACHIEVEMENTS

Critical acceptance and public acclaim have greeted Chaim Potok's novelistic explorations of the conflict between Orthodox Judaism and secular American culture. Potok received the Edward Lewis Wallant Award and a National Book Award nomination for *The Chosen*, his first novel. He received the Athenaeum Award for its sequel, *The Promise*. He also received the National Jewish Book Award for Fiction for *The Gift of Asher Lev* and the National Foundation for Jewish Culture Achievement Award for Literature. His sympathetic (critics would say sentimental) portrayal of Jewish fundamentalism and those who choose to leave it highlights the poignancy of an individual's break with tradition. Indeed, Potok's novels test the ability of traditional communities to contribute to the modern world without themselves being assimilated. His evocation of Jewish life in New York in the latter two-thirds of the twentieth century has universal appeal and disturbing implications.

BIOGRAPHY

Born of Orthodox Jewish parents in the Bronx in 1929, Chaim Potok was reared in a fundamentalist culture. Potok's father, Benjamin Potok, was a Polish émigré and no stranger to the pogroms of Eastern Europe. The young Potok was taught that the profound suffering of the Jews would one day transform the world. Yet, as Potok suggests in *Wanderings*, his service as a Jewish chaplain with the U.S. Army in Korea (1956-1957) confronted him with a world of good and evil that had never heard of Judaism. His attempt to come to terms with this larger world led Potok to a critical investigation of his own Jewish heritage and the limitations of the fundamentalist perspective. Though he was ordained a Conservative rabbi in 1954, attracted by doctrines more liberal than those of strict Jewish Orthodoxy, Potok continued his struggle to reconcile fundamental Judaism with the findings of science (as historiography and textual criticism shed new light on ancient traditions). *The Chosen* inaugurated his public search for a voice with which to speak to his heritage as well as to the larger world.

In the early 1960's, Potok taught at the Jewish Theological Seminary in New York and edited *Conservative Judaism*. In 1965, he became editor in chief at the Jewish Publication Society of Philadelphia, and in 1975, he took the position of special projects editor. He was married to Adena Mosevitzky in 1958, and they took up residence in Merion, Pennsylvania. The Potoks had three children: Rena, Naama, and Akiva. Potok served as a visiting professor at the University of Pennsylvania, Bryn Mawr College, and Johns Hopkins University.

ANALYSIS

In his novels, Chaim Potok returns again and again to the story of a young protagonist coming of age in a culture (usually Jewish) at once mysterious, beautiful, sad, and somehow inadequate. Usually told in the first person, Potok's stories surround the reader with forebodings of the larger, evil world (news of pogroms in Europe, the Holocaust, the first atom bomb) into which his characters are plunged. Potok creates a microcosm of feeling and reaction to events that shake the world. His sentences are simple and reportorial, at times almost a parody of the staccato style of Ernest Hemingway. The stories develop chronologically, though they are frequently invaded by dreams, visions, or voices from the "Other Side."

In each of his stories, Potok sets for himself a question to be answered and reworks his own experiences until he is satisfied with at least a provisional resolution. Controlling metaphors help shape the questions. In *The Chosen*, the baseball game symbolizes the competition between two Jewish cultures, the very strict Hasidic and the more openly assimilationist. What happens to those caught in between those two traditions? The vision of pups being born in *The Book of Lights* represents the entrance of fertile Kabbala mysticism into a world of strict Jewish law. How can Jewish mysticism enrich Orthodoxy? Asher Lev's dreams of his mythical ancestor foreshadow the young artist's confrontation with his own culture. What happens when art brings great hurt? The sound of a little door harp symbolizes the transforming power of the imagination for Ilana Davita Chandal (Potok's first female protagonist) of *Davita's Harp*. What is the place of the imagination in Jewish Orthodoxy? What is the place of women?

THE CHOSEN

The Chosen recounts the story of Danny Saunders, brilliant son of a Hasidic rabbi, chosen by tradition to one day succeed his father as leader of the fundamentalist community in Brooklyn, New York. Yet Danny is less interested in studying the Talmud (Jewish law) than in probing the works of Sigmund Freud and other secular psychologists. The story closes with the inevitable confrontation between Danny and his father, which is mediated by Danny's friend Reuvan Malter. In the climactic scene in Reb Saunders's office, the old rabbi turns to his son and addresses him as a father for the first time. (For years, Danny had been reared in silence, except for times of Talmud study.) With fatherly tears, Reb Saunders explains that the years of silence created a soul of compassion within his brilliant son. Though he may well leave the Hasidic community for secular studies, Danny will always carry with him the legacy of Jewish suffering. That legacy will provide the moral force to change the world.

Reuvan, son of a Talmud scholar of the new school of textual criticism, chooses to become a rabbi. The choices, for Reuvan and for Danny, do not, however, come easily. Reuvan faces ostracism by the Hasidic community for suggesting that some Talmudic texts were of inferior quality and subject to misinterpretation. Danny must seemingly turn against his father if he is to pursue secular studies and abandon his leadership obligations.

The novel is structured almost as a diary, with pages of detailed descriptions of schoolwork in the Jewish high school, visits to the local synagogue, and the ebb and flow of Reuvan's life. Though at times tedious, the very innocence of the language contributes to a certain dramatic intensity. The conflict in the novel is mirrored in the frequent news reports of World War II and in the ensuing controversy over the creation of a Jewish state, Israel, in 1949. The Hasidic community is content to wait for the Messiah to create such a state; Reuvan's father calls for an immediate political settlement. Political questions are present in each of Potok's novels and are of central interest in *Davita's Harp*.

THE PROMISE

Silence is again present in Potok's second novel, *The Promise*, which continues the story of Danny Saunders and Reuvan Malter as they enter their professional lives. The novel begins with shouts of rage from young Michael Gordon, the son of Professor Abraham Gordon, a controversial Jewish philosopher. Michael has been cheated at a carnival booth by an old Jewish man, and both Reuvan and his date, Rachel Gordon, Michael's cousin, stare in horror as Michael angrily denounces Orthodoxy. Michael's father had questioned the supernatural accounts in the Hebrew Bible and, as a result, was excommunicated from the Orthodox community; now Michael is releasing his hate on those who persecuted Professor Gordon. Subsequently, Michael is taken to Danny Saunders, now a psychologist at a residential treatment center. When the boy refuses to speak, Danny isolates him. The agonizing silence breaks Michael's will and he reveals the hate he feels for his father and his writings, writings that have brought condemnation to them both. Eventually, Michael is finally able to accept his own feelings and reconcile with his parents, and Danny and Rachel are married, the powerful coupling of the brilliant Hasid with the cosmopolitan daughter of a secularist philosopher.

The Promise continues the exploration of Reuvan's choice to receive his rabbinate from an Orthodox seminary and his refusal to become a secular Jew, as Professor Gordon has done. Yet Reuvan is uneasy with the traditional method of Talmud study advanced by Rav Kalman, one of his teachers. If the Talmud is the sacred oral tradition of the Jews in written form, contradictory commentaries from rabbis down through the centuries must always be reconciled by newer interpretations, so as not to call God's Word into question. For Reuvan, there is another possibility; a corrupt text could be the source of confusion. Any correction, however, would mean violence to sacred scripture. Reuvan will become a rabbi so that he might debate Rav Kalman and the others from within a common tradition.

Reuvan's father, David Malter, is the voice of quiet wisdom throughout both books. Though a proponent of the new Talmud studies, he is sympathetic toward those whose tightly knit culture is being threatened. As he tells Reuvan in *The Promise*, "We cannot ignore the truth. At the same time, we cannot quite sing and dance as they do. . . . That is the dilemma of our time, Reuvan. I do not know what the answer is." Earlier, Reuvan's father had challenged his son to make his own meaning in the world. Those who had committed themselves to the Hasidic traditions had kept the faith alive through incomprehensible persecution. Now, Reuvan must also choose with the greatest seriousness and fervency, for he, too, must make a mark on the world and endure hardship of his own.

MY NAME IS ASHER LEV

Potok picks up this theme in his third novel, *My Name Is Asher Lev*. Covering the period of the late 1940's through the late 1960's, the book is an apologia for the artist. The Orthodox Jewish surroundings are familiar, but this time the controversy is not over textual criticism but rather representational art. Painting is not strictly forbidden to the Orthodox Jew, but it is regarded as useless, as foolishness, as a waste of time better devoted to the study of the Torah, the five books of Moses. Moreover, certain pictures could come close to violating the commandment forbidding graven images. Asher Lev is a born painter, however, and throughout the novel, as he develops his talent, he is increasingly isolated from his family and culture.

Asher is born in Crown Heights in Brooklyn in 1943. His father travels extensively for the local Rebbe in an effort to establish Ladover Hasid communities throughout Europe and to aid families immigrating to the United States. Asher's mother must stay with her son in New York because Asher refuses to leave his familiar streets to join his father in Europe. There are long nights of loneliness, waiting for Asher's father to return from some mission or other. Asher's mother suffers a breakdown when her brother, also on a mission for the Rebbe, is killed. She begins to find herself again by plunging into her Russian studies, picking up the work her brother left unfinished. Metaphors of things unfinished and things completed permeate the novel. Asher's father is continually on the move because of the great unfinished work of the Ladover. Asher himself finds that he must bring some kind of completeness to the world by painting not only what he sees with his eyes but also what his inner vision reveals to him. Those visions are not always beautiful; his paintings can be like knives, plunging the reality of evil into the soul of the onlooker. The wise Rebbe, sensing Asher's vast talent, entrusts him to Jacob Kahn, himself an artistic genius and a nonobservant Jew. Kahn forces Asher to absorb the work of Pablo Picasso, especially *Guernica* (1937), a painting inspired by the German bombing of the Basque capital during the Spanish Civil War. In time, Asher begins to surpass his teacher.

Asher becomes virtually a stranger to his father. At the end of the novel, Asher's parents stare with mixed rage and amazement at the two crucifixions he has painted. Both are of his mother, looking in abstract fashion at Asher the stranger on one side and at the always-traveling husband on the other. The image of the cross for Asher has become the supreme symbol of suffering, devoid of any Christian preoccupation. The image is too much, however, for his parents, Orthodox Jews. As the Rebbe tells him, "You have crossed a boundary. I cannot help you. You are alone now. I give you my blessings."

There is a marked contrast between Asher's sensitive paintings (an effort to say what must be said about the evil in the world) and his selfish behavior toward his parents. He is one of the least sympathetic of Potok's protagonists because he struggles less with his own anguish than with his need to express his artistic gift at whatever cost. Jacob Kahn's advice, "Be a great painter, Asher Lev. . . . That will be the only justification for all the pain your art will cause," seems too facile. Asher is determined to remain an observant Jew, but he will do so on his own terms. The commandment about honoring one's parents must be radically reinterpreted. The book suffers from the technical difficulty that Asher Lev must be identified as a genius early in the story in order for Potok to create the kind of tension he needs to interest a reader. A mediocre artist who causes pain is merely self-indulgent.

Yet the book reveals something of Potok's larger purpose. Art must be true to itself even if that means surprise or hurt. The artist, painter, or writer must speak from the heart; anything else is mere propaganda. Potok sought to provide a rationale for his novelistic critiques of fundamentalist communities.

Potok introduces something else into Asher's story: Asher often dreams of his "mythic ancestor," a Jew who served a nobleman only to have the nobleman unleash evil upon the world. Just as Asher envisioned that ancient Jew traveling the world, seeking to redress the wrong he had a part in, so must the artist reshape evil into art and so bring a kind of balance to the world. Asher's visions are forerunners of Potok's use of mysticism or imaginative visions themselves as ways of coming to terms with a world gone crazy.

In the Beginning

In the Beginning is the story of young David Lurie and his childhood in an Orthodox family in the Bronx in the 1920's. The novel is patterned on the biblical book of Genesis: David falls from his mother's arms, develops a keen interest in the accounts of the Flood, and learns through the study of the Torah the power of words to shape a world. Potok's fourth novel was his most complex to date, departing from the forthright exposition found in *The Chosen* in favor of a more subtle panoply of impressions of growing up.

Like all Potok's protagonists, David is precocious, constantly questioning the world around him, trying to have it make sense. He is sickly, bullied by other boys, and plagued with recurring nightmares. David functions in the novel as an idealized figure to focus the reader's attention on how Orthodoxy confronts anti-Semitism and growing secularization. David imagines the Golem of Prague crushing those who would harm the Jews like some powerful living robot; as David grows, though, he learns that words can be more powerful than the Golem. Eventually, helped by those who practice textual critique of the Torah, David heads for graduate study at the University of Chicago. Yet, as in Potok's other works, there must also be some kind of reconciliation of the demands of Jewish Orthodoxy with those of secular learning. It is achieved through a vision David has years later as he tours the site of the Bergen-Belsen death camp. David's vision of his dead father, and of his father's brother, David's namesake, is a moving conclusion to the book. David's father despairs that he has lost his son to the evil world, to the very world that took the lives of millions of Jews. He is reassured by David's uncle, however, that the son must journey into that world in order to bring something back to enrich Orthodoxy, which has become moribund. The son must venture out but must never forget his own roots. No anger of humanity can strike evil from the world. Only the patient use of words, with faith in their power to transform creation, can accomplish the task. That will be a new beginning for the world, and for Orthodoxy.

Potok's earlier novels tell the story of those in conflict with their Orthodox heritage. For the first time, *In the Beginning* pictures a reconciliation as a vision or story within the context of the novel. It is a kind of blessing from the beyond; here is the artist at work, crafting the resolution to the story.

THE BOOK OF LIGHTS

The Book of Lights, narrated in the third person, uses the technique of mystical reconciliation for a more universal purpose. If the Master of the Universe truly exists, how is a believer to accept the death light of the twentieth century, the atomic bomb? Potok's answer is that through the imaginative use of Jewish mysticism, the spark of God can be found in an evil world.

The story departs from Potok's previous novels, which traced the childhood of the protagonist. Only a few pages are devoted to Gershon Loran's early life before his seminary days and subsequent chaplaincy in Korea. Those first pages, however, are significant. Gershon witnesses the birth of some pups on a rooftop in the midst of his rundown neighborhood; he is awed by the presence of life even amid wreckage.

In seminary, Gershon is introduced to the study of the Kabbala and its *Zohar*, a Jewish mystical work from the thirteenth century. The *Zohar* is the book of lights of the novel's title, describing the creation of the world through the emanations of God. There are places where God has withdrawn His light; that has enabled humankind to come on the scene but it has also ushered in great evil. Now the mystic is called to ascend through those emanations to find God.

Such mystical tradition is complex and even contradictory. For Gershon, however, it is the pounding heart of a living faith. Gershon's quiet moments of reverie serve him well during his chaplaincy. Though Potok paints a detailed picture of Gershon's activities in Korea, the crucial story is elsewhere. Gershon's seminary friend, Arthur Leiden, travels with him to Kyōto and Hiroshima. At the Hiroshima monument, Arthur reads from the Psalms and pleads to God in vain for some kind of atonement. Arthur's father had worked with other scientists in developing the atom bomb, and Arthur is haunted by the memory. Later, Arthur is killed in a plane crash; Gershon, visiting Arthur's parents, hears a portion of one of Arthur's letters: "All the world, it seems, is a grayish sea of ambiguity, and we must learn to navigate in it or be drowned." That is Potok's message in the novel; "Loran" is itself a navigational acronym. If Judaism were merely the law, the faith would break on the shoals of the gritty world. Its mystical tradition infuses the faith with the ambiguity of real life. It does not explain but rather affirms the nature of God's creation. The *Zohar* is an imaginative understanding of the nature of God; in it, God enfolds both good and evil. It is a light by which to view a decaying civilization, a light that will survive the death light. In his final mystical vision of his old Kabbala teacher, Gershon learns that the mystical light will help mend the world so that it can be broken again in yet new acts of creation.

DAVITA'S HARP

It is the "mending power" of imagination that is at the heart of *Davita's Harp*. The harp referred to is a small instrument that fits on a door, with little balls that strike piano wires when the door is opened or closed. Here Potok returns to the first-person narrative, tracing the childhood of Ilana Davita Chandal, his first female lead character. She is the daughter of a nonbelieving Jewish mother and a nonbelieving Christian father. Spanning the years from the mid-1930's to 1942, the novel speaks with a new voice yet recapitulates some familiar themes.

Davita grows up in the New York area; she remembers frequent moves, strange people coming and going, and the constant singing of the door harp. Her parents are involved in the Communist Party, attempting to fight fascism in Spain and in the United States. Davita is precocious and inquisitive and her mother intelligent and cool, forever supplying Davita with the meaning of new words: proletariat, strike, idea, magic, war. Davita is spurred in her imaginative development by Aunt Sarah, a devout Episcopalian nurse, who tells her Bible stories, and by Jakob Daw, an Austrian writer, now suffering from having been gassed in World War I, who had loved Davita's mother when they were both in Vienna. Daw is sheltered for a time by Davita's parents and spins odd stories for her. There is the story of the little bird, flying to find the source of a beautiful music that soothes the world from the horrors of war. Only if the bird could stop the deceitful music would the world wake to its pain.

Davita's father, Michael Chandal, a journalist with *New Masses*, is killed during the bombing of Guernica during the Spanish Civil War. Soon after, both Jakob Daw and Davita's mother, Channah, become disillusioned with the Stalinists because the Communists, too, have committed atrocities. Davita has taken to attending a Jewish high school and becomes an outstanding student. Jakob Daw returns to Europe, where he dies, though his stories live in Davita's heart. Not long afterward, Ezra Dinn, an Orthodox Jew who had loved Davita's mother years before, marries Channah. Slowly, Davita's mother regains her sense of place. Davita's time of innocence is over. Before Jakob Daw left for Europe, he finished his strange story of the bird. The bird, he said, gave up searching for the music of the world and became very small to fit inside the door harp. There, said Daw, the music was not deceitful but full of innocence. Now, however, Davita encounters something sinister in her adopted tradition. She is the most brilliant student at her yeshiva but she is passed over for the Akiva Award because, she is told, she is a woman. It is 1942. Another student is selected for the award but learns the truth and refuses it. He is Reuvan Malter, first introduced in *The Chosen*.

Ilana Davita had wanted the prize because it would have given her the opportunity to tell her Jewish community a few words of farewell. "I had made this community my home, and now I felt betrayed by it. . . . I felt suddenly alone. And for the first time I began to understand how a single event could change a person's life." Later, in a vision, Jakob Daw and Davita's father appear, as well as Aunt Sarah. They want to hear her words, and so Davita speaks. She does not understand a world that kills its very best. She had wanted to speak public words of good-bye to her father and Jakob Daw the storyteller. The harp appears in her vision as well, singing in memorial to all the Davitas who would never have an opportunity to "speak their few words to this century."

In the end, Davita will go on to public school, angry with "sacred discontent." In an interview, Potok explained that Davita's experience was based on that of his wife, who was passed over as valedictory speaker because of her gender. *Davita's Harp* is a new exploration for Potok, that of Orthodoxy and feminism. Yet the novel also draws from Gershon Loran, David Lurie, and Asher Lev in recognizing the power of the artist's imagination to transform pain and ambiguity into some kind of meaning. A writer is a kind of harp, playing new music that mends the world.

THE GIFT OF ASHER LEV

The Gift of Asher Lev is framed by death. It begins with the funeral of Yitzchok Lev, Asher's uncle, and the ending of Asher's exile in France to attend the services in Brooklyn. Asher Lev is forty-five; he is joined by his wife, Devorah; their daughter, Rocheleh, eleven; and five-year-old son, Avrumel. Though his family adapts well to the life of the Brooklyn Hasidim, Asher is haunted by the memory of a strange telephone call he received eighteen years earlier, the last time he had visited his parents in New York. It was a voice from the "Other Side," threatening death.

Asher is unable to paint (though he is given to sketching) and he seems to wander aimlessly through the local shops and galleries, as if waiting for a renewal of his gift. In the last year, critics had detected Asher's repetition of old themes, and he feels in danger of losing his gift should he become acclimated to his parents' community. Morose and determined to flee to France again, Asher is asked by the Rebbe to stay, at least for a while. Eventually it becomes clear to Asher that he and the aging Rebbe are woven inextricably together, as darkness and light. The Rebbe has no heir, and it is apparent that the leadership of the Ladover must pass soon to Asher's father; but there can be stability in the community only if there is assurance of the line of succession. If not Asher, then the next heir must be Avrumel, Asher's only son.

By the end of the novel, which takes Asher's story to the late 1980's, the artist has exiled himself again to France, but not without sacrifice. He has left his wife and children in New York, promising to return to them several months hence; yet in his isolation he has begun to paint again. "What kind of God creates such situations?" Asher asks himself as he walks with Devorah. "He gives me a gift and a son, and forces me to choose between them." Later, in France, Asher is visited by the image of the far-away Rebbe: "Slowly you begin to unravel the riddle," the vision says,

> Your answer may save us and return you to your work. . . . It is sometimes possible for a man to acquire all of the world to come by means of a single act in this world. . . . You will redeem all that you have done and all that you are yet to do.

Paradoxically, the sacrifice of Avrumel for the good of the community is a kind of death that redeems that artist himself; a gift on behalf of the world to come in exchange for the gift of the world as it is, in all its ambiguity and horror, and the ability to capture it on canvas.

I Am the Clay

Like *The Book of Lights*, *I Am the Clay* is a third-person narrative that grew in part from Potok's experiences in Korea. As they flee the North Korean and Chinese armies, a nameless old man and a woman named Gyu find a boy, Kim Sin, who is terribly wounded. The man wants to leave the boy, but the woman insists on taking him with them and heals him of his wounds. Eventually, they return to the village of the old couple to discover that it has not been destroyed. The boy then travels to his village, discovers that it has been razed, and returns to the village of the man and woman. Nearby is an American military installation where the boy gets a job, eventually working for a Jewish chaplain. After the boy reluctantly gets involved with a thief, the chaplain helps him escape by finding him a job in Seoul. By this time, the woman is dead, and the man has learned to love the boy.

The book treats the conflicts between the old, rural way of life and the new, technological way of life as well as between the old religious ideas and the reality of war. When the old man and woman return to their village, they think things will be the same because it has been spared, but they are wrong.

Like the biblical Job, to whom the novel's title alludes, the man, woman, and boy do not understand why they suffer. The woman has learned the words "I am the clay" from a missionary, from whom she has also learned to make the sign of the cross. Blending the sign of the cross into her own ideas about magic, she illustrates Potok's idea of the unity of all people. Although the novel has little to do with Jews, *I Am the Clay* treats one of Potok's central problems: testing one's beliefs in the face of an ambiguous, often harsh, and rapidly changing reality.

Dan Barnett
Updated by Richard Tuerk

Other major works

NONFICTION: *Wanderings: Chaim Potok's History of the Jews*, 1978; *Tobiasse: Artist in Exile*, 1986; *The Gates of November: Chronicles of the Slepak Family*, 1996; *My First Seventy-nine Years*, 1999 (with Isaac Stern); *Conversations with Chaim Potok*, 2001 (Daniel Walden, editor).

CHILDREN'S LITERATURE: *The Tree of Here*, 1993; *The Sky of Now*, 1995.

Bibliography

Abramson, Edward A. *Chaim Potok*. Boston: Twayne, 1986. The first book-length study of Potok, this volume is the fullest available introduction to his life and works. After a biographical sketch, Abramson discusses each of Potok's novels through *Davita's Harp*. Supplemented by a chronology, notes, an index, and a good selected bibliography, including a list of secondary sources with brief annotations.

Bloom, Harold, ed. *Chaim Potok's "The Chosen."* Philadelphia: Chelsea House, 2005. This student guide to the novel contains a biographical sketch of Potok, an account of the conditions under which the novel was written, a list of characters, a plot summary and analysis, and a critical opinion of the book. Also includes an annotated bibliography.

Daum, Robert A. "Crossing Cruci-Fictional Boundaries: Transgressive Tropes in Chaim Potok's *My Name Is Asher Lev*." In *Jesus in Twentieth-Century Literature, Art, and Movies*, edited by Paul C. Burns. New York: Continuum, 2007. This analysis of Potok's novel focuses on its treatment of a crucified Jesus. Part of a collection of essays that analyze the representation of Jesus in the work of twentieth century novelists, artists, and filmmakers.

Furman, Andrew. "Zionism in Chaim Potok's *The Chosen*, Messianic Complications and Current Crises." In *Israel Through the Jewish-American Imagination: A Survey of Jewish-American Literature on Israel, 1928-1995*. Albany: State University of New York Press, 1997. Furman analyzes *The Chosen* and works by seven other Jewish-American authors to chart the evolution of the relationship of American Jews with the state of Israel.

Shaked, Gershon. "Shadows of Identity: A Comparative Study of German Jewish and American Jewish Literature." In *What Is Jewish Literature?*, edited by Hana Wirth-Nesher. Philadelphia: Jewish Publication Society, 1994. Shaked briefly places *The Chosen* in the context of literature in which Jewish authors and their characters have a dual identity: Jewish as well as that of the country in which they live.

Sternlicht, Sanford. *Chaim Potok: A Critical Companion*. Westport, Conn.: Greenwood Press, 2000. A straightforward and useful guide to the novelist's works through *I Am the Clay*. Includes two biographical chapters and a bibliography of primary and secondary sources.

Studies in American Jewish Literature 4 (1985). This special issue devoted to Potok includes several valuable critical essays, an interview with Potok conducted in 1981 by S. Lillian Kremer, and an autobiographical essay by Potok, "The First Eighteen Years." An indispensable source.

University of Pennsylvania, Jewish Studies Program. *Chaim Potok and Jewish-American Culture: Three Essays*. Philadelphia: Author, 2002. These essays, delivered at a memorial symposium for Potok, reappraise *The Chosen*, discuss "Potok and the Question of Jewish Writing," and examine how the author was a *Zwischenmensch*, or a person who negotiated between two cultures.

Walden, Daniel, ed. *Conversations with Chaim Potok*. Jackson: University Press of Mississippi, 2001. Reprints numerous interviews with Potok, in which he discusses a range of topics, including his view on writing and other writers, his religious faith, and his novels.

MORDECAI RICHLER

Born: Montreal, Quebec, Canada; January 27, 1931
Died: Montreal, Quebec, Canada; July 3, 2001

PRINCIPAL LONG FICTION

The Acrobats, 1954 (also known as *Wicked We Love*)
Son of a Smaller Hero, 1955
A Choice of Enemies, 1957
The Apprenticeship of Duddy Kravitz, 1959
The Incomparable Atuk, 1963 (also known as *Stick Your Neck Out*)
Cocksure: A Novel, 1968
St. Urbain's Horseman, 1971
Joshua Then and Now, 1980
Solomon Gursky Was Here, 1989
Barney's Version, 1997

OTHER LITERARY FORMS

As a professional writer, spurning academic life for wider creative possibilities, Mordecai Richler (RIHCH-lur) was known for producing short stories, essays, articles, film scripts, television plays, and children's literature. Much of his work first appeared in prestigious magazines such as *The Atlantic Monthly*, *The New Yorker*, *New Statesman*, and *Encounter.* Some of his individual stories, many of which became chapters in his novels, have been collected in *The Street: Stories* (1969). A children's book, *Jacob Two-Two Meets the Hooded Fang* (1975), and two novels, *Joshua Then and Now* and *The Apprenticeship of Duddy Kravitz*, have been adapted into motion pictures. The film version of *The Apprenticeship of Duddy Kravitz*, directed by Ted Kotcheff, received the Golden Bear Award at the Berlin Film Festival in 1974; in addition, Richler's screenplay for the film was nominated for an Academy Award, and it won a Screenwriters Guild of America Award. The motion-picture adaptation of *Joshua Then and Now*, also directed by Kotcheff from a screenplay by Richler, was released in 1985.

ACHIEVEMENTS

Forsaking Canada for the more exciting atmosphere of Paris, Mordecai Richler struggled with his work and lived in poor circumstances, publishing very few stories. Here, however, he met some significant figures of the new literary set who reacted favorably to his work; among them were Allen Ginsberg, Herbert Gold, and Terry Southern. After returning to Canada for a short while, Richler finished his first novel, *The Acrobats*. As is often the case with Canadian writers, Richler preferred to publish outside his own country, where he felt more appreciated. His first effort was accepted by André Deutsch in London.

In later years, with his reputation secure, he decided to publish with the Canadian publishing house McClelland & Stewart.

In order to make a living exclusively as a writer, Richler left Canada again. Still using his Canadian experience as the substance of his work, Richler was very productive in England, publishing stories and novels that met with much acclaim. Even his film scripts for *No Love for Johnnie* (1961), *Young and Willing* (1964), and *Life at the Top* (1965), which Richler considered inferior work for an often superficial medium, were positively reviewed. Richler twice won Canada's foremost literary prize, the Governor-General's Award, for *Cocksure* and *St. Urbain's Horseman.* Although he achieved a certain notoriety for his searing portraits of Canadian life, he finally gained acceptance as one of Canada's most distinguished novelists. In 2001, not long before his death, he was made a Companion of the Order of Canada.

BIOGRAPHY

Mordecai Richler was born in Montreal, Canada, in 1931, in the heart of the Jewish ghetto. His father was a junk dealer and his mother was a housewife (in later years, she wrote a book about her life). Her father was a rabbi whose influence ensured an Orthodox household. By turning away from Orthodoxy at a young age, however, Richler ran into trouble at home, which perhaps accounts for some of his perceptive but acerbic reflections on family life. Further compounding his problems as a youth, his parents divorced when he was thirteen years old. As a response to the breakdown at home, Richler joined a Zionist labor group called Habonim and dreamed of settling in Palestine. Only later did he go to Israel as a journalist.

In his adolescent years, Richler attended Baron Byng High School, a predominantly Jewish school even though it was part of the Protestant school system. In his stories and novels it is transformed into Fletcher's Field High School and peopled with characters known to Richler in his youth. After high school, Richler attended Sir George Williams University in Montreal (now Concordia University) because his high school grades were not good enough to gain him admittance to McGill University. Although he later returned to Sir George as writer-in-residence, the academic life did not appeal to him. He once remarked that "academe, like girls, whiskey, and literature, promised better than it paid." Rejecting a life of scholarship, Richler decided on the uncertain life of a freelance writer in Europe, where he could develop his own style and not merely put a stamp of approval on someone else's. After living in Paris for two years, where he published his first story in a magazine called *Points* and got his first taste of expatriate life, Richler returned to Montreal. There he joined the Canadian Broadcasting Company for a short time, earning enough money to complete his first novel, *The Acrobats*. The novel aroused more attention in England than in Canada, which perhaps convinced him that the richer literary heritage there would fuel his talents. For the best part of twenty years, then, Richler lived in England, producing many novels, short stories, and film scripts.

Although Richler needed this geographical and cultural change to gain an ironic and critical distance in his work, he used his Canadian experience as the basis of his fiction; he once said that the first twenty years of a writer's life determine the character of his writing and inform his imaginative vision. Even after many years in England, Richler never felt sufficiently integrated into English society to capture the essence of that particular culture. Feeling himself an outsider in England and cut off from the social context of Canada, Richler returned in 1972 to settle with his wife and five children in Montreal. He died there in 2001.

ANALYSIS

In an article titled "Why I Write," Mordecai Richler repeats the honest answer given by George Orwell to the same question: sheer egotism, aesthetic enthusiasm, political purposes, and historical impulse. These reasons, modified by Richler's unique perception, are clues to the form and content of his work.

Richler's egotistical desire to be talked about was, no doubt, fulfilled, as he was the victim of attacks from both Jews and Protestants for what they considered to be unjust satiric portraits of their respective communities. He even said that to be a Jew and a Canadian is to emerge from the ghetto twice, as a sense of self-consciousness and envy pervades both societies. His satire, however, even when confined by the geography of Montreal, is more universal than some critics have assumed, and this element has enhanced his status as a significant writer. Although Richler never wanted to acquire the role of writer as personality (avoiding the talk-show circuit as much as possible and loathing being cast as the kind of figure Norman Mailer became), his fierce attacks on provincialism, pretension, community arrogance, envy, and class economic superiority marked him as a highly visible, eccentric, and often vicious outsider.

While there is a great deal of harshness in Richler's writing, it is not merely personal vindictiveness; rather, it is a narrative strategy of accurate observation informed by imagination. It is a grotesque comic style designed to emphasize the absurdity of the human condition and to mock those whose misdirected values merely cause suffering. In *The Acrobats*, Richler dissects a generation of hollow men who infest the corrupt world of Spain's festival time, in which a loss of belief is symbolized by *fallas*, empty wood and papier-mâché dolls. It is a nightmare world of confusion and fantasy that culminates in the death of antihero André Bennett. Without capturing the flavor and intensity of Ernest Hemingway's lost generation, Richler, in a limited way, sets the themes for his later novels by attacking all attitudes that he thinks are essentially destructive.

Richler admitted to a certain sense of guilt prompted by the discrepancy between his life at home facing a blank page and the memory of his father going to work in his junkyard in subzero weather. Perhaps this recognition of the severity of ordinary life gave him the focus of his work, the precisely observed but critically and ironically rendered life of the common man fighting circumstances greater than himself.

Richler's intelligence, however, did not allow him to glorify his protagonists uncritically. The tension between what is and what ought to be is always present in Richler's fiction; the result is a controlled realism balanced by a satiric distance that allows fantasy, nightmare, and a morally grounded sense of the ridiculous. As George Woodcock observed, Richler was influenced by the realism of André Malraux, Albert Camus, and Louis-Ferdinand Céline, but Richler himself praised Evelyn Waugh as the greatest novelist of his time, and there is in Richler's work much of the energy, sensibility, and bawdiness of American writers such as Philip Roth.

When Richler spoke of a political purpose, he followed Orwell's idea that a novelist should push the world in a certain direction, that in fact any serious novelist is therefore a moralist. Although many of his stories end tragically, there is still a sense that his characters exist not as victims of a cruel, impersonal fate but as victims of their own and others' actions. The choices they make are important ones and often lead to disaster when they are not based on a consistent moral viewpoint. Norman Price in *A Choice of Enemies* recognizes that choices are significant but no longer has the courage to make the difficult ones that confront his modern generation. He ends up complacently accepting values from his friends. In *The Apprenticeship of Duddy Kravitz*, Richler succeeds in making Duddy a partially sympathetic character, often a victim of powerful people even more ruthless than he is, but Duddy, blinded by ambition, is the indirect cause of his friend Virgil's paralysis from a motor accident. In his enthusiasm for the direct, specific attack, however, Richler takes a moral position that often seems diffuse or simply confusing. Two of his novels, *St. Urbain's Horseman* and *Joshua Then and Now*, manifest a more coherent intention that makes the satire even more meaningful.

Much of the force of Richler's work comes from his observation and memory of life in the Montreal ghetto of his youth. Even novels such as *Cocksure* and *The Acrobats* are distilled through the experience of the expatriate Canadian trying to make sense of a less provincial foreign world. Richler said that he felt rooted in Montreal's St. Urbain Street, and, because that was his time and place, he elected to get it right. To that end, Richler's fiction often concerns the same characters from Fletcher's Field High School as they experience life at different stages of intellectual and emotional growth. A peripheral character such as Jake Hersh, for example, in *The Apprenticeship of Duddy Kravitz* and *The Street*, becomes the focus of *St. Urbain's Horseman*.

THE APPRENTICESHIP OF DUDDY KRAVITZ

There is so much comic energy in *The Apprenticeship of Duddy Kravitz* that the reader can easily underestimate the social and moral implications of the work. Richler stated that to a certain extent the reader should sympathize with Duddy, who must rise above the poverty of the St. Urbain ghetto to challenge and defeat powerful manipulators such as Jerry Dingleman, the Boy Wonder. The ambiguity of Duddy's character creates a problem of moral focus, however, in that some of his victories are at the expense of truly kindhearted people, such as Virgil Roseboro and Yvette.

There are certainly many reasons for Duddy's aggressive, almost amoral behavior. His mother died when Duddy was very young, leaving him without the female stability he needed at the time. His father, Max the Hack, who drives a Montreal cab and pimps on the side, lets Duddy fend for himself, as most of his affection and attention goes to his elder son, Lenny. Duddy remembers that his father wrote many letters to Lenny when he worked at a resort, but Max refuses to write to Duddy. Max also encourages Lenny to go to medical school and is proud of his achievements; he makes it obvious that he expects little from Duddy and does not perceive the extent of Duddy's ambition or his loyalty to his family. Duddy is also often humiliated by the affluent university students with whom he works as a waiter at the Hotel Lac des Sables. Irwin Shubert, for instance, considers Duddy a social inferior and, using a rigged roulette wheel, cheats him out of three hundred dollars.

Although Richler elicits sympathy for Duddy by explaining his situation, he undercuts a completely sympathetic attitude toward Duddy by detailing the results of the character's actions. Duddy's exploitation of the other students of Fletcher's Field High School leads even his friend Jake Hersh to believe that Duddy makes everything dirty. Duddy's schemes to make money are clever enough; he works out a system to steal hockey sticks from the Montreal Canadiens, but he does not realize that the blame rests on the stick boy, who is trying to earn money through honest, hard work. More seriously, Duddy, through a cruel practical joke, is responsible for the death of Mrs. Macpherson, the wife of one of his teachers. Later, as he tries to make his dream of owning land come true, Duddy rejects his lover, Yvette, causes the paralysis of his friend Virgil, from whom he also steals money, and alienates his grandfather, Simcha, who cares for him more than anyone else.

Duddy's relationship with Simcha provides both the moral tone and the narrative drive of the novel. Simcha, a man trusted but not loved by the elders of the St. Urbain ghetto for his quiet, patient integrity, is loved by his favorite, Duddy. Like many others of his generation, Simcha feels the weight of the immigrant's fear of failure and instills in Duddy the idea that a man without land is a nobody. For Simcha, this cliché is a more complex concept associated with the traditional struggles of the Jews and presupposes a sense of responsibility. Duddy misinterprets the implications of his grandfather's advice and perceives it as a practical imperative. He determines to gain land at any cost, involving himself in many schemes—from importing illegal pinball machines to filming Bar Mitzvahs with a bizarre, alcoholic documentary director—in order to purchase land for commercial development.

For a short time, Duddy's plans misfire; he goes bankrupt and is unable to pay for the land he wants so badly. Upon hearing that the Boy Wonder, the ghetto "miracle" who has escaped his environment by drug peddling and other corrupt means, covets the same land, Duddy forges checks in Virgil's name to get enough money to make the purchase. In a closing scene, Duddy brings his family to see his property. By coincidence, the Boy Wonder arrives, and Duddy drives him away with verbal abuse. His father is more impressed with this act of defiance than with Duddy's achievement, and later, among his circle of friends, Max begins to create a legend about Duddy in much the same way he created the legend of the Boy Wonder. Although his victory has been effected through deceit and victimization, Duddy's behavior seems vindicated; he smiles in triumph, unaware that he continues only under the spell of a shared illusion. The reader is left elated to a certain extent at the defeat of the Boy Wonder, yet sobered by the figure of Simcha crying in the car after Yvette has informed him of Duddy's method of acquiring the land.

St. Urbain's Horseman

Unlike Duddy Kravitz, whose life is defined by the wealth he acquires, Jake Hersh of *St. Urbain's Horseman* is defined by the exploits of his cousin Joey, the "Horseman" of the title. In his quest for certainty and identity in a world of confusion and moral ambiguity, Jake chooses a dubious model of behavior that eventually becomes an obsession. Much of the comedy and much of the human drama in the book come from the discrepancy between Jake's illusions of the Horseman and the reality of his own life.

In this work Richler experiments with a cinematic style of flashbacks and flash-forwards, not only to create a sense of suspense but also to show the role memory plays in developing a character. It is obvious that Jake is involved in some sort of sex scandal that threatens his married and professional life. As the trial progresses, the narrative is punctuated by the events in Jake's life that have led him to this degradation. In his youth, he wanted to escape the St. Urbain ghetto and the provincial nature of Canada itself. Typically, however, he leaves Canada to escape boredom only to find it everywhere.

Although Jake's loving relationship with his wife offers the promise of real stability, Jake seems to believe that only his cousin Joey leads a meaningful life, fighting injustice wherever he can find it. Specifically, he thinks Joey is the lone avenger riding after Josef Mengele, the feared *Doktor* of the Nazi extermination camps. At first, Joey is simply the black sheep of the Hersh family, leaving home at a young age and returning periodically to disrupt the mundane lives of his relatives. Jake, who is eleven years younger than Joey, perceives him to be a hero and dismisses the accusations that he is just a criminal taking advantage of others for his own gain. Uncle Abe even tells Jake that the famed Horseman is more likely to blackmail Mengele than kill him.

By the time Jake reaches adulthood, his fantasies and nightmares about his cousin assume mythic proportions, and he incorporates this mythology into his daily concerns, measuring himself against the Horseman he has created. Jake's consequent search for Joey in Israel and Germany uncovers the grim reality of Joey's fraud, drug smuggling, and disastrous love affairs, but Jake only rationalizes his negative impression; he places the Horseman's quest for "justice" beyond the sphere of ordinary moral culpability or human responsibility.

Jake reasons that he is a product of his generation, conceived in the Great Depression. He and others like him lived through the Spanish Civil War, World War II, the Holocaust, the Israeli War of Independence, McCarthyism, the Korean War, and finally the Vietnam War. They were always the wrong age to be involved; they were merely observers, moral bystanders who could protest and give advice, but who were fundamentally impotent. Jake wants answers to his plight but feels even more alienated from the important issues of his time because he is a case history of the Jewish intellectual born into the Canadian working class. He finds his generation and its concerns trivial and peripheral, easily susceptible, in his thinking, to the guilt induced by the "injustice collectors"—the prison camp survivors and the starvelings of Africa.

These issues, these betrayals of age, are contrasted with the more personal betrayals of life: Jake's father rejects his marriage to a non-Jew; Luke Scott decides to choose a British director instead of Jake, his best friend, for his first major script; Jenny dismisses Jake as a lover because he is too young; and Harry Stein implicates Jake in the rape of a young woman. Jake is no more capable of understanding these events than he is capable of understanding historical events of more significant import.

After the trial, in which Jake is found guilty of indecent assault and fined, he receives word that the Horseman has been killed in a plane crash while smuggling cigarettes. He retreats to his attic and finds a gun hidden in the Horseman's saddle. It fires only blanks, its efficacy as illusory as the Horseman's exploits. Upon discovering this, Jake seems to return to reality, but later he dreams that he is the Horseman extracting gold fillings from Mengele's teeth with pliers. He wakes up and changes the Horseman's journal to read "presumed dead." The irony is that Jake will probably continue to search for certitude and will live a tolerable life based on illusion; he does not realize that the love of his wife is the stable point that will exist despite the illusion.

JOSHUA THEN AND NOW

There are many similarities between *St. Urbain's Horseman* and *Joshua Then and Now*: The time schemes of both works are not linear but rather shift backward and forward in a search for meaning that takes precedence over simple historical considerations; the characters are graduates of Fletcher's Field High School who gain obvious material success but are not immune to even the minor ravages of time; the major issues of the world are always present, but private and personal issues dominate; and Joshua Shapiro, like Jake Hersh, tries to make sense of his own life in terms of facing the past. The important difference between the two novels is that Richler's attitude toward life in *Joshua Then and Now* is much more humane, and love is seen as the moral imperative that makes all other attitudes seem trivial.

Joshua Then and Now begins close to the present with Joshua in a cottage retreat suffering from multiple fractures incurred in a car accident. Because of hints of a sex scandal, he is guarded from the press by his father, Reuben, and his father-in-law, Senator Stephen Hornby. Joshua reads many letters from his fans and colleagues who have scorned him for what they think is his atrocious behavior, but he is able to put this criticism into perspective. He believes this public display of disapproval is what he deserves for the roguish behavior of his youth. Reflecting on his life, he now is able to see clearly what was of real importance.

Joshua's background seems almost surreal; certainly it is more colorful than the lives of his friends in St. Urbain. Joshua's aspiration to be a sportswriter derived from his father, who was a Canadian boxing champion. After his retirement from the ring, Reuben became an enforcer for a gangster named Colucci. As a youngster, Joshua had to suffer both his father's long absences and the resentment of the neighborhood over Reuben's involvement with Colucci. Joshua's mother, Esther, is an eccentric who bewilders him even more than his father. At Joshua's Bar Mitzvah, Esther has too much to drink and decides to let the young boys see her perform as an exotic dancer. She shocks them with the explicitness of her movements and even lets them fondle her. Later in life, she gets involved in pornographic films and in running a massage parlor. It seems that Joshua's independent and sometimes improbable behavior is the logical result of his upbringing.

In trying to prolong his adolescence, Joshua becomes as ridiculous as his parents, and although his exploits seem harmless, they do have consequences; Joshua's fake letters about the novelist Iris Murdoch's homosexuality, written to make money at the expense of the University of Texas, end up being made public, to Joshua's disgrace. The pranks that he plays to gain revenge on his enemies—taking labels off Pinsky's valuable wine bottles, defacing Jonathan Coles's original painting, and planting illegal currency at Eli Seligson's house—conclude with Joshua's injuring himself in a high-speed car chase. For Joshua, at least, these episodes are a learning experience; they are stages on his way to maturity.

Joshua has many friends from his youth who still get together as the "Mackenzie King Memorial Society," the name being an ironic comment on a prime minister whom they consider a fraud. As successful as they are, however, in their middle age they are susceptible to lawsuits, tax-evasion inquiries, bypass operations, hair transplants, and cancer. The struggle for material wealth and its attainment now seem inadequate as values. More important is Joshua's involvement with the country-club circle. After marrying Pauline, Joshua is introduced to Jane and Jack Trimble and Pauline's brother Kevin. Joshua marries above his social class, but he takes a resentful and superior attitude to his wife's friends and relatives. He does as much as he can to sabotage a group that he believes has all the advantages. Through the years, however, he sees the disintegration of the Trimble marriage, the dashed hopes of the senator, and the death of Pauline's dependent brother, which precipitates her madness, and realizes that, even with their pretensions, they were only trying to survive.

The echoes of the past are most vividly sounded when Joshua returns to Ibiza, Spain, to confront Mueller, a German, who had disgraced him more than twenty-five years before. To gain revenge on Mueller, Joshua leaves his wife at a crucial time in her life, when she needs his comfort to fight off impending madness. In Spain, he notices remarkable changes: The friends he had are gone; many of his former haunts have been destroyed; the road to Almeria, the route of the retreating Republican army, is now dotted with hotels, condominiums, and commercial signs; and more significantly, Mueller is dead, a victim of cancer. To cleanse himself of the past, however, Joshua pays a price. His wife is institutionalized; then, after a prolonged stay at the hospital, she disappears. The novel ends with a loving reconciliation that suggests a change in Richler's perspective. Still on crutches as a result of his accident, Joshua recuperates at Hornby's cottage, accompanied by his children, the senator, and Reuben. In the final scene, Pauline returns, and Reuben sees Joshua in the vegetable garden without his cane, being supported by Pauline.

Solomon Gursky Was Here

Solomon Gursky Was Here is Richler's richest and most complex work, a 150-year chronicle of the ambitious and conniving Gursky family (loosely based on the real-life liquor kings of Montreal, the Bronfmans), weaving back and forth in time from the ill-fated Franklin Expedition in the Arctic to the political uncertainties of modern times. Beneath the surface of what is essentially a mystery story, a search for the elusive but seemingly ubiquitous Solomon Gursky, Richler examines the greed and corruption of society, the nature of the Jewish and Canadian peoples, mythological forces of the past, and the tenuous but compelling hold of love. Although uncompromising in his satiric portrait of the characters, Richter nevertheless alludes to the positive creative power of those who strive for understanding, however difficult the quest may be.

At the center of the novel stands writer Moses Berger, son of failed poet L. B. Berger, who has sold out to the Gurskys. Because of his father, Moses hears of Solomon Gursky at an early age and becomes obsessed with the almost mythical nature of this character. The alcoholic Moses, more a follower than the leader that his name suggests, investigates stories and documents and uncovers clues about why Solomon decided to resist the purely materialistic interests of his brothers Bernard, the ruthless businessman who has built his fortune by bootlegging, and Morrie, his unctuous partner. Moses discovers that Solomon's enigmatic grandfather, Ephraim, was a criminal once imprisoned on Botany Bay, by incredible ingenuity the only survivor of the Franklin Expedition, a shaman of Eskimos who taught them Yiddish, and an energetic profligate perplexing in his moral ambiguity. Ephraim is, however, both a comic manifestation and a serious vital force of Judaism, instilling imagination and realism in Solomon, his spiritual heir.

Moses' search for the "real" Solomon, then, is an attempt to reclaim his past as a Jew and participate in the redemptive value of this figure, who takes on the mythic qualities of the raven that insinuates itself into a diversity of situations to provoke the apathetic and the misguided. Although Moses cannot quite verify all the incarnations of the mysterious Solomon, he suspects that Solomon has influenced many of the nobler acts that occur: the attempt to take over Bernard's McTavish distillery, the creation of the Israeli Air Force, and the success of the raid on Entebbe. By trying to restore order in his own life, through research and the dogged pursuit of the truth concerning Solomon, Moses begins to understand that honest engagement, not exploitation of life, is a source of value and meaning. No one is spared in Richler's caustic view, but some can glimpse hope, however concealed it may be.

Barney's Version

In some respects, Moses' search for truth extends into *Barney's Version*, published almost a decade after *Solomon Gursky Was Here*. In this novel, however, Richler creates a character who risks becoming a parody not only of the author's earlier characters but also of the author himself. Barney Panofsky—"trash" television producer, lifelong Montrealer, and rabid hockey fan—is a man whose passions have often been too strong for his own good. Among other fiascoes, he drinks too much, smokes cigars obsessively, bungled three marriages, and potentially committed murder. His faults become an issue, however, only when he learns that Terry McIver, a friend from his youthful years in Paris, is about to publish an autobiography. Rightfully afraid of what Terry has to say about him, Barney immediately sets to penning his memoirs, his version of past events from which the novel's title is born.

The central action of *Barney's Version* is at turns poignant and hilarious. As expected, Barney recounts history much to his own benefit, including scorching depictions of his first two wives, a "martyred" feminist icon and a stereotypical Jewish princess. He rarely offers conscious insight into his own shortcomings and, in fact, often forgets or revises details of his life at its most crucial moments. Still, Barney manages to make his audience feel sympathy for him, especially in recalling his, Barney's "heart's desire," and his likely soul mate. What ultimately emerges from Barney's memoir is a credible protagonist—foul-mouthed, hedonistic, sometimes oblivious, infrequently accepting blame who manages to retain his desire for "true love" and for a creative outlet beyond the shallow commercialism of his television production company. As with Richler's other works, Barney becomes an enigmatic hero, tainted by his world experiences, yet still not devoid of hope.

Nevertheless, Barney's hope feels less substantial than the kind exhibited by characters in Richler's earlier fiction. One wonders if Barney truly longs for a better world, or simply for one in which people like Terry McIver do not threaten to reveal his secrets. This question is reinforced by the vitriol that Barney occasionally heaps on some of Richler's most familiar targets (feminists, Quebecer separatists, pretentious Jews, pseudointellectuals, vegetarians, antismoking zealots, and just about any other standard-bearer of political correctness). Despite the ongoing matter of whether Barney did or did not kill his former friend Boogie, the momentum of the novel sometimes lags, feeling less like a well-plotted story than like a meandering path between Barney's occasional rants. Though unequivocally humorous, such tirades sometimes feel more like a lecture from Barney (or perhaps straight from Richler himself) in which the protagonist's own foibles are tragically overlooked in his attempt to decimate his targets.

Whether he is a narrow-minded curmudgeon or a keen social satirist, Barney does extend Richler's quirky vision of the world with undeniable force. Perhaps it is a mistake to ask for moderation from a writer like Richler. His work has always been effective because of its raw power, its unsparing depiction of any character type that happened to drift beneath the author's lens. Richler was praised widely for the richness of his comic vision and for his keenly observed, unsentimental portrait of Montreal's inhabitants (Jew and non-Jew alike). Through an imaginative extension of this vision, Richler developed into a novelist of importance, with his message transcending the limited boundaries of St. Urbain Street to assume universal significance.

James C. MacDonald
Updated by J. David Stevens

Other major works

SHORT FICTION: *The Street: Stories*, 1969.

SCREENPLAYS: *No Love for Johnnie*, 1961 (with Nicholas Phipps); *Young and Willing*, 1964 (with Phipps); *Life at the Top*, 1965; *The Apprenticeship of Duddy Kravitz*, 1974 (adaptation of his novel); *Joshua Then and Now*, 1985 (adaptation of his novel).

NONFICTION: *Hunting Tigers Under Glass: Essays and Reports*, 1968; *Shovelling Trouble*, 1972; *Notes on an Endangered Species and Others*, 1974; *The Great Comic Book Heroes, and Other Essays*, 1978; *Home Sweet Home*, 1984; *Broadsides: Reviews and Opinions*, 1990; *Oh Canada! Oh Quebec! Requiem for a Divided Country*, 1992; *This Year in Jerusalem*, 1994; *Belling the Cat: Essays, Reports, and Opinions*, 1998; *Dispatches from the Sporting Life*, 2001; *On Snooker: The Game and the Characters Who Play It*, 2001.

CHILDREN'S LITERATURE: *Jacob Two-Two Meets the Hooded Fang*, 1975; *Jacob Two-Two and the Dinosaur*, 1987; *Jacob Two-Two's First Spy Case*, 1997.

EDITED TEXTS: *Canadian Writing Today*, 1970; *Writers on World War II: An Anthology*, 1991.

Bibliography

Benson, Eugene, and William Toye, eds. *The Oxford Companion to Canadian Literature*. Toronto, Ont.: Oxford University Press, 1998. Collection of essays is useful not only for general information on Richler but also for placing the author's work within context with a solid cross-index to related writers and literary movements in Canada.

Brenner, Rachel Feldhay. *Assimilation and Assertion: The Response to the Holocaust in Mordecai Richler's Writings*. New York: Peter Lang, 1989. Examines the portrayal of the Holocaust in Richler's fiction. Maintains that Richler's work reflects the powerlessness that Canadian Jews felt about the European tragedy, a feeling that was intensified by their experiences of anti-Semitism in the 1930's and 1940's.

Craniford, Ada. *Fiction and Fact in Mordecai Richler's Novels*. Lewiston, N.Y.: Edwin

Mellen Press, 1992. Devotes separate chapters to analyses of Richler's first nine novels, through *Solomon Gursky Was Here*. Also offers informative discussion of Richler's Jewishness and his identity as a Canadian. Includes bibliography and index.

Darling, Michael, ed. *Perspectives on Mordecai Richler.* Toronto, Ont.: ECW Press, 1986. Eight essays by different writers present analyses of Richler's craft and the moral vision expressed in his fiction. Some of the articles provide illuminating overviews of Richler's themes.

Kramer, Reinhold. *Mordecai Richler: Leáving St. Urbain.* Montreal: McGill-Queen's University Press, 2008. Demonstrates how Richler's life was the source of his fiction and argues that his Jewishness, "Canadianness," and secularism were central to both his life and his work. Includes notes, bibliography, and index.

McSweeney, Kerry. "Mordecai Richler." In *Canadian Writers and Their Works*, edited by Robert Lecker, Jack David, and Ellen Quigley. Vol. 6. Toronto, Ont.: ECW Press, 1985. Provides an orderly, lucid, and insightful analysis of Richler's fiction through *Joshua Then and Now.* Includes notes and select bibliography.

Posner, Michael. *The Last Honest Man: Mordecai Richler, an Oral Biography.* Toronto, Ont.: McClelland & Stewart, 2004. Recounts Richler's life through interviews with family members, friends, colleagues, editors, drinking and snooker companions, and others who discuss their experiences with and impressions of the author.

Ramraj, Victor J. *Mordecai Richler.* Boston: Twayne, 1983. Good introductory study of Richler's fiction (up to *Joshua Then and Now*) is enriched by an informative preface, a useful chronology of Richler's writing life, and a thorough select bibliography.

Woodcock, George. *Mordecai Richler.* Toronto, Ont.: McClelland & Stewart, 1970. Concise discussion of Richler's fiction presents analyses in a down-to-earth prose style accessible to student readers. Includes a bibliography.

HENRY ROTH

Born: Tysmenica, Galicia, Austro-Hungarian Empire (now in Ukraine); February 8, 1906

Died: Albuquerque, New Mexico; October 13, 1995

PRINCIPAL LONG FICTION

Call It Sleep, 1934

Mercy of a Rude Stream, 1994-1998 (includes *A Star Shines over Mt. Morris Park*, 1994; *A Diving Rock on the Hudson*, 1995; *From Bondage*, 1996; and *Requiem for Harlem*, 1998)

OTHER LITERARY FORMS

In addition to his novels, Henry Roth wrote a number of essays, short stories, and fragments that editor Mario Materassi collected and published in 1987 as *Shifting Landscape: A Composite, 1925-1987.*

ACHIEVEMENTS

With *Call It Sleep*, Henry Roth created a masterpiece of American Jewish fiction and a classic novel of immigration, one that brilliantly adapts the insights associated with Austrian psychoanalyst Sigmund Freud and the techniques associated with Irish writer James Joyce in order to recount the traumatic experiences of an impressionable young foreigner in New York City. However, it was not until thirty years after its publication that the book began to be widely read, studied, and admired. Discouraged by neglect of his first novel, Roth abandoned the literary life and did not return to writing novels until a prodigious burst of creativity in his final years yielded 3,200 manuscript pages of disturbing autobiographical fiction, the tetralogy titled *Mercy of a Rude Stream*, half of which appeared after the author's death at the age of eighty-nine. The sixty-year gap between publication of *Call It Sleep*, in 1934, and *A Star Shines over Mt. Morris Park*, the first volume of the tetralogy, in 1994, represents the most remarkable instance in American literary history of writer's block and late artistic renewal.

BIOGRAPHY

Like David Schearl, the young protagonist of *Call It Sleep*, Henry Roth was born in 1906 in the Galician region of the Austro-Hungarian Empire (now in Ukraine) but was brought to New York City when only two years old. Like many other working-class Jewish immigrants, the Roths settled on the lower East Side of Manhattan but later relocated to Harlem. Roth manifested talent with a story in the student magazine of New York's public City College. Eda Lou Walton, a professor at New York University who befriended Roth and encouraged him to write, became his mentor and lover. Eventually, Roth moved into her

Greenwich Village apartment, where he wrote *Call It Sleep*. Though Walton helped him find a publisher, the Depression year 1934 was not propitious for a literary debut, and, though the book received favorable reviews, its publisher was forced into bankruptcy.

Roth began a second novel but, convinced that it was unworthy of the Marxist ideals he then set for himself, he abandoned both it and the cosmopolitan ferment of New York. He married Muriel Parker, a composer he had met at the Yaddo artists' colony, and moved with her to rural Maine. Abandoning her own musical aspirations, Muriel supported him and their two sons by teaching school, while Roth helped by chopping wood, selling maple syrup, fighting forest fires, tutoring Latin and math, and serving as an attendant at a mental hospital. For most of a decade, he raised and slaughtered geese and ducks.

In 1964, *Call It Sleep* was rediscovered, and, at the age of fifty-eight, its obscure author suddenly found himself famous. Roth was plagued by persistent questions about his current projects. In 1968, after an abortive effort to write a novel set during the Spanish Inquisition, he and Muriel moved to Albuquerque, New Mexico. After Muriel's death in 1990, Roth attempted suicide but survived to complete his last great literary task at the age of eighty-nine. Despite agonizing rheumatoid arthritis, he managed to produce an enormous autobiographical fictional sequence, one that revisited its author's strained relationship with his abusive, embittered father and incestuous relationships with his sister and his cousin. Upon Roth's death in 1995, two of the four volumes of *Mercy of a Rude Stream* had been published, while the final two appeared posthumously, in 1996 and 1998, respectively. Enough material remained for two additional volumes, but Roth's publisher, St. Martin's Press, determined that they fell outside the *Mercy of a Rude Stream* cycle and remained uncertain about when or whether they would be published.

ANALYSIS

For much of the twentieth century, Henry Roth, the novelist who vanished for sixty years after a stunning debut, seemed a gloss on writer F. Scott Fitzgerald's quip that American lives lack second acts. Yet his long life offers enough acts to please the most garrulous of playwrights and challenge the most assiduous of biographers. He is at once salutatorian and valedictorian of twentieth century America, a contemporary of both William Faulkner and Don DeLillo. His pioneering use of stream of consciousness captured a newly urbanized, industrialized society undergoing massive transformation, but Roth survived into a very different era to write his own requiem.

In retrospect, *Call It Sleep* seems so unequivocally a major artistic achievement that it is difficult to understand why it was neglected for thirty years. However, in 1934, American culture lacked a category for American Jewish literature. By 1964, Roth fulfilled the need to anoint a worthy ancestor to Saul Bellow, Bernard Malamud, and Philip Roth, to legitimate a newly canonized tradition. It was only after ethnicity became a crucial issue in American society that Roth's novel could be appreciated for its pioneering embodiment of multiculturalism and multilingualism.

Mercy of a Rude Stream is of a different order of accomplishment than *Call It Sleep*. The fictional sequence that Roth created in his final years is of compelling interest to those fascinated by a tormented author's representation of his own compulsions and his desperate attempt to find closure. If Roth's virtuosic first novel appeared ahead of its time, his parting tetralogy was a throwback—a fictional sequence that not only is set in the 1920's but also employs the naturalistic style common to that era. From *Call It Sleep* to *Requiem for Harlem*, Roth's frustrated literary career is itself the most remarkable narrative he created.

CALL IT SLEEP

Call It Sleep begins in May, 1907, with the arrival by ship from Europe of two-year-old David Schearl and his mother, Genya. They are met at Ellis Island by David's father, Albert, a surly, abusive man who is embittered by disappointment. Albert is forever falling out with fellow workers and forced to seek new employment, as a printer and then as a milkman. The family moves from modest lodgings in Brooklyn's Brownsville neighborhood to a crowded tenement on the lower East Side of Manhattan. Roth's book focuses on young David's troubling experiences during the years 1911-1913, as a stranger in a strange land. *Call It Sleep* is a coming-of-age novel about a hypersensitive Jewish boy who is forced to cope alone with the mysteries of sex, religion, and love.

After a brief prologue recounting David's arrival in America, Roth organizes his story into four sections, each defined by a dominant image: "The Cellar," "The Picture," "The Coal," and "The Rail." What might otherwise seem casual details are magnified by refraction through the mind of an anxious child. Roth's use of stream of consciousness intensifies the sense of an unformed mind trying to assimilate the varied sensations that assault it. The family apartment is a haven for David, as long as his father, who even doubts his paternity of the boy, is not home and his doting mother can lavish her affections on him. When David ventures out into the clamorous streets, he encounters threats, from both rats and humans.

At the heder, the drab religious school where Jewish boys are given rote instruction in a Hebrew Bible they cannot understand, David is confused and inspired by Isaiah's account of the angel with a burning coal. Eavesdropping on a conversation between his mother and her sister, Bertha, he misconstrues an explanation for why Genya, disgraced after being jilted by a Gentile, married Albert. When Leo, an older Polish boy, persuades David to introduce him to his cousin, Esther, David is overwhelmed by incredulity and guilt over the sexual liberties that Leo takes. Fleeing his brutal father, David is shocked into unconsciouness after touching the live rail of a street car. Faced, like the reader, with sensory overload, David might as well call it sleep, embracing temporary oblivion as restoration after a long, disorienting day.

To explore the tensions among Albert, Genya, and David, a clanging family triangle rife with resentments and recriminations, Roth appropriates the theories of Freud, particularly in describing the powerful Oedipal bond between mother and son as well as the almost patricidal strife between Albert and David. The authority of Joyce asserts itself, not only in the fact that Roth's account of David Schearl, a surrogate for the author himself, is in effect another portrait of the artist as a young man but also in his lavish use of stream of consciousness and his meticulous deployment of recurrent imagery.

During the two decades surrounding the beginning of the twentieth century, massive, unprecedented migration from eastern and southern Europe was radically reshaping American society; more effectively than any other novel, *Call It Sleep* records the traumas experienced when the Old World met the New World. Many of Roth's immigrants are inspired by the American Dream of enlarged opportunity, while others are repulsed by an urban nightmare. Call *it*, too, sleep.

Though the Schearls are Polish Jews, the eclectic slum in which they live also serves as home to immigrants and natives from many other backgrounds. Not the least of Roth's accomplishments is his success at rendering the diversity of David's environs. Yiddish is the first language of the Schearls, but English, German, Hebrew, Italian, and Polish are also spoken, in varying registers, by characters in the story. In a novel designed for an Anglo reader, it would be misleading and demeaning to put fractured English into the mouths or minds of fluent Yiddish speakers when they are assumed to be using their native language. Instead, Roth fashions English prose supple enough to represent the varying speech and thoughts of those who speak and think in other tongues.

Call It Sleep is significant for reflecting a momentous phenomenon that transformed the United States but was ignored by many of Roth's literary contemporaries. In its vivid rendition of a child's-eye view, its dramatic exposure of family tensions, and its creation of a rich linguistic texture, Roth's first novel is an artistic triumph.

MERCY OF A RUDE STREAM

Though they were published separately and can be read independently and autonomously, the four novels that constitute *Mercy of a Rude Stream* are best understood together, as a single narrative sequence. The entire tetralogy follows the coming-of-age of Ira Stigman, a Jewish emigrant to New York, from 1914, when he is eight years old, until 1927, when he is twenty-one and a senior at City College. Despite the change in names and the addition of a younger sister, Minnie, Ira seems largely an extension of David Schearl from *Call It Sleep*. He is also a thinly disguised version of Roth himself. The autobiographical basis of the books is made even more apparent by interpolated sections in which an older Ira, an ailing octogenarian author living in Albuquerque, addresses his word processor, calling it Ecclesias. He comments on his own renewed, belated efforts at writing fiction. Ira as author poses the question that most readers will raise about Roth himself—Why, approaching death, does he struggle to record such lacerating memories?

In narrating his story, Ira forces himself to revisit an unhappy childhood and adolescence, in which he and his mother, Leah, are terrorized by his psychotic father, Chaim.

When the family moves from the lower East Side to a largely Irish neighborhood in East Harlem, Ira feels rudely wrenched out of an organic, nurturing Jewish community. He recalls the painful details of broken friendships and of his public disgrace when he was expelled from high school for stealing fountain pens. The most agonizing recollections—and the element that has drawn the most attention to Roth's final books—concern Ira's sexual transgressions. The second volume, *A Diving Rock on the Hudson*, offers the startling revelation that, beginning when he was sixteen years old and she was fourteen years old, Ira regularly, furtively committed incest with his sister, Minnie. He also maintained covert sexual relations with his younger cousin, Stella. Recollections of incest continue through volumes 3 and 4 and fuel the author's suicidal self-loathing. The older Ira longs to die but feels compelled to tell his story first, as though narration might bring purgation and even redemption.

Unlike the bravura *Call It Sleep*, much of *Mercy of a Rude Stream* is written in undistinguished prose that is at most serviceable in evoking working-class, urban life during and after World War I. Ira offers details of jobs he held, including stock boy in an upscale food store, soda peddler at Yankee Stadium and the Polo Grounds, and salesman in a candy shop. His sentimental education is very much connected to his intellectual one, and, though his grades are mediocre, Ira thrives in college. Publication of a short story in the student magazine awakens literary ambitions; his friendship with affluent Larry Gordon enlarges Ira's life beyond his own squalid situation. He begins to acquire social graces and to strike on ideas. Ira becomes inebriated with reading, particularly after Edith Welles, the professor who was Larry's lover, becomes Ira's mentor and lover. Edith, who is modeled on Roth's own Eda Lou Walton, introduces Ira to the most influential books and people of New York's bohemian culture.

In the final pages of the cycle's final book, *Requiem for Harlem*, Ira bids farewell to his dysfunctional, debilitating family and his loathsome sexual compulsions by moving down to Greenwich Village to live with Edith. The apprentice artist is finally ready to write a novel very much like *Call It Sleep*. Finally, after disburdening himself of excruciating secrets, the eighty-nine-year-old Roth finished writing and prepared at last to call it sleep.

Steven G. Kellman

OTHER MAJOR WORKS

SHORT FICTION: "Broker," 1938; "Somebody Always Grabs the Purple," 1940; "Petey and Yorsee and Mario," 1956; "At Times in Flight," 1959 (parable); "The Dun Dakotas," 1960 (parable).

MISCELLANEOUS: *Shifting Landscape: A Composite, 1925-1987*, 1987 (Mario Materassi, editor).

BIBLIOGRAPHY

Adams, Stephen J. "'The Noisiest Novel Ever Written': The Soundscape of Henry Roth's *Call It Sleep*." *Twentieth Century Literature* 35, no. 1 (Spring, 1989). Adams analyzes the power and integral role of sounds in Roth's novel *Call It Sleep*.

Buelens, Gert. "The Multi-Voiced Basis of Henry Roth's Literary Success in *Call It Sleep*." In *Cultural Difference and the Literary Text: Pluralism and the Limits of Authenticity in North American Literatures*, edited by Winfried Siemerling and Katrin Schwenk. Iowa City: University of Iowa Press, 1996. An examination of Roth's famous novel, focusing on the ways in which he represents different languages and voices.

Halkin, Hillel. "Henry Roth's Secret." *Commentary* 97, no. 5 (May, 1994). A study of Roth's novels and his homosexual experiences, in which Halkin compares the lives and works of Roth and British writer T. E. Lawrence.

Kellman, Steven G. *Redemption: The Life of Henry Roth*. New York: W. W. Norton, 2005. An engaging, readable account of the writer's life, particularly good in examining the long interim between Roth's novels. According to Kellman, Roth deliberately stopped writing because he did not want to confront his adolescent experiences with incest.

Lyons, Bonnie. *Henry Roth: The Man and His Work*. New York: Cooper Square, 1976. The first book-length study to address Roth's early work. Includes an interview with Roth, some biographical information, and a detailed reading of *Call It Sleep*.

Rosen, Jonathan. "Writer, Interrupted." *The New Yorker*, August 1, 2005. In his review of Kellman's biography (above), Rosen provides a detailed description of Roth's life, literary career, personality, and novels, and he recalls visiting Roth in Albuquerque in 1993.

Sokoloff, Naomi B. *Imagining the Child in Modern Jewish Fiction*. Baltimore: Johns Hopkins University Press, 1992. Roth's David Schearl is linked to representations of the child by other Jewish writers, including Sholom Aleichem, Hayim Nachman Bialik, Jerzy Kosinski, Aharon Appelfeld, David Grossman, A. B. Yehoshua, and Cynthia Ozick.

Walden, Daniel, ed. *Studies in American Jewish Literature* 5, no. 1 (Spring, 1979). A special issue of this journal devoted to essays on Roth. Includes a bibliography and an interview with the author.

Weber, Myles. *Consuming Silences: How We Read Authors Who Don't Publish*. Athens: University of Georgia Press, 2005. Roth figures prominently in Weber's discussion of four American authors who stopped writing for long periods of time. He argues that for some writers the decision to defer authorship can be an intelligent career move.

Wirth-Nesher, Hana, ed. *New Essays on "Call It Sleep."* New York: Cambridge University Press, 1996. A collection of some of the most engaging and useful analyses of Roth's first novel. Includes an essay by literary critic Leslie Fielder on the "many myths" of Roth and analysis of "language, nostalgic mournfulness, and urban immigrant family romance" in the novel.

PHILIP ROTH

Born: Newark, New Jersey; March 19, 1933
Also known as: Philip Milton Roth

PRINCIPAL LONG FICTION

Letting Go, 1962
When She Was Good, 1967
Portnoy's Complaint, 1969
Our Gang (Starring Tricky and His Friends), 1971
The Breast, 1972 (revised 1980)
The Great American Novel, 1973
My Life as a Man, 1974
The Professor of Desire, 1977
The Ghost Writer, 1979
Zuckerman Unbound, 1981
The Anatomy Lesson, 1983
Zuckerman Bound, 1985 (includes *The Ghost Writer*, *Zuckerman Unbound*, *The Anatomy Lesson*, and *The Prague Orgy*)
The Counterlife, 1986
Deception, 1990
Operation Shylock: A Confession, 1993
Sabbath's Theater, 1995
American Pastoral, 1997
I Married a Communist, 1998
The Human Stain, 2000
The Dying Animal, 2001
The Plot Against America, 2004
Everyman, 2006
Exit Ghost, 2007
Indignation, 2008

OTHER LITERARY FORMS

Five of Philip Roth's short stories are collected along with his novella *Goodbye, Columbus* in a volume bearing that title (1959). A number of his essays, interviews, and autobiographical pieces appear in *Reading Myself and Others* (1975). Roth's unproduced screenplay *The Great American Pastime* was anthologized in 1968, and several of his works, including *Goodbye, Columbus*, *Portnoy's Complaint*, and *The Human Stain*, have been adapted to film by others. In 1975, Roth began editing a series called Writers from the Other Europe for Penguin Books, to which he contributed several introductions. *The*

Facts: A Novelist's Autobiography appeared in 1988, and *Patrimony: A True Story*, a memoir of his father's life, was published in 1991. In 2001, Roth published *Shop Talk: A Writer and His Colleagues and Their Work*; seven of the ten chapters in this work are conversations that Roth had with other important authors, such as Primo Levi, Aharon Appelfeld, Milan Kundera, and Mary McCarthy.

ACHIEVEMENTS

Philip Roth emerged as a leading Jewish American writer when his first published book, *Goodbye, Columbus*, won the National Book Award in 1960. Many of his subsequent works have involved Jewish characters and specifically Jewish American dilemmas; novels such as *Portnoy's Complaint*, *The Counterlife*, and *Operation Shylock*, in particular, involve characters struggling to reconcile their desires to be fully American during the age of American triumphalism with their deeply ingrained sense of separateness. More than a touch of local color, Roth's depictions of Jewish communities form a base from which to spin—and unspin—national and personal narratives. Along with contemporary writers such as John Barth and Norman Rush, Roth has created some of American literature's most memorable and most self-conscious storytellers: the angst-ridden Alexander Portnoy, the irrepressible Nathan Zuckerman, and the outwardly controlled, inwardly crumbling Swede Levov.

Roth's special concern in his work is the relationship between writer and subject, which is often closely drawn from his own personal life. His fictional accounts of smothering Jewish mothers, harried Jewish fathers, and illicit love affairs involving Jews in his early work made him notorious among the conservative Jewish establishment during the 1970's. Subsequent depictions of family relationships bearing a close resemblance to his own drew fire from his ex-wife Claire Bloom, among others. In his later work, Roth has brilliantly presented the fascinating relationship between fiction and autobiography, using fictional surrogates, such as Nathan Zuckerman, to explore what he calls "counterlives," or the proliferation of possible lives one single person might have lived.

Throughout his fiction, Roth exhibits the abilities of a master comedian. His ear is arguably the best of any contemporary writer, capturing the spoken voice in a wide variety of accents, intonations, and cadences, but his facility with dialogue sometimes leads critics to miss the serious undercurrents of his work. Roth's fiction covers a variety of satiric modes, from the social (*Portnoy's Complaint*) to the political (*Our Gang*) to the literary and academic (*The Professor of Desire*). Whatever mode he adopts, he presents the objects of his satire or comedy in vivid and compelling fashion. Once referred to as preeminently a social realist (as in *Goodbye, Columbus*), he has transcended that mode successfully in such works as *The Counterlife* and *Deception*, which show him, as ever, both a consummate craftsman and a tireless experimenter with his medium.

Roth has won numerous prestigious awards for what constitutes one of the twentieth and twenty-first centuries' most impressive bodies of literary work in the English language. Among other honors, he received the National Book Critics Circle Award for *Patrimony*, the PEN/Faulkner Award for *Operation Shylock*, the National Book Award for *Sabbath's Theater*, the Pulitzer Prize for *American Pastoral*, and the Ambassador Book Award of the English-Speaking Union for *I Married a Communist*. He also received the Koret Jewish Book Award and awards from the *New York Times* and *Chicago Tribune*, the National Jewish Book Award, and the PEN/Faulkner Award for Fiction for *The Human Stain*. He won the Sidewise Award for Alternate History as well as awards from a number of periodicals for *The Plot Against America*, and he was honored with another PEN/Faulkner Award for *Everyman*. In 1998, he was presented the National Medal of Arts in a White House ceremony, and in 2002 he won the Gold Medal in Fiction from the American Academy of Arts and Letters, the highest award the academy gives. He received the United Kingdom's W. H. Smith Award, given for making a contribution of significance to literature, for *The Human Stain* and again for *The Plot Against America*; he was the first author ever to win that award twice. In 2005, he became the third living author to have his works published in a comprehensive edition by the Library of America.

BIOGRAPHY

Born in the Weequahic section of Newark, New Jersey, on March 19, 1933, Philip Roth learned very early what it was like to grow up Jewish in a lower-middle-class neighborhood of a large metropolitan area. His parents were Beth Finkel Roth and Herman Roth; his father was a salesman for the Metropolitan Life Insurance Company. After he graduated from Weequahic High School in 1950, Roth worked for a while at the Newark Public Library and attended Newark College of Rutgers University. A year later, he transferred to Bucknell University. Although the family could ill afford the expense of a private college, Herman Roth determined that if his son wanted to go there, he would go. At Bucknell, Roth began writing stories and edited the school's literary magazine. He also had his first love affairs, from which he drew incidents (fictionally transformed) for his subsequent novels. He received his B.A. in English, magna cum laude, in 1954, and he accepted a teaching fellowship at the University of Chicago for graduate work in English.

After receiving his M.A. in English from Chicago, Roth enlisted in the U.S. Army, but a back injury suffered during basic training resulted in an early discharge. He returned to Chicago to pursue doctoral studies in English and continued writing short stories; he had begun to get stories published as early as the fall of 1954 in small literary journals such as the *Chicago Review* and *Epoch*. Several of his stories were anthologized in Martha Foley's *The Best American Short Stories* and in *The O. Henry Prize Stories*. These honors, the success of his first published volume, *Goodbye, Columbus*, a Houghton Mifflin Literary Fellowship, and a Guggenheim Fellowship persuaded Roth to abandon graduate work in English for a career as a creative writer.

While a graduate student and instructor at the University of Chicago, Roth met and later married his first wife, Margaret Martinson Williams. The relationship was never a happy one, and after a few years they separated, Margaret steadfastly refusing to agree to a divorce. Meanwhile, they spent one year of their marriage (1960) at the Writers' Workshop at the University of Iowa, where Philip served on the faculty. After his first full-length novel, *Letting Go*, was published in 1962, he became writer-in-residence at Princeton University. He later taught English literature at the University of Pennsylvania. His experiences as an academic provided much material for his later novels, many of which have university settings or are otherwise peopled by academics.

The publication of *Portnoy's Complaint* in 1969, a year after his estranged wife was killed in an automobile accident, launched Roth's greatest notoriety, especially among the conservative Jewish community in the United States, and assured his fame as a novelist. He became an increasingly prolific writer, spending part of the year in his Connecticut home and part in London in an apartment near his writing studio. For years he shared his life with the British stage and screen actor Claire Bloom, whom he married in April, 1990. Their difficult relationship and 1995 divorce became a subject of Bloom's memoir, *Leaving a Doll's House* (1996) and received highly fictionalized treatment in Roth's 1998 novel *I Married a Communist*.

Around the end of the twentieth century, Roth began living alone in his house in the woods of northwest Connecticut. He continues to visit New York from time to time and has contact with other writers, including younger ones, but his main focus is on his writing.

ANALYSIS

While his early works clearly show the influence of his literary idols—Henry James, Leo Tolstoy, Gustave Flaubert, Thomas Wolfe, and Theodore Dreiser—Philip Roth came into his own as a novelist beginning with *Portnoy's Complaint*, which reveals a unique voice in American literature. His subsequent development parallels his growing interest in other Continental writers, such as Anton Chekhov, Franz Kafka, Fyodor Dostoevski, and particularly contemporary writers such as Milan Kundera, whom Roth assisted in getting his works published in the United States. Roth's first novels are set squarely in his native land: in Newark, where he was born and reared; in the great Midwest, where he went to graduate school; and in New York and Philadelphia, where he lived, wrote, and taught literature at several universities. The protagonists of his later fiction travel abroad to Western and Eastern Europe and as far as Hong Kong. Roth's development as a novelist is thus the development, in part, of a growing cosmopolitanism along with a deepening interest in basic human concerns and predicaments.

Chief among those predicaments is the endless struggle between the id and the superego, or, in less Freudian terms, between the drive for sensual gratification and the drive for moral uprightness. On one hand, pulling at his protagonists (most of whom are men) is the powerful desire for sexual conquest; on the other is the almost equally powerful desire to lead a morally self-fulfilling and decent life. These drives, conflicting at almost every turn, nearly tear his protagonists apart. Even when, as at the end of *The Professor of Desire*, a protagonist believes that he has at least achieved a reasonable equilibrium and found peace, a nagging unease enters the picture, upsetting his contentment and providing a presentiment of doom.

Indeed, Roth's heroes, if one can apply that term to such unlikely characters, all seem doomed in one way or another. Their pervasive sense of disaster, however, does not destroy Roth's comedy; it deepens it. A sense of the absurd, of the incongruities of human experience, also pervades Roth's novels and is the source of much rich humor. Moreover, his protagonists usually are fully self-aware; they understand their predicaments with uncommon self-perception, even if (more often than not) they are utterly baffled in trying to find a solution to or resolution of their dilemmas. Again, their awareness and frustration combine to make the reader laugh, though the reader must be careful not to let the laughter obscure or nullify the compassion that is also the character's due.

LETTING GO

Roth's first full-length novel, *Letting Go*, sets out all these themes and influences. The principal character, Gabe Wallach, is the educated, sophisticated young son of well-off middle-aged easterners. After a brief stint in the Army, Gabe pursues graduate studies in the Midwest. His mother has recently died, leaving her son with a heavy moral burden: not to interfere in the lives of others as she, regretfully, has done. It is a legacy Gabe finds almost impossible to live up to, until the very end, after he has nearly ruined the lives of several people close to him. Before that, he succeeds, however, in remaining aloof from his widower father, who is lonely and adrift and tries to persuade Gabe to return home. This is Gabe's only success, however, as eventually his father meets and marries a widow who helps him rediscover life's pleasures.

Meanwhile, Gabe has his affairs, none of which works out happily, and his friendships, especially with Paul and Libby Herz, whom he meets during graduate school in Iowa. Paul is a hardworking, highly principled young man who married Libby while they were still undergraduates at Cornell. Their mixed marriage—Paul is Jewish, Libby Catholic—is mainly the result of Paul's misguided sense of devotion and responsibility. Although the passion has long since gone out of their relationship, owing to Libby's poor health and neurotic disposition, Paul remains loyal. Together, they struggle with financial and other problems, including opposition from both sets of parents.

Gabe's life and the life of the Herzes intersect at various points, invariably with well-intentioned but almost disastrous consequences. At Iowa, Gabe tries to befriend the couple, offers various forms of assistance to them, and finds an unusual attractiveness in Libby, which culminates in little more than a kiss. Their affair, such as it is, focuses partly on Henry James's novel *The Portrait of a Lady* (1881), which Gabe lends to Paul; Libby reads the book and finds tucked into its pages the last letter Gabe's mother had written him when she lay dying. Both the novel and the letter help to form a bond between Gabe and

Libby that endures. Later, when Gabe is teaching at the University of Chicago, their relationship resumes when Gabe helps Paul get a job in his department.

Through Martha Reganhart, with whom Gabe has begun to live, Gabe finds someone who is willing to let her unborn baby be adopted by the Herzes. Paul and Libby have wanted a child and nearly had one, but poverty-stricken as they were, Paul persuaded Libby to have an abortion. The incidents surrounding that event are both comical and dreadful. Afterward, Libby's health never becomes robust enough for her to risk conceiving another child; hence, they hope to adopt one. The circumstances of trying to adopt a baby involve episodes best referred to as "deadly farce," including several in which Gabe intervenes on the couple's behalf. At the same time, Gabe's relationship with Martha, a divorcée with two young children, deepens and then falls apart, largely the result of his inability to make a full and lasting commitment.

Gabe and Paul thus represent contrasting studies in personality. At the end, Gabe finally learns to "let go," the lesson his mother tried to teach him from her deathbed, but letting go for him means abandoning lover, friends, family, and career to become a wanderer in Europe, whence he writes Libby a final letter. Forwarded many times, an invitation to her adopted daughter's first birthday party arrives with no other message in it. This Gabe takes as "an invitation to be forgiven" for his nearly catastrophic interference in their lives. Gabe, however, feels unable to accept forgiveness—not yet, anyway. He is not "off the hook," he says, and does not want to be let off it, not until he can make some sense of the "larger hook" he feels he is still on.

PORTNOY'S COMPLAINT

The larger hook on which Roth's later protagonists wriggle is precisely the dilemma between commitment and freedom that they all experience. Thus, Alexander Portnoy of *Portnoy's Complaint* finds himself torn between his desire to maintain his position as New York's assistant commissioner for human opportunity, a job of considerable responsibility as well as prestige, and his desire to enjoy the full sexual freedoms heralded by the 1960's. For a while he seems to manage both, until his affair with Mary Jane Reed develops into something else—Mary Jane's wish to get married. Her sexual adroitness—she is called "the Monkey"—has kept them together for more than a year, but this demand for full commitment proves too much for Alex, who abandons her in Athens during a trip to Europe in which they have experienced the ultimate of their sexual adventures. Alex flees to Israel, the land of his forefathers, only to find that when he tries to make love there he is impotent. The experience drives him to seek help from Dr. Otto Spielvogel, a New York psychiatrist.

The novel, in fact, is told as a series of confessions, or therapy sessions, and derives its title from the name Dr. Spielvogel gives to his patient's illness. "Portnoy's Complaint" is "a disorder in which strongly felt ethical and altruistic impulses are perpetually warring with extreme sexual longings, often of a perverse nature." The symptoms of the illness, Spielvogel believes, can be traced to the mother-child relationship, and indeed Portnoy's boyhood has been fraught with problems, often hilarious ones as he recounts them, occasioned by his stereotypical Jewish mother. Sophie Portnoy is a domineering, overprotective mother who frequently drives her young son to distraction as he tries in vain to understand her demands on him and her suffocating affection. Jack Portnoy, his father, long-suffering (mostly from constipation) and hardworking, seems unable to mitigate the family relationship, exacerbating Alex's quandary. No wonder he grows up as he does, afflicted with the dilemma, or the condition, that Dr. Spielvogel describes. By the end of the novel, after the long unfolding of his tales of woe, all Alex hears from his therapist is, "Now vee may perhaps to begin. Yes?"

My Life as a Man

In a sense, that *is* just the beginning. Roth tried hard to progress further in his next "family" novel, *My Life as a Man*, which took him years to write. Meanwhile, he wrote the pre-Watergate Nixon satire *Our Gang* and the satirical burlesque of American culture *The Great American Novel*, which takes the great American pastime, baseball, as its focus and its vehicle. Yet it was the fictionalized account of his marriage—or rather, the affair that turned into marriage through a masterful trick—that really preoccupied Roth in the years following *Portnoy's Complaint*. In *My Life as a Man*, Roth invents not one fictional surrogate but two: Peter Tarnopol, a writer, and Tarnopol's own fictional surrogate, Nathan Zuckerman. The two "useful fictions" that precede "My True Story," or the novel proper, are Roth's early experiments with "counterlives," which he developed at greater length and complexity in his later novel, *The Counterlife*. They provide alternative, "possible" accounts of Peter Tarnopol's early life—and, through Tarnopol's, Roth's.

Peter's problem is trying to discover how he ever got involved with Maureen, his wife of ten years, from whom he is finally separated but who refuses to grant him a divorce. Related to this problem is the current one he experiences with his beautiful and dutiful lover, Susan Seabury McCall, a young widow who provides Peter with apparently everything he wants; however, she is essentially too submissive, too dull. One part of Tarnopol misses the excitement—no, the frenzy—that Maureen brought into his life, while another part hates it. Though it does not follow a strict chronological sequence, the novel becomes an account of Peter's experience first with Maureen, then with Susan, whom he finally also leaves and determines to give up, despite her attempted suicide. Writing the novel in guarded solitude at an artist's colony called Quahsay, Tarnopol retrospectively tries to understand his plight.

The Breast

The Breast is another novel written during this period when Roth was trying to compose *My Life as a Man*. This book is the sequel to *The Professor of Desire*, written a few years later. Like Portnoy, Zuckerman, and Tarnopol, David Kepesh is a nice young Jewish man, brought up by caring parents in a sheltered Jewish environment, who early in life experiences the pleasures of emancipation and of the flesh, first as a Fulbright scholar living in London, then as a graduate student at Stanford University. Like Tarnopol, he becomes the victim of a femme fatale, a woman who, like Maureen, has "lived." Helen Baird is a striking beauty, but more than her beauty, her experience living abroad as the lover of a Hong Kong millionaire attracts Kepesh. They become lovers and later, disastrously, husband and wife. Gradually, Kepesh sinks into the condition of becoming Helen's servant, if not slave, until she flees once more to Hong Kong, hoping to reunite with her erstwhile lover. He will not have her, and David must rescue her, but in the process he becomes aware that their life together is over, and they get divorced.

David now moves back to New York, where he gets a job teaching comparative literature, meets Claire, a young schoolteacher, and falls in love with her. During this period he undergoes psychotherapy to "demythologize" his marriage to Helen; Dr. Klinger becomes Claire's advocate against David's brooding over Helen. During this period also, David's mother dies, and like Gabe Wallach in *Letting Go*, Kepesh has a widowed father on his hands. The elder Mr. Kepesh is by no means as demanding as Dr. Wallach, however; on the contrary, he is delighted with his son's liaison with Claire (as he was not with the marriage to Helen) and hopes that they will marry. The novel ends as the young couple, along with the elder Mr. Kepesh and a friend of his, a concentration camp survivor, spend a weekend in a bungalow in the Catskills, not far from where David grew up and where he now ponders his future. He seems to have everything he wants or needs, but somehow he feels dissatisfied, anxious, afraid that ennui will set in and destroy everything or that some other disaster will overtake him.

It does, but the disaster is hardly anything that David could anticipate. About a year later, as his lovemaking with Claire has almost ceased, he turns into a six-foot, 155-pound breast. In *The Breast*, Roth partly follows Franz Kafka's *Die Verwandlung* (1915; *The Metamorphosis*, 1936), an obvious, but not exact, source for this novella. Unlike Kafka, Roth tells the story from Kepesh's point of view, using the first-person narrator to convey something of the real anguish Kepesh feels and his amazement at his condition. If he was beset by a dilemma at the end of *The Professor of Desire*, his bafflement there is nothing to what he experiences now. Despite the aid and comfort that everyone—Claire, his father, Dr. Klinger—tries to give him, he remains at the end as bitterly confused and disturbed as ever, thoroughly unreconciled to his lot except as he vainly tries to persuade everyone that what has happened has not happened, that it is all a bad dream from which eventually he will awake, or that he has simply gone mad.

The Ghost Writer

Roth's next novels form a trilogy to which he has appended an epilogue, all under the title of *Zuckerman Bound*. Again, Roth borrows from autobiography to write his fiction, his own "counterlife." In *The Ghost Writer*, the first of the series that make up this portrait novel, Nathan Zuckerman is at the beginning of a promising career as a writer. He has published a few short stories and is now staying at an artist's colony (Quahsay again), trying to write more. Since he is not far from the home of E. I. Lonoff, a writer he much admires, he visits and is welcomed by the older writer and his wife. Zuckerman is surprised by them in many ways: first by Lonoff's austere life as a writer, spent endlessly turning his sentences around, and then by Hope Lonoff's conviction that her husband would be better off without her. By birth and upbringing far different from her husband—she is a New England Yankee as opposed to his immigrant origins—she is temperamentally unsuited to the kind of life they have led for many years. She is convinced, moreover, that Lonoff would be better off living with a younger woman, like Amy Bellette, a former student from the nearby women's college where Lonoff teaches, who obviously adores him. Lonoff refuses, however, to entertain any such thoughts of abandoning Hope or realizing his fantasy of living abroad in a villa in Italy with a younger woman.

Nathan is persuaded to stay the night, especially after he meets Amy Bellette, who is also staying there on a brief visit. Nathan has his own fantasy that evening, that Amy is really Anne Frank, author of the famous diary, who has miraculously survived the Nazi death camps. They fall in love, get married, and thus show his parents and other relatives that, despite what they may think from some of his stories, he is a good Jewish man, the worthy husband of the famous Jewish heroine. As a tribute to Roth's skill as a writer, the account of Amy's survival is quite credible; moreover, it shows Roth's understanding of compassion for the suffering in the death camps. At the same time, it supports Nathan Zuckerman's qualifications as a writer, justifying Lonoff's praise and encouragement of the young man.

ZUCKERMAN UNBOUND

Lonoff's belief in Nathan is borne out in *Zuckerman Unbound*, the second novel in the trilogy. By now Zuckerman is the author of several novels, including the notorious *Carnovsky*. This novel is to Zuckerman what *Portnoy's Complaint* is to Philip Roth, and *Zuckerman Unbound* recounts experiences similar to those Roth must have had, such as the notoriety that involved outsiders' mistaking his fictional characters for his real mother and father. Zuckerman is accosted in the streets, on the telephone, and apparently everywhere he goes by people who think they know him because they mistake his confessional novel for actual autobiography. Fiction and autobiography are at best distant relatives, however; for example, unlike Zuckerman's father, who is extremely upset by his son's novel and turns on him at his death, Roth's parents remained proud of their son's accomplishments and never took offense at what he wrote, notwithstanding the uproar in the Jewish community.

Zuckerman is beset by would-be hangers-on such as Alvin Pepler, the Jewish Marine, once a quiz-show winner but deprived of full fame by a scam reminiscent of the Charles Van Doren scandal. Zuckerman's brief affair (actually no more than a one-night stand) with the Irish actor Caesara O'Shea is a comic treatment of the adventures attributed to

Roth by columnists such as Leonard Lyons, who insisted he was romantically involved with Barbra Streisand, though actually Roth at that time had not so much as met her. Finally, Zuckerman's trip to Miami with his brother, Henry, which ends with their estrangement on the way home after their father dies of a stroke, is totally different from actual events in Roth's life. All these incidents are, after all, "counterlives," imaginative renderings of what might have or could have happened, not what did.

THE ANATOMY LESSON

Similarly, in *The Anatomy Lesson*, the third novel in the series, Roth borrows from incidents in his own life but fictionalizes them so that no one-to-one equivalence can be made. Now, some years later, Zuckerman is afflicted with a strange ailment that causes him intense pain, from which he gets temporary relief only from vodka or Percodan. He can no longer write, but four different women tend to his other needs, including his sexual ones. Among them are a young Finch College student who also works as his secretary, his financial adviser's wife, an artist in Vermont who occasionally descends from her mountaintop to visit, and a Polish émigré whom Zuckerman meets at a trichological clinic (in addition to everything else, Zuckerman is losing his hair).

In despair of his life and his calling, Zuckerman decides to give up writing and become a doctor. He flies to Chicago, where he hopes his old friend and classmate Bobby Freytag will help him get admitted to medical school. En route on the plane and later from the airport, Zuckerman impersonates Milton Appel, a literary critic modeled on Irving Howe, who early praised Roth's work and then turned against it. In this impersonation, however, Zuckerman pretends that Appel is a pornography king, editor and publisher of *Lickety Split*, and an impresario of houses of pleasure. The impersonation is triggered by Appel's appeal, delivered through an intermediary, to Zuckerman to write an op-ed article on behalf of Israel.

Zuckerman as the porn king Appel provides plenty of material for those who like to see Roth as antifeminist but who thereby miss the point of his fiction. It is a tour de force, a persona adopting a persona—miles away from the real Roth. At his office in the hospital, Bobby Freytag reminisces with Zuckerman for a bit and then tries to talk him out of his scheme. Only the next day, when, under the influence of too much Percodan and vodka, Zuckerman falls and fractures his jaw does the healing begin, in soul as well as body. Zuckerman learns what real pain and loss are as he walks the corridors of the hospital watched over by his friend, who also weans him from his drug addiction. At the end, Zuckerman is a chastened and more altruistic individual, though still deluded into thinking he could change into a radically different person.

THE PRAGUE ORGY

The epilogue, *The Prague Orgy*, shows Zuckerman not as a doctor but as a famous novelist undertaking an altruistic mission on behalf of an émigré Czech writer whose father had written some excellent, unpublished stories in Yiddish. Unfortunately, the Czech's estranged wife holds the stories but will not release them. Zuckerman manages to fetch them without having to sleep with her, despite her pleas, but the stories are immediately confiscated by the police, who then escort him out of the country (this is pre-1989 Czechoslovakia). Zuckerman thus learns to accept his limitations and to become reconciled to them. He accepts that he will not become "transformed into a cultural eminence elevated by the literary deeds he performs."

The Counterlife *and* Deception

In *The Counterlife*, Nathan Zuckerman and his brother are briefly reunited, mainly so that Roth can explore alternative versions of a fate that first befalls one and then the other. The plot thus doubles back on itself more than once and is too complex for summary treatment. Despite its complexity, the novel is not difficult to follow and is full of surprises that intellectually stimulate as they also amuse the reader. Particularly interesting are the episodes in Israel, where Henry has fled to start a new life, bringing Nathan after him to discover what is going on. Much is going on, including a considerable amount of discussion from characters on the left and right of the political spectrum, with Nathan clearly in the middle. The latter part of the novel finds Nathan in London, married to an English divorcée with a child and trying to come to grips with British anti-Semitism, including some in his wife's family. Throughout the novel, Roth implicitly and sometimes explicitly raises questions about the nature of fiction and the characters that inhabit it.

He does so, too, in *Deception*, though in that novel, written almost entirely in dialogue, the experiment takes on a different form. Here, Roth drops his surrogate, Nathan Zuckerman; his main character, present in all the dialogue, is called Philip, who also happens to be a novelist who has written about a character named Zuckerman. Thus Roth seems here to speak in his own voice, though of course he does not, quite: He merely makes the partition separating him from his characters that much thinner, almost to the point of transparency, as when he takes on the critics who claim that when he writes fiction, he does autobiography, and vice versa. The novel is filled with discussions between "Philip" and his lover, who proves to be the woman Nathan married in *The Counterlife*; thus, much of the talk is naturally about fiction.

Sabbath's Theater

Roth turned away briefly from his various author personas to write the wickedly funny *Sabbath's Theater*, a novel about an aging pornographic puppeteer obsessed with death and socially proscribed forms of sex. Mickey Sabbath's perverse confessions and the absurd situations Sabbath creates for himself may remind some of Roth's early novel *Portnoy's Complaint*, but whereas Alexander Portnoy was tortured by his conflicting desires to be a model American and to satisfy his sexual longings, there is no such conflict in Sabbath. He revels in his capacity to break bourgeois mores, becoming a cause célèbre for defenders of the First Amendment in the 1950's, when running his randy street theater resulted in his arrest.

Since that time, he has lived in a small New England town, teaching college drama, until he is forced to resign for sexually harassing female students. Now he is locked in an acrimonious marriage with his wife Roseanna, a recovering alcoholic, and mourning the death of his sexually adventurous mistress Drenka. If *Portnoy's Complaint* revolves around Portnoy's confessions, *Sabbath's Theater* revolves around Sabbath's unapologetic reveling in nastiness. Through Sabbath's repellent diatribes against the Japanese, women, and self-help groups, Roth draws a figure for whom readers will find little sympathy. Because Sabbath himself seems so thoroughly jaded, many critics have decried the novel's sentimental turn toward Sabbath's past, into the death of his much-admired brother in World War II and the resulting demise of his mother, to contextualize Sabbath's bitterness.

AMERICAN PASTORAL

Roth portrays another bitter and obsessed character in *American Pastoral*, but in this novel the stakes are higher and the perspective a degree removed. Merry Levov is the stuttering teenage daughter of a beauty queen and a successful assimilated American Jew. She grows up in a prosperous New Jersey suburb in a loving home, the center of her father Swede's ideal, his "American pastoral." Then life changes. Merry's protests against the Vietnam War turn into ever more violent, clichéd complaints against American imperialism, capitalism, bourgeois complacency, and, finally, her family's own success story. She bombs the town's post office, killing a well-loved doctor and challenging her father's understanding of his life and his country. The story is told through her father's tortured pursuit of both his daughter and the reasons for her rage.

Roth deftly weaves social criticism into this compelling story for an insightful depiction of an entire generation blindsided by the great upheavals of the 1960's. Zuckerman reappears to interpret Swede Levov's story as an epic clash between the American innocent pursuing upward mobility and the return of the repressed violence inherent in that American Dream. Merry Levov, Zuckerman says, "transports him out of the longed-for American pastoral and into everything that is its antithesis and its enemy, into the fury, the violence, and the desperation of the counterpastoral—into the indigenous American berserk."

I MARRIED A COMMUNIST

Just as ambitious as *American Pastoral*, Roth's next book, *I Married a Communist*, takes the 1950's as its historical backdrop. Nathan Zuckerman again acts partly as interpreter and partly as scribe, this time to his former high school teacher, Murray Ringold. Murray tells the story of his brother Ira, a radio actor who was blacklisted during the era of McCarthyism. Ira becomes a populist hero to many, including young Nathan, until his actor wife, exasperated by Ira's repeated betrayals with other women, exposes him by publishing a tell-all book, *I Married a Communist.* The book destroys not only Ira's heroic profile but also his career, for he becomes blacklisted.

The plot of this novel once again alludes to events in Roth's own life, particularly to his divorce from Claire Bloom. Like the character Eve Frame, Bloom had a talented teenage daughter from an earlier marriage who caused friction in the marriage. Also like Eve Frame, Bloom published a memoir in which she, like Roth in several of his novels, exposed intimate details of their personal life. Ira's unthinking acceptance of the Communist Party and his subsequent devolution into an angry, bitter cynic give this political novel a decidedly conservative overtone.

THE HUMAN STAIN

The Human Stain is the final work in the group of novels known as Roth's American trilogy, which includes *American Pastoral* and *I Married a Communist.* Coleman Silk, an African American who passes for white, loses his job as dean at Athena College when he asks the students in his class whether two students who do not attend his class are "spooks." The two students, who are African American, accuse Silk of having made a racist remark. Nathan Zuckerman, narrator of the tale, befriends Silk and guesses the secret of his true identity. Silk has a much younger mistress, Faunia Farley, whose husband kills both Faunia and Silk by forcing their car off an icy road. At Silk's funeral, faculty members who earlier distanced themselves from Silk finally speak in his defense. Zuckerman recognizes Silk's sister at the funeral and from her learns that many of his guesses about Silk's identity and about the irony of the accusations of racism are correct.

THE DYING ANIMAL

The narrator of *The Dying Animal* is David Kepesh, who also appears in *The Professor of Desire* and *The Breast.* Each year, David gets one student in the classes he teaches to become his mistress. Consuela Castillo is one of those mistresses. Years later, she returns to him and says that she faces a partial mastectomy. At the book's end, she calls him two weeks before she is scheduled for surgery and tells him the doctors have decided that they must remove the entire breast. She is alone and cannot eat. She needs David. At this point, the nameless person to whom David tells his tale advises David not to go. The reader does not know whether David goes. In this book, Roth challenges Kepesh's emphasis on the body alone while at the same time attacking what he considers to be American prudery.

THE PLOT AGAINST AMERICA

In *The Plot Against America*, Roth rewrites history, having Charles A. Lindbergh, the famous aviator and American hero, win the office of the U.S. presidency over Franklin D. Roosevelt in the election of 1940. The book focuses on seven-year-old Philip Roth and his family as they react to national events. An older Roth tells of the comfort he feels being an

American Jew in Newark, New Jersey, and of the way that feeling changes to discomfort and fear as Lindbergh campaigns and wins the presidency.

During the 1930's, the historical Lindbergh sympathized with the Nazis, finding their air force especially admirable. While in Germany, he dined with Hermann Göring, Adolf Hitler's air marshal, who bestowed on Lindbergh the Commander Cross of the Order of the German Eagle. In Roth's novel, the Lindbergh administration has close ties to Nazi Germany. Even though Lindbergh has as one of his advisers Philip's uncle by marriage, his mother's sister's husband, who is a rabbi and insists that Lindbergh means no harm to the Jews, Lindbergh institutes several anti-Semitic programs. One such program is intended to spread Jews throughout the country in order to dilute their voting power; another is to put Jewish children to work on farms, to make them more like other American children. Philip's brother Sandy goes to a farm and becomes a supporter of and spokesperson for the program. Philip's family comes further apart when his cousin Alvin, who lost a leg fighting for the Canadians against the Nazis, and Philip's father get into a fight because Alvin says he no longer has any concern for the Jews. Philip's parents are the real heroes of the novel. They protect and provide for their family, give love, and always try to do what they consider best and right in the face of tremendous chaos and evil.

Many critics have insisted that *The Plot Against America* is Roth's comment on the presidency of George W. Bush. Roth has denied this, but many critics have refused to accept what Roth says. It is fact that in 1940 groups of Americans tried to get Lindbergh to oppose Roosevelt for the presidency, and Lindbergh did more than just flirt with Nazism and anti-Semitism. For many readers, however, the most horrifying fact of the book is not its historical background but that the events are related by a young child who reacts with immaturity and often terror to what is going on around him.

EVERYMAN

The nameless narrator of *Everyman* tells of a nameless protagonist who faces the deterioration of his body. This novel is loosely based on a fifteenth century English morality play also called *Everyman*, in which Death unexpectedly comes to call on Everyman. All worldly things desert him; only Good Deeds will accompany him beyond the grave. Similarly, Roth's nameless protagonist, who is largely dedicated to serving carnal lust, dies when he least expects it, apparently taking nothing with him beyond the grave.

Over the course of the novel, the protagonist inherits a store that he names Everyman's Jewelry Store. He marries three times; each of the second two times he marries the woman with whom he has been having an affair while still married to the previous wife. After separating from his third wife, he moves to a retirement home on the New Jersey shore, where he is lonely; he is estranged from his children, except for his daughter who lives in New York. He dies of cardiac arrest during what was supposed to be a minor, safe operation—an operation about which he did not inform his daughter. The book ends without the promise of the possibility of immortality and salvation offered by the medieval play.

Exit Ghost

The title of *Exit Ghost* echoes stage directions in William Shakespeare's play *Hamlet, Prince of Denmark* (pr. c. 1600-1601). The words refer to the ghost of Hamlet's father, who was murdered by Hamlet's uncle. The ghost demands that Hamlet avenge the murder. Similarly, in Roth's book, ghosts from Nathan Zuckerman's past demand that he avenge the attempt of Richard Kliman to write a biography of one of Zuckerman's favorite authors, E. I. Lonoff, in which Kliman will expose to the world Lonoff's supposed incest with his half sister. The title also refers to Zuckerman himself, who is a kind of ghost. Having separated himself from the rest of the world by living in isolation in the Berkshires in Massachusetts and having hardly any relationship with the rest of humankind, he returns to New York for a procedure designed to end his incontinence from a prostate operation that has also rendered him impotent. At the book's end, he exits Manhattan to return to his rural retreat. The title also refers to Roth's earlier book *The Ghost Writer*, in which Zuckerman tells about a visit to Lonoff's house and his fantasy that Amy Bellette is really Anne Frank, the author of the famous diary.

Zuckerman, now a famous writer, meets a much older Amy Bellette, who is dying from a brain tumor. Zuckerman decides to protect her and the now-deceased Lonoff from Kliman but appears unable to succeed. He also meets Jamie Logon and Billy Davidoff, a married couple who know Kliman. In college, Jamie was Kliman's mistress, and Zuckerman fantasizes that she still is. Zuckerman finds her attractive but knows he is physically unable to do anything about it. Finally, he invites Jamie to come to his hotel room, but she refuses. He then flees from New York—the final exit of a ghost from the novel.

Surveying the corpus of Roth's long fiction, one may conclude that he is a novelist who rarely repeats himself, even as he reworks ideas, issues, and dilemmas and reintroduces characters and locales. This is the essence of the "counterlife" motif that has been present in Roth's work from the start but became explicit only later on.

Jay L. Halio; Julie Husband
Updated by Richard Tuerk

Other major works

SHORT FICTION: *Goodbye, Columbus, and Five Short Stories*, 1959; "Novotny's Pain," 1962 (revised 1980); "The Psychoanalytic Special," 1963; "On the Air," 1970; "'I Always Wanted You to Admire My Fasting': Or, Looking at Kafka," 1973.

NONFICTION: *Reading Myself and Others*, 1975 (expanded 1985); *The Facts: A Novelist's Autobiography*, 1988; *Patrimony: A True Story*, 1991; *Shop Talk: A Writer and His Colleagues and Their Work*, 2001.

Bibliography

Brauer, David. *Philip Roth*. Manchester, England: Manchester University Press, 2007. Study of some of Roth's later novels presents discussion of the paradoxes and other difficulties the works present as a way of illustrating how rewarding it is to read the works.

Cooper, Alan. *Philip Roth and the Jews.* Albany: State University of New York Press, 1996. Carefully researched volume examines Roth's life and work, with particular focus on the author's political views, which are evident in his writing.

Halio, Jay L. *Philip Roth Revisited.* New York: Twayne, 1992. Provides some biographical information as well as a solid overview of the critical response to Roth's fiction up to the early 1990's.

Halio, Jay L., and Ben Siegel, eds. *Turning up the Flame: Philip Roth's Later Novels.* Newark: University of Delaware Press, 2005. Collection of essays provides a wide range of critical discussion of Roth's novels since the mid-1980's.

Milowitz, Steven. *Philip Roth Considered: The Concentrationary Universe of the American Writer.* New York: Taylor & Francis, 2000. Explores Roth's writings on the "concentrationary" world of the "camps" of the Holocaust, how this world keeps revealing itself through memories and other reminders, and how the "shadowy presence" of the Holocaust refuses forgetting.

Omer-Sherman, Ranen. *Diaspora and Zionism in Jewish American Literature: Lazarus, Syrkin, Reznikoff, and Roth.* Hanover, N.H.: University Press of New England, 2002. Discusses in depth how Emma Lazarus, Marie Syrkin, Charles Reznikoff, and Roth have addressed the issue of Jewish nationalism and the fate of the Jewish Diaspora.

Parrish, Timothy, ed. *The Cambridge Companion to Philip Roth.* New York: Cambridge University Press, 2007. Collection of eleven original scholarly essays critiques all of Roth's fiction, examining the themes of sexuality, cultural identity, and the Holocaust in the works. Serves as an excellent introduction to Roth's works. Includes a chronology.

Posnock, Ross. *Philip Roth's Rude Truth: The Art of Immaturity.* Princeton, N.J.: Princeton University Press, 2006. Shows how Roth uses immaturity and the loss of propriety as central ideas and forces in his works.

Royal, Derek Parker, ed. *Philip Roth: New Perspectives on an American Author.* Westport, Conn.: Praeger, 2005. Collection of astute essays discusses his work through *The Plot Against America*. Includes an extensive bibliography.

Safer, Elaine B. *Mocking the Age: The Later Novels of Philip Roth.* Albany: State University of New York Press, 2006. Treats Roth in some of his later works as a creator of humor and comedy with tears just beneath the surface. Focuses on the novels from *The Ghost Writer* to *The Plot Against America*.

ISAAC BASHEVIS SINGER

Born: Leoncin, Poland; July 14 or November 21, 1904
Died: Surfside, Florida; July 24, 1991
Also known as: Isaac Bashevis; Isaac Warshawsky; Tse

Principal long fiction

Der Sotn in Gorey, 1935 (*Satan in Goray*, 1955)
Di Familye Mushkat, 1950 (*The Family Moskat*, 1950)
Der Hoyf, 1953-1955 (*The Manor*, 1967, and *The Estate*, 1969)
Shotns baym Hodson, 1957-1958 (*Shadows on the Hudson*, 1998)
Der Kuntsnmakher fun Lublin, 1959 (*The Magician of Lublin*, 1960)
Der Knekht, 1961 (*The Slave*, 1962)
Sonim, de Geshichte fun a Liebe, 1966 (*Enemies: A Love Story*, 1972)
Der Bal-Tshuve, 1974 (*The Penitent*, 1983)
Neshome Ekspeditsyes, 1974 (*Shosha*, 1978)
Reaches of Heaven: A Story of the Baal Shem Tov, 1980
Der Kenig vun di Felder, 1988 (*The King of the Fields*, 1988)
Scum, 1991
The Certificate, 1992
Meshugah, 1994

Other literary forms

The first work that Isaac Bashevis Singer published when he moved to the United States was the novel known as "Messiah the Sinner," which was serialized in 1936 but was never published as a book. It was serialized in three Yiddish daily papers: *Der Vorwärts* (the *Jewish Daily Forward*, in New York), the *Warshanahaint* (in Warsaw), and the *Pariser Haint* (in Paris). Singer himself considered this work a "complete failure" and never attempted to translate it. In addition to his novels, Singer wrote several memoirs: *Mayn Tatn's Bes-din Shtub* (1956; *In My Father's Court*, 1966), *A Little Boy in Search of God: Mysticism in a Personal Light* (1976), *A Young Man in Search of Love* (1978), and *Lost in America* (1980). He also wrote more than one hundred stories and numerous books for children. He wrote two works on Hasidism, one in collaboration with the artist Ira Moskowitz titled *The Hasidim* (1973). His Yiddish translations of works by such noted authors as Stefan Zweig, Knut Hamsun, Erich Maria Remarque, and Thomas Mann are well regarded, as are his many literary essays and reviews. Several of Singer's short stories have been adapted as plays; "Yentl der Yeshive Bocher" ("Yentl, the Yeshiva Boy"), which was written in Yiddish in the 1950's, became a Broadway play in 1975 and a film (*Yentl*) in 1983.

Isaac Bashevis Singer
(The Nobel Foundation)

ACHIEVEMENTS

Isaac Bashevis Singer has been acclaimed by some critics as a genius and referred to by others as one of the greatest writers of the modern world. In the aftermath of the Holocaust, which resulted in the obliteration of central and eastern European Jewry, the works of Isaac Bashevis Singer stand as monuments to a vibrant and vital world. Singer's writing does not idolize this community: He depicts it in its totality, in its full humanity. His people are saints and sinners, believers and heretics, fools and scholars, avaricious merchants and ineffectual rabbis, patient wives and termagants. His imaginative world includes demons, elves, dybbuks, and magicians, mystical figures from a lost folk culture. However, Singer's fiction does more than recall a world destroyed by the Holocaust. The power of his work, while remaining thoroughly Jewish, transcends the boundaries of cultural and religious ethnicity to raise questions about life that have been translatable across the changing contexts of twentieth century thought.

Singer's works are written in Yiddish, the language of the shtetl—the eastern European village or town. For Singer, Yiddish is more than the vernacular of the people of the central and eastern European Jewish community. It is, as he stated in his Nobel Prize lecture, "the wise and humble language of us all, the idiom of a frightened and hopeful humanity." His Yiddish reflects the influence of three languages, Yiddish, Hebrew, and Aramaic, and contains frequent allusions to rabbinic and talmudic lore. The richness of his prose and its texture, pace, and rhythm are not easy to capture in translation. Singer worked with his translators and participated in the editing. All of his major works first appeared in serial form in the *Forward* (originally a daily, the *Jewish Daily Forward*, then a weekly) prior to their translation and rendition into book form except for his first novel, *Satan in Goray*, which was serialized in the magazine *Globus* in Warsaw in 1934.

One of the outstanding characteristics of Singer's tales is his use of demoniac imagery. This motif does not represent a love of the bizarre, the occult, or the gothic, although Singer is interested in these aspects. His demons figuratively portray the evil side of human nature; moreover, Singer believed that supernatural powers—both good and evil—do exist, and he affirmed his ultimate faith in Providence.

Singer's vision is optimistic when it concerns cosmic matters but pessimistic in dealing with humanity. He differs from his Yiddish literary contemporaries or predecessors in that most have been secularists who relinquished the past in favor of the Enlightenment. Most Yiddish writers after the 1940's portrayed an idealized and sentimental view of the shtetl. Singer could not accept this tradition. He maintains that the greatest gift of God is freedom of choice. Where there is no evil, there is also no freedom. He is aware that good does not always triumph, so his Jews are not all good. His characters share the traits and illusions of all humankind.

Singer is a supreme storyteller. For him, the suspense, the adventure, the age-old pleasures of narrative are paramount. He leaves explanations and interpretations to his readers and critics. Singer achieved a popular success unusual for a writer of his distinction: His works have become best sellers and have been translated into fifty-eight languages. He won the National Book Award twice, three of his works were named Newbery Honor Books, and he was awarded the Nobel Prize in Literature in 1978. A number of his works have been dramatized and widely performed; some have also been made into motion pictures. He was an engaging and popular figure on the campuses of colleges and universities and a favorite of interviewers; he served as writer-in-residence at Oberlin College, at the University of California, and at Bard College. In 1989, the American Academy and Institute of Arts and Letters bestowed on Singer its highest award, its Gold Medal.

BIOGRAPHY

Isaac Bashevis Singer was born in Leoncin, Poland. There has long been some uncertainty as to the date of his birth; in *Isaac Bashevis Singer: The Magician of West Eighty-sixth Street* (1979), biographer Paul Kresh quotes Singer as stating that November 21 was, as far as he knew, "more or less" the actual date of his birth. For many years, however, he had celebrated July 14 because his parents had told him that was his birthday to cheer him up after they moved.

He was the third child in a family of four siblings, who included an older sister, Hinde Esther, an older brother, Israel Joshua, and a younger brother, Moishe. His parents were Pinchas Mendel Singer, a Hasidic rabbi from Tomoszov, and Bathsheba Zylberman, the daughter of the *Mitnagid*—the opposing sect—rabbi of Bilgoray. The couple seemed to be mismatched. Pinchas Mendel, a gentle, pious, spiritual man, was an ardent follower of Hasidism. Bathsheba, a learned, strong-minded woman, was a rationalist and a pragmatist. Israel Joshua, eleven years Singer's senior, inherited his mother's rationalism; Moishe, two years Singer's junior, inherited his father's piety. The confluence of parental legacies—the mysticism of Singer's father and the rationalism of his mother—was Singer's inheritance, reflected in the tensions of his fictive characters: conflicts between the heart and the head, the sacred and the profane, the spiritual and the secular.

Four years after Singer's birth, the family moved to Warsaw, to an apartment on Krochmalna Street. Rabbi Pinchas Mendel became the rabbi of Krochmalna Street, and the Singer home served as its *bet din*, or rabbinic court. Singer's memoirs *In My Father's Court* and *A Day of Pleasure: Stories of a Boy Growing Up in Warsaw* (1969) and the novels *Shosha* and "Yarme and Kayle" (serialized in the *Forward* in 1977 but never published in book form) re-create the intricate life that existed on this cobblestoned shtetl street, a "literary gold mine" to which Singer regularly returns.

In 1917, World War I forced Singer, his mother, and his younger brother to flee the city. They went to Bilgoray, where they stayed for four years. The visit was crucial in his development as a writer. The village of Bilgoray, far removed from the bustle of cosmopolitan Warsaw, appeared to be untouched by modernity. Young Singer witnessed Old World spirituality unblemished by the encroaching Enlightenment. This experience remained with him as an eternal reminder of his rootedness—indeed, humankind's rootedness—in the past, in history, in that which transcends human nature. Bilgoray plays an important role in many of his works; Singer once said that he could never have written *Satan in Goray* without having been there. In Bilgoray, he studied the Talmud and modern Hebrew, which in turn he taught in private homes. He also studied the Kabbalah, read the works of philosopher Baruch Spinoza, and studied German and Polish. He became immersed in the rural Hasidic folk culture that would permeate his work.

In 1921, Singer entered a rabbinical seminary in Warsaw. He remained for a year and then went back to Bilgoray and supported himself by teaching Hebrew. Shortly afterward, he joined his parents in Dzikow, a shtetl close to Bilgoray, where his father had accepted a position as a rabbi. He found this village stifling and depressing, and he was delighted when his older brother, who was coeditor of the *Literarische Bleter*, offered him a job as proofreader for the journal. In 1923, Singer moved back to Warsaw to take up this new position. His family was settled in Dzikow, and he never saw his mother or younger brother again.

Singer's brother Israel Joshua was also a writer and served as Singer's mentor. He was the person who exerted the greatest influence on the young Singer, encouraging him when he began to write and instructing him in the rules of good storytelling. Although Isaac was given to mysticism, Israel Joshua was a realist who became part of the Jewish Enlightenment, the *Haskalai*, which was overtaking the shtetl at the beginning of the twentieth century. This situation had caused friction in the Singer home, especially with their father, who was a traditionalist. Joshua—no one called him by his first name—moved out of the house, becoming an artist and then a writer. Singer often visited his brother and discovered, in his studio, a whole new world. He describes the experience of going from his father's house to his brother's studio in *In My Father's Court*, saying: "It is just one step from the study house to sexuality and back again. Both phases of human existence have continued to interest me." Through his brother, he was introduced to secular literature. Singer lived, for the most part, in his brother's literary shadow. He used pseudonyms for his early writings; some stories were signed "Isaac Bashevis" (a form of his mother's first name in Yiddish) to distinguish his works from those of Joshua, while some were signed "Isaac Warshawsky" ("man of Warsaw").

In 1925, Singer made his fiction debut in Yiddish with a short story, "Oyf der elter" (in old age), which won a prize in *Literarishe bleter*'s literary contest. It was published under the pseudonym "Tse." In 1935, it was reprinted in the *Jewish Daily Forward*. His second published story, "Nerot" (candles), appeared in 1925 in *Ha-yon*. In 1932, Singer edited, with Aaron Zeitlin, a magazine called *Globus*, which printed several of Singer's short stories and in 1933 serialized his first novel, *Satan in Goray*, which was published in book form by the Warsaw PEN Club in 1935. In these early years, Singer also began a series of translations into Yiddish, which by 1935 included Hamsun's *Pan* and *Victoria*, Remarque's *All Quiet on the Western Front*, and Mann's *The Magic Mountain*.

Singer fell in love with Runya, the mother of his only child, Israel, who was born in 1929, the year of Singer's father's death. Runya was an avid communist and wanted to live in Russia. She and Singer quarreled heatedly, frequently about political issues. Runya finally took their child and left for Russia in 1934. She was expelled shortly thereafter and went to join her mother in Palestine. Once settled there, she sent their son to Kibbutz Bet Alpha. He changed his name to Israel Zamir—the Hebrew equivalent of Singer. Singer did not see his son until 1955, when Zamir decided to visit his father; this episode is described in the short story "The Son" in the collection *A Friend of Kafka, and Other Stories* (1970).

Joshua Singer emigrated to the United States with his family in 1933 and found a job on the Yiddish daily, the *Jewish Daily Forward*. He urged his brother to do likewise. With the shadow of Adolf Hitler extending over most of Europe, Singer did not need much coaxing, and in 1935 he followed his brother. He never returned to Poland. Singer's acclimation to America was difficult. English was a strange language to him, and Yiddish, his mother tongue and his literary language, did not seem to have a future in America. *Lost in America* records this transitional period. He reviewed plays for the *Jewish Daily Forward* but could not resume his writing. At the urging of his Warsaw friend Aaron Zeitlin, he completed a novel, begun in Warsaw, known as "Messiah the Sinner." It was not a success.

In 1937, Singer met Alma Haimann Wasserman at a summer resort in the Catskill Mountains in New York State. She had emigrated from Germany the previous year. Theirs was an attraction with "telepathic qualities," Singer would reminisce in his later years. They married on February 14, 1940. For many years, Alma supported Singer's writing by working in sales positions in New York department stores. She tended to all their financial concerns and served as one of his translators.

The "greatest misfortune" of his life, according to Singer, was the death of his brother Joshua in 1944. In the dedication to the English version of *The Family Moskat*, he extols his brother as his "spiritual father and master." Singer's family sagas, *The Family Moskat*, *The Manor*, and *The Estate*, are efforts to emulate his brother's work; critics agree that they do not represent the best of Isaac Bashevis Singer and are not typical of his work. However, these novels do present a historical overview of Jewish life in Poland, beginning with the Polish uprising of 1863 in *The Manor* and culminating in the catastrophe of the Holocaust during World War II in *The Family Moskat*.

In 1943, *Satan in Goray, and Other Tales* was published in New York in Yiddish, and in the mid-1940's Singer's fiction began appearing regularly. In 1945, "Gimpel Tam" ("Gimpel the Fool"), perhaps Singer's most famous story, was published in *Yidisher kemfe*. In the 1950's a range of Singer's work—long and short novels, a novella, and a collection of short stories—was brought before an English-speaking public. The May, 1953, publication of "Gimpel the Fool," translated by Saul Bellow in the *Partisan Review*, was a crucial breakthrough for Singer. Thereafter, his work appeared widely in English in magazines such as the *Partisan Review*, *Commentary*, *The New Yorker*, *Harper's*, and *Esquire*. In 1960 Singer began his long affiliation with the publishing house of Farrar Straus Giroux. With the publication by *The New Yorker* of "The Slaughterer" in 1967, later collected in *The Séance, and Other Stories* (1968), Singer began his exclusive association with that magazine that lasted until his death.

At the suggestion of a friend, Elizabeth Shub, Singer started writing children's books; the first, *Zlateh the Goat, and Other Stories*, appeared in 1966. He published more than fifteen books for children. Singer's books for children are not written with the left hand; indeed, the format is particularly congenial to certain aspects of his genius. His children's books have been extremely popular and have won numerous prizes; they have been translated into a dozen languages in addition to the usual English, French, Spanish, Japanese, and Hebrew. Singer worked with a variety of translators, including his wife, Alma, and his nephew, Joseph.

ANALYSIS

An oft-quoted line from Isaac Bashevis Singer's story "Gimpel Tam" ("Gimpel the Fool") epitomizes the author's theory of fiction and his worldview: "No doubt the world is entirely an imaginary world, but it is only once removed from the real world." His approach to his material is both imaginative and historical. Sometimes these strains run concurrently; at other times, one is subdued by the other. Through his use of the supernatural, he imaginatively portrays the Jewish community from the seventeenth to the twentieth century.

Singer's concern is not only with Jewish destiny but also with the destiny of any individual. He believes that the soul is a battleground for good and evil impulses. His use of the fantastic suggests the tenuous line between reality and fiction; it also provides what Singer termed a "spiritual stenography" of human behavior. He suggests that the perversions in which humans engage are otherworldly, that people are not always in control of their actions. Although individuals have freedom of choice, this freedom may be illusory because the forces of evil, if allowed to prevail, can be stronger than the forces of good. Ultimately, however, a desire for good can triumph if people can exert all their efforts to that end. The struggle between good and evil, between the spiritual and sensual, supplies the tension in his works. Singer contends that humankind cannot be separated from its passions; they are one and the same. His early novels, especially *Satan in Goray* and *The Magician of Lublin*, illustrate the problem of passions ruling the individual. Singer's solution to human problems is a return to one's ancestral heritage.

SATAN IN GORAY

Singer's first novel, *Satan in Goray*, written while he was still in Poland, is a gothic tale, commingling the historical with the phantasmagoric, the mysticism of Hasidism with the influences of Fyodor Dostoevski and Edgar Allan Poe, the sacred with the profane. The work is historical, contemporary, and prophetic. Its vision is dark, its tone harsh, and it deals with eternal conflicts: between good and evil, between predestination and freedom of choice. Two historical events constitute the background of this novel: The first is the Cossack rebellion (1648-1649) led by Bogdan Chmielnicki against the Polish landowners, which resulted in the destruction of 100,000 Jews. This was a period of Jewish history remembered for its tremendous loss of life and for its acts of absolute barbarism, surpassed only by the Holocaust of World War II. The second is the messianic movement known as Shabbeteanism, after its originator Shabbetai Zvi (1626-1676). Historically, these movements converged when Shabbetai Zvi, in Smyrna, Turkey, proclaimed himself messiah in the year 1648, the time of the Chmielnicki massacres.

For Singer, however, historical events are important only in their effects upon individuals. His interest, at all times, lies with the passions that govern individuals and engage them in a continuous struggle. In this early work, Singer presents the shtetl of Goray in the aftermath of the Chmielnicki pogrom and indicates how the spiritual decline of the community is related to its physical destruction. The action of the novel takes place in the year 1666 as the survivors of the massacre move back to Goray and attempt to resume their lives. The village, however, cannot be resuscitated. Its people are maimed; its leaders are ineffectual; all are vulnerable. Singer focuses on what happens to people during a time of utmost vulnerability. He presents a good but misguided community, easily led astray by promises of redemption and the cessation of their earthly travails. The community has suffered much, and its prospects for the future are bleak. Its roads and its earth are drenched with the blood of recently murdered people. Life appears meaningless. The inhabitants move about sluggishly. It would seem that the guardian of Israel slumbers, while her adversaries are on the alert.

The work is divided into two parts. The first deals with the struggle between good and evil as represented by the opposing factions within the community. Rabbi Benish Ashkenazi, the spiritual leader of this enervated community, one of its last survivors to return, represents the forces of good within the shtetl. His is the voice of traditionalism. He was a strong leader before the events of 1648. He did not allow the study of the Kabbala, with its promise of messianic redemption and with the asceticism of its adherents. At present, he can resume certain rabbinic functions within the community, he can deal with legal matters, but he cannot handle the spiritual and social problems of the villagers. He cannot control the dissension within his family; likewise, he cannot control the growing dissension in Goray. In both situations, he retreats into his own chambers and ultimately is concerned only with his own salvation. Meanwhile, rumors of the new messiah have filtered into the secluded village, injecting into it a vitality heretofore absent, resurrecting the shtetl as only messianism can. It is, however, a destructive messianism, one that must be preceded by absolute evil, an abrogation of societal restraints, an immersion in sexual perversity and religious heresy. Part 1 ends with the rabbi's leaving town, after being wounded in a battle with Satan, because he does not want to be buried in Goray. He fears that the evil that has overtaken Goray will contaminate even the dead.

Part 2 concerns the spiritual decline of the community through lack of leadership and perversions of the Law in the name of Shabbeteanism. The battle has been lost. Once the rabbi leaves, total chaos ensues. Part 2 begins with Rechele's marriage to an impotent ascetic—who is also a believer in Shabbeteanism—and ends with her death, after the dybbuk (a form of satanic possession) in her body was exorcised. In the interim, the community gets a new leader, Reb Gedaliya, an emissary who proclaims the news of the crowning of the messiah. He is a ritual slaughterer by trade, a charlatan by profession. One of Singer's many perverted religious functionaries, his lust for blood is exceeded only by his lust for Rechele, who is the innocent victim of life's misfortunes. Gedaliya persuades the community that its redemption can take place only upon the abandonment of traditional Jewish life. Singer vividly portrays the manner in which the community loses sight of the relationship between traditional Judaism and redemption and the depths of moral turpitude into which it has plunged. Ultimately, evil—the dybbuk—is exorcised, together with the remaining Shabbeteans, and good returns to Goray. The novel ends in the spirit of a morality tale with these words: "Let none attempt to force the Lord. . . . The Messiah will come in God's own time."

Satan in Goray is a bleak tale in which the forces of good and evil fight for the human soul; humankind, maimed, vulnerable, and misguided, easily succumbs to the passions of lust and perversity. Critics have seen this work as adumbrating events that were soon to take place in Europe. The strength of this early novel lies in its use of demonology and the supernatural, which became a distinctive feature of Singer's fiction.

THE MAGICIAN OF LUBLIN

Written in 1958, serialized in 1959, and published in English in 1960, *The Magician of Lublin* also deals with human passions, but it is not overcast with the gloom of past events. It reflects an expansiveness often missing in Singer's works. Its focus is not on the Jewish community itself but on the individual in a timeless context. Singer's magician-protagonist is well cast. On a literal level, he is representative of the artist. On a symbolic level, every person may be seen as a magician, living life, like Yasha Mazur, the novel's protagonist, "as if walking the tightrope merely inches from disaster." The variegated personality of the hero, "religious and heretical, good and evil, false and sincere," and the lack of dates in the work lend themselves to a symbolic interpretation. Singer focuses on the single individual and the choices he or she makes. In *Satan in Goray*, historical events negate options. In *The Magician of Lublin*, Singer removes the encumbrances of history and allows his hero to make conscious decisions that determine the progress of his life.

Yasha Mazur is a complex person, vital, exuberant, intense—above all, a man with a personal destiny. Unlike Jacob, the protagonist of *The Slave*, for example, who is a good person, motivated to do right no matter what the circumstances are, Yasha has an intricate personality. It engages him constantly in a struggle of opposing forces. In *Satan in Goray*, the opposing forces are presented as two distinct elements within the community. The triumph of one necessitates the removal of the other. When evil was victorious, Rabbi Benish Ashkenazi had to leave Goray. In *The Magician of Lublin*, however, these forces exist within the individual, enduring aspects of human nature. Yasha Mazur's entire life is a battle. He can never conquer the evil drive. He can only negotiate with it, appease it, or in some other way deal with it, so that it remains dormant. He never knows, however, when it will awaken to begin another round.

Yasha Mazur was reared in a pious Jewish home, studied the Talmud until his father died—his mother died when he was seven—and then joined the circus. He maintains a home in Lublin with his wife, Esther, but roams the Polish countryside as a "circus performer and hypnotist." As an artist or magician, he moves in various worlds, assumes various guises or personalities, and has a different mistress in each world. He aspires to higher things: He is a successful artist and would like to perform in Warsaw, in the summer theater of the prestigious Saxony Gardens. He is barred from doing so because he is Jewish. The closest he comes to achieving this goal is at the apartment of the middle-class Gentile Emilia, located on a street opposite the Saxony Gardens. Yasha's relationship with Emilia focuses the tensions of the work. He thinks he is in love with her, but she refuses the role of mistress. She wants to be his wife. To marry her, Yasha would have to divorce Esther, convert to Christianity, and procure great wealth to maintain the facade he has established in his courting of Emilia. These are formidable decisions that will determine his future.

Singer establishes the dichotomy of predestination and free will early in the work in the contrasting attitudes toward life represented by Yasha and his wife. Esther is a religious woman, married twenty years to Yasha; they have no children. Her entire life consists of making a home for a husband who returns to it only on holidays. She loves him but regrets, at times, not having married someone more stable. The thought of changing her life, however, never crosses her mind. She is a strong believer in Providence and accepts her fate as a lonely woman.

Yasha, although he says that "everything is fate," realizes that he shapes his own destiny in all his choices. He is a magician who consorts with thieves, but he refuses to use his powers for evil purposes. He will not become a thief. When he finally attempts it, out of a desperate need to support Emilia, he fails and injures himself. The man who is so agile that he can walk a tightrope to the awe of his audience becomes a shlemiel and bungles a simple act of burglary. Although he is Jewish by birth, he is a nonbeliever—or says he is—by choice. He does not pray, because God does not answer the prayers of his supplicants: his "gifts" are "plagues, famines, poverty, and pogroms." Nevertheless, to become a Christian for Emilia is a difficult choice for him. He is a libertine, yet he considers the institution of marriage sacred and cannot easily make the decision to break up his home for his new infatuation. He is faced with the dilemma of choosing "between his religion and the cross, between Esther and Emilia, between honesty and crime." These choices will "seal his destiny." He finally chooses to remain with his own religion and decides also that traditionalism is more meaningful than assimilationism.

Yasha is aware that life is the most powerful seductress. He returns to his home and builds for himself a doorless brick prison, which frees him from temptation and allows him to meditate on his past actions, yet he discovers that as long as he is alive, he cannot shut out the world. As an artist or a magician, he went out into the world, succumbing to carnal pleasures, drinking, eating, loving unrestrainedly. Having come to the realization that "there must be discipline," he undergoes the transformation from sinner to saint. As an ascetic, in the confines of his self-imposed banishment, considered by all a "holy man," the world comes to him. Even his past love writes him a letter. Yasha's imprisonment has been only partially successful. He has turned his intense feelings in another direction, moving from the sensual to the spiritual. In this work, Singer suggests that people cannot escape their essence: They and their passions are one. *The Magician of Lublin* presents a positive outlook even though it concludes (as does Singer's novel *Shosha*) in a dark cell or room.

ENEMIES

Singer's novels *Enemies* and *Shosha* directly address the most tragic time of Jewish history, the Holocaust. *Enemies*, ironically subtitled *A Love Story*, is Singer's only novel set in the United States; it deals specifically with survivors of the Holocaust. In *Shosha*, Singer returns for another nostalgic look at the destroyed world in which he grew up and attempts to capture the spirit of his people as the perimeters of death close in on them.

Like *The Magician of Lublin*, *Enemies* is written on two levels. It fills a gap in Singer's canon. Until this work, Singer's literary aim was to re-create the destroyed world of eastern European Jewry, to present the pulsating life that existed specifically in his native Poland. *Enemies* acknowledges the destruction of his fictive world and deals with problems confronting those who survived. In a note that precedes the work, Singer asserts that although he has lived with survivors for years, this work is in no way typical of the Holocaust experience. The novel presents the "exceptional case," he says, unique to an individual who is a victim both of his own personality and of his persecutors. Certainly, this can be said of all victims, and the novel, despite his abjuration, is a moving depiction of the varied problems many survivors have encountered. Singer's note cautions the reader against a rigorous historical interpretation. The Holocaust serves as a framework within which Singer presents his perennial concern: humankind battling its adversaries in the dark of night, in the fashion of Jacob and the angel. In the biblical narrative, Jacob is not overcome; he walks away, at daybreak, limping but unvanquished. Singer's hero also walks away, but not as a victor.

Enemies bears a similarity to *Satan in Goray* both in its focus on an individual who lives a tormented life, burdened with the knowledge of the tragic destruction of all that is meaningful to him, and in its use of the supernatural. In this work, the spiritual powers that represent the forces of good and evil also reflect a movement away from traditionalism. In addition, they indicate the extent to which the characters, through their previous experiences, have lost touch with reality. *Enemies* also has affinities with *The Magician of Lublin*: The multiple personalities of the protagonist are reflected in his relationships with three strikingly different women.

Enemies is a ghostly story. Herman Broder, the protagonist, is defined through his actions in the Holocaust. He spent those years hiding in a hayloft and has acquired a negative identity in the Holocaust's aftermath. Now, as a survivor, he is psychologically warped and socially maimed. He lacks the courage to commit suicide, hides behind schizophrenia to "deaden" his consciousness, and assumes the guise of a demon. In New York, Broder becomes a ghostwriter for a rabbi. He shuns contact with others to preserve his anonymity and lives a life of haunting duplicity with his second wife and his mistress. The tensions in his spiritual juggling act are intensified by the appearance of his wife from the Old World—he had assumed her to be dead. Ultimately, he disappears, vanishing like a ghost.

The work is divided into three parts. Part 1 establishes the diverse personalities of Herman Broder, "a fraud, a transgressor—a hypocrite," as he sees himself, and the complications they create. Broder's current life in New York is eclipsed by the terrifying experiences of his past. He lives in Brooklyn with his second wife, Yadwiga, the Polish woman who worked for his family before the war and who hid him in a hayloft during the Nazi occupation. He married her in gratitude for saving his life, but his relationship with her is deceitful. She does not know about his professional life or about his mentally disturbed mistress, Masha, who shares with him her experience of the Holocaust. He spends as much time with Masha as he does with Yadwiga, always telling Yadwiga that, as a book salesman, he must go out of town to sell books.

The tangled web of Broder's relationships is further complicated when his first wife, Tamara, who has survived being shot twice—one bullet still lodged within her—comes to New York and seeks him out. Part 1 ends with an additional complication when Masha claims to be pregnant and Broder promises to marry her.

Part 2 attempts a resolution of the problems. Through Broder's conversations with Masha and Tamara, much of the Holocaust experience is re-created. Like Elie Wiesel and other writers of the Holocaust, Singer points out that the full enormity of the Holocaust can never be expressed, because words are inadequate to the task. That which is related, however, is extremely powerful. Singer deals with the theological, social, and philosophical problems, both individual and universal, that confront humankind in coming to terms with the Holocaust. While presenting the myriad issues with which survivors have been faced—equivocal attitudes toward faith, a missing spouse who turns up after the other has remarried, disorientation in a new environment, reestablishing an identity that was nonexistent for a time, relating to people as human beings within a society rather than as individuals competing for survival—Singer indicates that the individual is also his or her own victim, governed by passions he or she cannot or will not control. Broder would not have married Yadwiga if he had thought that Tamara were alive. Now, however, he wants to hold on to all three women. They satisfy different needs: Yadwiga cares for him and worships him with a childlike simplicity; Masha fulfills his sexual desires and fires his imagination with her nightlong storytelling; Tamara is his wife, to whom he feels committed.

When the intricacies of his life seem overwhelming, he resorts to traditionalism as a life-sustaining measure, yet he cannot maintain his resolve to be a good Jew. He is a weak person by nature, and the impact of the Holocaust has left him without a will, without the power to make meaningful choices and decisions. He is, as he tells Tamara, a "corpse." His only alternative is to vanish. Herman Broder joins Singer's other eternal wanderers, the most famous of whom is Gimpel the Fool. The epilogue, in an almost Darwinian statement, attests the insignificance of the individual in the larger scheme of things by confirming Herman Broder's disappearance and suggesting that life nevertheless continues for those who can battle their enemies successfully.

SHOSHA

Shosha is narrated in the first person, unusual in Singer's novels that have been translated into English. Originally appearing in the *Forward* under the title *Neshome Ekspeditsyes* (soul expeditions) in 1974, it is considered a fictionalized and expanded version of the memoir *A Young Man in Search of Love*, which appeared almost simultaneously in 1978. A beautifully wrought work, it is one of the most poignant of all of Singer's novels. Set in Poland in the 1930's, the novel portrays the plight of the Jewish community, overcast with the gloom of the Nazi invasion, yet it brims with the lives, loves, and hopes of its characters. It combines realism with humor and pathos. It is another nostalgic glance at a decimated world, but it is not a gloomy work. It is, as the Yiddish title indicates, the journey of the author's soul, in an affectionate tribute to the vitality of the shtetl, and stands in defiance of his statement at the end of the work: "Time is a book whose pages you can turn forward, not back." *Shosha* presents a marvelous picture of Warsaw before the war, focusing on its Yiddish cultural and intellectual life, its writers, artists, philosophers, actors, critics, and dilettantes, as well as its simple people. Within this historical framework, Singer presents his protagonist's life in Poland at the time of greatest stress, a time when Jewish life and culture were disintegrating.

In *Shosha*, the conflict between good and evil that animates all of Singer's works takes the form of the relationship between victim and persecutor. All of the characters are concerned with their immediate gratification. They arouse the reader's sympathy because they become victims of their own blindness and naïveté. In their determination to live normally, they love, argue, philosophize, celebrate holidays. They write plays about dybbuks and talk about dybbuks within themselves. They do not recognize the external evil, the phantom that surrounds them or pursues them.

The first part of the novel charts the circular movement of the protagonist as he attempts to reestablish a sense of belonging, transporting the reader to the halcyon days of the narrator's childhood and moving forward to the period preceding the destruction of the shtetl by Hitler. The ancestors of the protagonist, Aaron Greidinger, have lived in Poland for seven hundred years. Krochmalna Street, already familiar to Singer's public through his memoir *In My Father's Court*, is not only a place housing his father's judiciary but also the scene of the narrator's first love, for Shosha—his neighbor, his playmate, his first audience—who believes and trusts him implicitly and unconditionally.

The work delineates the maturation of the narrator, as the serenity of his youthful universe is quickly replaced by the turmoil of world events with their disquieting effect upon the Jews of Poland. The first twenty years of his life pass rapidly as he moves from Krochmalna Street and attempts to define himself as a writer. In Warsaw, the Writers' Club becomes the focal point for the intellectuals, much as the synagogue was the focal point of the traditional Jewish community. It is through the people whom he meets at the Writers' Club that Aaron Greidinger works out his role as writer and lover.

Greidinger's destiny and identity are intimately bound to his youth on Krochmalna Street, and after twenty years, he returns to the area and visits Shosha and her mother. He is amazed that Shosha has changed only slightly during the years: She and Greidinger are the same age, but she looks like a child. Greidinger falls in love with her immediately. He explains to Betty Slonim, the Yiddish actor from America for whom he is writing a play, that he sees himself in Shosha. Shosha represents the naïveté and gentleness of his childhood, a phase of his life that he wants to recapture and repossess. She is Krochmalna Street. She is the shtetl. She is the traditionalism that refuses to keep in step with modernity but is beautiful nevertheless. She also represents the sources of his creativity, the childlike wonder that Singer the writer still possesses in old age. Part 1 ends with Greidinger's movement back in time, his failure as a playwright, his proposal to Shosha, and his spending most of his time in the small apartment on Krochmalna Street as the political situation worsens for the Jews in Poland.

Part 2 develops the protagonist's affirmation of his unity with his people. It is Yom Kippur, a day of judgment and reckoning for all Jews. The war is getting closer, Poles are more outspoken in their anti-Semitism, and Greidinger spends the day with Shosha, fasting. He marries Shosha two months later during the festival of Hanukkah. By doing so, he forgoes the opportunity to leave Warsaw before the Germans enter. He will not forsake Shosha, knowing that she could not survive by herself during these times. His writing career has improved; he is writing novels that have been accepted by his publisher. Part 2 concludes with the war imminent but with everyone presenting reasons for not leaving Warsaw prior to the German invasion. The epilogue ties the loose ends together. It takes place thirteen years later, during Greidinger's trip to Israel, where he meets his Warsaw friend, Haiml. While seated in the dark, each tells the story of what happened to his family, his friends, and how he escaped. Shosha died, as expected, because in her fragility she could not keep ahead of the march of malevolence pursuing her and overtaking Europe.

THE KING OF THE FIELDS

Singer's last novel to be published before his death in 1991 was *The King of the Fields*, set in prehistoric Poland, a violent, animalistic place where tribes of cave-dwelling hunters struggle against Poles who cultivate the land. Singer seems to have dipped into a nightmare world so embedded in the past as to be unrelated to the present, yet the hellish qualities of this Stone Age Poland and the brutality of its inhabitants conjure up the Poland of the Holocaust—a wilderness of corruption, a wasteland for humanity.

SCUM

Scum, written in the late 1960's and published in English the year of Singer's death, recreates pre-Holocaust Warsaw at the beginning of the twentieth century. Max Barabander, a thief turned businessman, returns to Singer's famous Krochmalna Street after decades in Argentina. His son has died, and his grieving wife ignores him; he has become impotent. His journey backward to Krochmalna Street is his attempt to journey toward renewed health, or at least toward a new life.

Barabander becomes involved both with Shmuel Smetena, the central figure in Krochmalna Street mobster activities, and with a saintly rabbi whose daughter, Tsirele, he wants to marry. He poses as a grieving widower to win Tsirele while working with Shmuel

Smetena's mistress on a scheme to seduce unsuspecting young women and ship them off to an Argentinian brothel. The project has a restorative effect on Max's virility, but when the web of lies he must weave begins to unravel, he is exposed as bereft of moral character, one for whom life—his or another's—is devoid of meaning. His only dreams are of "shady deals." *Scum* is Singer's version of the underworld; the literal underworld of gangsters mirrors the underworld of demons and dybbuks that make no appearance in this novel. When human beings are such scum, there seems to be no need for the Evil One.

THE CERTIFICATE

The Certificate, serialized in the *Forward* in 1967, was published posthumously in 1992. Its protagonist, David Bendinger, an eighteen-year-old would-be writer, arrives in Warsaw in 1922 with an unfinished novel, an essay on Spinoza and the Kabbala, and a collection of prose poems. Like so many of Singer's males, David soon finds himself involved with three women: Sonya, his old girlfriend; Minna, a woman whom he agrees to marry in order to obtain immigration papers for Palestine; and Edusha, his Marxist landlady. Like the youthful Singer, whom he resembles, David turns every event, no matter how seemingly insignificant, into an occasion for philosophical musing. Unlike Max Barabander of *Scum*, David Bendinger dreams of more than shady deals, and he believes that those around him have worth. No matter how complicated his life becomes, he dreams of writing and he thinks of God.

MESHUGAH

Meshugah, which means crazy, was first called *Lost Souls*, a title that connects this novel with *Shosha*, which was first called *Neshome Ekspeditsyes* (soul expeditions). Serialized in the *Forward* in the early 1980's and appearing in English in 1994, the novel brings Aaron Greidinger, the protagonist of *Shosha*, into a post-Holocaust 1950's setting. This most Singer-like character is a Polish exile who serializes novels in Yiddish for the *Forward*. While Aaron has his series of women, his primary mate, Miriam Zalkind, who is writing her dissertation on his work, juggles her own set of men. All are "lost souls" harboring memories of the Holocaust, mourning loved ones, contemplating suicide. Aaron discovers that the real truth of human suffering defies the power of writing—the world is meshugah.

SHADOWS ON THE HUDSON

Shadows on the Hudson was originally serialized in Yiddish twice a week in the *Forward* between January, 1957, and January, 1958. Singer had long wanted this novel to be published in English, but the project was undertaken only years after his death. It is set in the 1940's in Manhattan, and the lives of its characters are, like those in *Meshugah*, overshadowed by the Holocaust. As bleak as *Scum* but without its sordid underworld, *Shadows on the Hudson* deals with characters who strive for some sense and meaning in a world that continuously trips them up. Hertz Dovid Grein rotates among wife, mistress, and lover, always yearning for the one who is not there. His lover, Anna, juggles him along with her first and second husbands. His mistress, Esther, marries another, divorces, flees with Grein, and, in turn, flees him.

In the second part of this three-part novel, these chaotic couplings seem to be headed for resolution in a return to the past and traditional values. Grein returns home to his wife and to orthodoxy, Anna returns to her first husband, Esther marries, and even Anna's long-widowed father marries and has a son. The hope that a retreat from the secular will result in a return to meaning is demolished in part 3, however, when the new couplings are undone and the newborn child is recognized as severely retarded. The shadows of the Holocaust stretch over the Hudson and into the future. What saves this novel, and much of Singer's fiction, from a darkness too intense to bear is his extraordinary ability to create comic situations from the bleakest of moments. Whether caricaturing secondary characters or rendering outlandish a protagonist's rationalization of his or her latest sexual exploit, Singer's comic touch lightens his vision. Except in a few novels such as *Scum* and *The King of the Fields*, there is a redemptive quality in the very need his characters display for meaning and for love.

Singer occupies a unique place in the literary world. His works transcend the barriers of age, education, and culture, and they appeal to all peoples. Singer was a chronicler, historian, spiritualist, and moralist, and his writings are informed by a deep compassion for men and women who are, after all, only human. Singer may admit to a pessimistic view of humankind, but it is a sympathetic rather than a cynical pessimism. Throughout the darkness of his presentation, there flickers a spark of faith in the basic goodness of humankind, the promise of a universal and eternal light.

L. H. Goldman
Updated by Grace Farrell

OTHER MAJOR WORKS

SHORT FICTION: *Gimpel the Fool, and Other Stories*, 1957; *The Spinoza of Market Street*, 1961; *Short Friday, and Other Stories*, 1964; *The Séance, and Other Stories*, 1968; *A Friend of Kafka, and Other Stories*, 1970; *A Crown of Feathers, and Other Stories*, 1973; *Passions, and Other Stories*, 1975; *Old Love*, 1979; *The Collected Stories of Isaac Bashevis Singer*, 1982; *The Image, and Other Stories*, 1985; *The Death of Methuselah, and Other Stories*, 1988.

PLAYS: *The Mirror*, pr. 1973; *Shlemiel the First*, pr. 1974; *Yentl, the Yeshiva Boy*, pr. 1974 (with Leah Napolin); *Teibele and Her Demon*, pr. 1978.

NONFICTION: *Mayn Tatn's Bes-din Shtub*, 1956 (*In My Father's Court*, 1966); *The Hasidim*, 1973 (with Ira Moskowitz); *A Little Boy in Search of God: Mysticism in a Personal Light*, 1976; *A Young Man in Search of Love*, 1978; *Isaac Bashevis Singer on Literature and Life*, 1979 (with Paul Rosenblatt and Gene Koppel); *Lost in America*, 1980; *Love and Exile*, 1984; *Conversations with Isaac Bashevis Singer*, 1985 (with Richard Burgin); *More Stories from My Father's Court*, 2000.

TRANSLATIONS: *Romain Rolland*, 1927 (of Stefan Zweig's biography); *Di Vogler*, 1928 (of Knut Hamsun's novel); *Victoria*, 1929 (of Hamsun's novel); *All Quiet on the Western Front*, 1930 (of Erich Maria Remarque's novel); *Pan*, 1931 (of Hamsun's novel); *The Way Back*, 1931 (of Remarque's novel); *The Magic Mountain*, 1932 (of Thomas Mann's novel); *From Moscow to Jerusalem*, 1938 (of Leon Glaser's memoir).

CHILDREN'S LITERATURE: *Zlateh the Goat, and Other Stories*, 1966; *The Fearsome Inn*, 1967; *Mazel and Shlimazel: Or, The Milk of a Lioness*, 1967; *When Shlemiel Went to Warsaw, and Other Stories*, 1968; *A Day of Pleasure: Stories of a Boy Growing Up in Warsaw*, 1969; *Elijah the Slave*, 1970; *Joseph and Koza: Or, The Sacrifice to the Vistula*, 1970; *Alone in the Wild Forest*, 1971; *The Topsy-Turvy Emperor of China*, 1971; *The Wicked City*, 1972; *The Fools of Chelm and Their History*, 1973; *Why Noah Chose the Dove*, 1974; *A Tale of Three Wishes*, 1975; *Naftali the Storyteller and His Horse, Sus, and Other Stories*, 1976; *The Power of Light: Eight Stories*, 1980; *The Golem*, 1982; *Stories for Children*, 1984.

BIBLIOGRAPHY

Allentuck, Marcia, ed. *The Achievement of Isaac Bashevis Singer*. Carbondale: Southern Illinois University Press, 1969. Collection of eleven essays addresses various aspects of Singer's work. Most of the essays focus on themes in individual novels, but the collection also includes pieces on Singer's memoirs and children's stories as well as examinations of "The Spinoza of Market Street" and "Gimpel the Fool."

Farrell, Grace, ed. *Critical Essays on Isaac Bashevis Singer*. New York: G. K. Hall, 1996. Collection of essays provides an extensive introduction to Singer's critical reception and the issues that have preoccupied him and his critics. Includes both contemporary reviews and essays on a wide range of topics, including Leslie Fiedler's "I. B. Singer: Or, The American-ness of the American Jewish Writer."

_______. *Isaac Bashevis Singer: Conversations*. Jackson: University Press of Mississippi, 1992. Collection of interviews with Singer enables readers to draw connections among the writer's philosophy of life, his perspective on literature, and his mode of living.

Hadda, Janet. *Isaac Bashevis Singer: A Life*. New York: Oxford University Press, 1997. Examines both the forces of family and the social environment that influenced Singer, uncovering the public persona to reveal a man who was more complex than many had previously understood.

Kresh, Paul. *Isaac Bashevis Singer: The Magician of West Eighty-sixth Street*. New York: Dial Press, 1979. Provides a lively account of Singer's first seventy-five years, incorporating refreshing quotes and anecdotes, creating a delightful sense of intimacy for the reader. Careful attention to facts clarifies the often ambiguous details of Singer's works in terms of creation, translation, publication, and reissue. Includes photographs, bibliography, and index.

Mulbauer, Asher Z. *Transcending Exile*. Miami: Florida International University Press, 1985. Presents a thoughtful contemplation of exile in the works of three writers: Joseph Conrad, Vladimir Nabokov, and Singer. The discussion of Singer focuses on three novels—*Shosha*, *The Slave*, and *Enemies*—and also is mindful of thematic parallels to Singer's short stories.

Noiville, Florence. *Isaac B. Singer: A Life*. Translated by Catherine Temerson. New York: Farrar, Straus and Giroux, 2006. For those unfamiliar with Singer, this concise, easy-to-read biography serves as an excellent introduction to the man and his works. Noiville gleans information from interviews with Singer's wife, son, friends, and colleagues as well as his memoir *In My Father's Court*. Focuses on Singer's life struggles, his relationships with others, and the adversity he had to overcome as a Jewish writer.

Qiao, Guo Qiang. *The Jewishness of Isaac Bashevis Singer*. New York: Peter Lang, 2003. Analyzes Singer's work and finds a unique place for the writer within American Jewish literature. Addresses Singer's depiction of past and present Jewish assimilation in both Poland and the United States, examines Singer's narrative strategies, and compares the Jewish identity and Jewish historical consciousness in works by Singer, Saul Bellow, Bernard Malamud, and Philip Roth.

Sinclair, Clive. *The Brothers Singer*. London: Allison & Busby, 1983. Presents a fascinating examination of Singer and his work in the context of one of the most important personal and literary relationships of the author's life. Effectively interweaves biography and literary analysis, conveying a deep understanding of the lives and works of Isaac and Joshua Singer.

Wolitz, Seth L., ed. *The Hidden Isaac Bashevis Singer*. Austin: University of Texas Press, 2001. Collection of essays covers such topics as Singer's use of Yiddish language and cultural experience, themes that persist throughout his writing, his interface with other times and cultures, his autobiographical work, and a translation of a previously unpublished "gangster" novel.

LEON URIS

Born: Baltimore, Maryland; August 3, 1924
Died: Shelter Island, New York; June 21, 2003
Also known as: Leon Marcus Uris

PRINCIPAL LONG FICTION

Battle Cry, 1953
The Angry Hills, 1955
Exodus, 1958
Mila 18, 1960
Armageddon, 1964
Topaz, 1967
QB VII, 1970
Trinity, 1976
The Haj, 1984
Mitla Pass, 1988
Redemption, 1995
A God in Ruins, 1999
O'Hara's Choice, 2003

OTHER LITERARY FORMS

Leon Uris (YEWR-ihs) is known primarily for his novels, but he wrote for films as well. He wrote the screenplay adaptation of his first novel, *Battle Cry*, in 1955, and he wrote the screenplay for the 1957 American Western classic *Gunfight at the OK Corral*. He also wrote the script for the short documentary film *Israel*, which was released in 1959.

ACHIEVEMENTS

Perhaps Leon Uris's greatest achievement was the novel for which he is most remembered, *Exodus*. Published in 1958, *Exodus* was an international sensation. It was translated into more than fifty languages, and millions of copies were sold. Hailed as Uris's best work, it was on the *New York Times* best-seller list for more than a year, staying at number one for five months. Inside the Soviet Union, where it was forbidden reading, smuggled copies of the 599-page paperback edition of *Exodus* were translated and then typed by hand because citizens were not allowed access to copy machines or duplicating equipment. The 1960 film adaptation of *Exodus*, directed by Otto Preminger and starring Paul Newman, was a blockbuster success.

Biography

Leon Marcus Uris was born in Baltimore, Maryland, to William and Anna Uris in 1924. His father, a paperhanger by trade, had immigrated to the United States from Poland after having spent a year in Palestine. The author once said of his father, "He went from failure to failure." Leon Uris was a failure himself in high school, having failed English three times. He dropped out of high school and joined the U.S. Marine Corps at the age of seventeen.

Uris served in World War II as a radioman in Tarawa, Guadalcanal, and New Zealand. After his service, while recovering from malaria in San Francisco, Uris met the first of his three wives, Betty Beck. Uris used his war experiences extensively, especially in his first novel, *Battle Cry*. Before he became a successful writer, Uris was employed in California as a newspaper delivery driver for the *San Francisco Call-Bulletin* in the late 1940's.

Battle Cry was written when Uris was twenty-nine years old, after he had a story published in *Esquire* and was encouraged by the editors to write a novel. After 1950, Uris was a full-time writer. Living in California, he also became a screenwriter, penning *Gunfight at the OK Corral*, a film directed by John Sturges. Uris could be a difficult man to work with, and he often found himself at odds with Hollywood directors, including Sturges. Later he fought with two directors who filmed adaptations of his novels: Otto Preminger, who directed *Exodus* (1960), and Alfred Hitchcock, who directed *Topaz* (1969).

In 1958, *Exodus* made Uris's reputation as a writer. Having served as a war correspondent during the Arab-Israeli conflict of 1956, Uris once again turned to his personal experience for the basis of his next novel. In only his third book, Uris displayed a tremendous work ethic and attention to detail, sending an unlikely epic about the founding of the state of Israel to the top of the best-seller lists. Uris's career as a writer centered on the blockbuster, the large, sweeping saga that brings history to life; examples include *Mila 18*, which centers on the Warsaw ghetto uprising, and *Trinity*, an epic novel that focuses on Ireland under English rule and covers generations.

Hard to live with as well as to work with, Uris admitted to being difficult and sometimes ruthless. His first marriage ended in divorce in 1965 after twenty years and three children. Uris married Margery Edwards in 1968 and she died in 1969, apparently a suicide. Uris married for a third time, to Jill Peabody, in 1970, when Uris was forty-six and his bride was twenty-four. They had two children before divorcing in 1989. Uris died of congestive heart failure in June, 2003, in his home in Shelter Island, New York, at the age of seventy-eight.

Analysis

The historical novel is neither strictly history nor strictly novel. The best writers in this genre, of which Uris was certainly one, are skilled enough to blur the lines between fiction and history. If all one knows about the founding of Israel or life in Ireland under English occupation is what one has read in Uris's *Exodus* or *Trinity*, then one has only a rudimentary understanding of the subject, and that understanding is likely to be biased by the author's own prejudices.

It is a testament to Uris's power as a writer and thoroughness as a researcher that he was able to present his works in such a convincing light as to persuade his readers that they have gained a useful knowledge of the subject at hand. Literary critics, whose job it is to dissect works of fiction, point out Uris's complete lack of objectivity. For example, Uris spoke on behalf of Jewish interests around the world, raising money for Jewish causes during his career, and his portrayals of Jewish soldiers and settlers in works such as *Exodus* must be accepted as the products of a man who was a devout Zionist. This observation, however, is not really criticism as much as truth. Uris was a Jew, and he sympathized with the plight of European Jews especially, and his novels reflect this.

Uris was a great storyteller, if somewhat overly melodramatic at times. He did not graduate from high school, and he earned his writer's reputation on the job. The lack of polish, the brute force of his prose, shines through at times. His treatment of women characters in his novels, for example, is a product of his lack of sophistication. Women in his early novels, such as Kitty Fremont and Jordana Ben Canaan in *Exodus*, struggle with the role of the feminine. Jordana wants to be the equal of any man, but she resents Kitty's frilly dresses, cosmetics, and demure attitude in the company of men. Kitty, meanwhile, resents Jordana and Dafna, Ari Ben Canaan's first wife, for their strength and uncompromising personalities. In later novels, Uris moved away from this dichotomy and presented women as more modern, less inhibited, and more likely to engage men on a level playing field.

EXODUS

Exodus is the story of the founding of the state of Israel, including almost one hundred years of history before the Jewish state was founded in 1948. Full of great detail, this work is typical and the best example of Uris's historical novels. The amount of background work that Uris invested and his extensive research into the supporting documents that went into the writing of *Exodus* are impressive.

While *Exodus* is a famous novel, it must be viewed in the context of its time. Published only ten years after the founding of the state of Israel, *Exodus* was particularly significant in its day because it gave Jewish people a sense of their history and chronicled their struggles, not only in Nazi Germany and Eastern Europe but also around the world. In the year of its publication, Israeli prime minister David Ben-Gurion has been quoted as saying about *Exodus*, "As a piece of propaganda, it's the greatest thing ever written about Israel."

Exodus presents Jewish characters in a light that up to the time of its publication was unusual—one of heroic stature. The novel's main character, Ari Ben Canaan, is a sort of Jewish superman. Tall, dark, handsome, fearless, decisive, bold, and daring, Ari is a far cry from the Jewish stereotype presented in previous popular fiction. Uris addresses this difference in his foreword to the novel, noting that the characters in *Exodus* do not include shrewd businessmen, intelligent doctors, or humorous, self-deprecating Jewish men who have been in therapy for years.

This sweeping epic begins on the island of Cyprus only a couple of years after the end of World War II. The refugee problem, the issue of where to resettle millions of displaced Jews, many of them survivors of Nazi concentration camps, is vexing Europe. For generations, Jews have been slowly returning to Palestine; however, the large number of Jews needing relocation could overwhelm the resources of the Middle East and aggravate Arabs who already live there. Great Britain has control of the region and must walk a tightrope between appeasing Arab interests and allowing Jewish settlement in Palestine. In the meantime, Cyprus serves as a holding pen for tens of thousands of displaced persons.

Since the end of the war, Jewish financiers in the United States and Europe have paid to have ships outfitted for the purpose of transporting illegal immigrants to Palestine. Jewish underground agents, including Ari Ben Canaan, have been secreting Jews aboard ships, evading British barricades, and grounding their crafts on the beaches of Palestine. Ben Canaan's latest idea is to smuggle thousands of children out of Cyprus on a ship the Jews have named *Exodus*. This time, however, the aim is not to run the British blockade but to gain worldwide sympathy for the plight of displaced Jews and win the battle of public opinion. To accomplish his mission, Ben Canaan must be willing to risk the lives of the children to bluff the British and embarrass them on the world's stage so that the ship *Exodus* will be allowed to sail to Palestine without conflict.

Aside from Ari Ben Canaan, other important characters in *Exodus* include Katherine "Kitty" Fremont, an American nurse from Indiana who is falling in love with Ben Canaan and who dotes on a young Jewish girl named Karen Clement Hansen. Karen, who has lost her family in the Holocaust, was smuggled out of Germany by her parents before the war and was raised in Denmark. She has come to Palestine to find her father, who was an important German scientist and professor before the war. Karen has a fondness for young Dov Landau, a survivor of a Polish concentration camp and the Warsaw ghetto uprising. He has been emotionally scarred by his horrid past and withdraws from everyone except Karen. *Exodus* also explores the story of Ari Ben Canaan's family, including his father and uncle, who have conflicting ideas about how Jews should bring about the state of Israel. The stories of Ari's family, of Karen Clement Hansen, of Kitty Fremont, and of Dov Landau are all told through long flashbacks. These four people and their intertwining relationships serve as the pattern that carries the novel's story.

The novel has been criticized for its sexism and for its blatant anti-Arab bias as well as for what many critics contend are oversimplified themes, unrealistic portrayals, trite dialogue, and shoddy sentence structure. Although it is perhaps not a great work of literature, *Exodus* stands as an important document in the history of Israel and in the world's understanding of Jews and their passion for a Jewish state. In a way that no pure historical work could convey, *Exodus* gives readers a feeling for how Jews were treated by the world after World War II and how they responded with great persistence, bravery, and ingenuity.

QB VII

One of the main characters of Uris's 1970 novel *QB VII* is Abe Cady, an American Jew who has written a best-selling book titled *The Holocaust*. Some of Cady's family members died in Jadwiga, a Nazi concentration camp in Poland that was known for the medical experiments performed there on twins, including Jews. In adHdition to the Nazi doctors in the camp there were also some prisoner-surgeons, including a Pole named Adam Kelno. In 1947, at Poland's insistence, Kelno became a wanted man for his part in the war crimes committed at the camp. Kelno was living in England by this time, however, and the British were reluctant to send a physician, even one accused of war crimes, to Communist Poland. The evidence against Kelno had to be overwhelming to speed his extradition to Poland. After spending two years in an English prison awaiting evidence, Kelno was finally brought face-to-face with an accuser. At a legal hearing, the accuser could not pick Kelno out of a lineup of suspects, and Kelno was set free. Shortly thereafter he left England with his wife and young son, bound for Borneo in the South Pacific.

The novel moves to the past to relate Kelno's life in Borneo, which is above reproach. For seventeen years he fights to improve the living conditions of the local tribespeople, introducing medicines, working to change dangerous customs that are based on tribal superstitions, altering the diet of the tribe and improving nutrition—single-handedly saving the lives of a generation of Borneo natives. Word spreads of his accomplishments, and scientific papers are written on his work. Finally, the world learns about the British doctor performing miracles in the farthest reaches of the empire.

Kelno is afraid of returning to Western civilization, afraid of the accusations that might have been lying dormant through the years. He feels that he cannot risk his hard-earned good name, and he does not want to bring shame upon his family. The groundswell of recognition proves too much, however, and Kelno moves his family back to England. He is knighted for his service to the Crown and its subjects. Kelno avoids the spotlight as much as he can, preferring to run his clinic in London's poorest neighborhood. His instincts tell him to keep a low profile. Kelno's son Stephan and his apprentice Terrence are in awe of Kelno's work and aspire to be like him. This admiration means everything to Kelno, who believes that Jews hate him and will not rest until he is punished for crimes he never willingly committed. After all, he was a prisoner, the same as they were.

Cady's book, an in-depth chronicling of Nazi atrocities, has become a worldwide best seller. Kelno learns of the book, and he is particularly disturbed by one paragraph in it that identifies him as a butcher, a killer of innocents. Kelno brings a libel suit against Cady in the English courts, and the trial is heard by a jury in a courtroom designated Queen's Bench VII (QB VII).

This is a novel about forgiveness and redemption. Are there some human acts that are beyond the pale, that can never be forgotten or forgiven, no matter how many years have passed or what circumstances may have prevailed or what good deeds may have been performed in the interim? Is there a limit to the power of denial and self-delusion? Is there an ultimate accountability for one's actions, even those performed under the most extreme duress?

Randy L. Abbott

Other major works

SCREENPLAYS: *Battle Cry*, 1955 (adaptation of his novel); *Gunfight at the OK Corral*, 1957.

NONFICTION: *Exodus Revisited*, 1959 (photographs by Dimitrios Harissiadis; also known as *In the Steps of Exodus*); *Ireland, a Terrible Beauty: The Story of Ireland Today*, 1975 (photographs by Jill Uris); *Jerusalem: Song of Songs*, 1981 (photographs by Jill Uris).

Bibliography

Cain, Kathleen Shine. *Leon Uris: A Critical Companion*. Westport, Conn.: Greenwood Press, 1998. Provides biographical information and presents critical analysis of each of Uris's novels, discussing plot, characterization, and major themes.

Gonshak, Henry. "Rambowitz Versus the Schlemiel in Leon Uris' *Exodus*." *Journal of American Culture* 22, no. 1 (Spring, 1999): 9-16. Offers in-depth discussion of the characterization of Jews in Uris's *Exodus*.

Salt, Jeremy. "Fact and Fiction in the Middle Eastern Novels of Leon Uris." *Journal of Palestine Studies* 14, no. 3 (Spring, 1985): 54-63. Examines the historical accuracy of Uris's novels, particularly *Exodus* and *The Haj*.

Weissbrod, Rachel. "*Exodus* as a Zionist Melodrama." *Israel Studies* 4, no. 1 (Spring, 1999): 129-153. Discusses *Exodus* in its capacity as a historical novel—a work of fiction that is more easily digested than actual histories or sacred works that include a history of Palestine.

Whitfield, Stephen J. "Necrology: Leon Uris, 1924-2003." *Jewish Quarterly Review* 94, no. 4 (Fall, 2004): 666-671. Traces Uris's writing career, including *Exodus*, which Whitfield terms a propaganda novel.

EDWARD LEWIS WALLANT

Born: New Haven, Connecticut; October 19, 1926
Died: Norwalk, Connecticut; December 5, 1962

PRINCIPAL LONG FICTION

The Human Season, 1960
The Pawnbroker, 1961
The Tenants of Moonbloom, 1963
The Children at the Gate, 1964

OTHER LITERARY FORMS

The brevity of Edward Lewis Wallant's literary career did not allow for a long list of publications. He did contribute three short stories to the *New Voices* series: "I Held Back My Hand" appeared in *New Voices 2* (1955), "The Man Who Made a Nice Appearance" in *New Voices 3* (1958), and the posthumously published "When Ben Awakened" in *American Scene: New Voices* (1963). Wallant also wrote an essay on the art of fiction that was published in the *Teacher's Notebook in English* (1963). In addition, a sizable collection housed at the Beinecke Library at Yale University includes unpublished manuscripts, the final drafts of Wallant's first two unpublished novels, about one-half dozen short stories, various drafts of his published novels, the first act of a play, his journal and his notebooks, and miscellaneous loose notes and fragments.

ACHIEVEMENTS

Edward Lewis Wallant's literary output was so small and his career so short that it is difficult to assess his place in postwar American fiction. Wallant's work is best seen in its relationship to kindred works in the late 1950's and early 1960's. Although he is still little known to the public, Wallant's four novels rank with J. D. Salinger's *Franny and Zooey* (1961), Saul Bellow's *Henderson the Rain King* (1959), Bernard Malamud's *A New Life* (1961), and Ken Kesey's *One Flew over the Cuckoo's Nest* (1962) as examples of what has been described as the "new Romanticism." Wallant's novels reflect an outlook on life that led him to write about the unfortunate, the outcast, and the common person, whom he portrayed with compassion and dignity. His unwaveringly realistic perception of life and its often painful demands leaven his general optimism. In each of his fictions, Wallant's central character is shocked out of a moral lethargy and into action on behalf of his fellow human beings. This shock is preceded by a submersion into the contemporary human condition, which provides Wallant the opportunity to explore the interconnections and disconnections of modern urban life.

Wallant was a committed writer whose commitment acknowledged the darker side of the lives of his characters. It is not surprising, then, that while some critics should emphasize the positive nature of Wallant's work, his "happy endings" and his optimism, there should also be those who find in his work a note of despair and a presentiment of his own early death. It was Wallant's achievement to fuse the qualities of an old-fashioned novelist with the perceptions of a modern urban realist. The combination resulted in novels that offer a particularly clear view of the 1960's.

Biography

Edward Lewis Wallant was born in New Haven, Connecticut, on October 19, 1926. His father, who was disabled by a mustard-gas attack during World War I, was almost continuously hospitalized during Wallant's early years, and he died when his son was six years old. Wallant, an only child, was reared in a shabby although respectable middle-class neighborhood by his mother, Anna, and two aunts. Except for his Russian-born grandfather, who told him stories of the old country, it was a household without adult males. During his years at New Haven High School, Wallant held a number of jobs, including plumber's assistant, delivery boy for a drugstore across the street from a Catholic hospital, and hot-dog hawker at Yale football games. Although his academic career in high school was not remarkable, he did attend briefly the University of Connecticut. He soon left, however, to join the U.S. Navy.

The final months of World War II found Wallant serving as a gunner's mate in the European theater of operations; after his discharge from the Navy in 1946, he enrolled in Pratt Institute to prepare for a career as an artist. In 1947, he married Joyce Fromkin, a woman he had known since childhood; in 1948, they moved to Brooklyn. After his graduation from Pratt in 1950, he was hired by the L. W. Frohlich advertising agency, where he became art director for a Westinghouse account. In the same year, he also enrolled in creative writing courses at the New School for Social Research in New York City, where he studied with Charles Glicksberg and Don Wolfe. Under their guidance, Wallant wrote a group of short stories and an unpublished novel, "Tarzan's Cottage."

In 1953, Wallant moved to the advertising agency of Doyle, Kitchen, and McCormick. He also moved his family from New Rochelle, New York, where a son, Scott, had been born in 1952, to Norwalk, Connecticut. In 1954, his daughter, Leslie, was born. In 1955, his short story "I Held Back My Hand" appeared in *New Voices 2: American Writing Today*, edited by his writing instructor, Wolfe. It was Wallant's first publication. During the late 1950's, Wallant submitted to various publishers his early novels *Tarzan's Cottage* and *The Odyssey of a Middleman*, but neither met with any success. Wallant changed jobs a third time in 1957, moving to McCann Erikson as an art director, a position he was to hold until shortly before his death. His second daughter, Kim, was also born the same year. Another story, "The Man Who Made a Nice Appearance," was published in 1958 in *New Voices 3*, edited by Glicksberg.

Wallant's third novel was accepted within twenty-four hours of its submission to Harcourt, Brace. Originally titled "A Scattering in the Dark," it appeared in 1960 as *The Hu-*

man Season. Although it received few reviews, some were enthusiastic and helped to create a small, underground reputation for his work. In spite of its limited commercial success, the novel received the Harry and Ethel Daroff Memorial Fiction Award from the Jewish Book Council for the best novel on a Jewish theme. The publication of *The Pawnbroker* in 1961, also by Harcourt, Brace, established Wallant's reputation as a novelist. The book was nominated for a National Book Award, and the screen rights were sold to Sidney Lumet, who in 1965 made a critically acclaimed film starring Rod Steiger.

The modest success of *The Pawnbroker* came at a crucial period in Wallant's life. For years, he had balanced his work as an advertising art director with his after-hours vocation of writing, and he was having increasing difficulty in reconciling his two lives. A resolution of sorts seemed imminent when he received a Guggenheim Fellowship in 1962, which allowed him to travel in Europe and to write full time. For three months, he traveled abroad. Joyce joined him briefly in Italy, and then Wallant went on to Spain. He returned home with the idea for a comic novel, to be called *Tannenbaum's Journey*, based on his travels. He also resolved to devote his life to full-time writing and resigned his position with McCann Erikson. He took a small room in New York to use as a retreat for his work. In spite of feeling tired, Wallant was excited by his prospects; the European trip had given him inspiration. Then, quite suddenly, he was stricken by a viral infection and lapsed into a coma. He died of an aneurysm of the brain a week later on December 5, 1962.

At the time of his death, Wallant had two novels, *The Tenants of Moonbloom* and *The Children at the Gate*, under consideration by Harcourt, Brace, and it fell to his editor, Dan Wickenden, to finish these projects. *The Tenants of Moonbloom* was published in 1963, as were two other pieces: a story, "When Ben Awakened," in *American Scene: New Voices*, again edited by Wolfe, and an essay, "The Artist's Eye," for the *Teacher's Notebook in English. The Children at the Gate*, although written before *The Tenants of Moonbloom*, was not published until 1964.

ANALYSIS

Just before his death, Edward Lewis Wallant wrote, "I suggest that most people are nearsighted, myopic in their inability to perceive the details of human experience." It was a condition he found perfectly normal; there is simply too much energy used up in everyday life, having families, supporting oneself, and living in a community, for much insight into the lives of fellow human beings, except as they relate to one's own immediate needs. Yet there are times, Wallant noted, when people experience an unrecognized yearning to "know what lies in the hearts of others." "It is then," he wrote, "that we turn to the artist, because only he [sic] can reveal even the little corners of the things beyond bread alone." It is revealing that Wallant, first trained as a graphic artist, should title the one essay in which he set forth his artistic credo "The Artist's Eye." In this essay, Wallant explores the relationship between the observable, everyday world and the interpretation of that world through the writer's heightened sense of awareness.

In all four of Wallant's published novels, this theme of heightened perception is central. The protagonist, who has become emotionally insulated from life, experiences a reawakening of feelings and rejoins the world around him. This spiritual and emotional rebirth comes as the result of the death of someone who has become close to the protagonist. The impact of this death, which often happens in a shocking way and with suddenness, penetrates the emotional barriers Wallant's characters erect against the onslaught of modern, urban life: Joe Berman escapes the past, Sol Nazerman is rescued from both the past and the dim recesses of his pawnshop, Angelo DeMarco gets beyond his streetwise sassiness, and Norman Moonbloom overcomes his inertia and learns to act. In each case and with each novel, Wallant takes his readers into the lives of his characters and reveals the little corners of the human heart.

THE HUMAN SEASON

Wallant's first novel, *The Human Season*, is the story of a middle-aged, middle-class man who must come to grips with himself following the death of his wife, Mary. Joe Berman is recognizably a twentieth century Everyman who lives a life barely distinguishable from that of his neighbors. He is a Russian Jew who immigrated to the United States when he was a little boy, and he seemingly has attained the American Dream, founding his own plumbing business, owning his own modest home, marrying, and fathering three children.

Mary, of "obligatory blonde, American prettiness," as one critic has described her, dies prior to the beginning of the novel, leaving Berman alone to face life and his largely unrecognized emotions. The structure of the novel intensifies the tension between past and present by alternating scenes from the present, in which Wallant skillfully renders Berman's daily life through a series of highly detailed episodes, with incidents from the past, each of them exposing some traumatic memory. In their reverse progression into the earlier years of Berman's life, these dreams deepen one's understanding not only of Berman's character but also of the formation of his emotional paralysis. Beginning on April 30, 1956, the day of Mary's fatal stroke, the dreams go back to September, 1907, when Berman was a little boy of nine years living in Russia. The dreams contrast sharply in their emotional vividness with the increasingly comatose quality of Berman's present life. He has become an automaton, living without connection in an environment increasingly alien to him. He lashes out at the objects that remind him of his wife's delicacy and sensitivity as he succumbs to his "numbing, disorienting grief." Finally, Berman tries to kill himself.

As he becomes more and more blind to the real world, the world of his dreams, his past, becomes more vivid until it begins to intrude into his present, waking life. Increasingly, Wallant returns to images of the natural sources of Berman's earlier feelings in his memories of his father and of his life in Russia. Although there is a pastoral quality to these memories. Wallant does not suggest a return to some agrarian ideal. Berman's dreams remind him of his human capacities and inaugurate his search for something that will approximate the bond with the nature of his youth. Among the dreams are recollections of his father and Judaism. Berman realizes how neglectful he was of his own son, who was killed in the war, and how estranged from the healing qualities of his Jewishness he had become. The death of his wife, after all, merely provides a catalyst for his sickness, causing his self-doubt and sense of alienation to surface. The initial moment of his illumination quite literally comes as a shock: In an attempt to fix a faulty television set, Berman is thrown across the room, and in his fear and astonishment, he begins to pray in a jumble of English, Yiddish, and Russian. In that moment, he discovers the meaning of all the months of his suffering: He is alone.

It is from this revelation that he begins to reconstruct his life, one that will be authentic and will result in a new self. He discovers a craving for people; his dreams no longer haunt him but rather provide him with soothing images that strengthen his zest for self-renewal. In a scene that elevates the fiction to a mythical dimension, Berman is born again as he walks home in the rain after having "witnessed" the life around him. As the novel ends, Berman is waiting in his empty house for his son-in-law to take him home for a family dinner. In this final chapter, Wallant convincingly depicts a poignant example of people's infinite capacity for self-renewal.

The Pawnbroker

Wallant abandoned work on a comic fiction, *Gimple the Beast*, to write his second novel, *The Pawnbroker.* As in his first novel, the central character is a middle-aged Jewish immigrant. Sol Nazerman, however, did not arrive in the United States as a youth; instead, the forty-five-year-old former professor from the University of Kraków fled Europe and the death camps in which he had been a prisoner during World War II. Now he is the operator of a pawnshop in a black ghetto in New York City. The shop is owned by a minor underworld figure who uses it as a drop point for the transferral of illegal money. Nazerman is aware of the criminality of the operation but does not protest. He uses his income to support his sister and her family, who live in the suburbs. He also contributes to the support of his mistress, Tessie Rubin, who lives with her dying father. The novel brings together the nightmare world of the concentration camp as Nazerman remembers it with the corrupt urban world of the pawnshop.

As in *The Human Season*, the central character has walled himself off from the pain and suffering of the world around him. Amid the grotesques who visit his shop, Nazerman remains private and isolated. The novel is the story of his spiritual reawakening, which is largely brought about through the intervention of Jesus Ortiz, the black, Catholic assistant who works in the business, and whose energy and ambition awaken sympathy from Nazerman. The death of Ortiz during an attempted robbery of the shop, which occurs on the fifteenth anniversary of the destruction of Nazerman's family in the death camps, provides the shock that penetrates the insulation with which Nazerman has wrapped his feelings in order to maintain his delicate sense of survival. He recognizes the part he willingly plays in the chain of human exploitation of which his pawnshop is a microcosm, and he is forced to acknowledge the community of grief to which he belongs and from which he has so long isolated himself.

The novel concludes with three acts of atonement for Nazerman as he rejoins the world. He telephones his nephew, Morton, and asks him to become his new assistant, thereby opening a father-son relationship with the young man who has been wanting it for so long. After the phone call, Nazerman sleeps and dreams, not a nightmare as he usually does, but a dream in which he is able to lay the dead past to rest. Finally, he, like Berman, learns to mourn and goes to Tessie to help her grieve over the death of her father. As in the previous novel, this act is an important sign of his rebirth.

The connections between Wallant's first two novels are more than superficial. The two protagonists, who have much in common, experience similar awakenings. Both novels interweave dreams with the narrative thread. Both men must expiate their guilt over the death of their sons. Berman never did respond to his son, who died in the war unaware of his father's love; Nazerman must seek forgiveness for the guilt he feels for the death of his son, who slipped out of his grasp and suffocated on the floor of a cattle car on their way to the death camp. Both men are finally free from their past when they can fully and properly mourn the dead; then they can rebuild their lives again in the present. *The Pawnbroker* is the darkest of Wallant's books and seems to have provided a release for the marvelously comic voice of the last two novels.

THE CHILDREN AT THE GATE

During the summer of 1961, while he was awaiting the outcome of his Guggenheim application, Wallant underwent a radical shift in attitude concerning his vocation as a writer. In the little more than six months he took to complete the manuscript of *The Pawnbroker*, he drafted the first version of *The Children at the Gate*, a completed version of which was left with his editor before he began his European travels with the fellowship money.

The novel concerns the relationship between the literal-minded, nineteen-year-old Angelo DeMarco, who makes the rounds of a Catholic hospital to take orders among the patients for the pharmacy where he works, and Sammy Cahan, a clownish Jew who is an orderly in the hospital. DeMarco, who clings to a rationalism as a defense against the horrors of his life—his disabled sister, his fatherless home, his obsessively religious mother, and the dying patients among whom he must spend his days—is redeemed by the antics of Cahan, whose essentially emotional view of life provides DeMarco with his spiritual change. Unlike Berman and Nazerman, Cahan seems to have inherited his life-giving vision, which he is able to spread throughout the hospital. As with the pawnshop and later the apartment houses of *The Tenants of Moonbloom*, the hospital setting provides a microcosm for the world's suffering humanity against which the drama of the central character's spiritual growth can take place.

Once again, it is a death, Cahan's, that shocks DeMarco awake to the final recognition of his stifling life and the possibility of rebirth, a recognition that is made concrete in DeMarco's ministrations to his developmentally disabled, childlike sister, who has been raped by their father. Like Berman and Nazerman before him, DeMarco reveals his growing humanity through his acts of kindness and tenderness.

The centrality of the dreamworld that played so important a part in the previous novels is replaced here by a living world of dreams that DeMarco must shatter before abandoning his barricade of toughness. It is no coincidence that he first discovers Cahan in the children's ward at the hospital, for it is the childlike simplicity of the orderly, his trust and innocence, that DeMarco must rediscover in order to be reborn. *The Children at the Gate* reveals the intermingling of Christian and Jewish myths that Wallant used to such great effect in all of his novels. It is not only the accumulation of religious artifacts or references in the novel but also Cahan's portrayal as the religious fool and his martyrdom in the Christlike crucifixion on the hospital gates that sets the tone. Just as the death of the assistant, Ortiz, in *The Pawnbroker* precipitated Nazerman's rebirth, so here Cahan's death reveals to DeMarco the path he must follow. The roles of teacher and priest, the relationship between suffering and redemption, and the confluence of death and rebirth form a religious nexus that gives this book its especially powerful message of commitment, community, and love.

Although there were comic elements in *The Children at the Gate*, it was only in *The Tenants of Moonbloom* that Wallant's comic genius flowered. His last novel exhibits a certainty of handling and a smoothness of execution that were the results of his growing confidence as a writer. Wallant had thrown over his job in advertising and had made a commitment to literature.

THE TENANTS OF MOONBLOOM

The Tenants of Moonbloom traces the emergence of Norman Moonbloom, an introverted rent collector who manages four decrepit apartment buildings for his brother, and who emerges from his passivity as the result of his contact with the urban flotsam and jetsam who inhabit his apartments. Moonbloom, who is thirty-three at the time of the story, has finally settled down after years of college and a number of majors. He is a rather average young man who has spent his life retreating from people, and although he would prefer to hide in the womblike security of his apartment, his tenants persistently intrude on his consciousness. Finally unable any longer to retreat from the world, Moonbloom plunges into his past, like Berman and Nazerman, to search for a base on which he can build a relationship with life. Through a series of seemingly disconnected visions, Moonbloom awakens to an understanding of the humanity that he shares with even the most bizarre of his tenants. He launches a "holy war" of rehabilitation in order to try to respond to the needs of those human beings placed into his trust.

Through a series of jolts, not unlike the ones received by Wallant's other antiheroes, delivered by the various inhabitants of Moonbloom's apartments, he is transformed. This is accomplished during three visits he makes to his tenants. Each successive visit further shocks him into responding. His reaction culminates in the frenzy of activity in which he engages to bring the buildings and by extension the lives of his tenants up to some sort of standard. Although Moonbloom, a former rabbinical student, is Wallant's final Christ figure, this novel relies far less than its predecessors, most notably *The Children at the Gate*, on biblical imagery and allusions, despite Moonbloom's messianic zeal to convert his tenants into full-blown human beings. In his last novel, Wallant was to integrate the comic and the tragic. As one critic has written, Wallant moved from being a cautious optimist to become "the comic celebrant of man's capacity to live an energetic, courageous, and spiritually dedicated existence."

Wallant's reputation rests firmly on a small body of fiction that he wrote with much passion and energy. Necessarily, this reputation has been enhanced by the tragedy of his untimely death and the unfulfilled promise of his career. His prose reflects a joyful celebration of life, life in all of its manifest complexities. Although he has often been compared to two other Jewish writers, Bruce Jay Friedman and Nathanael West, Wallant did not succumb to the absurd fantasies of the first or to the despair of the second. Perhaps his importance as a modern novelist is best summarized by a critic who wrote that it was Wallant's cautious refusal to accept "the existential despair and the universal isolation of modern man" that distinguished him from his contemporaries and led him to affirm quietly the worth and joy of life. Wallant's novels are a testament to the continuing resilience of the human spirit.

Charles L. P. Silet

BIBLIOGRAPHY

Ayo, Nicholas. "The Secular Heart: The Achievement of Edward Lewis Wallant." *Critique: Studies in Modern Fiction* 12 (1970): 86-94. Focuses on the religious element in Wallant's characters. Compares Wallant to Fyodor Dostoevski, maintaining that Wallant has Dostoevski's ability to convey grim realism and to emphasize changes of heart.

Codde, Philippe. *The Jewish American Novel.* West Lafayette, Ind.: Purdue University Press, 2007. Codde analyzes the unprecedented success of novels written by Jewish Americans in the years following World War II. He focuses on the work of several novelists of the era, including Wallant.

_______. "'No Enemy, No Betrayer, No Bearded Torturer': The Death of God, the Holocaust, and Existentialism in Wallant's *The Human Season*." *English Language Notes* 43, no. 1 (September, 2005): 63-77. Codde examines Wallant's novel, providing an overview of the book and analyzing its use of Holocaust imagery and its representation of the death of God and of existentialism.

Galloway, David. *Edward Lewis Wallant.* Boston: Twayne, 1979. A full-length treatment of Wallant's life and writings. Includes a chronology, notes, and an annotated bibliography. A good introduction to his work.

Gurko, Leo. "Edward Lewis Wallant as Urban Novelist." *Twentieth Century Literature* 20 (October, 1974): 252-261. Examines Wallant's metaphoric use of the city: ugly, perverted, dangerous, and cruel. Gurko claims, however, that in its sprawling vitality, the city also contains "seeds of its own reconstruction."

Kerner, Howard A. "*The Pawnbroker*." In *Holocaust Literature*, edited by John K. Roth. Pasadena, Calif.: Salem Press, 2008. An overview and analysis of the novel, describing its characters, stylistic influences, and place within Jewish American literature. Includes a bibliography.

Lewis, Robert W. "The Hung-Up Heroes of Edward Lewis Wallant." *Renascence* 24 (1972): 70-84. This substantial discussion examines all of Wallant's novels, especially *The Pawnbroker*, paying particular attention to his sensitive, intellectual characters and his themes of suffering and rebirth. Also looks at Wallant's use of myth.

McDermott, John V. *Flannery O'Connor and Edward Lewis Wallant: Two of a Kind*. Lanham, Md.: University Press of America, 2005. A comparison of the works of the two American writers, focusing on their philosophical views. McDermott demonstrates how both writers are concerned with spirituality, the meaning of existence, and humankind's relationship to God.

Schulz, M. F. "Wallant and Friedman: The Glory and Agony of Love." *Critique: Studies in Modern Fiction* 10 (1968): 31-47. Compares Wallant and Bruce Jay Friedman, particularly in their use of humor and the theme of love. Finds Wallant's characters examples of growth in sensibility and his novels affirmations of order and rebirth.

Stanford, Raney. "The Novels of Edward Wallant." *Colorado Quarterly* 17 (1969): 393-405. Examines some of Wallant's characters and themes, concentrating especially on *The Tenants of Moonbloom* and *The Pawnbroker*. Maintains that Wallant's characters tend to undergo rebellion that leads to their rebirth.

ELIE WIESEL

Born: Sighet, Transylvania, Romania; September 30, 1928
Also known as: Eliezer Wiesel

PRINCIPAL LONG FICTION

L'Aube, 1960 (novella; *Dawn*, 1961)
Le Jour, 1961 (novella; *The Accident*, 1962)
La Ville de la chance, 1962 (*The Town Beyond the Wall*, 1964)
Les Portes de la forêt, 1964 (*The Gates of the Forest*, 1966)
Le Mendiant de Jérusalem, 1968 (*A Beggar in Jerusalem*, 1970)
Le Serment de Kolvillàg, 1973 (*The Oath*, 1973)
Le Testament d'un poète juif assassiné, 1980 (*The Testament*, 1981)
Le Cinquième Fils, 1983 (*The Fifth Son*, 1985)
Le Crépuscule, au loin, 1987 (*Twilight*, 1988)
L'Oublié, 1989 (*The Forgotten*, 1992)
Les Juges, 1999 (*The Judges*, 2002)
Le Temps des déracinés, 2003 (*The Time of the Uprooted*, 2005)

OTHER LITERARY FORMS

Since the appearance in 1956 of *Un di Velt hot geshvign* (in French as *La Nuit*, 1958; *Night*, 1960), Elie Wiesel (vee-ZEHL) has published many works of fiction and nonfiction. Among these are *Les Juifs du silence* (1966; *The Jews of Silence*, 1966), a personal testimony of his trip to Russia; *Le Chant des morts* (1966; *Legends of Our Time*, 1968), *Entre deux soleils* (1970; *One Generation After*, 1970), and *Un Juif aujourd'hui* (1977; *A Jew Today*, 1978), collections of essays and short stories; several volumes of biblical portraits and Hasidic tales; the plays *Zalmen: Ou, La Folie de Dieu* (pb. 1968; *Zalmen: Or, The Madness of God*, 1974) and *Le Procès de Shamgorod tel qu'il se déroula le 25 février 1649* (pb. 1979; *The Trial of God: As It Was Held on February 25, 1649, in Shamgorod*, 1979); and a cantata, *Ani Maamin: Un Chant perdu et retrouvé* (1973; *Ani Maamin: A Song Lost and Found Again*, 1973). Some of his later works, the biblical portraits and Hasidic tales, although written in French, were originally published in the English translation by his wife, Marion Wiesel.

ACHIEVEMENTS

Elie Wiesel is one of the most important figures in the genre known as "the literature of the Holocaust." He brings to literature a new literary vocabulary, rooted in the Bible, that is at once mystical, legalistic, theological, and historical. As a survivor of the Holocaust, Wiesel considers himself to be a messenger from the dead to the living, and, as a witness, he bears testimony both to the unfathomable events of the death camps and to the current,

Elie Wiesel
(The Nobel Foundation)

unfolding history of his people. Wiesel's work, parochial in context, is universal in perception. It speaks to all humankind, for all participated, either actively or silently, in the supreme trial of their humanity. He views the Holocaust as touching upon every facet of one's life and interests, and he perceives humanity's major problem to be survival in the post-Holocaust world.

As a writer, Wiesel is preoccupied with the inadequacy of language, but not in the abstract manner of many contemporary writers. Language affirms a belief in humankind and attests its grandeur. The Holocaust negates humanity. It represents a misuse of language; the failure of imagination; the rule of the depraved; the suspension of the senses, of beliefs, of time; the inversion of order. To capture the Holocaust in language is to impose upon it a decorum that in itself is a betrayal of those victimized by this satanic maelstrom. Wiesel believed, when he began to write, that the tale nevertheless must be told, because the murderer murders not only his victim but also himself. He says, "At Auschwitz, not only man died, but also the idea of man." Awareness of the Holocaust may save the world from self-obliteration.

Wiesel raises questions that are unanswerable, questions intended to arouse the consciousness of a people, the progeny of the indifferent observers of the decade of the

1940's. He also vies with God, not as a defiant disbeliever but as a believer in the biblical tradition of the prophets who have challenged God, remonstrated with him, and protested heavenly decrees. There is no gaiety in Wiesel's works. There is laughter, but it is not a joyous laughter. It is the laughter of a madman defying his creator. Writers, theologians, and humanists of all faiths have attempted to come to terms with the problems that Wiesel presents.

Writing, for Wiesel, is not simply intended as a moral lesson for the post-Holocaust generations. It is also, and perhaps primarily—as he explains in the essay "Mes Maîtres" ("My Teachers"), in *Legends of Our Time*—a monument to the unburied dead, to the millions whose celestial cemeteries are bereft of tombstones.

Wiesel's first publication, *Night*, is in the form of a memoir of his Holocaust experiences. Wiesel did not have an easy time publishing his initial work. It originally appeared in 1955 as an eight-hundred-page manuscript in Yiddish titled *Un di Velt hot geshvign* (and the world was silent) and was published in Argentina by a Yiddish press. It was then condensed to a little more than one hundred pages, translated into French, given the title *La Nuit*, and, with the help of Wiesel's close friend François Mauriac, published in France in 1958. It was an instant success. Stella Rodway translated the French version into English, but major publishing houses in the United States rejected the manuscript because the subject matter was "too sad" to appeal to the general public. Finally, in 1960, the publishing company Hill & Wang accepted the manuscript for publication. Wiesel would continue to write in French; his later books were translated into English by his wife, Marion. The exception is his eyewitness account of his trip to Russia, *The Jews of Silence*, which was originally written in Hebrew as a series of journalistic articles for an Israeli newspaper. It was thereafter put together in its present form. Some of Wiesel's essays first appeared in various magazines prior to their appearance in *Legends of Our Time* and *A Jew Today*.

Wiesel is a celebrated lecturer sought after by various organizations, conferences, and campuses, and he has served on the boards of numerous national and international organizations. He holds honorary doctoral degrees from more than forty colleges and universities and has received awards for literary, academic, and humanitarian contributions from numerous organizations. In 1983 he won the Belgian International Peace Prize, and in 1986 he received the Nobel Peace Prize.

In the period since he received the Nobel Prize, Wiesel has been honored with a great many other awards and recognitions, chief among them the Janusz Korczak Humanitarian Award from Kent State University (1989), named for the Polish teacher and author of children's books who chose to march into the gas chambers at Treblinka with his young students so that they would not have to die alone; the first Raoul Wallenberg Medal from the University of Michigan (1990), named for the Swedish diplomat who attended the university in the 1930's and later saved more than one hundred thousand Hungarian Jews from the Nazis; and the first Primo Levi Award (1992), named for the Italian chemist/author and Auschwitz survivor whose writings have served as testimony to the atrocities of the Holocaust. In 2006, Wiesel was made an Honorary Knight of the British Empire, a title bestowed on him in recognition of his vital contribution to Holocaust education worldwide. Wiesel has also been honored by university chairs and distinguished service awards named for him at such prestigious institutions as the University of Haifa, the University of Florida, and Connecticut College.

BIOGRAPHY

Eliezer Wiesel, the third child and only son of Shlomo and Sarah Wiesel, was born in the village of Sighet, in Transylvania, Romania, on September 30, 1928. He had two older sisters, Bea and Hilda, and one younger one, Tzipporah. His parents were Orthodox Jews. As a child, Eliezer was a profound believer in God and spent his days in religious studies. His father, though religious, was a man of culture and a rational humanist. He taught his son to believe in humanity and saw to it that he learned secular subjects, such as Latin, mathematics, and physics, as well as religious ones. His mother was more spiritual. She taught her son a love of God. The constant argument in the Wiesel home was whether their son should be a professor or a rabbi.

Wiesel's maternal grandfather, Dodye Feig, was a Hasid. The young boy would visit with his grandfather to listen to the tales of the Hasidim and the miracles wrought by the rabbis. Eliezer's talent as a storyteller had its beginnings in the stories told to him by his grandfather. He also evinced an appreciation for music and took violin lessons at an early age. After the war, he earned his keep as a choirmaster. His cantata, *Ani Maamin*, with a musical score by Darius Milhaud, is one of the most moving works to be produced about the Holocaust. At the age of twelve, he studied the Kabbala under the tutelage of his master, Moshe. Wiesel's first literary work, *Night*, commences with the serenity of his youth. The portrait of his grandfather and the conflicting attitudes of his parents are subjects of essays to be found in *Legends of Our Time* and *A Jew Today*.

The tranquillity of Wiesel's life was disturbed in the spring of 1944. Although the war in Europe had been going on since 1939, Hungary was one of the last countries to be invaded by the Germans. The inhabitants of the town of Sighet, protected as they were by the Carpathian Mountains and isolated from the events taking place, did not recognize or believe that disaster was imminent. Immigration, when it was still possible, had never been seriously considered. Suddenly, in a matter of weeks, ten thousand Jews were first placed in ghettos and then deported to Auschwitz. For Wiesel, one of the most bizarre aspects of the deportation was the apathy and indifference of the general public. Friends and neighbors turned their backs on people who had lived with them for generations. Wiesel deals with this in his novel *The Town Beyond the Wall* and also in various essays and lectures.

The four-day ride in a sealed boxcar, the arrival at Auschwitz, the separation of families, his last glimpse of his mother and younger sister, the concentration camp experience (including the loss of faith), the stripping away of his humanity, the march to Buchenwald, the death of his father, and finally liberation by the Americans in April, 1945, are tersely rendered in *Night*. Various aspects of this experience are reflected upon by some of the characters of his other novels and by Wiesel directly in some of his essays. The Holocaust itself, while it remains the impetus and muted background of all his writings, does not appear again as the bulk of any particular work. Instead, Wiesel turns from the memoir to the novel form, from fact to fiction, as his protagonists search, as he has done, for a way to live in the post-Holocaust world with the burden of the unimaginable behind them and with the guilt of living confronting them.

When Wiesel was liberated, at the age of sixteen and a half, he refused to be repatriated to the town that had evicted its Jews one year earlier. Instead, he joined a transport of children that was going to France at the invitation of Charles de Gaulle. Upon his arrival in France, he made the decision that he must testify to what he had experienced, but not until he understood it fully himself. He knew it would take him a long time to prepare himself for that testimony, perhaps ten years. He realized that he needed better communication skills and a keener understanding of what had happened. Meanwhile, he vowed not to speak of his experience of the Holocaust. (This vow of silence later became the subject matter for his novel *The Oath*.) In France, Wiesel learned that his two older sisters were alive. At Versailles, he became acquainted with François Wahl, a young philosopher at the Sorbonne, who taught him French by having Wiesel read French classical literature and classics translated into French.

Wiesel moved to Paris in 1946. There, he earned his livelihood as a choir director and as a teacher of the Bible. In 1948, he enrolled at the Sorbonne to study philosophy, the humanities, and literature, hoping to find the answers to the theological, philosophical, and humanistic questions that were plaguing him. His studies broadened his horizons but did not present him with solutions, and he was becoming restless. Fortunately, he landed a job as Paris correspondent for the Israeli newspaper *Yediot Aharonot*, and he spent the next few years traveling in North America, South America, Europe, North Africa, Asia, and the Middle East. As a journalist, Wiesel covered the Israeli War of Independence, which forms the background of his novella *Dawn*. In 1952, Wiesel traveled to India on an assignment. While in India, he wrote a dissertation comparing the Hindu, Christian, and Jewish religions. He also decided to teach himself English at that time.

One of Wiesel's assignments brought him back to Paris, where he met François Mauriac, who convinced him that he must break his vow and start telling his story. The result of this meeting was *Night*, a memoir in the form of a novella. The years after his liberation and the meeting with Mauriac are reflected in his essay "An Interview Unlike Any Other," in *A Jew Today*.

In 1956, Wiesel was sent to New York to cover the United Nations. He also began writing articles in Yiddish for the *Jewish Daily Forward*. During his first summer in New York, he was almost killed when he was struck by a taxicab while crossing Times Square.

He required weeks of hospitalization and months of recuperation during which he could move about only with the help of a wheelchair. This experience became the subject of the novella *The Accident*, which he wrote while he was housebound. During that time, his French visa expired, and he applied for American citizenship.

Wiesel returned to Sighet in 1965. He arrived in the middle of the night. It was an unbearable experience for him, which he poignantly and searingly relates in an essay titled "Le Dernier Retour" ("The Last Return"). The retailing of this incident also appears in the collection *Legends of Our Time* and in "The Watch," in *One Generation After*, and it is recorded with great accuracy in his novel *The Town Beyond the Wall*. Wiesel could not bring himself to spend more than twenty-four hours in the city he had left so abruptly some twenty years before.

Wiesel's first visit to Russia, in 1965, resulted in three works, each in a different form: *The Jews of Silence*, a compilation of newspaper articles concerning the trip; *Zalmen*, a play dealing with the anguish of the rabbi of the Moscow synagogue; and *The Testament*, a novel begun during his trip but set against the background of the Stalinist purge of Jewish writers and poets in 1952. Wiesel returned to Russia again in 1979.

From 1948 on, Wiesel made several trips to Israel in his capacity as correspondent for *Yediot Aharonot*. His participation in the June, 1967, war provided the impetus for the novel *A Beggar in Jerusalem*. He returned to Israel in 1968, this time to be married in Jerusalem, to Marion Erster Rose, a Viennese, a concentration camp survivor also, and a linguist.

Wiesel joined the faculty at City College of New York in 1972, first as a visiting professor teaching courses on Jewish literature, the Holocaust, and Hasidism, and then, in 1973, as Distinguished Professor. Thereafter, he would teach at Boston University, as Andrew Mellon Professor of the Humanities.

In 1979, Wiesel was selected by President Jimmy Carter to chair the U.S. President's Commission on the Holocaust, which eventually created the United States Holocaust Memorial Museum, dedicated in 1993, in Washington, D.C. In 2004, the country of Romania, where Wiesel's hometown of Sighet is located, published a report on the truth about Holocaust atrocities committed against Jews in that region; Wiesel headed the group that researched and wrote this important report.

In 2006, a new edition of *Night* was published, retranslated by Wiesel's wife, Marion. Concurrent with this new edition, television talk-show host Oprah Winfrey chose *Night* as the featured selection of her book club and traveled with Wiesel to the site of the Auschwitz death camp, an event and interview that was later televised on Winfrey's show. At that time, Wiesel stated that he would probably never return to that horrific place. On another Winfrey show shortly after, Wiesel looked on proudly while student essayists, inspired by *Night*, received recognition for their antihate writings.

In 2007, Wiesel was violently assaulted in a San Francisco hotel elevator by a young American Holocaust denier who demanded that Wiesel recant his shattering Holocaust memoir *Night* and publicly assert that the Holocaust never occurred. The attacker was later captured after posting details of the attack on an anti-Semitic Web site. Ironically, when he was attacked, Wiesel was in San Francisco to speak at a conference on conflict resolution; he returned to the city three months later, heavily guarded, to accept a $250,000 award for his Elie Wiesel Foundation for Humanity.

Wiesel continues to be a passionately caring international educator, scholar, spokesman, and public intellectual. He has engaged and interacted with many other scholars, philosophers, and public figures to study and elucidate the genesis and texture of, and potential cures for, hate and its equally evil twin, apathy.

ANALYSIS

Elie Wiesel has said that all his works are "commentary" on *Night*, his one work that deals directly with the Holocaust. His novels are odysseys of a soul fragmented by the Holocaust, in quest of tranquillity, an attempt to move away from the night, reaching the shores of day. The key to understanding Wiesel, then, is his memoir in the form of a novella, *Night*. It is a slim volume that records his childhood memories of his hometown and his experiences in the concentration camp. It also contains the themes, images, and devices that recur throughout his novels.

NIGHT

The opening chapter of *Night* begins with the social setting of Wiesel's native village of Sighet in Transylvania—its inhabitants, their customs, their beliefs—and his first meeting with Moché, the beadle, a character who forms a link to all his other works. Events occur rapidly. The disruption of normalcy with the invasion of the Germans, the forcing of the Jews into ghettos, their deportation, and the obliteration of the Jewish community are recorded tersely but accurately.

From the moment the Jews of Sighet leave the tranquil setting of their native village until they are liberated, time is suspended. The concentration camp is a universe like no other. There, every day is a waking nightmare. Each day is a repetition of deprivation, starvation, cremation; death, either by torture, gunshot, or fire, is the only certainty. The boys look like old men; the men cry like children. Existence depends on endurance, regardless of age.

Not only is the town obliterated and time obliterated, but also the individual is transformed into an unrecognizable substance. The bestial inhumanity of the victimizers, the divorce from social, moral, and humanistic constraints, marks their apotheosis in the kingdom of Hell. The inmates of the concentration camp's universe are metamorphosed also. The tattooing of numbers on their arms indelibly brands them as objects of inventory, to be used as long as they work well and to be disposed of when they malfunction. *Night* describes this transformation. Early in the work, Wiesel says of himself that he "had become a completely different person."

The work ends after the war. He has survived and has been liberated; he looks into the mirror and sees a corpse staring back at him. The corpse becomes part of his life, and the tension of his works rests on his separating himself from the corpse, which means finding a place for himself among the living and giving the corpse a proper burial in the form of a literary monument. Separating himself from the corpse is not an easy task. It involves personal, social, and theological issues: assuaging his own guilt for having survived and coming to terms with an indifferent society and an indifferent God, who allowed the Holocaust to take place. His future works chart his attempt at reconciliation with life, reintegration into society, rediscovery of his religious heritage, and reaffirmation of his belief in God, in spite of everything. This is accomplished by the use of a dual character or alter ego. In each novel, the personality of the protagonist, a survivor of the Holocaust, is complemented by that of the antagonist, usually someone who was not directly involved in the war. They lead separate lives until their paths cross and their souls fuse. The antagonist then disappears; his existence is no longer necessary.

Within the biographical-historical-psychological framework of Wiesel's works are recurring metaphors, characters, and themes. The Holocaust, the overriding presence in Wiesel's oeuvre, is metaphorically night. The sealed, unlit boxcar bearing Wiesel and his townspeople arrived at Auschwitz at midnight. For the victims, night describes the abyss to which they were consigned; for the oppressors, it indicates the depravity of the soul; for the world, it represents the failure of enlightenment, the blackness in which the world was engulfed during the Holocaust period. For Wiesel, night is a physical and psychological condition. As a victim, he moved like a shadow through the kingdom of Death, communicating with corpses. As a survivor, the corpses still haunt him. In Auschwitz, time lost its significance, and night became the only frame of reference. Night continues to circumscribe the parameters of confinement for the protagonists in *The Town Beyond the Wall*, *The Gates of the Forest*, *A Beggar in Jerusalem*, *The Oath*, and *The Testament*.

The lasting effects of the devastation on the psyche are summed up by Wiesel in an incantatory paragraph that appears early in *Night*:

> Never shall I forget that night, the first night in camp which has turned my life into one long night, seven times cursed and seven times sealed. Never shall I forget that smoke. Never shall I forget the little faces of the children, whose bodies I saw turned into wreaths of smoke beneath a silent blue sky.

Having pledged never to forget, Wiesel makes memory an important aspect of all his writings. His characters, especially his protagonists, are haunted by their memories. Memory controls their lives and motivates their actions. It is also a bridge to their future.

Moché, the beadle of *Night*, survives the massacre of the first roundup of Jews and returns to Sighet to tell the tale and warn the others concerning their impending doom. The townspeople, however, refuse to believe him and think he has gone mad. Moché appears in every book; his role is usually that of messenger in the tale he tells. Madness is an essential element in all Wiesel's works. On the one hand, it is indicative of the malady that struck the world during the Holocaust years. Wiesel, however, treats his madmen sympathetically. Their madness is not clinical but mystical. They are visionaries, saints, or messengers, endowed with the task of saving the world. As such, they become one with humankind, God, and creation. Wiesel's point is that madness can be a force of evil or good. Hitler and his Nazis were mad. Their madness was employed to destroy the world. Most of Wiesel's madmen want to bring about the Messiah; they want to redeem the world.

Another theme that is paramount in Wiesel's works is that of silence. Wiesel's ten years of silence after his liberation afforded him the opportunity for reflection and meditation on past events and future actions. He followed a carefully conceived plan not to speak. It was not that he had nothing to say or that he was indifferent; his decision was prompted by the knowledge that no words could describe what had taken place. His silence was intended as an "eloquent silence, a screaming silence, a shouting silence." Wiesel broke his silence when he decided to write, and in each of his novels, excepting *The Town Beyond the Wall*, the protagonist is confronted with a similar problem and makes a similar decision. Related to the theme of silence is the theme of responsibility, which is expressed in breaking the silence.

To evoke accurately the ravaged soul of the survivor in the post-Holocaust world, Wiesel creates a society of characters different from those one is used to meeting in novels. The characters are beggars, witnesses, messengers, storytellers, and chroniclers

The Town Beyond the Wall

The Town Beyond the Wall, Wiesel's first novel after his three novellas, depicts his attempt to go home again. After his liberation from Buchenwald, Wiesel refused to return to his native town. He became, like the beggars or messengers in his stories, a *navenadnik*, a wanderer, a lost soul traveling throughout the world to find an inner peace and a place that he could call home. He traveled for ten years and finally, albeit accidentally, settled in the United States. It became home for him, however, only when he could totally and irrevocably sever his ties with his hometown. No matter where he went, he was drawn to the memories of his childhood, the familiarity and tranquillity of those days. He had to return at least once in order to realize that the Sighet of his youth no longer existed. It was a journey, as Wiesel says, to "nothingness."

The Town Beyond the Wall is divided into four parts and is presented in a series of reveries that help the protagonist cope with the torture imposed on him by his captors during his confinement in prison. Michael, a survivor of the Holocaust, has returned to his hometown of Szerencseváros with the aid of his friend, Pedro. The town is now under Communist rule, and he has entered it illegally. He is betrayed, imprisoned, and—because he remains silent and will not inform on his friend—is given the standard treatment, a torture called "The Prayer," which consists of keeping a prisoner on his feet facing a wall until he speaks or loses consciousness. To surmount the pain, Michael devises a method of transcending time by moving back and forth in his consciousness so that the present recedes to his subconscious level and the past moves forward into his consciousness. The reflections relating to his hometown are twice filtered, first as they are told to Pedro and then as he recalls them during his "prayers."

The pendular movement between different levels of consciousness, so that time is obliterated, is suggestive of Wiesel's imprisonment in the concentration camp. It is as if Wiesel is saying that time exists only in society. Once removed from society, people are also removed from time. In fact, they have no need for it. Time stops for them, but because time continues to move on for the world beyond their confinement, they will never be able to retrieve it.

Night hovers over *The Town Beyond the Wall*, as it hovered over Wiesel's first work. The protagonist is enveloped in a physical and psychological darkness. With his eyes closed, shutting out all light and consciousness, he evokes the nightmare world of his past, the fears of his childhood, his reflections on the Holocaust, the death of those who influenced him—Moché, the madman; Varady, his neighbor; Kalman, his teacher; his father; Yankel, his friend from the concentration camp—and the bleakness of life in France. An aspect of this nightmare world is his divided consciousness. This is suggested by the time and place in which he meets Pedro: in Tangiers, an hour before midnight in a dimly lit café, which is under a sign of a black cat. Pedro is his antagonist. He is what Saul Bellow would call "the Spirit of Alternatives." They walk the city together late at night. Pedro listens to Michael, providing him with alternatives to his dilemmas, answers to his questions, and a *modus vivendi*. He is a good friend. Their identities, at the conclusion, fuse, and when Michael is imprisoned, Pedro disappears, living only in Michael's memory in the form of an attitude toward life.

Through his relationship with Pedro, Michael comes to realize that silence in the form of indifference is destructive. People affirm their humanity when they involve themselves with or share in the anguish of humankind. To be a spectator of life is to deny life. That was the reason for Michael's return to Szerencseváros. He wanted to confront the spectator, the man who watched his Jewish neighbors being humiliated, looked on as the children cried of thirst, and then turned his back without any expression of emotion. That is why, at the end of the novel, he decides that he must reach out to his cell mate, who has rejected the world and now exists as a mute on the periphery of life. Michael knows that by restoring an interest in existence to his silent companion, he is also asserting his own essence, giving meaning to his own life. Wiesel later expands on this theme in *The Oath*.

In *The Town Beyond the Wall*, silence is viewed as detrimental. In the opening section, when Michael reflects on his childhood friendship with the renegade Varady, he notes that the community expresses its hatred for him through silence. In the next chapter, Michael's failure to respond to his friend's need results in Yankel's committing suicide. In the third section, Michael tells the tale of a mother and child who attempt to flee the Germans by hiding in the wagon of hay owned by a friendly neighbor who offers to take them to safety.

He tells them that their lives depend on their being silent. Silence, however, did not help them; they were killed when the Hungarian officers repeatedly stuck their bayonets through the hay. In the conclusion, Michael's silence, while it may have saved the life of Pedro, may also have cost him his own life.

Wiesel expresses his own equivocation regarding silence in this novel. Words may betray, words may deceive, but speech remains the only expression of civilized people. Language, when properly used and properly understood, is instructive and a means of creating a bond between people. It may not save the world, but it may save one human being. This is the lesson Wiesel learned from Mauriac, which caused him to break his vow.

Madness is presented as the opposite of silence. One takes refuge in being mute, the other in being vocal. The silent one sees without responding; the madman sees and reacts, usually through the use of words that other characters cannot comprehend or that they refuse to comprehend. Wiesel elaborates on this theme in the scene at the insane asylum in *A Beggar in Jerusalem*. In *The Town Beyond the Wall*, Pedro prevents Michael from joining the cadre of madmen. He tells him, "To see liberty only in madness is wrong." Madness is seen as a force of evil in this work. Michael's cell mate is mad; he sees things that are not there and says things that do not make sense, and he finally attempts to kill a third cell mate, Menachem.

It is significant that *The Town Beyond the Wall* ends in the cell. Michael is still a prisoner of his past. He is reaching out toward others, attempting to find his own identity, but he has not yet been able to do so. Wiesel's next novel deals with this problem; each of his novels, excluding *The Testament*, charts his journey away from *Night*.

THE GATES OF THE FOREST

While *The Town Beyond the Wall* examines the possibility of going home and acknowledges the impossibility of doing so, *The Gates of the Forest* concentrates on retrieving a lost name and the identity that goes with it. This novel also begins with night and imprisonment. The opening setting is not a cell but a cave in the forest. It is springtime, with its intimations of rebirth and regeneration, but the war once again casts its shadowy reflection over the entire work. Gavriel, a seventeen-year-old Jewish youth, has escaped deportation and is hiding from the German and Hungarian police. He has assumed the name of Gregor to increase his chances of remaining alive. His father was with him in hiding but had gone in search of food three days earlier, and he has not returned. Prior to his leaving, he had admonished his son not to break his silence and betray his whereabouts. A stranger, another Jew, makes his way to Gregor's hideout. The man has no name, and Gregor gives him his. The entire work is devoted to searching out the efficacy of silence and its relationship to an individual's identity.

The Gates of the Forest is also divided into four sections, alternating between the forest and the city. The first two sections establish the protagonist as a man of various masks. In the first section, he gives his name to a stranger who first jeopardizes and then saves his life. In section 2, he assumes two guises: that of a deaf-mute bastard child and that of the betrayer of Christ. After escaping from the forest, Gregor seeks refuge with Martha, the peasant woman who used to work for them. It is her idea that he disguise his identity and become the child of her wayward sister, Ileana. He assumes yet another identity in this village, when the school principal decides to stage a Passion play and bestows on him the part of Judas. Section 2 concludes with Gregor proclaiming his true self—Gavriel.

Now that he has pronounced his name, he has to labor at reclaiming his identity. The second half of the work is devoted to transforming the personality of Gregor into that of Gavriel: the estranged individual into a man of God. He does this by intimately relating to his own people and by refusing to be other than what he is. He joins a Jewish partisan group in the forest. When the war is ended, he meets Clara, who was also a partisan, and marries her. In New York, Gregor joins in a Hasidic celebration and gains an audience with a Hasidic Rebbe. He confronts him with all the problems that have afflicted him since the war, especially his inability to believe in God after what has happened. The Rebbe's answers provide him with a "gate" to the future. It is in the synagogue after his meeting with the Rebbe that Gavriel reclaims his name and his identity as a man of God.

The Rebbe and the stranger are Gregor's antagonists. The stranger at the beginning of the novel has the name Gavriel—"Man of God"; the Rebbe, at the end of the work, *is* the man of God. The stranger disappears early in the work, and Gregor's search for him proves futile. He thinks he sees Gavriel at the Rebbe's house of study, but it is an illusion, a dream. He sees, or dreams that he sees, only another stranger. He insists that the stranger listen to his story. The act of telling the story restores Gavriel's identity. He awakens from his dream knowing what he has to do: help Clara lay her ghosts to rest and restore his relationship with God. The work ends with his recitation of Kaddish, which, while it is a prayer for the dead, affirms the greatness of God. Once again, Wiesel concludes that silence is not a solution. Through the use of words, people not only speak to God but also become "messengers to heaven."

There is in this novel, as in all of Wiesel's novels, much autobiographical detail. Wiesel, as Gavriel-Gregor, the storyteller, presents his attitude toward the Germans, the Christians, and Europe itself, as well as the humanism of his father, the mysticism of his childhood, the isolation and ignorance of the Jews of Transylvania regarding their fate, his inability to cry, his guilt as a survivor, his going to France immediately after the war, his becoming a journalist and traveling to North Africa, the Far East, and the United States, his refusal to say Kaddish upon the death of his father, and his inability to believe in a God who remained silent during the Holocaust. Above all, this work charts the author's slow but certain return to religion and the Hasidism of his childhood. The visits to the Hasidic Rebbe are autobiographical, as is the search for a master or teacher. Wiesel continues to study with a Talmudic master and maintains a close relationship with a Hasidic rebbe in Brooklyn, New York.

Night, in this work, is significant as a general obfuscation of identity. The novel begins at night, in the cave with the protagonist who bears an assumed name, and it concludes in the morning, as Gavriel finds himself. Madness is a force of evil. It connotes the failure of rationality and describes the malady of the times, the frenzy of the mob. It is a condition from which one must be saved. Clara is on the verge of madness, and Gregor attempts to rescue her. The masters (or teachers), the stranger Gavriel, and the Rebbe are storytellers, and storytellers always bear messages. Gregor is both witness and messenger. In his role as Judas, he is witness to the madness of the peasants. Upon entering the partisan camp, he is a messenger bearing news from the outside, telling the group about the massacre of the townspeople. Later, he brings word of the death of Leib, leader of the partisans.

The work concludes in the season of winter with the ushering in of a new day. In its reconciliation with the past, the "gates of the forest" open onto a new life for Wiesel and his protagonists while not fully closing on the darkened phase of his youth.

A BEGGAR IN JERUSALEM

A Beggar in Jerusalem is a difficult novel. It is lyric, mystical, sensitive, yet powerful. Written in a mood of ecstasy, the seven-hundred-page first draft was condensed to its present length of slightly more than two hundred pages.

A Beggar in Jerusalem was galvanized by two crucial events in Wiesel's post-Holocaust life: a trip to Israel in 1967 and his marriage in 1968. At the outbreak of the Six-Day War in 1967, between the Arabs and Israelis, with its threat of extermination of the Jews once again, Wiesel went to Israel as a journalist. This work captures and records a victorious moment in Jewish history, the reunification of Jerusalem and, with it, the securing of the Wailing Wall. It also transmits the texture of this experience, the significance that Jerusalem embodies for Wiesel and the Jewish people. It is an emotional presentation, communicating the yearning of a people, the fulfillment of dreams, the "returning" home to Jerusalem. Wiesel was married in 1968 in a synagogue near the Wall. The novel is also a dedication to his wife, Marion. As such, it looks backward into his past and forward into the future. Like *The Town Beyond the Wall* and *The Gates of the Forest*, it, too, is a quest. In this novel, the search is for a new being. Wiesel does not want to rid himself of his past; it becomes an integral part of his life. The new being has to integrate his past experiences with his present identity and his future with his wife.

Silence is not a major issue in this work. It is the telling of tales and memory that are paramount. *A Beggar in Jerusalem* shifts between time periods, suggesting that contemporary events are meaningful only in the perspective of history. The joy of conquest is tempered with the sadness of two millennia of Jewish suffering. As in all Wiesel's works, the Holocaust forms the background and molds and shapes the events of this hauntingly beautiful novel. It is a paean to Jerusalem, but it does not extol the victors. There is no gaiety, no victory celebration. It is a somber novel that concentrates on the anticipation and fear that precede war, acknowledges the human torment that follows war, and focuses on the collective responsibility of humankind.

The aftermath of war is not glorious; instead of heroes, the novel offers a strange array of beggars, vagabonds, madmen, and storytellers. All are Holocaust survivors who left the camps with nothing, had no homes to which to return, were unwanted by everyone, and were treated like beggars everywhere—displaced persons whose lives take on meaning in the sharing of experiences. The beggars—Moché, the madman, among them—meet at night. They exchange tales of anguish as they debate God's justice and their own human condition.

David, the narrator of the work, is also a survivor of the Holocaust. As a representative of the past, he is the witness and the teller of tales. He interrupts the present tale of the Six-Day War with memories, the collective experiences of his people, and stories he has heard from others. He is a beggar and seeks out the company of other beggars, survivors like himself. This narrator-beggar ironically bears the name of the king of Israel, David. David's antagonist, Katriel, is an Israeli officer. He represents the present, a new generation that believes that it can alter its destiny. The work begins as a search for Katriel, who disappears after the war. David's and Katriel's stories move along separate lines, yet they are related. They meet during the war in the army camp and enter into a pact whereby they will remain together, each helping the other to conquer his fear. The survivor will bear witness for the other.

They remain together for the war and the victory. They are together at the Wailing Wall, and both observe the custom of writing a wish on a piece of paper that is slipped into a crack in the wall. The destiny of the antagonists of *The Town Beyond the Wall* and *The Gates of the Forest* befalls Katriel: He vanishes. No one knows what has happened to him. Actually, the personalities of Katriel and David have fused at the Wall in Jerusalem. The present has joined the past to create a new being. That David and Katriel are now one is suggested when David repeats to Malka, Katriel's wife, a story about a beggar told to him by Katriel. He then asks her, "But do you know who the beggar was? Sometimes I tell myself he was Katriel, he was I."

In this novel, Wiesel ends his quest. He no longer searches for a home. He has come to realize the validity of the words of a wandering preacher whom he met as a young boy—that all roads lead to Jerusalem. He also recalls the words of Katriel: "One doesn't go to Jerusalem, one returns to it." He no longer searches for identity or a new being; it has been reshaped by Jerusalem, "the city which miraculously transforms man into pilgrim; no one can enter it and go away unchanged." At the conclusion of *A Beggar in Jerusalem*, both the protagonist and his creator find that Jerusalem, the city of peace, is a concept one carries within oneself.

In *The Town Beyond the Wall* and *The Gates of the Forest*, the protagonists learn of the necessity to involve themselves in the life of other human beings. In *A Beggar in Jerusalem*, Wiesel moves from the single individual to the community: The beggars are comforted by the others in their group, Jewish people everywhere offer their support to the threatened Jewish state, and Israel wins the war, as the narrator states, with the aid of the six million who died.

THE OATH

Responsibility, both individual and collective, is the major theme of *The Oath*. In the works that preceded *The Oath*, especially *The Town Beyond the Wall* and *The Gates of the Forest*, the dramatic tension created by the desire for silence gave way to the practical need to speak, yet Wiesel continued to question his decision to speak. In *One Generation After*, he suggests that the horrors of the Holocaust might have been transmitted more eloquently and consequently more effectively by the abjuration of speech. Had the survivors "remained mute, their accumulated silences would have been unbearable: the impact would have deafened the world." *The Oath* addresses itself to this issue. It, too, is a personal statement in which Wiesel works out his own problems regarding his decision to break his vow of silence. *The Oath* seems to resolve the tensions created in the desire for silence, recognizing the futility of explanation and the need for speech. It does not, however, conclude Wiesel's concern with the issue, which he takes up once again in *The Testament*.

THE TESTAMENT

The Holocaust marked the destruction of East European Jewish life and culture. Not long after World War II, another area of Jewish culture was liquidated. On August 19, 1952, Stalin climaxed his infamous purge of Yiddish artists in the Soviet Union. On that day, thirty Yiddish writers were executed simply because they were Jewish. Hundreds more had been murdered earlier or were killed shortly afterward. These artists were consigned to oblivion, but Wiesel commemorates their achievements and bemoans their loss in *The Testament*. In so doing, he helps "the dead vanquish death."

Like Wiesel's earlier novels, *The Testament* is animated by the dramatic and dialectical tension between silence, or the "futility of all explanation," and the need to recount or bear witness. In this work, father and son are in opposition to each other. The father, Paltiel Kossover, an obscure poet, has substituted the god of Communism for the God of his forefathers, only to realize, too late, that his zeal is misdirected, that the new god has rejected him, and that his destiny is linked to his own people. This is the legacy he transmits to his son, in the form of a testament written in jail prior to his execution. The son, Grisha, a mute—he bit off his tongue so that he would not be able to testify against his father—reads the father's testament in an apartment in Jerusalem, to which he has come in 1972. The document was saved by a witness to the execution, Zupanev, a jailer who is determined not to allow Paltiel Kossover's memory to be obliterated.

The testament binds the present to the past, links the current tragedy to its historical predecessors. Zupanev says that Grisha, as a mute, is an "ideal messenger"—ideal because no one suspects him—who will be able to assimilate the events of the document into his consciousness and then recount them to future generations. Grisha's role as an effective witness is diminished, nevertheless, by his inability to speak.

Among Wiesel's novels, *The Testament* is the harshest in outlook and the darkest in vision. All his other works end on a note of optimism. This one does not. Only the setting of

Jerusalem illuminates the night of the novel. The work begins in hope, at the Lod airport, with the ingathering of the Russian exiles. It ends in death and in memory and indicates that Wiesel has little faith in the writer's ability to change humanity and human nature. It is his testament that "mankind didn't change." Nevertheless, Wiesel continues to write. One explanation for his persistence is suggested by the prologue to *The Testament*, which recounts an anecdote concerning a Just Man and his desire to correct injustice. He says: "In the beginning, I thought I could change man. Today, I know I cannot. If I still shout today, if I still scream, it is to prevent man from ultimately changing me."

THE FORGOTTEN

The Holocaust and its aftermath would remain powerful themes in Wiesel's writings, as he shows again in *The Forgotten*. The title refers to the things that are forgotten as well as to who is forgotten, for memory, remembrance, and mental and psychological forgetting are all important leitmotifs. Professor Elhanan Rosenbaum, Malkiel's increasingly sick and senile father, is rapidly losing his memory. To hold on to his dissolving past, he sends Malkiel to his native Carpathian village to retrace the family origins, a mission for which the son is highly qualified. As a *New York Times* reporter, Malkiel specializes in the dead, whether the victims of the Cambodian killing fields or the mighty of the obituary page. In President Nicolae Ceauşescu's Romania the reporter meets a philosophical Jewish gravedigger, who, through his tales told in the style of Hebraic storytellers, is both a witness of Nazi horrors and Jewish heroism and a repository of Jewish folklore and memory. Malkiel learns of his grandfather's self-sacrifice and of his father's courage and also of the fact that, as in so many German-occupied countries, most people actively participated in tracking and killing Jews or did nothing to save them. He also learns that the young Elhanan did not speak out while a comrade took revenge on their worst enemy by raping his widow, a silence that would haunt his father forever.

During lucid moments the father tells the son of his illegal entry into Palestine with Talia, his future wife, and of the intoxicating first days of Israel's independence, which symbolically and dramatically coincide with Malkiel's birth and Talia's death. Woven with the moving and passionate plea not to forget the dead are Malkiel's torturing liaisons with Inge the German and Leila the Arab, each of whom revives a special memory of hatred and pain. On the other hand, Tamar, his Jewish colleague and lover, presents him with a more difficult dilemma when she questions the conduct and ethics of modern-day Israel.

Only through legends, stories, eyewitness accounts—in short, words—can one hope to triumph over forgetfulness and ultimately death itself. From the power of words the spinner of tales survives, and so does his message, however incomplete and lost in the fog of memory. To seize and reassemble those shattered fragments of Elhanan's failing memory, Wiesel uses various narrative devices—letters, flashbacks, journal entries, tape recordings, prayers, unspoken dialogues—complemented by parables taken from Hasidic and Talmudic scholars.

Beginning with the publication of *Night* in 1956, Wiesel established himself as the bard of the Holocaust. *The Forgotten*, though, shines with a luminosity that was often absent from his earlier works, as if Wiesel had come out of his own Night Kingdom, scathed of course, but also full of hope and optimism. All is remembered; nothing is forgotten: "Thanks to him [Elhanan's grandson yet to be born], I shall live on; thanks to you, Abraham lives."

THE TIME OF THE UPROOTED

The Time of the Uprooted begins in 1939 as Gamaliel, a five-year-old Jewish boy, is spirited out of Nazi-overrun Czechoslovakia by his parents and taken to temporary safety in Hungary. When the Nazis overtake Hungary in 1944, Gamaliel's parents leave him with a cabaret singer, Ilonka, who lovingly rears the boy as a Christian, thereby protecting him from certain death in the Holocaust. After the war, Gamaliel is able to return the favor by saving Ilonka from the Russians, who think she was a German collaborator. In 1956, after the failed Hungarian Revolution, Gamaliel leaves Ilonka for a transcontinental odyssey through Vienna and Paris during which he has several unhappy affairs and a failed marriage that results in his wife's suicide and twin daughters who hate him. He drifts to New York City, where he has an unfulfilling career as a ghostwriter and, late in life, associates mostly with fellow refugees. A possible "ghost" from Gamaliel's past unexpectedly returns, however, when a doctor, Lili Rosenkrantz, draws him to the hospital bedside of a disfigured, silent, old Hungarian woman. Could this be Ilonka, his surrogate mother who saved him and whom he saved? The unidentified dying woman brings Gamaliel and Lili closer, and they are soon celebrating the Sabbath together.

In *The Time of the Uprooted*, Wiesel explores the themes of statelessness, perpetual itinerancy, and exile, both physical and psychic, and their damaging effects on the personal identity of the wanderer. Most of Gamaliel's problems, including his seeming incapacity for emotional intimacy, result from his being "uprooted" at an early age and therefore unable to feel that he truly belongs anywhere. Torn from his family's roots in Czechoslovakia, Gamaliel is searching, lost, and disconnected, a drifter from one random location and unfulfilling relationship to another. Even his career as a ghostwriter, in which his name fails to appear on his writing, symbolizes that he is hiding behind someone else, never feeling fully legitimate as his own person.

Wiesel also shows how, mostly without awareness, a person's past shapes who he or she is and who he or she becomes. In this powerful novel, as in all of his works, Wiesel explores the ways in which memory both holds humans captive to our pasts and reminds us of the courage and strength required to live nobly and fully despite our pasts. Through his attempts to explain Ilonka's goodness and heroism to Lili, Gamaliel begins to face where he comes from and who he is. He searches for the courage not to shove the past away but to accept it, to push through it and to find possible redemption for his failed life by beginning to live again. Gamaliel's powerful struggle parallels the challenging conundrum articulated by Wiesel in his Nobel Prize lecture. Wiesel implicitly addressed all Holocaust survivors, all of the cruelly "uprooted," when he said, "Because I remember, I despair. Because I remember, I have the duty to reject despair."

L. H. Goldman; Pierre L. Horn
Updated by Howard A. Kerner

Other major works

short fiction: *Le Chant des morts*, 1966 (essays and short stories; *Legends of Our Time*, 1968); *Entre deux soleils*, 1970 (essays and short stories; *One Generation After*, 1970); *Un Juif aujourd'hui*, 1977 (essays and short stories; *A Jew Today*, 1978).

plays: *Zalmen: Ou, La Folie de Dieu*, pb. 1968 (*Zalmen: Or, The Madness of God*, 1974); *Le Procès de Shamgorod tel qu'il se déroula le 25 février 1649*, pb. 1979 (*The Trial of God: As It Was Held on February 25, 1649, in Shamgorod*, 1979).

nonfiction: *Un di Velt hot geshvign*, 1956 (in Yiddish; in French as *La Nuit*, 1958; *Night*, 1960); *Les Juifs du silence*, 1966 (travel sketch; *The Jews of Silence*, 1966); *Discours d'Oslo*, 1987; *Le Mal et l'exil: Recontre avec Élie Wiesel*, 1988 (*Evil and Exile*, 1990); *From the Kingdom of Memory: Reminiscences*, 1990; *A Journey of Faith*, 1990 (with John Cardinal O'Connor); *Tous les fleuves vont à la mer*, 1994 (memoir; *All Rivers Run to the Sea*, 1995); *Et la mer n'est pas remplie*, 1996 (*And the Sea Is Never Full: Memoirs*, 1999); *Le Mal et l'exil: Dix ans après*, 1999; *Conversations with Elie Wiesel*, 2001 (Thomas J. Vinciguerra, editor); *After the Darkness: Reflections on the Holocaust*, 2002; *Elie Wiesel: Conversations*, 2002 (Robert Franciosi, editor); *Wise Men and Their Tales: Portraits of Biblical, Talmudic, and Hasidic Masters*, 2003; *Confronting Anti-Semitism*, 2006 (with Kofi Annan).

children's literature: *King Solomon and His Magic Ring*, 1999.

miscellaneous: *Célébration hassidique*, 1972-1981 (2 volumes; biographical sketches and stories; volume 1, *Souls on Fire*, 1972; volume 2, *Somewhere a Master: Further Hasidic Portraits and Legends*, 1982); *Ani Maamin: Un Chant perdu et retrouvé*, 1973 (cantata; *Ani Maamin: A Song Lost and Found Again*, 1973); *Célébration biblique*, 1975 (biographical sketches and stories; *Messengers of God: Biblical Portraits and Legends*, 1976); *Four Hasidic Masters and Their Struggle Against Melancholy*, 1978 (biographical sketches and stories); *Images from the Bible*, 1980 (biographical sketches and stories); *Five Biblical Portraits*, 1981 (biographical sketches and stories); *Paroles d'étranger*, 1982 (biographical sketches and stories); *Somewhere a Master*, 1982 (biographical sketches and stories); *The Six Days of Destruction: Meditations Towards Hope*, 1988 (with Albert H. Friedlander); *Silences et mémoire d'hommes: Essais, histoires, dialogues*, 1989; *Célébration talmudique: Portraits et légendes*, 1991; *Sages and Dreamers: Biblical, Talmudic, and Hasidic Portraits and Legends*, 1991; *Célébration prophétique: Portraits et légendes*, 1998; *Celebrating Elie Wiesel: Stories, Essays, Reflections*, 1998 (Alan Rosen, editor).

Bibliography

Berenbaum, Michael. *Elie Wiesel: God, the Holocaust, and the Children of Israel.* West Orange, N.J.: Behrman House, 1994. Reprint of *The Vision of the Void*, Berenbaum's thoughtful 1979 study of Wiesel, emphasizes Wiesel's insights about Jewish tradition.

Bloom, Harold, ed. *Elie Wiesel's "Night."* New York: Chelsea House, 2001. Collection of critical essays represents the spectrum of responses to Wiesel's memoir, which holds an important place in his body of work.

Cargas, Harry James. *Conversations with Elie Wiesel.* South Bend, Ind.: Justice Books, 1992. Updated and expanded edition of Cargas's 1976 interviews with Wiesel features Wiesel's own words on topics that include the Holocaust as well as his audience, his craft, and his mission as a witness and writer.

Downing, Frederick L. *Elie Wiesel: A Religious Biography.* Macon, Ga.: Mercer University Press, 2008. Analyzes Wiesel's life and writings, with a focus on the influence of his profound religious faith.

Horowitz, Rosemary, ed. *Elie Wiesel and the Art of Storytelling.* Jefferson, N.C.: McFarland, 2006. Collection of scholarly essays focuses on the ways in which Wiesel's cultural background has influenced his writing and how he maintains the Jewish storytelling tradition. Provides a critical examination of his writing style and the content of his works.

Katz, Steven, and Alan Rosen, eds. *Obliged by Memory: Literature, Religion, Ethics.* Syracuse, N.Y.: Syracuse University Press, 2005. In honor of Wiesel's seventieth birthday, such renowned scholars as Geoffrey Hartman and Cynthia Ozick contribute valuable essays to this collection of insights into the core of Wiesel's writing.

Kolbert, Jack. *The Worlds of Elie Wiesel: An Overview of His Career and His Major Themes.* Snelinsgrove, Pa.: Susquehanna University Press, 2001. Offers a useful starting point for the beginning student of Wiesel's work. Combines biography with literary and philosophical analysis.

Mass, Wendy, ed. *Readings on "Night."* New York: Greenhaven Press, 2000. Includes biographical chapters, a summary of the plot and characters of Wiesel's book, and discussion of the major themes, the author's art, relationships in the novel, literary interpretation, and the legacy of the book.

Rosen, Alan, ed. *Celebrating Elie Wiesel: Stories, Essays, Reflections.* Notre Dame, Ind.: University of Notre Dame Press, 1998. Distinguished scholars reflect on the ethical and religious dimensions of Wiesel's essays and novels.

Sibelman, Simon P. *Silence in the Novels of Elie Wiesel.* New York: St. Martin's Press, 1995. Presents a thorough, intelligent, and stimulating discussion of a dominant theme in Wiesel's fiction.

Sternlicht, Sanford. *A Student Companion to Elie Wiesel.* Westport, Conn.: Greenwood Press, 2003. Presents critical analysis of all of Wiesel's major fiction and nonfiction works and relates the works to Wiesel's own life stories. Intended for general readers.

HERMAN WOUK

Born: New York, New York; May 27, 1915

PRINCIPAL LONG FICTION

Aurora Dawn, 1947
The City Boy, 1948
The Caine Mutiny, 1951
Marjorie Morningstar, 1955
Slattery's Hurricane, 1956
Youngblood Hawke, 1962
Don't Stop the Carnival, 1965
The Lomokome Papers, 1968
The Winds of War, 1971
War and Remembrance, 1978
Inside, Outside, 1985
The Hope, 1993
The Glory, 1994
A Hole in Texas, 2004

OTHER LITERARY FORMS

Herman Wouk (wohk) wrote several plays; the first, *The Traitor*, was produced on Broadway in 1949 and was published by Samuel French the same year. His most successful theatrical work, *The Caine Mutiny Court-Martial* (based on his novel published in 1951), appeared on Broadway in 1954 and was published by Doubleday the same year. *Nature's Way* was produced on Broadway in 1957 and was published by Doubleday the following year. Eric Bentley, speaking of *The Caine Mutiny Court-Martial*, said that Wouk showed a gift for crisp dialogue that no other regular writer for the American theater could rival. The musical *Don't Stop the Carnival*, a collaboration with pop musician Jimmy Buffett, was produced in 1998. Wouk collaborated with Richard Murphy in writing the screenplay for *Slattery's Hurricane* (1949). Wouk also wrote teleplays, for *The Winds of War* (1983) and *War and Remembrance* (1988). *This Is My God*, which Wouk first published in 1959 and followed with a revised edition in 1973, is a description and explanation of Orthodox Judaism, especially as it is practiced in America. The volume was a Reader's Digest Condensed Book Club selection and an alternate selection for the Book-of-the-Month Club in 1959.

ACHIEVEMENTS

It is a peculiarity of American criticism to denigrate popular success in literature. Almost from the outset of his career, Herman Wouk was a very popular writer; putting aside prejudicial presuppositions, this can be acknowledged as a genuine achievement, for Wouk did not attain his popular status by catering to the baser tastes of his readers. Beginning with *The Caine Mutiny*, his books appeared regularly on best-seller lists. Several of his titles were selections of major book clubs. Wouk was awarded the Pulitzer Prize for fiction in 1952 for *The Caine Mutiny*. That same year, Columbia University presented him its Medal of Excellence, an honor extended to distinguished alumni. Several universities awarded him honorary doctorates.

Wouk might be described as a traditional novelist, in that his writing does not reflect the experimental qualities that are to be found in so much twentieth and twenty-first century American fiction. As with John Updike, he gives primacy of place to the narrative element in fiction; he brings to the novel his own peculiar brand of rough-hewn vigor. At a time when conventional wisdom judged it bad form for a novelist to take a clear stand on moral issues—as if ambiguity itself were a virtue—Wouk consistently declared his moral position in his writings. This was not always to the benefit of his fiction, but by and large, his novels are stronger for his conviction that literary art does not subsist in a vacuum but is part of a larger moral universe.

BIOGRAPHY

Herman Wouk was born in New York City on May 27, 1915, the son of Abraham Isaac and Esther (Levine) Wouk. Wouk's father, an industrialist in the power laundry field, started out as an immigrant laundry worker earning three dollars a week. Wouk was educated at Townsend Harris Hall and at Columbia University, where he graduated with honors in 1934. While at Columbia, he studied philosophy and comparative literature and was editor of the *Columbia Jester*. From 1934 to 1935 he worked as a gag writer for radio comedians, and from 1936 to 1941, he was a scriptwriter for Fred Allen. In 1941, Wouk moved to Washington, D.C., following his appointment to the U.S. Treasury Department as a dollar-a-year man; his job was to write and produce radio shows to sell war bonds.

Wouk left this work to join the Navy. After completing Officer Candidate School, he was commissioned an ensign and assigned to mine sweeper duty in the Pacific fleet. He served in the Navy from 1942 to 1945, first aboard the USS *Zane* and then aboard the destroyer-minesweeper USS *Southard*. Eventually, he was promoted to the position of executive officer of the *Southard*. He was decorated with four campaign stars during the war, and received a unit citation as well. When Wouk was processed out of the Navy in 1945, he held the rank of lieutenant. Wouk married Betty Sarah Brown in December, 1945. They had three sons, Abraham Isaac (who died before reaching his fifth birthday), Nathaniel, and Joseph.

Wouk began his career as a serious writer while he was in the Navy; before his release from the service, he had completed a good portion of his first novel. That novel, *Aurora Dawn*, was published by Simon and Schuster in 1947. The following year he published his second novel, *The City Boy*. Neither of these works gained a great deal of attention for

Wouk, but with the publication of *The Caine Mutiny* in 1951 (awarded the Pulitzer Prize the following year), he was quickly established as a writer of consequence. His play *The Caine Mutiny Court-Martial* began its successful run on Broadway in 1954. *Marjorie Morningstar* appeared in 1955 and his nonfiction work on Jewish culture and religion, *This Is My God*, appeared in 1959. The 1960's saw the publication of *Youngblood Hawke* and *Don't Stop the Carnival*. Wouk's sprawling two-volume fictional account of World War II, which he began writing in 1962, was published in the 1970's; the first volume, *The Winds of War*, appeared in 1971, and the second, *War and Remembrance*, was published in 1978. Wouk wrote the teleplay for the eighteen-hour television film based on *The Winds of War*, which was broadcast during the week of February 6-13, 1983. He was coauthor of the teleplay for the television adaptation of *War and Remembrance*, which appeared in 1988.

Unlike many contemporary popular novelists, Wouk shunned the public spotlight throughout his career. Though the Wouks spent more than a decade after they were married in New York, they moved to the Virgin Islands in 1958, partly so that Wouk could find a place to write free of interruptions. In 1964, the family moved to Georgetown, a Washington, D.C., suburb, so that he could be closer to archival materials he needed to consult to write *The Winds of War* and *War and Remembrance*. During the next three decades, Wouk divided his time between his home in the nation's capital and one in Palm Springs, California, occasionally appearing at public events to accept awards or participate in fund-raising or religious events. In 1995, Wouk entered into an agreement with popular singer Jimmy Buffett to write the book for a musical based on *Don't Stop the Carnival*. Featuring a number of Caribbean songs composed by Buffett, the musical opened in Florida in 1997 and moved to Broadway in 1998.

Wouk's great popular success enabled him to devote his full time to his craft, but on occasion he took academic or semiacademic positions. From 1953 to 1957, he was a visiting professor of English at Yeshiva University, and during 1973-1974, he was scholar-in-residence at the Aspen Institute for Humanistic Studies. He was a member of the Authors Guild and the Dramatists Guild, and he served on the board of directors for institutions and organizations such as the College of the Virgin Islands, the Washington National Symphony, and Kennedy Center Productions.

Analysis

Herman Wouk is a novelist in the tradition of the great English novelists of the nineteenth century; he is also a spiritual descendant of such American writers as James Fenimore Cooper, William Dean Howells, Theodore Dreiser, and James T. Farrell. What he has in common with these writers is narrative prowess, a commitment to realism, and a lively moral consciousness. Furthermore, like these writers, Wouk addresses himself to the population at large. Since World War II, American fiction has seen a distinction between writers who seem inclined to write primarily for other writers or for academic critics and those inclined to write for a general audience. That Wouk is numbered among the latter would appear to be traceable to a definite decision on his part.

Wouk's first novel, *Aurora Dawn*, has the flavor of the experimental fiction that began to proliferate in the postwar period. If one were to have speculated in 1946 on the course that Wouk's literary career was going to take, it would have been a safe guess to say that he would probably continue down the road of experimentation, that he would become more and more concerned with language as an end in itself, and that eventually, he would be writing books destined to be read only in upper-division English courses in universities. This was not what happened, however; in his second novel, *The City Boy*, Wouk followed a conventional narrative pattern and told his story in language that was not constantly calling attention to itself.

In *Aurora Dawn* and *The City Boy*, Wouk was still stretching his muscles and attempting to find his proper level as a writer. He came into his own with *The Caine Mutiny*. In that novel, and in every novel that followed for the next four decades, there is the presence of a central theme, treated in various ways and from varying perspectives. The theme is the conflict between traditional values and a modern consciousness that is either indifferent to those values or flatly antipathetic toward them. The conflict is not treated in abstract terms, but in terms of individuals who are caught up in it, and how the individual fares is in great part determined by the side with which he chooses to ally himself.

AURORA DAWN

Aurora Dawn, which Wouk began writing while serving as an officer in the Navy, is an effort at satire. The butt of the satire is the advertising industry and, more generally, the foolishness of anyone in business whose ethical consciousness is dimmed by avarice. The moral of the story is explicit: Greed is the root of all evil. Andrew Reale, the novel's young protagonist, is bright, energetic, and imaginative, but until he undergoes a conversion at novel's end, his primary concern is getting ahead. He wants to be successful above all else, and to him, success means money. In his scramble to get to the top as quickly as possible, his myopia becomes acute and his values are severely twisted. He is willing to make compromises where compromises should not be made. A connection is intimated between Reale's moral weakness and his failure to continue to adhere to the religious principles according to which he was reared, a recurring theme in Wouk's fiction.

Reale's obsessive pursuit of success leads him to jilt his fiancé, the beautiful and innocent Laura Beaton, so that he can take up with the beautiful but frivolous Carol Marquis, daughter of the despicable but very rich Talmadge Marquis. It leads him to be crassly manipulative in his dealings with the Reverend Calvin Stanfield, who is simple, straightforward, and a good man. Finally, it leads him, in a move of pure expediency, to quit an employer who has been generous with him so that he can join forces with Talmadge Marquis. All Reale's machinations, however, are to no avail. The hastily courted Carol Marquis runs off with an eccentric painter, and Laura Beaton, brokenhearted at Reale's rejection of her, marries an older man. In the end, Reale gets better than he deserves. His thwarted attempt to blackmail Father Stanfield proves to be the occasion of a conversion experience for him. He suddenly sees the wickedness of his ways and decides to alter his course. Laura Beaton is miraculously released from her unconsummated marriage, so that Reale is able to get the woman of his dreams after all. Fleeing the wicked city, the bride and groom go off to live together in New Mexico.

The novel is not realistic and cannot be judged according to the criterion of verisimilitude. It is a light, playful work in which humor plays an important part. Despite several brilliant passages, however, the novel does not come across as successful satire, and that would seem to be attributable to the fact that Wouk is vacillating and hesitant in what he wants to say. What he takes with one hand, he gives back with the other. The novel is clever, in both good and bad senses. While its language is often lively, it can as well be pretentious and self-conscious at times. The anachronistic devices of addressing the reader directly, inserting explicit authorial commentary on the action, and interspersing the narrative with short philosophical asides do not always work to maximize the effect. The humor of the novel is capable of being right on the mark, but for the most part it is a bit forced; Wouk, the radio gagman, is too much in evidence. The flaws to be found in *Aurora Dawn* are flaws that are not uncommon in a first novel. Despite its weaknesses, however, already in evidence in this work are the two traits that have subsequently become the chief strengths of Wouk's fiction: a vigorous talent for narrative and a lively sensitivity to moral issues.

THE CITY BOY

Perhaps the most striking thing about Wouk's second novel, *The City Boy*, is that, stylistically, it represents a marked departure from the standards he had established in his first novel. The language of the work does not call attention to itself; it is clear, straightforward, and unpretentious. The novel is humorous in tone, and its plot structure is loose.

The book revolves around the adventures—most of which take place in an upstate summer camp—of a New York City boy, Herbie Bookbinder. John P. Marquand's comparison of this novel with Mark Twain's *The Adventures of Tom Sawyer* (1876) is well-founded. In many respects, Herbie is an urban version of the scamp from the midwestern frontier. He is a bright and enterprising lad, and if he is mischievous at times, it is seldom with malice. Much of what he does is calculated to impress Lucille Glass, the object of his single-minded puppy love. Herbie is unlike Tom Sawyer in that he is an outsider as far as other boys are concerned, largely because of his poor athletic skills and his penchant for things intellectual. A goodly number of Herbie's efforts in the novel are given over to his attempts to gain the status of a regular guy. He succeeds, finally, and as a result is welcomed into the full fellowship of his peers. *The City Boy* is a light novel—in some respects a boy's book—but in it, Wouk's moral consciousness is manifested by his underscoring the difference between good and evil in the actions of the characters.

THE CAINE MUTINY

The Caine Mutiny is Wouk's best novel, the work on which his reputation rests. The novel takes place against the backdrop of war, but it cannot be regarded as a "war story" in any simplistic sense. It is a story about the subtle and complicated relationships that exist among men who are part of the enclosed world that constitutes the military establishment. One of its central themes concerns the matter of authority—how it is exercised within a military context, and how it is abused. The novel explores the manner in which various personality types act and react within a hierarchical, authoritarian structure. In addition, it examines the ways in which the lives of those caught up in the trauma of war are altered, sometimes profoundly. Other themes that the novel treats are loyalty and disloyalty, patriotism, doers versus sayers, personal integrity, and the process by which young men are tested in stressful situations.

The Caine Mutiny can easily be misread. One might conclude that its chief concern is the everlasting battle between despotism and democracy, that Captain Queeg therefore is clearly the villain of the piece, and that its heroes are Lieutenant Maryk, Willie Keith, Tom Keefer, and the others who were involved in the mutiny. It is not that simple. If it were, *The Caine Mutiny* would be little more than a melodrama. Captain Queeg is not a hero, but neither is he a diabolical type. He is a sorry human being; he has serious personal problems (his eccentricity is not amusing—he is, in fact, a sick man); and, perhaps most serious, given his status as a commanding officer, he is incompetent professionally. For all that, he is consistent in trying to do his job to the best of his ability. Queeg's problem is that he is in over his head; he can at times scarcely cope with situations that are his duty to control. The circumstances surrounding the event that lead to the mutiny are sufficiently ambiguous as to render doubtful the claim of the mutineers that, had they not relieved Queeg of command when they did, the ship would have been lost.

Wouk's assessment of the situation seems to be communicated most directly through the character of Lieutenant Greenwald, the young aviator-lawyer who defends Maryk at the court-martial. Greenwald is not sympathetic with the mutineers, but he decides to defend Maryk because he respects the executive officer's personal integrity and because he is convinced that Maryk, in assuming command of the *Caine* during the typhoon, was acting in good faith. Greenwald succeeds in having Maryk acquitted of the charge of mutiny, mainly by drawing out of Queeg in the courtroom telltale signs of his emotional instability, but he takes no joy in his victory.

After the trial, Greenwald puts the damper on the victory celebration being staged by the *Caine*'s officers when he gives them a stinging tonguelashing. His ire is directed particularly at Tom Keefer, whom he perceives correctly as being the chief instigator of the mutiny, but one who refused, when the matter came to a head, to put himself on the line. Greenwald's position seems to be that, while the *Caine*'s officers are legally innocent, they are morally guilty. However sophisticated a rationale they might provide for their actions, what was at the bottom of those actions, in his view, was disloyalty, and disloyalty, for a military officer, is an unforgivable sin. One might say that the trial does not prove either clear-cut guilt or innocence. If anything, it demonstrates the complexity and ambiguity of all human situations. Greenwald's position is that, given the ambiguity, it is always better not to second-guess legitimately constituted authority. It is the chief responsibility of the naval officer to do his duty through thick and thin.

If there is a clear villain in *The Caine Mutiny*, Tom Keefer would appear to be the most likely candidate for the role. Keefer is, in many respects, a preeminently modern man. He is committed to what he presumably regards as the absolute truths of Freudian psychology, which he employs in a reductionist way, as weapons against those who do not share his worldview. He is in the Navy, but not of it, and, in fact, he rather enjoys and exploits his position as an iconoclastic outsider. He maintains an attitude of supercilious superiority toward people such as Queeg, and toward everything that the Navy represents. His view is narrow, restricted by the dictates of his overriding egotism. Keefer is a carping critic of the Navy, but he does not hesitate to take selfish advantage of what the Navy can offer him at every turn. His hypocrisy allows him to talk a big game, but when the pressure is on and when circumstances call for words to be translated into action, he invariably backs off. Perhaps the most damning thing that could be said of Keefer is that he is a coward, as he demonstrates when he is captain of the *Caine* and precipitously abandons ship. By the novel's end, however, Keefer seem to have arrived at a degree of self-awareness that hitherto had eluded him; he confesses to Willie Keith, who succeeds him as commanding officer, that Keith is a better man than he. He is right.

Willie Keith is the central character of the novel; his moral education is the real subject of *The Caine Mutiny*. Willie is an aristocratic rich kid from New York who comes to learn, among other things, the value of democracy. His relationship with Maria Minotti, alias May Wynn, can be interpreted in this way. The bulk of Keith's education, however, takes place in the Navy. When he first comes aboard the *Caine*, he is very much under the influence of Keefer, and he accepts Keefer's cynical interpretation of things as the correct one. Eventually, Keith realizes that the Navy, though imperfect, is not a bad organization. What is more, given the realities of the modern world, it is a necessary organization. Unlike Keefer, Keith is prepared to acknowledge that the Navy in World War II is contributing toward the preservation of the way of life into which both men have been born and to which they are devoted, and that, excepting a total transformation of human nature, navies will probably always be needed to ensure the protection of people's freedom. Keith is not changed into a mindless patriot and militarist, but his criticism of the Navy and its personnel becomes more discriminate, more intelligent, more responsible. He learns to judge matters according to criteria that are not self-centered and develops an appreciation for the larger scheme of things. He takes pride in his work, and, as he rises in rank, his conscientiousness increases; he tries to be the best officer he can.

The world of the Navy in *The Caine Mutiny* is in certain respects a microcosm of the world at large. It is beset by all sorts of problems, but there is no perfect alternative somewhere to which one might flee. A person's maturity is measured by his or her ability to establish standards of excellence and to work assiduously to achieve them in spite of various limitations, sometimes severe—limitations in him- or herself, in others, and in the situation.

MARJORIE MORNINGSTAR

On the surface, Wouk's fourth novel, *Marjorie Morningstar*, would seem to lead nowhere. It is the story of a young Jewish woman, the daughter of immigrants established comfortably in the middle class of New York, who has been sufficiently Americanized as to have for her chief ambition the desire to become a famous actor, a star. Marjorie Morningstar (née Morgenstern) is a beautiful woman whose theatrical talent, while not scintillating, is probably sufficient to underwrite the realization of her dream, given a lucky break here and there. She is willing to make the sacrifices, within certain bounds, and to invest the hard work that the ascent to stardom inevitably entails. If Marjorie is determined about anything, it is that she is not going to allow herself to lapse into the staid, conventional life that is the destiny of the vast majority of nice, middle-class Jewish girls. She is going to be different; she is going to break out of the mold.

After several fruitless efforts to break into the theater and to make it big, after a sequence of adventures with an assortment of men, chiefly with Noel Airman, Marjorie ends up doing what she vowed she would never do. She marries a Jew, a successful lawyer by the name of Milton Schwartz, and she retires to a plush suburb to live the most conventional of conventional lives. The novel, then, would seem to end on an almost laughably anticlimactic note, but only if one fails to perceive the kind of statement that it is attempting to make.

If *The Caine Mutiny* delineates the education of Willie Keith, the education of Marjorie Morningstar is the primary concern of the novel that bears her name. If Marjorie comes full circle, as it were, and ends by embracing the conventional, it is because she discovers that the conventional is worthy of being embraced, the conventional not only as representing middle-class morality but also, and much more important, as embodying traditional cultural and religious values. The glamorous life to which Marjorie aspired, whether or not she was always fully conscious of the fact, was a life that repudiated traditional values. As a teenager and young woman, she fought her own tradition, particularly as manifested in the Jewish religion; she viewed it as crude and superstitious, a carryover from humankind's primitive past. This tradition, however, was more deeply embedded in her, was more integral a part of her identity, than she was willing to admit, and throughout her various experiences it guided her actions more than she knew.

Marjorie's failure to realize her dream of becoming a star actually represents the triumph of her better, truer self. Her concern shifts from thin, superficial values to those with substance and depth. The drama of her quest for self-realization is played out principally around her long and erratic affair with Noel Airman. When she first meets Noel, who is some ten years her senior, she is scarcely more than a girl, and she is completely enamored of him. He is handsome, intelligent, urbane, and witty, a talented composer of popular songs who shows promise of becoming a success in the theater. Noel represents much of what she wants to become, and all of what she has decided is most valuable in life, which is emphasized by the fact that she throws decorum to the winds and pursues him actively. When she finally catches him, however, she realizes that she does not really want him. The man who was once her ideal, her hero, the man whom she wanted to marry more than anyone else, is at last perceived, albeit faintly, as a god with clay feet.

Who is this Noel Airman? He is Saul Ehrmann, one who has actively repudiated his Jewish identity and its associated traditions but who has failed to come up with a viable substitute for either. He is a rootless vagabond, a shameless Casanova, one who eschews commitment as a matter of principle, and who tries hard to make a profession of cynicism. It would be wrong, however, to think of him entirely in negative terms. He is not a character lacking in complexity, and he is not devoid of critical self-knowledge, which at times can be acute and penetrating. Still, this self-awareness serves only to accentuate his pathetic quality, for in the final analysis, he is impotent to act on his better impulses. He does not have the moral stamina to follow through, and this is so, Wouk implies, precisely because he has cut himself off from his tradition.

The fact that Marjorie arrives at a new state of consciousness that allows her to see Noel for what he is, and accordingly to reject him, is attributable in part to her brief but fateful acquaintance with Michael Eden. Michael, like Noel, is a Jew, but, unlike Noel, he is not in flight from the fact. He is a strong, taciturn man whose personal sufferings have led him to dedicate himself to a melancholy but determined altruism. He is involved in the very risky business of rescuing Jews from Nazi Germany. He is every bit as bright and talented as Noel but has what Noel lacks—integrity and a sense of purpose in life. Although it is not Marjorie's destiny to marry Michael, meeting him has the effect of altering her perception of Noel. Milton Schwartz, the person she marries, has in common with Michael a fundamental decency.

YOUNGBLOOD HAWKE

Wouk's sixth novel, *Youngblood Hawke*, based to some extent on the life of Thomas Wolfe, could be the story of many young American writers of the twentieth century, and for that reason, the novel, besides its intrinsic worth as a work of fiction, has considerable value as a historical document. The story of Arthur Youngblood Hawke is a success story, but it is a story of failure as well. Indeed, Hawke's case is in many respects a tragic one. Hawke is a lanky, down-home Kentuckian who, after being released from the Navy at the end of World War II, moves to New York to conquer the city and the country, by his pen. He comes to his task with a spotty education, with an explosive imagination, and with a seemingly boundless store of energy. Writing is his life, and his engagement in it is passionate.

There is much about Hawke that smacks of the all-American boy. He is crude and unpolished, but straightforward and gentle in his dealings with people—except with those who deserve otherwise. He is honest, in his way, and an assiduous worker. He wants to be a success as a writer. He wants to become a millionaire, not so that he can give up writing but so that, freed from financial worries, he can devote himself to it without distractions. Hawke is in the mold of the rustic innocent who has long played a part in American literature.

Hawke's early success works against him in the long run. His first novel, though receiving rough treatment at the hands of the critics, gains a large popular audience; his second novel wins the Pulitzer Prize and increasing respect from the critics. He is associated with a solid, respectable publishing house whose head values his work, has faith in his future, and is willing to be very generous in making contractual arrangements with him. Hawke's obsessional longing for financial independence, however, prompts him to break ties with his publisher and begin publishing his own books; he also makes some risky investments. His luck turns, and in a matter of months he finds himself on the threshold of bankruptcy. He determines that he is going to write his way out of his debts; leaving behind the plush life that he enjoyed only too briefly in New York, he returns to Kentucky, and there, living in a cabin in the woods, he works furiously to complete what proves to be his final novel. In fact, he overworks, devoting himself not only to the novel but also, earlier, to a theatrical production that he hopes will strike it rich. The strain brought about by his frenetic activities exacerbates an old head injury, and, after a wild chase to South America made in a state of delirium, he ends up back in New York. He is hospitalized there and dies at the age of thirty-three.

As Hawke lies dying, his vaguely addressed prayer is that he might be given more time so that he can work. Everything that he has done he considers as only preparatory exercises to his great multivolume *Comedy*. That his magnum opus was never written is not simply attributable to the fact that Hawke showed poor business sense or that he was careless of his health. There is evidence in the novel to warrant the conclusion that Hawke's failure to fulfill his chief artistic ambition amounts to an exacting payment he has had to make for his sins. There have been two principal women in his life but, by his own admission, there should have been only one.

In the beginning of the novel, before he bursts upon the American literary scene, Hawke meets a young editor, Jeanne Green, who subsequently becomes for him what Maxwell Perkins was for Thomas Wolfe. Jeanne, besides being a very talented editor, is, like Hawke, essentially a small-town person. She is simple, unpretentious, genuine. Hawke falls in love with her almost immediately—his better self tells him that this is the woman in his life, the woman he should marry—but he becomes involved in a torrid affair with a wealthy, sophisticated, fundamentally selfish New Yorker, Frieda Winters. Winters is older than he; she is married, has three children, and is no stranger to adulterous affairs. Hawke is honest enough with himself to admit that he is involved in adultery; the reader is told that he hates both the word and the fact. He does not have the moral courage, however, to extricate himself from the affair—not until, as it turns out, it is too late. His relationship with Winters proves to be an enervating experience; if it does not exactly destroy him, it contributes substantially toward his destruction.

What allowed Hawke to become involved in an affair that he knew to be wrong? One explanation is that he failed to be true to the basic religious principles that he had been taught as a boy but that in his impetuous youth he attempted to reject. Unlike Marjorie Morningstar, whose roots in a religious tradition were sufficiently deep and tenacious to carry her through the hard times, Hawke succumbs to the facile moral standards of a secularized society.

DON'T STOP THE CARNIVAL

Wouk's next novel, *Don't Stop the Carnival*, is the weakest of his entire corpus. It is a comic novel and it would seem to have some kind of satiric intent, but the humor, instead of carrying the moral import of the tale, more often than not obstructs it. The work's humor is hampered by obtrusive, heavy-handed moralizing, and its seriousness is trivialized by a humor that too often degenerates into tedious slapstick. Most damaging for the novel is that Wouk's narrative talent, which is his forte, serves him poorly here. The plot is too often based on contrivance, and in some instances blatant authorial manipulation is very much in evidence. Add to this fact that characterization is unconvincing, and the sum total is a generally undistinguished piece of fiction that holds the reader's attention only by an adamant act of will. It is not that the novel is completely lacking in substance, but the detectably substantive elements are not allowed to emerge fully. There is, for example, a statement being made about the haplessness of "liberal" types who are awash in a world that in many respects is the result of their own brand of thinking, but the message is befuddled by static of various kinds and one must strain to detect it.

THE WINDS OF WAR *and* WAR AND REMEMBRANCE

Wouk's impressive companion novels, *The Winds of War* and *War and Remembrance*, published in 1971 and 1978, respectively, are in effect a single, sustained work of fiction, and therefore can be discussed together. Wouk spent sixteen years in completing the work, and it seems likely that he regards it as his magnum opus. *The Winds of War* is focused primarily on the European theater during World War II, beginning with the German invasion of Czechoslovakia and Poland, putting special emphasis on the latter. The Battle of Britain is also treated at close range. The book ends with the bombing of Pearl Harbor, the point at which *War and Remembrance* takes up the story. This book, while continuing to trace the course of events in Europe, especially those events having to do with the systematic extermination of the Jews by the Nazis, shifts attention to the Pacific theater and provides poignant descriptions of the major naval battles fought there. The book ends with the dropping of the atomic bombs and the Japanese acceptance of unconditional surrender.

In these two massive volumes, which constitute a single work, an ambitious fictional history of World War II, Wouk once again shows himself to be a master of narrative. This is not a mere chronicle of events; rather, major events of the war are given dramatic immediacy by the tactic of having one of the many key characters in the narrative involved in those events. One is even provided access to the Axis point of view through excerpts from the analytic histories of the German general Armin von Roon, interspersed throughout the work.

The key character in the work is Victor "Pug" Henry, a naval officer who has given thirty years of his life to military service. He is a staid, conservative man, a patriot but not a jingoist, dedicated to professional excellence and quietly guided by deeply embedded religious principles. Following his various adventures in Europe and in the Pacific, one is not only brought into direct contact with important historical personages but treated to his thoughtful reactions to them as well. Wouk is the type of artist who likes to paint on a large canvas, but the canvas he is covering in this work is of mammoth proportions. All the more remarkable, then, is the control he exercises here; nothing gets away from him. There is about this wide-ranging tour de force a satisfying unity and completeness. It is thickly peopled with a vast array of characters, and their attitudes toward the war run the full gamut from self-sacrificing heroism to cold-blooded murderousness.

One of the most interesting characters in the work is Aaron Jastrow, a Jewish American, world renowned scholar and former Yale professor who at the outbreak of the war is living in active retirement in Italy. In tracing the story of Aaron Jastrow, and that of his Polish cousin Berel, Wouk recounts in moving fashion the sickening circumstances of the infamous "final solution." Aaron himself was born in Poland and reared in a strict Orthodox tradition. As he reached young manhood, he put aside his religion and settled into a benevolent agnosticism. Accompanied by his niece Natalie, he is hounded by the Nazis throughout Europe for years, until he finally ends up in the land of his birth, in a death camp. His life is choked out in the gas chambers. He speaks to the reader directly through *A Jew's Journey*. What one learns from this document is that the most significant journey in the waning months of Jastrow's life is a spiritual one. His personal confrontation with the horrors of Nazism has the effect of returning him to the religion of his birth. When he comes to die, he is possessed of an inner peace his murderers could never know, and he represents a basic human dignity that they have chosen to abandon for themselves and to attempt to destroy in others.

The Winds of War and *War and Remembrance* are about a specific war, but they are about war in general as well. Wouk does not romanticize World War II, but he suggests that it was absolutely essential that the Allied forces emerge as victorious. It was an unspeakably grim yet nevertheless necessary struggle. The bombs that ended the war, however, changed the nature of war forever. If humankind were capable before Hiroshima and Nagasaki of arguing that all-out war, however cruel and crude, was a workable solution to human problems, that argument proved no longer tenable. World War II was perhaps the most gruesome war that human beings have ever inflicted on themselves. Wouk's thesis is that wars in the future will not be avoided simply by proclaiming them to be unthinkable. One must think about them; one must think especially about the most gruesome of wars. Through memory, perhaps a pathway to peace can be found.

INSIDE, OUTSIDE

Wouk's *Inside, Outside* appeared in 1985. *The Caine Mutiny* is by consensus Wouk's single best work of fiction, but *Inside, Outside* could arguably be offered as a legitimate contender for that honor. Here one finds all Wouk's considerable skill in operation: his commanding ability to create characters that live and breathe and convince, telling their interesting and interlocking stories within the context of a fictional world that, while complex, never degenerates into incoherence. Wouk's characters move and make their marks in a world that can be as confused and disorienting as that created by any other modern fictionist. However, the core, the center, of Wouk's world, although subjected to great strain, always manages to hold; that is, although Wouk's characters live in an extremely difficult and demanding world, that world preserves its essential meaningfulness. Wouk does not burden himself with the absurd task of attempting to populate an absurd universe.

It is difficult to specify what makes for the peculiar success of this novel, but certainly at work is Wouk's uncanny ability—which is singularly devoid of self-advertising and therefore easy to overlook—to create what one might call fictional immediacy. Wouk can effect the magic of bringing into being a fictional world that more than half persuades the reader that it is not fictional at all. In other words, he is a maker of art.

Inside, Outside revolves around the life and times of one Israel David Goodkind. It is principally his story, and he tells it with verve. The novel is interestingly structured. The time frame of the narration is 1973. In that year, Goodkind, a successful New York lawyer, finds himself in the rather unusual position—given the fact that he has been a lifelong Democrat—of serving in Washington as a special assistant to President Richard Nixon. The job, though flattering in its way, is anything but exacting, and Goodkind begins to expend his considerable free time in writing; however, this activity is not simply an idle exercise with which to fill the gaps in his undemanding day. He takes his writing quite seriously, and he intends to produce something of real literary worth. He endeavors to fulfill an ambition he has harbored since his youth but that thus far he has not managed to accomplish. He writes about his own life, which takes him back to the turn of the century and the stories of his parents, two Jewish emigrants from Russia. They both arrive in New York; there they meet and marry, and there their children, Israel and Lee, are born.

The reader follows the entire course of Goodkind's life as he recounts its developments, its delays, its assorted dramatic and melodramatic reversals, with meticulous and loving detail. The reader is brought into the very center of Goodkind's world and discovers it to be a world that is at once intensely provincial and intensely cosmopolitan—the kind of combination that is possible perhaps only in New York City. It is a wide world, thickly populated with a rich variety of relatives and friends. The reader is given the opportunity to meet them all and, with differing degrees of completeness, to come to know their stories, too.

Such is the main strand of the novel's narrative. Its secondary strand is no less compelling. Goodkind is interrupted periodically in his recounting of his past by the pressing events that take place around him in 1973 as he continues his writing project. Two significant historical events mark that time period. One is the Israeli-Egyptian War and the other is the resignation of President Nixon in the wake of the Watergate scandal. The first event takes place within the time frame of the novel, and Goodkind reports on it as he writes. The second event draws closer and closer, but the novel ends without the president's resignation having yet taken place. The Israeli-Egyptian War plays an important symbolic role in the narrative because one of the central themes of the novel is the situation of Jews in the modern world.

The "inside" of the novel's title refers to the somewhat self-enclosed, clearly identifiable, but far from homogeneous world of Jewish religion and culture, whereas the "outside" refers to the world at large. Wouk is something of an oddity among contemporary American novelists because of his open and unapologetic commitment to his religious convictions. This fact largely explains the decided and persistent moral tone of his fiction. One can find expressions, more or less strong, more or less developed, of his commitment to Judaism throughout his fiction, but in no other novel, it seems, does his religious faith play so central and integral a part than in *Inside, Outside*.

What Wouk gives the reader in this novel, along with much else, is a dynamic and dramatic picture of the manifold consciousness that constitutes late twentieth century Judaism. The picture he presents is intricate, complicated, and in some respects even contradictory. Wouk deals with the rich reality that is Judaism in a manner that is—variously—intensely objective and intensely subjective. He seems to leave nothing out of the picture; negative elements are treated with as much thoroughness as are positive elements. Nevertheless, Wouk does not treat the heart of his subject matter, the essential identity of Judaism, with anything but respect and reverence.

If by novel's end one cannot identify its protagonist as a typical modern Jew, that is only because one has come to understand that there is no such thing. Goodkind is a representative modern Jew, but so are many who are quite different from him, and Goodkind himself is far from simple. On one hand, Goodkind reflects the "inside" component of his world, but a distinct "outside" dimension to his personality exists as well. Both together, "inside" and "outside," make up who he is. Goodkind is a religious Jew who faithfully practices his religion. He is also a political Jew who sympathizes with the Zionist tradition and takes great patriotic pride in the state of Israel. At the same time, Goodkind is a thorough American. In a larger sense, he is an eminently modern man, one who, even in spite of himself at times, reflects the consciousness of the contemporary Western intellectual, with all the limitations peculiar to it. His judgments on the major issues that impinge on his life have to them a ring of confident cosmopolitanism, which disguises their lack of substantial metaphysical foundations. For example, although he is in many respects exemplary for his perspicacity and sensitivity, he is obtuse in response to some of the clear signs of decadence in modern culture.

Mention might be made of the unorthodox manner in which the novel deals with the character of Nixon. Wouk goes beyond the crude journalistic stereotypes to discover in Nixon not merely a caricature but a real human being. Finally, *Inside, Outside* is simultaneously a serious and a humorous work, and both of these faces complement each other, helping to bring each into greater relief. In some of his other novels, Wouk has demonstrated his facility in handling humor, but that skill is especially in evidence in *Inside, Outside*.

THE HOPE *and* THE GLORY

Unfortunately, Wouk was not able to sustain in his next two novels the high level of artistry he achieved in *Inside, Outside*. In *The Hope* and *The Glory* he continues to exploit his interest in Judaic issues, using the techniques that proved successful in *The Winds of War* and *War and Remembrance*. Though published separately, *The Hope* and *The Glory* are much like Wouk's two-volume romance about World War II; collectively they provide a portrait of the early years of the state of Israel, depicting the struggles of the Jewish people to establish a new independent country in their ancestral homeland.

The Hope is set in the years immediately following World War II, when a small but determined group of Zionist freedom fighters ousted the British from Palestine and declared the foundation of the new state of Israel. As he did in *The Winds of War* and *War and Remembrance*, Wouk creates a number of fictional characters whose lives intersect with the real-life heroes and heroines of the new Jewish nation. Wouk offers a vivid account of the 1948 War of Independence, focusing on the struggles of leaders such as David Ben-Gurion and Moshe Dayan to unite the disparate political and paramilitary groups in the region. The climax of the novel is the stunning victory of the Israelis over their Arab enemies in the Six-Day War of 1967. *The Glory* is a sequel, containing many of the same characters. In recounting the tale of the Jewish nation from 1967 to the announcement of the Camp David Peace Accords, Wouk has his fictional characters support the likes of Golda Meir and Menachem Begin.

Though with less success than he realized in his World War II novels, Wouk gives his narrative a sense of immediacy by concentrating his attention on the effects of the Israelis' struggle on the lives of common men and women. To accomplish this, he creates four families whose fortunes are intertwined not only with historical personages of note but also with each other: the Baraks, the Blumenthals, the Pasternaks, and the Luries. Among them are fighters, local politicians, businessmen, and even ambassadors who represent Israel in the United States and at the United Nations. Political issues are paralleled by small acts of love and vengeance, bringing a certain degree of humanity to the large historical canvas on which Wouk depicts the nation he loves.

Like most novels published by Wouk since the appearance of *The Caine Mutiny*, both *The Hope* and *The Glory* attracted a large readership, but neither received praise from critics. The negative critical reaction seems justified. While the historical accounts are accurate and presented with a strong sense of control, at least one reviewer found this extremely complex political subject treated with "only slightly more subtlety than a grade-school Thanksgiving pageant." Knowing that he would be open to criticism because of his strong partisan views, Wouk was careful to offer a note in *The Hope* that he worked hard not to present a caricature of Arabs. Unfortunately, there is a general laxity in dealing with both major and minor Jewish figures. Instead of striving for complexity, Wouk often resorts to stereotypes that create heroes and villains more commonly found in melodrama or popular romances. His men are almost all superhuman, his women submissive handmaids. What could have been a wonderful final performance in a distinguished career as a popular novelist seems to have emerged as little more than a drifting away into contemporary cliché.

Despite his broad popular appeal, Wouk has generally not found favor with the critics, especially academic critics. The common response of the latter has been simply to ignore him. It is difficult to explain precisely why this is so. Perhaps Wouk's very popularity militates against him, as if there existed a necessary relationship between popularity and artistic worth: The more popular a writer, the poorer the quality of what he writes. Perhaps Wouk's traditionalist worldview and forthright advocacy of Judeo-Christian moral principles, to which many critics today are hostile, account in part for the critical neglect of his work.

In any case, Wouk deserves more critical attention than he has received. He is not the greatest among the many fine novelists to appear in the United States since World War II, but neither is he an inconsequential figure. His prose is solid and vigorous, eschewing precosity and self-indulgence. Writing with intelligence and sensitivity, he appeals neither to a small clique of literary aesthetes nor to the lowest common denominator of a general audience. His attitude toward fiction is that shared by all the major novelists of literary history; his fiction is not concerned with itself but with the world at large. His fiction does not attempt the irrelevant task of creating a moral universe from scratch, but accepts and responds to the moral universe that is already in place.

Dennis Q. McInerny
Updated by Laurence W. Mazzeno

OTHER MAJOR WORKS

PLAYS: *The Traitor*, pr., pb. 1949; *The Caine Mutiny Court-Martial*, pr., pb. 1954; *Nature's Way*, pr. 1957; *Don't Stop the Carnival*, pr. 1998 (adaptation of his novel; musical with Jimmy Buffett).

SCREENPLAY: *Slattery's Hurricane*, 1949 (with Richard Murphy).

TELEPLAYS: *The Winds of War*, 1983; *War and Remembrance*, 1988.

NONFICTION: *This Is My God*, 1959; *The Will to Live On: This Is Our Heritage*, 2000.

BIBLIOGRAPHY

Beichman, Arnold. *Herman Wouk: The Novelist as Social Historian*. New Brunswick, N.J.: Transaction Books, 1984. A lifelong friend of Wouk, Beichman offers a strident defense of the novelist against those who fault him for his conservative political stance and his decision to stress narrative and action over complex characterization.

Darby, William. *Necessary American Fictions: Popular Literature of the 1950's*. Bowling Green, Ohio: Bowling Green State University Press, 1987. Examines *The Caine Mutiny* as a mirror of 1950's popular values in the United States.

Gerard, Philip. "The Great American War Novels." *World and I* 10 (June, 1995): 54-63. Gerard notes that World War II was "the last public event that defined a generation of novelists." In this essay, he looks at the works of many of these novelists, including Wouk's *The Caine Mutiny*.

Klingenstein, Susanne. "Sweet Natalie: Herman Wouk's Messenger to the Gentiles." In *Talking Back: Images of Jewish Women in American Popular Culture*, edited by Joyce Antler. Hanover, N.H.: University Press of New England, 1998. Klingenstein examines Natalie Jastrow, the American Jewish heroine of *The Winds of War* and *War and Remembrance*. She describes how Wouk uses his character to personalize the Holocaust for non-Jewish readers.

Mazzeno, Laurence W. *Herman Wouk*. New York: Twayne, 1994. Offers a brief biographical sketch and analyses of the major novels through *Inside, Outside*. The book contains excerpts from hundreds of reviews of Wouk's fiction, providing a sense of the contemporary reaction to each of his major works.

Shapiro, Edward S. "The Jew as Patriot: Herman Wouk and American Jewish Identity." In *We Are Many: Reflections on American Jewish History and Identity*. Syracuse, N.Y.: Syracuse University Press, 2005. This collection of Shapiro's previously published essays includes a retrospective review of Wouk's career. Shapiro argues persuasively that Wouk is concerned principally with defining American Jewish identity.

Shatzky, Joel, and Michael Taub, eds. *Contemporary Jewish-American Novelists: A Bio-critical Sourcebook*. Westport, Conn.: Greenwood Press, 1997. Includes an entry on Wouk's life, major works, and themes, with an overview of his critical reception and a bibliography of primary and secondary sources.

A. B. YEHOSHUA

Born: Jerusalem, Israel; December 9, 1936
Also known as: Abraham Ben Yehoshua; Avraham B. Yehoshua; Boolie

PRINCIPAL LONG FICTION

Mot ha-zaken, 1962 (novella)
Sheloshah yamim ve-yeled, 1967 (novella; *Three Days and a Child*, 1970)
Bi-tehilat kayits 1970, 1972 (novella; *Early in the Summer of 1970*, 1977)
Ha-meahev, 1977 (*The Lover*, 1978)
Gerushim me'uharim, 1982 (*A Late Divorce*, 1984)
Molkho, 1987 (*Five Seasons*, 1989)
Mar Mani, 1990 (*Mr. Mani*, 1992)
Shivah me-hodu, 1994 (*Open Heart*, 1996)
Masa' el tom ha-elef, 1997 (*A Journey to the End of the Millennium*, 1999)
Ha-Kalah ha-meshahreret, 2001 (*The Liberated Bride*, 2003)
Shelihuto shel ha-memuneh al mashabe enosh, 2004 (*A Woman in Jerusalem*, 2006)
Esh yedidutit, 2007 (*Friendly Fire*, 2008)

OTHER LITERARY FORMS

The writer and philosopher A. B. Yehoshua (yeh-HOH-shew-uh) first came to critical attention with short-story collections he published in the 1960's, such as *Mul ha-ye'arot* (1968; facing the forests). English translations of many of these early stories are collected in *The Continuing Silence of a Poet* (1988). By the 1980's, in addition to novels, Yehoshua began to publish essays and to write plays, among the most notable of which is *Hafatzim* (pr. 1986; *Possessions*, 1993); he has also written children's books. Yehoshua holds strong, and often controversial, political views, which he has defined in his collections of essays as well as through media and academic appearances and interviews.

ACHIEVEMENTS

A. B. Yehoshua is one of the most acclaimed and translated of the Hebrew novelists, known for his carefully observed portraits of Jewish life in Israel, with all its moral, political, and psychological conflicts. Among the many literary honors and awards Yehoshua has received in Israel and elsewhere are the Brenner Prize, the Bialik Prize, and the Alterman Prize. *Mr. Mani* was named "Best Novel of the Year" in England in 1992, and Yehoshua has also won the National Jewish Book Award twice (1990 and 1993), the Israeli Prize for Literature (1995), and Italy's Giovanni Boccaccio Prize (2005). In 2003 he received both the Premio Napoli and the Lampedusa Literary Prize for his novel *The Liberated Bride*. In 2005 he was among the nominees for the first Man Booker International

Prize, and he was presented with the Viareggio Prize for Lifetime Achievement (Italy). In 2006 his novel *A Woman in Jerusalem* won the Los Angeles Times Book Prize, and in 2008 *Friendly Fire* received the Premio Roma.

BIOGRAPHY

Abraham Ben Yehoshua was born a Sephardic Jew. His father's family was originally from Salonica and his mother's from Morocco, but the families had resided in Jerusalem for five generations, and Yehoshua considers himself simply an Israeli. His family was educated; his grandfather was a rabbi and his father, Yakov Yehoshua, was an Orientalist who wrote twelve books about the history of Sephardim in the Old City of Jerusalem. Historians have a certain prominence in Yehoshua's work, as many characters return to the past in their efforts to understand it.

The young Yehoshua fulfilled his military service as a paratrooper from 1954 to 1957 and then started to publish fiction. He soon became known as one of a "new wave" of Israeli writers whose emphasis on individuals and their relationships contrasted with the social concerns of earlier writers.

In June of 1960 he married Rivka Kirsninski, a psychoanalyst, with whom he eventually had three children. He studied Hebrew literature and philosophy at Hebrew University in Jerusalem, graduating with a B.A. in 1961, and he graduated from Teacher's College a year later. He taught in Paris from 1963 to 1967 and served as dean of students at Haifa University in Haifa, Israel, upon his return. He was promoted to professor of literature at Haifa University in 1997, where he worked until his retirement. Throughout his career he also served as visiting professor at many institutions, including St. Cross College, Oxford, Harvard University, the University of Chicago, and Princeton University.

ANALYSIS

A. B. Yehoshua is sometimes called Israel's best living novelist, and judging from the variety and complexity of his work, this may be true. His art fictionalizes the controversies that are ever present in Israel: the tensions between European-born and native-born Israelis, the tensions between those who live in Israel and those who choose to live in the Diaspora, the conflicts between Sephardic and Ashkenazi Jews, and the conflicts between Arabs and Israelis. Against the opposing forces of such conflicts, Yehoshua delves deeply into his characters' inner lives with astute psychological understanding, using certain archetypal and mythic patterns as well.

The Lover, his first full-length novel, immediately brought him international recognition; this work delineates the disintegration of an Ashkenazi family. Not until he wrote *Mr. Mani*, however—a family epic that spans six generations—did Yehoshua create a protagonist who is Sephardic and whose Sephardic roots play an important role in the story. The technique he employs in *Mr. Mani* is unusual; the novel is composed of five different conversations at five significant moments of history, but only one side of the dialogue is given in each of these conversations, while the other side must be assumed. In this way Yehoshua combines a long historical span with the personal perspectives of the members of the Mani family. The theme of the disintegration of the family is seen here as well as in many of his novels, such as *A Late Divorce* and *The Liberated Bride*. Yehoshua has often been called the Hebrew Faulkner, and in many of his books he deals with the same issues of guilt and penance that are addressed in the works of William Faulkner. The novelist credits Faulkner as one of his sources of inspiration, along with Albert Camus and Franz Kafka.

Always interested in history, Yehoshua switched from contemporary Israeli society with *A Journey to the End of the Millennium*, a historical novel that takes place in the year 999. The novel tells the story of a merchant traveling from Africa to Europe who has taken a second wife, a custom that was accepted in North African Jewish communities but forbidden in Europe. When he sets out on his journey, Ben Attar, the protagonist, intends to persuade the Jews of Europe to his way of thinking about polygamy. The novel is rich with the colorful appearance and sophisticated ideas of the African visitors, against which the drab costumes and narrow beliefs of the Rhineland towns Ben Attar visits seem provincial indeed. Ben Attar fails to persuade, however.

THE LIBERATED BRIDE

The Liberated Bride centers on Yochanan Rivlin, a professor of Near Eastern studies at Haifa University. Rivlin is determined to find out the cause of the divorce of his eldest son, Ofer, and he is also determined to find out the root cause of the ferocity of the Algerian war of the 1990's for a book he is writing. These two quests form the narrative arc of the novel, as they lead Rivlin into adventures that find him far from home and the constraints of his beloved wife, Hagit, a well-respected district judge. Hagit's position involves making judgments on those who break the boundaries of the law and trains her to respect privacy.

When Rivlin is dispatched to Jerusalem to pick up his visiting sister-in-law from the airport, he happens to hear that his former daughter-in-law, Galya, is in mourning for her suddenly deceased father. Seizing on this as an opportunity to see Galya, he stops in to pay his respects while Galya's family is receiving guests. He not only discovers that Galya has remarried but also comes to believe that she is pregnant. These facts do not quench his desire to discover the cause of his son's divorce from Galya five years previously, but he receives no satisfaction. Still obsessed with his hunger to know the causes of Ofer and Galya's divorce, he writes to Ofer and suggests that his son write a letter of condolence to Galya.

Later, when his wife leaves him for a few days to attend a trial in Europe, Rivlin calls Ofer in France to try again to find out the cause of his son's divorce, although Hagit has told Rivlin several times to leave their son in peace. Meanwhile, Ofer sends a letter to his mother telling her of his accidental discovery of his former father-in-law's dalliance with a woman who is not his wife, which led to the breakup of his own marriage when he told Galya.

Hagit returns from Europe and, her suspicions aroused regarding her husband's meddling, cross-examines Rivlin, which leads to a bitter fight about Ofer. Eventually, they declare a truce, and Ofer comes to Israel for a diving expedition with his younger brother, Tsakhi, an officer in the Israeli army. Hagit considers her younger son almost a saint because he has a sense of boundaries and knows right from wrong. Rivlin, who has no sense of boundaries, tries to question Ofer regarding his marriage to Galya, after which his son attacks him as a domineering, pushy traitor and returns to France, where he lives. In the final section of the book, titled "The Liberation," Galya, about to give birth at any moment, shows up at Rivlin and Hagit's home, to which she has summoned Ofer from Paris. She asks his forgiveness for dismissing his report of her father's dalliance, which caused the divorce. She has learned the truth from an employee at her father's hotel. She will not reunite with Ofer, however. While she is in labor at a Haifa hospital, Galya's husband and sister show up there to take her back to Jerusalem.

The Liberated Bride includes a rich subplot concerning Rivlin's graduate student Samaher, which brings Rivlin to cross the line between Israel and the Palestinian Territories in the middle of the night with Rashid, an Arab driver. Rivlin is amazed at how quickly Rashid kicks in the dividing fence, another boundary that Rivlin crosses. The novel is also embellished with acts of plays performed in the novel, with bits of Arabic conversation and Algerian poetry and stories, and with letters written from various characters to other characters. The narrative is further enriched by the differences Rivlin has with his colleagues, their discussions centering on the meaning of "national identity" and minority points of view. The point of view of the novel is always Rivlin's, usually told in the third person by an omniscient narrator and occasionally told in the second person.

Rivlin, driven by a thirst to know facts and causes—owing to his training as a historian—is insatiable, but he is willing to deal with real people in all their confusion and complexity, a character trait that is endearing. Constantly traveling Israeli roads and highways, the professor crosses borders both emotional and physical, annoying his family and friends in his quest for answers. He does not find them, however; he never learns the cause of Ofer and Galya's divorce, and he never learns to respect boundaries. At the end he is seen meddling in his younger son's new occupation as a housepainter, passing himself off as the young man's boss.

A WOMAN IN JERUSALEM

As *A Woman in Jerusalem* begins, a past employee of a bakery, a woman in her forties, has died as the result of a bombing. The only identification found with her body is a pay slip from the company, dated after she had quit her job a month previously. Nobody had noticed that she was still on the payroll. Stung by a forthcoming newspaper article about the inhumanity of the company, the prosperous, eighty-seven-year-old owner dispatches his human resources manager (unnamed) to investigate the woman so that he can make a public gesture on her behalf. The human resources manager, himself recently divorced and interested only in rearing his daughter, discovers a romantic entanglement between the worker and the bakery's night supervisor, which accounts for her continuing paychecks. The manager soon becomes obsessed with the deceased, Yulia Ragayev, an engineer from Russia who worked as a cleaner in the bakery. Negative newspaper publicity prods the owner to send the human resources manager to escort Yulia's body back to her home village on the steppes of Russia to be buried, thinking this will exonerate him of his company's former neglect of the woman.

The manager and the body are accompanied on the trip by the newspaper reporter who has been covering the story and his photographer. Their journey becomes saturated with irony and dark humor, and it is in dealing with the absurdities of the journey that the timid and nonassuming human resources manager finds himself, displaying resources of his own that he never knew he possessed. Along the way, as the group travels in a demobilized armored personnel carrier, the manager is forced to pay bribes to the authorities, fends off Yulia's ferocious ex-husband, lives for a time underground in a former bomb shelter because of the onslaught of a fierce winter storm, and survives a devastating illness. The novel turns into a comic tour de force, told mainly from the manager's point of view except for a series of brief, italicized passages that act as a kind of Greek chorus by giving outsiders' views of the action.

The change in the manager's character from a man intimidated by his mother, his ex-wife, and his secretary to a hero of staunch moral integrity is the main trajectory of the novel. The overarching theme of *A Woman in Jerusalem* is the question of responsibility, an issue revisited again and again by the human resources manager, by his mother, by the owner of the bakery, and by Yulia's relatives in Russia. In the final scene, the human resources manager asserts his humanity and, with great honor, resolves the question.

Sheila Golburgh Johnson

OTHER MAJOR WORKS

SHORT FICTION: *Mul ha-ye'arot*, 1968; *Three Days and a Child*, 1970 (selection of short stories, including the novella *Three Days and a Child*); *Tishah sipurim*, 1970; *The Continuing Silence of a Poet: The Collected Short Stories of A. B. Yehoshua*, 1988; *Kol ha-sipurim*, 1993.

PLAYS: *Layla be-May*, pr. 1969 (*A Night in May*, 1974); *Tipolim acharonim*, pr. 1973 (*Last Treatments*, 1974); *Two Plays*, 1974 (includes *A Night in May* and *Last Treatments*); *Hafatzim*, pr. 1986 (*Possessions*, 1993); *Tinokot laylah*, pr. 1992.

NONFICTION: *Bi-zekhut ha-normaliyut*, 1980 (*Between Right and Right*, 1981); *Israel*, 1988; *Hakir v-h-har*, 1989; *Kohah ha-nora shel ashmah ketanah*, 1998 (*The Terrible Power of a Minor Guilt*, 2000); *Essays*, 2006; *Achizat moledet*, 2008.

CHILDREN'S LITERATURE: *Ha-Achbar shel Tamar ve-Gaya*, 2005; *Chaiat ha-machmad shel Ofri*, 2007.

BIBLIOGRAPHY

Band, Arnold J. "The Archaeology of Self Deception: A. B. Yehoshua's *Mar Mani*." In *Studies in Modern Jewish Literature*. Philadelphia: Jewish Publication Society, 2003. Provides an in-depth discussion of *Mr. Mani* as part of a larger work concerned with contemporary Jewish literature in general.

Bayley, John. Review of *Mr. Mani*, by A. B. Yehoshua. *The New Republic*, November 5, 1992. Unravels the complexities of this novel, which jumps around in time and point of view.

Ellis, Samantha. "Fiction Turbulent as Life." *Jewish Quarterly*, no. 201 (Spring, 2006): 1-6. Presents an informative survey of Yehoshua's career, with special emphasis on the novels *The Lover* and *Mr. Mani*.

Essex, Ruth. "The Eastern Influence." In *Israeli Writing Against Itself: The Clash of Hellenism and Judaism in Modern Israeli Narrative*. New York: Peter Lang, 2001. Presents analysis of Yehoshua's novel *Open Heart* as part of an examination of the meeting of ancient lore and modern narrative in ten novels by Israeli writers.

Halkin, Hillel. "Politics and the Israeli Novel." *Commentary* 117, no. 4 (April, 2004). A frequent translator of Yehoshua's work offers an insightful discussion of how Israel's political climate determines the fate of many of the characters in the author's novels.

Horn, Bernard. *Facing the Fires: Conversations with A. B. Yehoshua*. Syracuse, N.Y.: Syracuse University Press, 1997. A recognized expert on Yehoshua presents his own interviews with the author that cover many topics, including books, nostalgia, politics, Sephardic Jewry in Israel, and writing.

Morahg, Gilead. "Testing Tolerance: Cultural Diversity and National Unity in A. B. Yehoshua's *A Journey to the End of the Millennium*." *Prooftexts* 19, no. 3 (September, 1999): 235-256. Examination of Yehoshua's novel focuses on the allegorical nature of the work and its depictions of cultural diversity.

Newton, Adam Zachary. "Not Quite Holocaust Fiction: A. B. Yehoshua's *Mr. Mani* and W. G. Sebald's *The Emigrants*." In *Teaching the Representation of the Holocaust*, edited by Marianne Hirsch and Irene Kacandes. New York: Modern Language Association of America, 2004. Compares and contrasts Yehoshua's novel and Sebald's *Die Ausgewanderten* (1992; *The Emigrants*, 1996) from within the context of fiction about the Holocaust.

Bibliography

Every effort has been made to include studies published in 2000 and later. Most items in this bibliography contain a listing of secondary sources, making it easier to identify other critical commentary on novelists, movements, and themes.

Theoretical, Thematic, and Historical Studies

Altman, Janet Gurkin. *Epistolarity: Approaches to a Form.* Columbus: Ohio State University Press, 1982. Examines the epistolary novel, explaining how novelists use the letter form to develop characterization, further their plots, and develop meaning.

Beaumont, Matthew, ed. *Adventures in Realism.* Malden, Mass.: Blackwell, 2007. Fifteen essays explore facets of realism, which was critical to the development of the novel. Provides a theoretical framework for understanding how novelists attempt to represent the real and the common in fiction.

Brink, André. *The Novel: Language and Narrative from Cervantes to Calvino.* New York: New York University Press, 1998. Uses contemporary theories of semiotics and narratology to establish a continuum between early novelists and those of the postmodern era in their conscious use of language to achieve certain effects. Ranges across national boundaries to illustrate the theory of the development of the novel since the seventeenth century.

Brownstein, Rachel. *Becoming a Heroine: Reading About Women in Novels.* New York: Viking Press, 1982. Feminist survey of novels from the eighteenth century through the latter half of the twentieth century. Examines how "becoming a heroine" defines for women a sense of value in their lives. Considers novels by both men and women, and discusses the importance of the traditional marriage plot.

Bruzelius, Margaret. *Romancing the Novel: Adventure from Scott to Sebald.* Lewisburg, Pa.: Bucknell University Press, 2007. Examines the development of the adventure novel, linking it with the medieval romance tradition and exploring readers' continuing fascination with the genre.

Cavallaro, Dani. *The Gothic Vision: Three Centuries of Horror, Terror, and Fear.* New York: Continuum, 2005. Study of the gothic novel from its earliest manifestations in the eighteenth century to the early twenty-first century. Through the lenses of contemporary cultural theories, examines readers' fascination with novels that invoke horror, terror, and fright.

Doody, Margaret Anne. *The True Story of the Novel.* New Brunswick, N.J.: Rutgers University Press, 1996. Traces the roots of the novel, traditionally thought to have been developed in the seventeenth century, to classical Greek and Latin texts that exhibit characteristics of modern fiction.

Hale, Dorothy J., ed. *The Novel: An Anthology of Criticism and Theory, 1900-2000.* Malden, Mass.: Blackwell, 2006. Collection of essays by theorists and novelists. Includes commentary on the novel form from the perspective of formalism, structuralism, poststructuralism, Marxism, and reader response theory. Essays also address the novel through the lenses of sociology, gender studies, and feminist theory.

_______. *Social Formalism: The Novel in Theory from Henry James to the Present*. Stanford, Calif.: Stanford University Press, 1998. Emphasizes the novel's special ability to define a social world for readers. Relies heavily on the works of contemporary literary and cultural theorists. Provides a summary of twentieth century efforts to identify a theory of fiction that encompasses novels of many kinds.

Hart, Stephen M., and Wen-chin Ouyang, eds. *A Companion to Magical Realism*. London: Tamesis, 2005. Essays outlining the development of Magical Realism, tracing its roots from Europe through Latin America to other regions of the world. Explores the political dimensions of the genre.

Hoffman, Michael J., and Patrick D. Murphy, eds. *Essentials of the Theory of Fiction*. 2d ed. Durham, N.C.: Duke University Press, 1996. Collection of essays by influential critics from the late nineteenth century through the twentieth century. Focuses on the essential elements of fiction and the novel's relationship to the world it depicts.

Lodge, David. *The Art of Fiction: Illustrated from Classic and Modern Texts*. New York: Viking Press, 1993. Short commentaries on the technical aspects of fiction. Examples from important and minor novelists illustrate literary principles and techniques such as point of view, suspense, character introduction, irony, motivation, and ending.

Lynch, Deirdre, and William B. Walker, eds. *Cultural Institutions of the Novel*. Durham, N.C.: Duke University Press, 1996. Fifteen essays examine aspects of long fiction produced around the world. Encourages a redefinition of the genre and argues for inclusion of texts not historically considered novels.

Moretti, Franco, ed. *The Novel*. 2 vols. Princeton, N.J.: Princeton University Press, 2006. Compendium exploring the novel from multiple perspectives, including as an anthropological, historical, and sociological document; a function of the national tradition from which it emerges; and a work of art subject to examination using various critical approaches.

Priestman, Martin, ed. *The Cambridge Companion to Crime Fiction*. New York: Cambridge University Press, 2003. Essays examine the nature and development of the genre, explore works by writers (including women and ethnic minorities) from several countries, and establish links between crime fiction and other literary genres. Includes a chronology.

Scaggs, John. *Crime Fiction*. New York: Routledge, 2005. Provides a history of crime fiction, explores key subgenres, and identifies recurring themes that suggest the wider social and historical context in which these works are written. Suggests critical approaches that open crime fiction to serious study.

Shiach, Morag, ed. *The Cambridge Companion to the Modernist Novel*. New York: Cambridge University Press, 2007. Essays explaining the concept of modernism and its influence on the novel. Detailed examination of works by writers from various countries, all influenced by the modernist movement. Includes a detailed chronology.

Vice, Sue. *Holocaust Fiction.* New York: Routledge, 2000. Examines controversies generated by novels about the Holocaust. Focuses on eight important works, but also offers observations on the polemics surrounding publication of books on this topic.

Zunshine, Lisa. *Why We Read Fiction: Theory of Mind and the Novel.* Columbus: Ohio State University Press, 2006. Applies theories of cognitive psychology to novel reading, explaining how experience and human nature lead readers to constrain their interpretations of a given text. Provides numerous examples from well-known novels to illustrate how and why readers find pleasure in fiction.

JEWISH NOVELISTS

Chertok, Haim. *We Are All Close: Conversations with Israeli Writers.* New York: Fordham University Press, 1989. Thorough and detailed discussion of themes, techniques, and ideological positions that have become the hallmark of such Israeli writers as David Grossman, Amos Oz, Abraham Yehoshua, and Aharon Appelfeld.

Fuchs, Esther. *Israeli Mythogynies: Women in Contemporary Hebrew Fiction.* Albany: State University of New York Press, 1987. Thought-provoking study that surveys Israeli literature from a feminist perspective. Examines the representation of gender and related issues in the works of male and female writers of Hebrew fiction.

Japtok, Martin. *Growing Up Ethnic: Nationalism and the Bildungsroman in African American and Jewish American Fiction.* Iowa City: University of Iowa Press, 2005. Comparative study of the literary similarities between African Americans and Jews in interpreting "ethnicity"—in the early decades of the twentieth century—through their writing of bildungsromans, or coming-of-age novels.

Shatsky, Joel, and Michael Taub, eds. *Contemporary Jewish-American Novelists: A Bio-Bibliographical Critical Sourcebook.* Westport, Conn.: Greenwood Press, 1997. Reference guide outlining the careers and accomplishments of more than sixty Jewish American writers, most of whom wrote during the decades following World War II.

Silberschlag, Eisig. *From Renaissance to Renaissance: Hebrew Literature in the Land of Israel.* New York: KTAV, 1977. A solid and thorough discussion of the origins, developments, themes, and circumstances of early Israeli literature, with a long chapter on the novel.

Laurence W. Mazzeno

Glossary of Literary Terms

absurdism: A philosophical attitude, pervading much of modern drama and fiction, that underlines the isolation and alienation that humans experience, having been thrown into what absurdists see as a godless universe devoid of religious, spiritual, or metaphysical meaning. Conspicuous in its lack of logic, consistency, coherence, intelligibility, and realism, the literature of the absurd depicts the anguish, forlornness, and despair inherent in the human condition. Counter to the rationalist assumptions of traditional humanism, absurdism denies the existence of universal truth or value.

allegory: A literary mode in which a second level of meaning, wherein characters, events, and settings represent abstractions, is encoded within the surface narrative. The allegorical mode may dominate an entire work, in which case the encoded message is the work's primary reason for being, or it may be an element in a work otherwise interesting and meaningful for its surface story alone. Elements of allegory may be found in Jonathan Swift's *Gulliver's Travels* (1726) and Thomas Mann's *Der Zauberberg* (1924; *The Magic Mountain*, 1927).

anatomy: Literally the term means the "cutting up" or "dissection" of a subject into its constituent parts for closer examination. Northrop Frye, in his *Anatomy of Criticism* (1957), uses the term to refer to a narrative that deals with mental attitudes rather than people. As opposed to the novel, the anatomy features stylized figures who are mouthpieces for the ideas they represent.

antagonist: The character in fiction who stands as a rival or opponent to the *protagonist*.

antihero: Defined by Seán O'Faoláin as a fictional figure who, deprived of social sanctions and definitions, is always trying to define himself and to establish his own codes. Ahab may be seen as the antihero of Herman Melville's *Moby Dick* (1851).

archetype: The term "archetype" entered literary criticism from the psychology of Carl Jung, who defined archetypes as "primordial images" from the "collective unconscious" of humankind. Jung believed that works of art derive much of their power from the unconscious appeal of these images to ancestral memories. In his extremely influential *Anatomy of Criticism* (1957), Northrop Frye gave another sense of the term wide currency, defining the archetype as "a symbol, usually an image, which recurs often enough in literature to be recognizable as an element of one's literary experience as a whole."

atmosphere: The general mood or tone of a work; atmosphere is often associated with setting but can also be established by action or dialogue. A classic example of atmosphere is the primitive, fatalistic tone created in the opening description of Egdon Heath in Thomas Hardy's *The Return of the Native* (1878).

bildungsroman: Sometimes called the "novel of education," the bildungsroman focuses on the growth of a young *protagonist* who is learning about the world and finding his or her place in life; typical examples are James Joyce's *A Portrait of the Artist as a*

Young Man (1914-1915, serial; 1916, book) and Thomas Wolfe's *Look Homeward, Angel* (1929).

biographical criticism: Criticism that attempts to determine how the events and experiences of an author's life influence his or her work.

bourgeois novel: A novel in which the values, preoccupations, and accoutrements of middle-class or bourgeois life are given particular prominence. The heyday of the bourgeois novel was the nineteenth century, when novelists as varied as Jane Austen, Honoré de Balzac, and Anthony Trollope both criticized and unreflectingly transmitted the assumptions of the rising middle class.

canon: An authorized or accepted list of books. In modern parlance, the literary canon comprehends the privileged texts, classics, or great books that are thought to belong permanently on university reading lists. Recent theory—especially feminist, Marxist, and poststructuralist—critically examines the process of canon formation and questions the hegemony of white male writers. Such theory sees canon formation as the ideological act of a dominant institution and seeks to undermine the notion of canonicity itself, thereby preventing the exclusion of works by women, minorities, and oppressed peoples.

character: Characters in fiction can be presented as if they were real people or as stylized functions of the plot. Usually characters are a combination of both factors.

classicism: A literary stance or value system consciously based on the example of classical Greek and Roman literature. While the term is applied to an enormous diversity of artists in many different periods and in many different national literatures, "classicism" generally denotes a cluster of values including formal discipline, restrained expression, reverence for tradition, and an objective rather than a subjective orientation. As a literary tendency, classicism is often opposed to *Romanticism*, although many writers combine classical and romantic elements.

climax/crisis: The term "climax" refers to the moment of the reader's highest emotional response, whereas "crisis" refers to a structural element of plot, a turning point at which a resolution must take place.

complication: The point in a novel when the *conflict* is developed or when the already existing conflict is further intensified.

conflict: The struggle that develops as a result of the opposition between the *protagonist* and another person, the natural world, society, or some force within the self.

contextualist criticism: A further extension of *formalist criticism*, which assumes that the language of art is constitutive. Rather than referring to preexistent values, the artwork creates values only inchoately realized before. The most important advocates of this position are Eliseo Vivas (*The Artistic Transaction*, 1963) and Murray Krieger (*The Play and Place of Criticism*, 1967).

conventions: All those devices of stylization, compression, and selection that constitute the necessary differences between art and life. According to the Russian Formalists, these conventions constitute the "literariness" of literature and are the only proper concern of the literary critic.

deconstruction: An extremely influential contemporary school of criticism based on the works of the French philosopher Jacques Derrida. Deconstruction treats literary works as unconscious reflections of the reigning myths of Western culture. The primary myth is that there is a meaningful world that language signifies or represents. The deconstructionist critic is most often concerned with showing how a literary text tacitly subverts the very assumptions or myths on which it ostensibly rests.

defamiliarization: Coined by Viktor Shklovsky in 1917, this term denotes a basic principle of Russian Formalism. Poetic language (by which the Formalists meant artful language, in prose as well as in poetry) defamiliarizes or "makes strange" familiar experiences. The technique of art, says Shklovsky, is to "make objects unfamiliar, to make forms difficult, to increase the difficulty and length of perception. . . . Art is a way of experiencing the artfulness of an object; the object is not important."

detective story: The so-called classic detective story (or mystery) is a highly formalized and logically structured mode of fiction in which the focus is on a crime solved by a detective through interpretation of evidence and ratiocination; the most famous detective in this mode is Arthur Conan Doyle's Sherlock Holmes. Many modern practitioners of the genre, however, such as Dashiell Hammett, Raymond Chandler, and Ross Macdonald, have de-emphasized the puzzlelike qualities of the detective story, stressing instead characterization, theme, and other elements of mainstream fiction.

determinism: The belief that an individual's actions are essentially determined by biological and environmental factors, with free will playing a negligible role. (See *naturalism.*)

dialogue: The similitude of conversation in fiction, dialogue serves to characterize, to further the *plot*, to establish *conflict*, and to express thematic ideas.

displacement: Popularized in criticism by Northrop Frye, this term refers to the author's attempt to make his or her story psychologically motivated and realistic, even as the latent structure of the mythical motivation moves relentlessly forward.

dominant: A term coined by Roman Jakobson to refer to that which "rules, determines, and transforms the remaining components in the work of a single artist, in a poetic canon, or in the work of an epoch." The shifting of the dominant in a *genre* accounts for the creation of new generic forms and new poetic epochs. For example, the rise of *realism* in the mid-nineteenth century indicates realistic conventions becoming dominant and *romance* or fantasy conventions becoming secondary.

doppelgänger: A double or counterpart of a person, sometimes endowed with ghostly qualities. A fictional character's doppelgänger often reflects a suppressed side of his or her personality. One of the classic examples of the doppelgänger motif is found in

Fyodor Dostoevski's novella *Dvoynik* (1846; *The Double*, 1917); Isaac Bashevis Singer and Jorge Luis Borges, among others, offer striking modern treatments of the doppelgänger.

epic: Although this term usually refers to a long narrative poem that presents the exploits of a central figure of high position, the term is also used to designate a long novel that has the style or structure usually associated with an epic. In this sense, for example, Herman Melville's *Moby Dick* (1851) and James Joyce's *Ulysses* (1922) may be called epics.

episodic narrative: A work that is held together primarily by a loose connection of self-sufficient episodes. *Picaresque novels* often have episodic structure.

epistolary novel: A novel made up of letters by one or more fictional characters. Samuel Richardson's *Pamela: Or, Virtue Rewarded* (1740-1741) is a well-known eighteenth century example. In the nineteenth century, Bram Stoker's *Dracula* (1897) is largely epistolary. The technique allows for several different points of view to be presented.

euphuism: A style of writing characterized by ornate language that is highly contrived, alliterative, and repetitious. Euphuism was developed by John Lyly in his *Euphues, the Anatomy of Wit* (1578) and was emulated frequently by writers of the Elizabethan Age.

existentialism: A philosophical, religious, and literary term, emerging from World War II, for a group of attitudes surrounding the pivotal notion that existence precedes essence. According to Jean-Paul Sartre, "Man is nothing else but what he makes himself." Forlornness arises from the death of God and the concomitant death of universal values, of any source of ultimate or a priori standards. Despair arises from the fact that an individual can reckon only with what depends on his or her will, and the sphere of that will is severely limited; the number of things on which he or she can have an impact is pathetically small. Existentialist literature is antideterministic in the extreme and rejects the idea that heredity and environment shape and determine human motivation and behavior.

exposition: The part or parts of a fiction that provide necessary background information. Exposition not only provides the time and place of the action but also introduces readers to the fictive world of the story, acquainting them with the ground rules of the work.

fantastic: In his study *The Fantastic* (1970), Tzvetan Todorov defines the fantastic as a *genre* that lies between the "uncanny" and the "marvelous." All three genres embody the familiar world but present an event that cannot be explained by the laws of the familiar world. Todorov says that the fantastic occupies a twilight zone between the uncanny (when the reader knows that the peculiar event is merely the result of an illusion) and the marvelous (when the reader understands that the event is supposed to take place in a realm controlled by laws unknown to humankind). The fantastic is thus essentially unsettling, provocative, even subversive.

feminist criticism: A criticism advocating equal rights for women in political, economic, social, psychological, personal, and aesthetic senses. On the thematic level, the feminist reader should identify with female characters and their concerns. The object is to provide a critique of phallocentric assumptions and an analysis of patriarchal ideologies inscribed in a literature that is male-centered and male-dominated. On the ideological level, feminist critics see gender, as well as the stereotypes that go along with it, as a cultural construct. They strive to define a particularly feminine content and to extend the *canon* so that it might include works by lesbians, feminists, and women writers in general.

flashback: A scene in a fiction that depicts an earlier event; it may be presented as a reminiscence by a character in the story or may simply be inserted into the narrative.

foreshadowing: A device to create suspense or dramatic irony in fiction by indicating through suggestion what will take place in the future.

formalist criticism: Two particularly influential formalist schools of criticism arose in the twentieth century: the Russian Formalists and the American New Critics. The Russian Formalists were concerned with the conventional devices used in literature to defamiliarize that which habit has made familiar. The New Critics believed that literary criticism is a description and evaluation of its object and that the primary concern of the critic is with the work's unity. Both schools of criticism, at their most extreme, treated literary works as artifacts or constructs divorced from their biographical and social contexts.

genre: In its most general sense, this term refers to a group of literary works defined by a common form, style, or purpose. In practice, the term is used in a wide variety of overlapping and, to a degree, contradictory senses. Tragedy and comedy are thus described as distinct genres; the novel (a form that includes both tragic and comic works) is a genre; and various subspecies of the novel, such as the *gothic* and the *picaresque*, are themselves frequently treated as distinct genres. Finally, the term "genre fiction" refers to forms of popular fiction in which the writer is bound by more or less rigid conventions. Indeed, all these diverse usages have in common an emphasis on the manner in which individual literary works are shaped by particular expectations and conventions; this is the subject of genre criticism.

genre fiction: Categories of popular fiction in which the writers are bound by more or less rigid conventions, such as in the *detective story*, the *romance*, and the *Western*. Although the term can be used in a neutral sense, it is often used dismissively.

gothic novel: A form of fiction developed in the eighteenth century that focuses on horror and the supernatural. In his preface to *The Castle of Otranto* (1765), the first gothic novel in English, Horace Walpole claimed that he was trying to combine two kinds of fiction, with events and story typical of the medieval romance and character delineation typical of the realistic novel. Other examples of the form are Matthew Gregory

Lewis's *The Monk: A Romance* (1796; also known as *Ambrosio: Or, The Monk*) and Mary Wollstonecraft Shelley's *Frankenstein: Or, The Modern Prometheus* (1818).

grotesque: According to Wolfgang Kayser (*The Grotesque in Art and Literature*, 1963), the grotesque is an embodiment in literature of the estranged world. Characterized by a breakup of the everyday world by mysterious forces, the form differs from fantasy in that the reader is not sure whether to react with humor or with horror and in that the exaggeration manifested exists in the familiar world rather than in a purely imaginative world.

Hebraic/Homeric styles: Terms coined by Erich Auerbach in *Mimesis: The Representation of Reality in Western Literature* (1953) to designate two basic fictional styles. The Hebraic style focuses only on the decisive points of narrative and leaves all else obscure, mysterious, and "fraught with background"; the Homeric style places the narrative in a definite time and place and externalizes everything in a perpetual foreground.

historical criticism: In contrast to *formalist criticism*, which treats literary works to a great extent as self-contained artifacts, historical criticism emphasizes the historical context of literature; the two approaches, however, need not be mutually exclusive. Ernst Robert Curtius's *European Literature and the Latin Middle Ages* (1940) is a prominent example of historical criticism.

historical novel: A novel that depicts past historical events, usually public in nature, and features real as well as fictional people. Sir Walter Scott's Waverley novels established the basic type, but the relationship between fiction and history in the form varies greatly depending on the practitioner.

implied author: According to Wayne Booth (*The Rhetoric of Fiction*, 1961), the novel often creates a kind of second self who tells the story—a self who is wiser, more sensitive, and more perceptive than any real person could be.

interior monologue: Defined by Édouard Dujardin as the speech of a character designed to introduce the reader directly to the character's internal life, the form differs from other kinds of monologue in that it attempts to reproduce thought before any logical organization is imposed on it. See, for example, Molly Bloom's long interior monologue at the conclusion of James Joyce's *Ulysses* (1922).

irrealism: A term often used to refer to modern or postmodern fiction that is presented self-consciously as a fiction or a fabulation rather than a mimesis of external reality. The best-known practitioners of irrealism are John Barth, Robert Coover, and Donald Barthelme.

local colorists: A loose movement of late nineteenth century American writers whose fiction emphasizes the distinctive folkways, landscapes, and dialects of various regions. Important local colorists include Bret Harte, Mark Twain, George Washington Cable, Kate Chopin, and Sarah Orne Jewett. (See *regional novel*.)

Marxist criticism: Based on the nineteenth century writings of Karl Marx and Friedrich Engels, Marxist criticism views literature as a product of ideological forces determined by the dominant class. However, many Marxists believe that literature operates according to its own autonomous standards of production and reception: It is both a product of ideology and able to determine ideology. As such, literature may overcome the dominant paradigms of its age and play a revolutionary role in society.

metafiction: This term refers to fiction that manifests a reflexive tendency, such as Vladimir Nabokov's *Pale Fire* (1962) and John Fowles's *The French Lieutenant's Woman* (1969). The emphasis is on the loosening of the work's illusion of reality to expose the reality of its illusion. Other terms used to refer to this type of fiction include "irrealism," "postmodernist fiction," "antifiction," and "surfiction."

modernism: An international movement in the arts that began in the early years of the twentieth century. Although the term is used to describe artists of widely varying persuasions, modernism in general was characterized by its international idiom, by its interest in cultures distant in space or time, by its emphasis on formal experimentation, and by its sense of dislocation and radical change.

motif: A conventional incident or situation in a fiction that may serve as the basis for the structure of the narrative itself. The Russian Formalist critic Boris Tomashevsky uses the term to refer to the smallest particle of thematic material in a work.

motivation: Although this term is usually used in reference to the convention of justifying the action of a character from his or her psychological makeup, the Russian Formalists use the term to refer to the network of devices that justify the introduction of individual *motifs* or groups of motifs in a work. For example, "compositional motivation" refers to the principle that every single property in a work contributes to its overall effect; "realistic motivation" refers to the realistic devices used to make a work plausible and lifelike.

multiculturalism: The tendency to recognize the perspectives of those traditionally excluded from the canon of Western art and literature. In order to promote multiculturalism, publishers and educators have revised textbooks and school curricula to incorporate material by and about women, members of minority groups, persons from non-Western cultures, and homosexuals.

myth: Anonymous traditional stories dealing with basic human concepts and antinomies. According to Claude Lévi-Strauss, myth is that part of language where the "formula *tradutore, tradittore* reaches its lowest truth value. . . . Its substance does not lie in its style, its original music, or its syntax, but in the story which it tells."

myth criticism: Northrop Frye says that in myth "we see the structural principles of literature isolated." Myth criticism is concerned with these basic principles of literature; it is not to be confused with mythological criticism, which is primarily concerned with finding mythological parallels in the surface action of the *narrative*.

narrative: Robert Scholes and Robert Kellogg, in *The Nature of Narrative* (1966), say that by "narrative" they mean literary works that include both a story and a storyteller. The term "narrative" usually implies a contrast to "enacted" fiction such as drama.

narratology: The study of the form and functioning of *narratives*; it attempts to examine what all narratives have in common and what makes individual narratives different from one another.

narrator: The *character* who recounts the *narrative*, or story. Wayne Booth describes various dramatized narrators in *The Rhetoric of Fiction* (1961): unacknowledged centers of consciousness, observers, narrator-agents, and self-conscious narrators. Booth suggests that the important elements to consider in narration are the relationships among the narrator, the author, the characters, and the reader.

naturalism: As developed by Émile Zola in the late nineteenth century, naturalism is the application of the principles of scientific *determinism* to fiction. Although it usually refers more to the choice of subject matter than to technical conventions, those conventions associated with the movement center on the author's attempt to be precise and scientifically objective in description and detail, regardless of whether the events described are sordid or shocking.

New Criticism: See *formalist criticism*.

novel: Perhaps the most difficult of all fictional forms to define because of its multiplicity of modes. Edouard, in André Gide's *Les Faux-monnayeurs* (1925; *The Counterfeiters*, 1927), says the novel is the freest and most lawless of all *genres*; he wonders if fear of that liberty is the reason the novel has so timidly clung to reality. Most critics seem to agree that the novel's primary area of concern is the social world. Ian Watt (*The Rise of the Novel*, 2001) says that the novel can be distinguished from other fictional forms by the attention it pays to individual characterization and detailed presentation of the environment. Moreover, says Watt, the novel, more than any other fictional form, is interested in the "development of its characters in the course of time."

novel of manners: The classic examples of this form might be the novels of Jane Austen, wherein the customs and conventions of a social group of a particular time and place are realistically, and often satirically, portrayed.

novella, novelle, nouvelle, novelette, novela: Although these terms often refer to the short European tale, especially the Renaissance form employed by Giovanni Boccaccio, the terms often refer to that form of fiction that is said to be longer than a short story and shorter than a novel. "Novelette" is the term usually preferred by the British, whereas "novella" is the term usually used to refer to American works in this *genre*. Henry James claimed that the main merit of the form is the "effort to do the complicated thing with a strong brevity and lucidity."

phenomenological criticism: Although best known as a European school of criticism practiced by Georges Poulet and others, this so-called criticism of consciousness is also propounded in the United States by such critics as J. Hillis Miller. The focus is less on individual works and *genres* than it is on literature as an act; the work is not seen as an object but rather as part of a strand of latent impulses in the work of a single author or an epoch.

picaresque novel: A form of fiction that centers on a central rogue figure, or picaro, who usually tells his or her own story. The plot structure is normally *episodic*, and the episodes usually focus on how the picaro lives by his or her wits. Classic examples of the mode are Henry Fielding's *The History of Tom Jones, a Foundling* (1749; commonly known as *Tom Jones*) and Mark Twain's *Adventures of Huckleberry Finn* (1884).

plot/story: "Story" refers to the full *narrative* of *character* and action, whereas "plot" generally refers to action with little reference to character. A more precise and helpful distinction is made by the Russian Formalists, who suggest that "plot" refers to the events of a narrative as they have been artfully arranged in the literary work, subject to chronological displacement, ellipses, and other devices, while "story" refers to the sum of the same events arranged in simple, causal-chronological order. Thus story is the raw material for plot. By comparing the two in a given work, the reader is encouraged to see the narrative as an artifact.

point of view: The means by which the story is presented to the reader, or, as Percy Lubbock says in *The Craft of Fiction* (1921), "the relation in which the narrator stands to the story"—a relation that Lubbock claims governs the craft of fiction. Some of the questions the critical reader should ask concerning point of view are the following: Who talks to the reader? From what position does the narrator tell the story? At what distance does he or she place the reader from the story? What kind of person is he or she? How fully is he or she characterized? How reliable is he or she? For further discussion, see Wayne Booth, *The Rhetoric of Fiction* (1961).

postcolonialism: Postcolonial literature emerged in the mid-twentieth century when colonies in Asia, Africa, and the Caribbean began gaining their independence from the European nations that had long controlled them. Postcolonial authors, such as Salman Rushdie and V. S. Naipaul, tend to focus on both the freedom and the conflict inherent in living in a postcolonial state.

postmodernism: A ubiquitous but elusive term in contemporary criticism, "postmodernism" is loosely applied to the various artistic movements that followed the era of so-called high modernism, represented by such giants as James Joyce and Pablo Picasso. In critical discussions of contemporary fiction, the term "postmodernism" is frequently applied to the works of writers such as Thomas Pynchon, John Barth, and Donald Barthelme, who exhibit a self-conscious awareness of their modernist predecessors as well as a reflexive treatment of fictional form.

protagonist: The central *character* in a fiction, the character whose fortunes most concern the reader.

psychological criticism: While much modern literary criticism reflects to some degree the impacts of Sigmund Freud, Carl Jung, Jacques Lacan, and other psychological theorists, the term "psychological criticism" suggests a strong emphasis on a causal relation between the writer's psychological state, variously interpreted, and his or her works. A notable example of psychological criticism is Norman Fruman's *Coleridge, the Damaged Archangel* (1971).

psychological novel: A form of fiction in which *character*, especially the inner lives of characters, is the primary focus. This form, which has been of primary importance at least since Henry James, characterizes much of the work of James Joyce, Virginia Woolf, and William Faulkner. For a detailed discussion, see *The Modern Psychological Novel* (1955) by Leon Edel.

realism: A literary technique in which the primary convention is to render an illusion of fidelity to external reality. Realism is often identified as the primary method of the novel form: It focuses on surface details, maintains a fidelity to the everyday experiences of middle-class society, and strives for a one-to-one relationship between the fiction and the action imitated. The realist movement in the late nineteenth century coincides with the full development of the novel form.

reception aesthetics: The best-known American practitioner of reception aesthetics is Stanley Fish. For the reception critic, meaning is an event or process; rather than being embedded in the work, it is created through particular acts of reading. The best-known European practitioner of this criticism, Wolfgang Iser, argues that indeterminacy is the basic characteristic of literary texts; the reader must "normalize" the text either by projecting his or her standards into it or by revising his or her standards to "fit" the text.

regional novel: Any novel in which the character of a given geographical region plays a decisive role. Although regional differences persist across the United States, a considerable leveling in speech and customs has taken place, so that the sharp regional distinctions evident in nineteenth century American fiction have all but disappeared. Only in the South has a strong regional tradition persisted to the present. (See *local colorists*.)

rhetorical criticism: The rhetorical critic is concerned with the literary work as a means of communicating ideas and the means by which the work affects or controls the reader. Such criticism seems best suited to didactic works such as satire.

roman à clef: A fiction wherein actual people, often celebrities of some sort, are thinly disguised.

romance: The romance usually differs from the novel form in that the focus is on symbolic events and representational characters rather than on "as-if-real" characters and events. Richard Chase says that in the romance, character is depicted as highly stylized, a function of the plot rather than as someone complexly related to society. The romancer is more likely to be concerned with dreamworlds than with the familiar world, believing that reality cannot be grasped by the traditional novel.

Romanticism: A widespread cultural movement in the late eighteenth and early nineteenth centuries, the influence of which is still felt. As a general literary tendency, Romanticism is frequently contrasted with *classicism.* Although many varieties of Romanticism are indigenous to various national literatures, the term generally suggests an assertion of the preeminence of the imagination. Other values associated with various schools of Romanticism include primitivism, an interest in folklore, a reverence for nature, and a fascination with the demoniac and the macabre.

scene: The central element of *narration*; specific actions are narrated or depicted that make the reader feel he or she is participating directly in the action.

science fiction: Fiction in which certain givens (physical laws, psychological principles, social conditions—any one or all of these) form the basis of an imaginative projection into the future or, less commonly, an extrapolation in the present or even into the past.

semiotics: The science of signs and sign systems in communication. According to Roman Jakobson, semiotics deals with the principles that underlie the structure of signs, their use in language of all kinds, and the specific nature of various sign systems.

sentimental novel: A form of fiction popular in the eighteenth century in which emotionalism and optimism are the primary characteristics. The best-known examples are Samuel Richardson's *Pamela: Or, Virtue Rewarded* (1740-1741) and Oliver Goldsmith's *The Vicar of Wakefield* (1766).

setting: The circumstances and environment, both temporal and spatial, of a *narrative.*

spatial form: An author's attempt to make the reader apprehend a work spatially in a moment of time rather than sequentially. To achieve this effect, the author breaks up the *narrative* into interspersed fragments. Beginning with James Joyce, Marcel Proust, and Djuna Barnes, the movement toward spatial form is concomitant with the *modernist* effort to supplant historical time in fiction with mythic time. For the seminal discussion of this technique, see Joseph Frank, *The Widening Gyre* (1963).

stream of consciousness: The depiction of the thought processes of a *character*, insofar as this is possible, without any mediating structures. The metaphor of consciousness as a "stream" suggests a rush of thoughts and images governed by free association rather than by strictly rational development. The term "stream of consciousness" is often used loosely as a synonym for *interior monologue*. The most celebrated example of stream of consciousness in fiction is the monologue of Molly Bloom in James Joyce's *Ulysses* (1922); other notable practitioners of the stream-of-consciousness technique include Dorothy Richardson, Virginia Woolf, and William Faulkner.

structuralism: As a movement of thought, structuralism is based on the idea of intrinsic, self-sufficient structures that do not require reference to external elements. A structure is a system of transformations that involves the interplay of laws inherent in the system itself. The study of language is the primary model for contemporary structuralism. The structuralist literary critic attempts to define structural principles that operate intertextually throughout the whole of literature as well as principles that operate in *genres* and in individual works. One of the most accessible surveys of structuralism and literature available is Jonathan Culler's *Structuralist Poetics* (1975).

summary: Those parts of a fiction that do not need to be detailed. In *Tom Jones* (1749), Henry Fielding says, "If whole years should pass without producing anything worthy of . . . notice . . . we shall hasten on to matters of consequence."

thematics: According to Northrop Frye, when a work of fiction is written or interpreted thematically, it becomes an illustrative fable. Murray Krieger defines thematics as "the study of the experiential tensions which, dramatically entangled in the literary work, become an existential reflection of that work's aesthetic complexity."

tone: The dominant mood of a work of fiction. (See *atmosphere*.)

unreliable narrator: A narrator whose account of the events of the story cannot be trusted, obliging readers to reconstruct—if possible—the true state of affairs themselves. Once an innovative technique, the use of the unreliable narrator has become commonplace among contemporary writers who wish to suggest the impossibility of a truly "reliable" account of any event. Notable examples of the unreliable narrator can be found in Ford Madox Ford's *The Good Soldier* (1915) and Vladimir Nabokov's *Lolita* (1955).

Victorian novel: Although the Victorian period extended from 1837 to 1901, the term "Victorian novel" does not include the later decades of Queen Victoria's reign. The term loosely refers to the sprawling works of novelists such as Charles Dickens and William Makepeace Thackeray—works that frequently appeared first in serial form and are characterized by a broad social canvas.

vraisemblance/verisimilitude: Tzvetan Todorov defines vraisemblance as "the mask which conceals the text's own laws, but which we are supposed to take for a relation to reality." Verisimilitude refers to a work's attempts to make the reader believe that it conforms to reality rather than to its own laws.

Western novel: Like all varieties of *genre fiction*, the Western novel—generally known simply as the Western—is defined by a relatively predictable combination of *conventions*, *motifs*, and recurring themes. These predictable elements, familiar from many Western films and television series, differentiate the Western from *historical novels* and idiosyncratic works such as Thomas Berger's *Little Big Man* (1964) that are also set in the Old West. Conversely, some novels set in the contemporary West are regarded as Westerns because they deal with modern cowboys and with the land itself in the manner characteristic of the *genre*.

Charles E. May

Guide to Online Resources

Web Sites

The following sites were visited by the editors of Salem Press in 2009. Because URLs frequently change, the accuracy of these addresses cannot be guaranteed; however, long-standing sites, such as those of colleges and universities, national organizations, and government agencies, generally maintain links when sites are moved or updated.

American Literature on the Web
http://www.nagasaki-gaigo.ac.jp/ishikawa/amlit

Among this site's features are several pages providing links to Web sites about specific genres and literary movements, southern and southwestern American literature, minority literature, literary theory, and women writers, as well as an extensive index of links to electronic text collections and archives. Users also can access information for five specific time periods: 1620-1820, 1820-1865, 1865-1914, 1914-1945, and since 1945. A range of information is available for each period, including alphabetical lists of authors that link to more specific information about each writer, time lines of historical and literary events, and links to related additional Web sites.

Books and Writers
http://www.kirjasto.sci.fi/indeksi.htm

This broad, comprehensive, and easy-to-use resource provides access to information about hundreds of authors throughout the world, extending from 70 B.C.E to the twenty-first century. Links take users from an alphabetical list of authors to pages featuring biographical material, lists of works, and recommendations for further reading about individual authors; each writer's page also includes links to related pages on the site. Although brief, the biographical essays provide solid overviews of the authors' careers, their contributions to literature, and their literary influences.

The Canadian Literature Archive
http://www.umanitoba.ca/canlit

Created and maintained by the English Department at the University of Manitoba, this site is a comprehensive collection of materials for and about Canadian writers. It includes an alphabetical listing of authors with links to additional Web-based information. Users also can retrieve electronic texts, announcements of literary events, and videocasts of author interviews and readings.

A Celebration of Women Writers

http://digital.library.upenn.edu/women

This site presents an extensive compendium of information about the contributions of women writers throughout history. The "Local Editions by Authors" and "Local Editions by Category" pages include access to electronic texts of the works of numerous writers, including Louisa May Alcott, Djuna Barnes, Grazia Deledda, Edith Wharton, and Virginia Woolf. Users can also access biographical and bibliographical information by browsing lists arranged by writers' names, countries of origin, ethnicities, and the centuries in which they lived.

Contemporary Writers

http://www.contemporarywriters.com/authors

Created by the British Council, this site offers "up-to-date profiles of some of the U.K. and Commonwealth's most important living writers (plus writers from the Republic of Ireland that we've worked with)." The available information includes biographies, bibliographies, critical reviews, news about literary prizes, and photographs. Users can search the site by author, genre, nationality, gender, publisher, book title, date of publication, and prize name and date.

Internet Public Library: Native American Authors

http://www.ipl.org/div/natam

Internet Public Library, a Web-based collection of materials, includes this index to resources about writers of Native American heritage. An alphabetical list of authors enables users to link to biographies, lists of works, electronic texts, tribal Web sites, and other online resources. The majority of the writers covered are contemporary Indian authors, but some historical authors also are featured. Users also can retrieve information by browsing lists of titles and tribes. In addition, the site contains a bibliography of print and online materials about Native American literature.

LiteraryHistory.com

http://www.literaryhistory.com

This site is an excellent source of academic, scholarly, and critical literature about eighteenth, nineteenth, and twentieth century American and English writers. It provides numerous pages about specific eras and genres, including individual pages for eighteenth, nineteenth, and twentieth century literature and for African American and postcolonial literature. These pages contain alphabetical lists of authors that link to articles, reviews, overviews, excerpts of works, teaching guides, podcast interviews, and other materials. The eighteenth century literature page also provides access to information about the eighteenth century novel.

Literary Resources on the Net

http://andromeda.rutgers.edu/~jlynch/Lit

Jack Lynch of Rutgers University maintains this extensive collection of links to Internet sites that are useful to academics, including numerous Web sites about American and English literature. This collection is a good place to begin online research about the novel, as it links to hundreds of other sites with broad ranges of literary topics. The site is organized chronically, with separate pages for information about the Middle Ages, the Renaissance, the eighteenth century, the Romantic and Victorian eras, and twentieth century British and Irish literature. It also has separate pages providing links to Web sites about American literature and to women's literature and feminism.

LitWeb

http://litweb.net

LitWeb provides biographies of more than five hundred world authors throughout history that can be accessed through an alphabetical listing. The pages about each writer contain a list of his or her works, suggestions for further reading, and illustrations. The site also offers information about past and present winners of major literary prizes.

The Modern Word: Authors of the Libyrinth

http://www.themodernword.com/authors.html

The Modern Word site, although somewhat haphazard in its organization, provides a great deal of critical information about writers. The "Authors of the Libyrinth" page is very useful, linking author names to essays about them and other resources. The section of the page headed "The Scriptorium" presents "an index of pages featuring writers who have pushed the edges of their medium, combining literary talent with a sense of experimentation to produce some remarkable works of modern literature." The site also includes sections devoted to Samuel Beckett, Umberto Eco, Gabriel García Márquez, James Joyce, Franz Kafka, and Thomas Pynchon.

Novels

http://www.nvcc.edu/home/ataormina/novels/default.htm

This overview of American and English novels was prepared by Agatha Taormina, a professor at Northern Virginia Community College. It contains three sections: "History" provides a definition of the novel genre, a discussion of its origins in eighteenth century England, and separate pages with information about genres and authors of nineteenth century, twentieth century, and postmodern novels. "Approaches" suggests how to read a novel critically for greater appreciation, and "Resources" provides a list of books about the novel.

Outline of American Literature

http://www.america.gov/publications/books/outline-of-american-literature.html

This page of the America.gov site provides access to an electronic version of the ten-chapter volume *Outline of American Literature*, a historical overview of prose and poetry from colonial times to the present published by the U.S. Department of State. The work's author is Kathryn VanSpanckeren, professor of English at the University of Tampa. The site offers links to abbreviated versions of each chapter as well as access to the entire publication in PDF format.

Voice of the Shuttle

http://vos.ucsb.edu

One of the most complete and authoritative places for online information about literature, Voice of the Shuttle is maintained by professors and students in the English Department at the University of California, Santa Barbara. The site provides thousands of links to electronic books, academic journals, association Web sites, sites created by university professors, and many, many other resources about the humanities. Its "Literature in English" page provides links to separate pages about the literature of the Anglo-Saxon era, the Middle Ages, the Renaissance and seventeenth century, the Restoration and eighteenth century, the Romantic age, the Victorian age, and modern and contemporary periods in Britain and the United States, as well as a page focused on minority literature. Another page on the site, "Literatures Other than English," offers a gateway to information about the literature of numerous countries and world regions.

ELECTRONIC DATABASES

Electronic databases usually do not have their own URLs. Instead, public, college, and university libraries subscribe to these databases, provide links to them on their Web sites, and make them available to library card holders or other specified patrons. Readers can visit library Web sites or ask reference librarians to check on availability.

Canadian Literary Centre

Produced by EBSCO, the Canadian Literary Centre database contains full-text content from ECW Press, a Toronto-based publisher, including the titles in the publisher's Canadian fiction studies, Canadian biography, and Canadian writers and their works series, *ECW's Biographical Guide to Canadian Novelists*, and *George Woodcock's Introduction to Canadian Fiction*. Author biographies, essays and literary criticism, and book reviews are among the database's offerings.

Literary Reference Center

EBSCO's Literary Reference Center (LRC) is a comprehensive full-text database designed primarily to help high school and undergraduate students in English and the humanities with homework and research assignments about literature. The database contains massive amounts of information from reference works, books, literary journals, and other materials, including more than 31,000 plot summaries, synopses, and overviews of literary works; almost 100,000 essays and articles of literary criticism; about 140,000 author biographies; more than 605,000 book reviews; and more than 5,200 author interviews. It also contains the entire contents of Salem Press's MagillOnLiterature Plus. Users can retrieve information by browsing a list of authors' names or titles of literary works; they can also use an advanced search engine to access information by numerous categories, including author name, gender, cultural identity, national identity, and the years in which he or she lived, or by literary title, character, locale, genre, and publication date. The Literary Reference Center also features a literary-historical time line, an encyclopedia of literature, and a glossary of literary terms.

MagillOnLiterature Plus

MagillOnLiterature Plus is a comprehensive, integrated literature database produced by Salem Press and available on the EBSCO*host* platform. The database contains the full text of essays in Salem's many literature-related reference works, including *Masterplots*, *Cyclopedia of World Authors*, *Cyclopedia of Literary Characters*, *Cyclopedia of Literary Places*, *Critical Survey of Long Fiction*, *Critical Survey of Short Fiction*, *World Philosophers and Their Works*, *Magill's Literary Annual*, and *Magill's Book Reviews.* Among its contents are articles on more than 35,000 literary works and more than 8,500 writers, poets, dramatists, essays, and philosophers, more than 1,000 images, and a glossary of more than 1,300 literary terms. The biographical essays include lists of authors' works and secondary bibliographies, and almost four hundred overview essays offer information about literary genres, time periods, and national literatures.

NoveList

NoveList is a readers' advisory service produced by EBSCO. The database provides access to 155,000 titles of both adult and juvenile fiction as well information about literary awards, book discussion guides, feature articles about a range of literary genres, and "recommended reads." Users can search by author name, book title, or series title or can describe the plot to retrieve the name of a book, information about the author, and book reviews; another search engine enables users to find titles similar to books they have enjoyed reading.

Rebecca Kuzins

GEOGRAPHICAL INDEX

SUBJECT INDEX